Vegetarian New York City

Help!

You hold in your hands what some might call an impossibility: an attempt to pin down the vegetarian scene in an incredibly dynamic, fast-changing tourist center.

We're going to be honest from the get-go and admit that—although every effort was made to ensure accuracy—some of the information in this volume will be imprecise, outdated, and just plain wrong. It's the nature of the game: restaurants close, menus change, chefs move on, and sometimes (but very rarely) sources lie. Because there are so many variables involved, you should always verify our recommendations before you make your travel plans.

Submit!

That's why we need to hear from you: whether you've had a bad experience at a restaurant we recommend, or a great experience at a restaurant we missed, or no experience at all because a restaurant, grocery store, or hotel closed down between the time of our last visit and yours.

Please send your comments and suggestions to the following address:

The Globe Pequot Press
Reader Response/Editorial Department
P.O. Box 480
Guilford, CT 06437

Or you may e-mail us at:

editorial@GlobePequot.com

We can't wait to hear from you!

Vegetarian New York City

The Essential Dining, Shopping,
and Lodging Guide

Foreword by Paul McCartney

Suzanne Gerber

The
Globe
Pequot
Press

GUILFORD, CONNECTICUT

The prices and rates listed in this guidebook were confirmed at press time. We recommend, however, that you call establishments to obtain current information before traveling.

INSIDERS'GUIDE®

Copyright © 2004 by The Globe Pequot Press

Text design: Nancy Freeborn
Photo credits: Jane Krenova, p. 399; Photographs by Zeva Oelbaum: pp. 20, 49, 69, 96, 149, 176, 291, 327, 372; Jane Booth Vollers: p. 228; all spot photos by Photodisk.
Maps: Rusty Nelson © The Globe Pequot Press

Library of Congress Cataloging-in-Publication Data
Gerber, Suzanne.
   Vegetarian New York City: the essential guide for the health-conscious
traveler/Suzanne Gerber; foreword by Paul McCartney.
      p. cm.
   Includes index.
   ISBN: 0-7627-2852-3
      1. Vegetarian restaurants–New York (State)–New York–Guidebooks. I. Title.

TX907.3.N72N437 2003
647.95747'1—dc22

                                                          2003056847

Manufactured in the United States of America
First Edition/First Printing

This series is dedicated to the memory of Linda McCartney,

whose commitment to compassionate living

continues to inspire vegetarians around the world.

For my parents,

who haven't always agreed with my decisions

but have always supported them.

—Suzanne Gerber

Contents

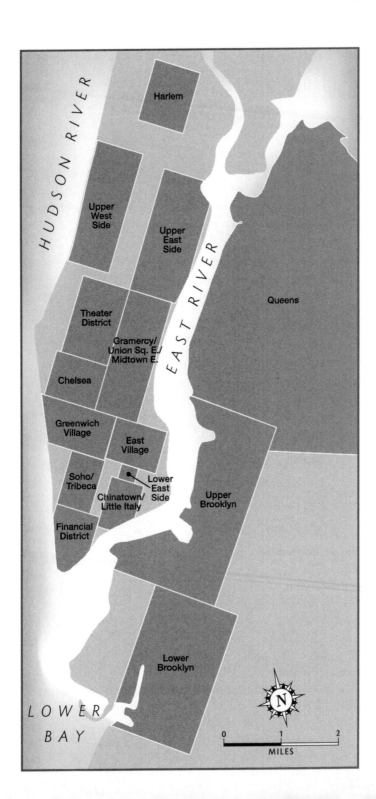

Foreword

As any traveling vegetarian can tell you, this series has been sorely needed for quite some time. Veggies on the road often have to make a special effort to eat right, what with steak houses and fast-food chains dominating the landscape. Even in big cities, the healthy choices are often severely limited.

On our group's world tours, I was blessed to have Linda and the great vegetarian chefs we took on the road with us preparing our meals—and every night the catering room was full of beefy riggers wolfing down the fantastic food! But it's a bit difficult to imagine Mum and Dad finding a way to squeeze the luggage, kiddies, Fido and Chef Jacques into the minivan for a holiday at the beach.

That's where these new Vegetarian World Guides come in. With one of these books in your suitcase, backpack, or glove box, you'll be able to find really great food on the road, without compromising your ideals.

In fact, it was while traveling that Linda and I often reaffirmed our commitment to a vegetarian diet and to the animals it saves. Driving through the agricultural regions of England and America, passing truckloads of sheep and cows headed for the "processing plant," our hearts were broken time and again. But experiences like those just made it that much more satisfying to tuck into a really delicious veggie meal at the end of the day.

After all, as Linda used to say, "Being vegetarian is about living life, not ending it." And veggies have known for years that it's a lot easier to end the suffering of others if you don't have to suffer yourself to do it! Back in the '60s, you'd order a sandwich at a vegetarian café, and this piece of dried bread with a bit of lettuce on it would come back. You'd be thinking, "Ooo, er, dear me, don't think I could ever go vegetarian!" But these days the idea of the vegetarian as some sort of dour, suffering martyr is long gone, thanks to the wonderful variety of food that we veggies can easily prepare or find on a menu.

Not only is it a lot easier to choose vegetarian meals, it just makes a lot of sense. Vegetarianism takes care of so many things in one shot: ecology, famine, cruelty, health—and it's great to see that nowadays more and more people are looking for kinder ways of living.

So if you haven't given vegetarianism a try, now is the time to do it: while you're on a trip and can look forward to really incredible meals prepared by some of the world's best chefs. You're sure to pick up a few great ideas to make your own meals at home more exciting, too. Linda and I often noticed that people who went veg ended up rediscovering their passion for food and all the varied and wonderful flavors that they'd lost while stuck in the rut of "meat and two veg."

For you vegetarians who've bought this guide, I don't need to convince you of the benefits of the veggie lifestyle. But I do want to tell you that this series is a sign that things are getting better—for vegetarians, for the animals, and for the planet. And as a part-time New Yorker, I can attest to the incredible vegetarian meals this city has to offer.

You've made the right choice. There are more options than ever, more vegetarians than ever, and now there are these great new Vegetarian World Guides. Linda was right when she said, "Going veggie is the single best idea for the new century." So what are you waiting for? Get out there and eat!

—PAUL McCARTNEY
London, England

Preface

This series is based on a radical notion: Vegetarians love food, and they recognize and appreciate good food.

When people choose to alter their diet—for health, compassion, or environmental reasons—they do not suddenly lose their sense of taste or their desire for comfy or elegant or serene environs, exciting creations, or knowledgeable, compassionate servers.

In addition to loving food, vegetarians know food. They've been forced to experiment with "exotic" cuisines and to learn how to make great food at home, throwing themselves into the lifestyle with gusto. Indeed, many vegetarian diners know more about certain ingredients and techniques than the chefs who cook their meals.

Thankfully, healthful choices have become more commonplace on menus over the past several years, and today almost every restaurant offers at least one meatless meal. But with greater awareness comes higher standards, and every vegetarian has a few war stories about meatballs in the marinara sauce or fish in the we-swear-it's-veggie kimchee. If you're not willing to settle for such fare, you still have to do an awful lot of legwork to find a really good meal, whether on vacation at Walt Disney World or in the middle of Manhattan. And wading through listings on Web sites isn't always much help—or much fun—when you want to know which Indian restaurant uses the freshest spices or whose vegan cookies aren't the consistency of rocks.

That's where we come in.

Vegetarian Guides are for people who love to travel but want to maintain their commitment to living well—a demographic that includes more than one-third of all Americans today. As the first mainstream, internationally marketed guides devoted to healthful travel and great veg dining, our books offer a fresh, sometimes irreverent, perspective. And instead of focusing on esoteric retreat centers, we start with a popular travel destination—like Disney World or New York City—and find the best places for vegetarians to eat, sleep, and shop for food.

Like a conventional travel guide, Vegetarian Guides paint a portrait of the destination, but with an emphasis on healthful, veg-friendly establishments. Unlike conventional travel guides, Vegetarian Guides will tell you whose "vegetarian" soup is made with chicken stock and whose refried beans are cooked with lard. And unlike any other vegetarian publication, we rate establishments with our vegebility index: a simple but effective method of evaluating the veg-friendliness of mainstream restaurants and an indispensable aid when you're dining with folks who eat meat. We provide at-a-glance information grids at the beginning of each review to help you choose a restaurant as painlessly as possible, with a plethora of information at your fingertips. We help you get to the restaurant with maps. We also give you lots of insider information by including reviews by locals, profiles of master chefs, and roundups of the best veggie sushi, lunch carts, and mock meat restaurants in town.

We approach the researching and recommending of establishments with two aims. First, we want to provide as many options as possible in a given destination, so we recommend outstanding vegetarian choices at restaurants that also serve meat—as well as tactful ways to let the management know you prefer meatless selections. Second, we want to further conscious dining by suggesting completely vegetarian restaurants so good that they don't require a cultural paradigm shift on the part of one's meat-eating companions. Many a longtime vegetarian has relished hearing a carnivorous relative wonder aloud, "Are you *sure* this is vegetarian?"

Acknowledgments

A truly great meal is measured not by just the quality of one dish, but by the progression of tastes from one course to the next, by gracious service, and by exceptional atmosphere. In the same way, this work has benefited from the hands and hearts of many individuals, without whose help and encouragement the book would not exist. First of all, I wish to thank Susan Shumaker and Than Saffel, creators of this series, gifted editors and reviewers in their own rights, and warm and dear friends. Their idea for a series of vegetarian world guides is indeed visionary, and their sustained dedication to the project is inspirational. On a more personal note, I am grateful to them for offering this project to me—originally they had planned to do it themselves. I'm glad they decided that writing this book from their farm in West Virginia was just slightly impractical. Susan, in particular, was a tremendous source of help, inspiration, and support at every turn.

An enormous debt of thanks is also due to The Globe Pequot Press, especially editors Laura Strom, whose enthusiasm, advice, patience, and support are a big reason this book exists in the first place, and Gillian Belnap, whose devotion to this project has been a godsend. And a very special place in editors' heaven is no doubt being reserved for Elissa Curcio, who copyedited this book with extraordinary care.

They've heard it from me a dozen times, but I must put in writing my deep appreciation for our talented team of volunteer reviewers, who endured meal after incredible meal to bring you this information, which you will not find anywhere else. But it wasn't just a gravy train of fabulous dinners for them: They interrogated and cross-examined servers and cooks with skills that top litigators would envy. I'd like to think they've sniffed out every last, lurking piece of bacon and cube of chicken bouillon in all of New York City. In alphabetical order, those indefatigable souls are Alia Akkam, Phil Andrews, Blair Barnette, Diana Bocco, Antrim Caskey, Sezin Cavusoglu, Brian Cazeneuve, Mary Margaret Chappell, Eureka Freeman, Rebecca Gould, Julie Hollar, Esther James, Carlos and Kathleen Lopez, Christina Massey, Lara Olchanetzky, Emily Park, Jewel Elizabeth Partridge, Lisa Poliak, Eileen Regan (who really deserves an assistant editor credit on this book for not just going beyond the call of duty but for bringing so much talent and enthusiasm to the project), Emily ("Emu") Rubin, Melena Z. Ryzik, Marianne Semchuk, Rebecca Krasney Stropoli, and Jessica Wurwarg. These people amazed me with their knowledge, dedication, and talent; it's an understatement to say this book could not have been done without their help.

Though less directly involved with the project, some people provided invaluable advice, support or necessary infusions of humor. Heartfelt thanks to Medéa ("Ms. Second Amendment") Eder, Charles ("Chuck") Isaacs, Diane ("Magic Fingers") Gerber, John ("Ol' Buck") Ross, Peter ("Sorvino") Cervoni, Joy Pierson and Bart Potenza, Rachel and Danny Tove, and everyone at Greenmarket. I also wish to express gratitude to my various dining companions, who would slam the brakes on intense personal discussions to help me deconstruct entrées or find yet another synonym for *delicious*. More indirect appreciation must be given to Donna Sapolin and Toni Apgar, who hired, nurtured, and mentored me during my four wonderful years at Vegetarian Times, in effect my training ground for this book. Gratitude, also, to my former colleagues there, for both sharing the mission of bringing great vegetarian food to the public and for making the daily grind more fun than a job has any business being.

But the most important acknowledgment must be saved for the restaurants and health food stores themselves. To all the shop owners, restaurateurs, chefs, cooks, servers, and even publicists who helped make this book a reality, thank you. Thanks not just for welcoming us into your restaurants, feeding us like kings, and patiently answering every question we could throw at you, but for doing what you do on a daily basis. You are the true heroes, and without you we'd all be warming up soup at home. And a big shout out to the farmers and producers of good food everywhere. By providing us with such healthy fare, you are surely doing God's work.

Last but hardly least, thank you, reader, for buying—and using—this book. We really do vote with our dollars, so let's support the people who devote their lives to bringing us fresh, clean plant food. Thank you all from the bottom of the food chain.

About This Book

This book was written with one purpose: to help vegetarians, vegans, and just health-minded people have the best vegetarian dining experiences possible in New York City. Period. That could mean eating at one of our many wonderful all-veg places, or at one of the hundreds of veg-friendly places, or even at a place that's decidedly not veg in the least but offers the greatest veg tasting menu on Earth or the most romantic setting (or just the best pizza). This book is intended to provide ideas and information not just for visitors, but for New Yorkers who love great food and need some new suggestions.

THE METHODOLOGY

The entries in this book were selected using very scientific principles: what I've liked in my own twenty years in New York City—all of them as a vegetarian—and the suggestions of local vegetarians and foodies. Aided by two dozen able-bodied contributors, I wrote this guide based on personal visits and tastings. When we visited, we doggedly interrogated the waitstaff and kitchen help (and often the head chefs and owners themselves) with the same questions: Are the veggies grilled on the same surface as the lamb chops? Are the beans cooked in lard? Bacon fat? Monkey grease? Does the soup have chicken stock in it? Fish stock? Chunks of beef left over from yesterday's soup du jour? What are the ingredients in the bread? Is the crust brushed with egg or butter? And so on. In the process we learned a lot more than we ever thought possible (and perhaps more than we ever wanted to) about vegetarian dining in the greatest city in the world.

And yet, even we have our limits. We are not chefs. We do not claim to be experts in every cuisine or cooking technique. But we do love good food, and we do hate bad food, especially when it's served to vegetarians. And we certainly do claim to have done an enormous amount of research, to care about our readers' experience, and to be a waiter's worst nightmare no matter where we go.

HOW TO USE THIS GUIDE

Because we've cross-referenced almost everything and included maps of every neighborhood, you can approach this book from a few different directions, so to speak. If you're looking for something in a particular neighborhood, go directly to the appropriate chapter and read through the reviews, or check out our star-rated suggestions for "Best of Best" on the chapter map. There's also an "Editor's Picks" section in the Introduction.

If you've heard of a particular place but don't know where it is or whether it'll suit your tastes, check the index, find it alphabetically, and go to the full review. The indexes also list restaurants by "vegebility," price, and type of food, so if you have a taste for Tibetan, a craving for Korean, an itch for Italian, or a yen for Japanese, check out those lists and narrow your search.

Of course, if you have a bit more time on your hands, skim—or, heck, read all the way through—the reviews until you find something that perfectly suits your fancy. We've done the hard part for you, culling the best of the best, so chances are you won't be disappointed with anything in this book.

Then again, if you're on West 13th Street and your blood sugar level starts to crash, flip straight for the maps and work backward from there. That is, check to see what places are closest and use the reviews to find your best bet. The good news: This is New York City. Any time, any neighborhood—you're never more than a few paces from something edible.

If you find a place we haven't reviewed, chances are there was nothing fabulous available for vegetarians there at the time of our research. Or it could be a new restaurant that has opened since the book was published. If the restaurant looks appealing, check it out! The culinary world is mercurial, and new chefs or new management—many with a vegetarian bent—could now be in place.

Symbols

In each chapter of the guide, a restaurant, market, or lodging is assigned a distinct number, repeated in the review and on the map for easy reference. A number in a black circle indicates a reviewed and recommended location that we consider among the "best of the best."

Ratings

PLACES TO EAT

Vegebility Index

The "vegebility" index provides a quick and accurate indication of a reviewed establishment's vegetarian-friendliness. Ratings are based upon the number of vegan and ovo-lacto (o/l) choices available, either on the menu or through the willingness of the kitchen staff to invent along with you. In a few cases there are a more limited number of options, but those dishes are so fabulous, or the kitchen is so flexible, that we felt obliged to mark on a curve.

EXCELLENT: Completely vegetarian or vegan

VERY GOOD: More than eight o/l and four vegan choices

GOOD: four to seven o/l and two to three vegan choices

FAIR: two to three o/l choices and one vegan choice

Dining Prices

The pricing of each restaurant has been categorized according to the average cost of a vegetarian entrée on the menu at breakfast, lunch, and dinner. Please note that nonvegetarian entrées at the same establishment are often much more costly and that fluctuations in price occur frequently.

INEXPENSIVE:
Breakfast/Lunch: . . . . less than $6.00
Dinner: . . . . less than $9.00

MODERATE:
Breakfast/Lunch: . . . . $6.01 to 10.99
Dinner: . . . . $9.01 to $16.99

EXPENSIVE:
Breakfast/Lunch: . . . . $11.00 to $20.00
Dinner: . . . . $17.00 to $25.00

VERY EXPENSIVE:
Breakfast/Lunch: . . . . more than $20.00
Dinner: . . . . more than $25.00

PLACES TO SHOP

How many times have you arrived at your destination only to find that you're almost out of your favorite cruelty-free shampoo or that it's 9:00 P.M. and little Amanda needs her organic banana yogurt *right now?* That's why we've included health food stores in nearly every chapter. But because New York has so many supermarkets with organic sections, delis (often called by their Spanish name, *bodega*), and greengrocers, we've just given health stores overall ratings of Excellent, Very Good, Good, and Fair. With food shops on nearly every block, one could write an entire book on such stores in this city alone!

PLACES TO STAY

Lodging Rates

The hotels and inns included in this guide span a wide range of affordability, depending upon amenities, location, and time of year. In New York City you can spend a king's ransom for a tiny room. We tried to find you clean, well-located, reasonably priced accommodations, paying special attention to places that offer kitchenettes and permit pets. Our classification is based upon the nightly cost of a double room with standard amenities, averaged across low, moderate, and high seasons. Tax is not included. Please note that fluctuations in price and availability occur frequently.

INEXPENSIVE: . . . . $50 to $100

MODERATE: . . . . $101 to $150

EXPENSIVE: . . . . $151 to $250

VERY EXPENSIVE: . . . . more than $250

Introduction: Out of the Pantry!

It's hard to quantify anything in New York City, but the Board of Health estimates that the total number of restaurants is somewhere between 12,000 and 13,000. That means if you ate out three times a day, 365 days a year, for the next ten years, you still wouldn't hit all the city's eateries. And that's assuming no new ones were to open. Locals take the vast number of options for granted, but visitors from towns where you couldn't get veggie pad thai at midnight if your life depended on it—let alone a Tibetan momo—are regularly blown away by the culinary offerings of this city. I've lived here for twenty years, and I'm still amazed at what's available. Ninth Avenue in the 40s and 50s, for example, has become a gastronomic Union Nations over the past decade, and there's one strip that's not to be believed: Mexican, Afghani, Caribbean, Spanish, Thai, Irish, diner, Middle Eastern, sushi, Vietnamese, lounge food, New American, pizza, Brazilian, wine bar, tapas, Greek, Szechuan, and Indian all peacefully coexist within two city blocks. And in my little Brooklyn neighborhood, the former no-man's-land of Smith Street has morphed into one of the hottest food destinations in the five boroughs, with some three-dozen restaurants and watering holes along a half-mile stretch.

Those might be some kind of records, but the rest of the city is no less impressive. In fact, the veg-friendly dining options are so enormous, it would be impossible to include all of them in one book. Out-of-towners often report having one good pizza place back home; here there's one good pizza place every two and a half blocks. Whether you want fast and cheap Chinese delivered to your door or to sit down to the most elegant six-course veg tasting menu paired with exquisite organic wines, you can do it in the Big Apple. Want an entire menu of truffles? How about a gourmet meal prepared with all raw food? You've come to the right city. Here "melting pot" takes on a new meaning; literally every cuisine from Azerbaijan to Zimbabwean can be found. In fact, there are probably a couple of each (two brothers feuding over great-granddad's kebab recipe, no doubt). In New York a meal can set you back half a week's pay, or you can fill yourself to the gills for a fiver. (Of course, if you're like some people we know and couldn't tell the difference, go for the second option.)

Editor's Picks: Best of the Best in NYC

PLACES WE RAVE ABOUT
Angelica Kitchen
Bonobo
Candle Café
Candle 79
Cho Dang Gol
Counter
Gobo
The Green Table
Hangawi
Ilo
Josie's (both)
Kapodoyka
Otto Enoteca Pizzeria
Quintessence
Rose Water

BEST SPLURGES
Anissa
Aureole
Café Boulud
Craft
Franchia
Gramercy Tavern
Hangawi
Ilo
66
Union Pacific

BEST BARGAINS
Ayurveda Café
Café Mogador
18 Arhans
Guru
Madras Café
Mei Ju Vege Gourmet
Thali
The Temple in the Village

BEST AMBIENCE
Angelica Kitchen
Aureole
Balthazar
Candle 79
Craft

Dawat
The Odeon
Oznot's Dish
The Pink Pony
Rice
Tabla
Turkish Kitchen
Vatan

BEST SOUTHERN
Counter
Jezebel
Old Devil Moon

BEST PLACES FOR TEA
Counter
Franchia
Jenny's Café
Teany's
T Salon and Emporium
Wild Lily

BEST PIZZA
Grimaldi's Pizza
Otto Enoteca Pizzeria

BEST HOTEL DINING
Heartbeat
Ilo

MOST ELEGANT
Anissa
Aureole
Café Boulud
Craft
Candle 79
Hangawi
The Odeon
Tabla
Zen Palate

MOST ROMANTIC
Anissa
Balthazar
Capsouto Frères
Gramercy Tavern

Il Cortile
Jezebel
Periyali

MOST PLAYFUL DECOR
Burrito Bar
Cicciolino
Old Devil Moon

BEST WINE LIST
Anissa
Aureole
Balthazar
Café Boulud
Capsouto Frères
Counter
Gramercy Tavern
The Green Table
Otto
Oznot's Dish

BEST-LOOKING PLATES
Candle 79
The Green Table
Hangawi

BEST KARMA
Ayurveda Café
Bonobo
18 Arhans
Franchia
The Sanctuary
Tiengarden

BEST PLACES TO BLOW A DIET
Chinatown Ice Cream Factory
Grimaldi's Pizza

BEST REASONS TO GO TO QUEENS
Oneness Fountain Heart
S'Agapo

In putting together this book, we joked that there are many places in America where a vegetarian dining guide would be a photocopied 8½-by-11-inch sheet of paper. (Folded in half, in the case of my hometown.) We had the exact opposite problem in creating this guide: how to limit the number to fit into a book that wouldn't require a U-Haul to transport it. We started with the top-flight vegan places (the Angelica Kitchens and Candle Cafés, the Quintessences and Counters), branched out to all the vegetarian places, then made a list of all the veg-friendly ethnic places we knew personally as well as the "regular" places that have been wonderfully accommodating to our veg concerns over the years. Coming up with the first hundred was easy. Then we hit a wall: How could we possibly whittle the rest down to just another hundred?

Since there was no way to include everyone, we sought to create a balance. But first and foremost: All the food had to be exemplary. We tried to include some of everything: different ethnicities, neighborhoods, price ranges, atmospheres, and dining experiences. And yet, we had to work with what was out there. Across the board, Indian and Chinese are always going to provide the best (and most plentiful) options for vegetarians because those culinary traditions are veg-based. Also, because rents are typically cheaper downtown— and because, for the most part, there's a younger and "artsier" indigenous customer base—you'll find more and better veg options south of 23rd Street. Of course, some of the very best places are (way) north of 23rd Street, so don't hesitate to jump on a subway or hail a cab to get to them. We included Brooklyn and Queens for two reasons: They're chock-full of incredible restaurants, and (for the most part) they're quick and easy to get to. So apologies to the wonderful places in the Bronx and Staten Island that we left out.

A word about the research: As we disclaimed earlier, we are just a bunch of regular New Yorkers who sampled some 200 meals in the spring of 2003. We know a lot about food and veg issues, but with very few exceptions, we are not professional chefs, detectives, or psychics. When we went to press, every fact was correct: addresses, phone numbers, days and hours, menu items, etc. But this being New York City and the food business, some things could well have changed by the time you pick this book up. Yet an overwhelming majority of places we reviewed have been around for years and years and aren't going anywhere—and aren't planning to change (thank goodness). Still, before you get all gussied up and drop in unannounced to celebrate Aunt Ellen's ninetieth birthday, do call ahead. Check the hours, check the address, check the menu items. Our mission is to help you get the best vegetarian food possible, and we'd hate to think we've misled you.

Here's the bottom line: New York is the greatest city in the world for a vegetarian to dine in, and, since many restaurateurs and chefs truly understand our dietary choices, you almost can't go wrong. But armed with this guide, you will eat like princes and princesses. Vegetarianism is not weird in NYC; in fact, many restaurant owners told us they'd go all veg (or vegan) if it were more economically feasible. So here's a radical notion: Since demand creates supply, let's start making our voices heard by patronizing the great veg places—often—and when we eat in wonderful non-veg places, let's not do so anonymously. Let's find the praiseworthy stuff and acknowledge it. Tell the server or inform the kitchen that we appreciate the veg options they have on the menu. Let them know, for example, that using separate grills or fryers for meat and veggies is not being done for nothing. Thank them for preparing that special risotto without the meat broth. And so on. Of course, if there are minor adjustments that could be made for vegetarians, there's no reason to sulk quietly in our steamed greens. If we are gentle about sharing our suggestions, they might just be acted upon. Unless kitchens learn that things are unsatisfactory, they will never be motivated to make changes. This is how progress occurs. Over the past twenty-five years, discriminating vegetarian diners have come a long way. Finally we're out of the pantry! Let's stay out.

Who Knew? Hidden Ingredients and Other Bugbears

As vegetarians we often turn to ethnic cuisine for tasty, exciting and veg-friendly meals. But hidden in many of those dishes are the very things we seek to avoid. Here's a good reference section for things to ask about when eating different cuisines.

CHINESE

Chinese restaurants, as with all Asian eateries, can be treasure troves for vegetarian diners—if you know what to ask for and what to avoid. Egg roll wrappers are made of wheat flour, water, and—as one might guess—egg; spring roll wrappers, however, are usually comprised of wheat flour and water only. Most Asian soups start with an animal base; egg drop soup, for instance, is often made with chicken stock, and hot-and-sour soup typically has a beef base. When asking about stocks at Chinese restaurants, use the word "broth," a term more commonly used in Asian cooking.

Certain noodle and rice dishes—including the ubiquitous Chinese fried rice—are often simmered in a meat broth as well, whether they are listed on the "vegetarian" menu or not. Many Chinese noodle dishes, including vegetarian lo mein, are made with oyster sauce, a popular Cantonese table and cooking condiment made by reducing oysters, water, and salt to a thick concentrate.

One major drawback to eating at a Chinese restaurant is the high level of fat, cholesterol, and sodium in typical menu items, including lo mein, mu shu, and fried rice. To eat healthfully, order meals that are more like those you'd find on a typical dinner table in China: steamed or "dry wok" vegetables over plain brown rice (and ask your server to please hold the

MSG). If you have the chance, sample some fu yu: wine-fermented soybean curd that tastes remarkably like cheese.

CUBAN

There are two common hobgoblins for vegetarians in all Hispanic restaurants: chicken stock in the rice and pork (or lard) in the beans. Sadly, this is true in many Cuban restaurants. We'd love to sample plato after plato of moros y cristianos ("Moors and Christians," better known as black beans and white rice), but a Cuban restaurant that serves a vegetarian version is devilishly hard to find. If you suspect they don't understand you in English, tell them in Spanish "No como carne" (I don't eat meat). Or you can get even more specific: "¿Hay pollo en los arroz?" (¿eye poy-o en los ARE-ros?; Is there chicken in the rice?) and "¿Hay manteca en los frijoles?" (¿eye mon-TAKE-a en los free-HOLE-ez?; Is there lard in the beans?). This usually works.

Another fabulous Cuban specialty is the sandwich cubano: a half loaf of French bread filled with ingredients and grilled in a sandwich press until its contents are hot. Most contain generous amounts of ham, pork, and cheese, but there are precious few places that will make meatless versions to order. Just be sure to check that the bread doesn't contain lard. Ai yai yai!

FRENCH

With its emphasis on meats and heavy cream sauces, traditional French cooking wasn't typically associated with healthful dining, but with the explosion of nouvelle cuisine in the early 1970s—thanks to chefs like Paul Bocuse and Roger Vergé and more recent missionaries like Patricia Wells—French food suddenly became lighter, fresher, simpler, and much more vegetarian-friendly. It even inspired our most favorite of food revolutionaries, Alice Waters, to craft California produce into a full-fledged cuisine.

When dining at a French restaurant, be on the lookout for the use of meat glazes on vegetables and for meat-based reduction sauces. French onion soup—a staple of French cooking and a great way to use up that stale baguette—is almost always made with a beef stock. Quiche lorraine, a savory egg and cream tart, contains bacon. Strict vegetarians who eat no eggs or dairy should ask about the use of egg washes on breads.

GREEK, MIDDLE EASTERN, AND MOROCCAN

Middle Eastern restaurants are among the most enjoyable places for vegetarians to dine. Vegetable and salad dishes usually take up a large portion of the menu, and high-protein legumes and whole grains have been a staple of the Greek and Middle Eastern diet since the dawn of civilization.

A Greek appetizer not to be missed is dolmadakia, or dolmades: savory stuffed grape leaves. Ask for the vegetarian version, traditionally served cold; meat-filled dolmades are usually hot. If you're concerned about sodium, ask if the grape leaves are fresh or from a can or jar (canned grape leaves are often packed in brine). A wonderful and simple meatless Greek entrée is fava: a puree of yellow split peas blended with onions and garlic, popular among Hellenes during Lent. One warning: Greek rice is often cooked in chicken stock; ask to be sure.

Vegetarian stuffed grape leaves are a common item on Middle Eastern menus as well, often part of a meze, or appetizer, platter that includes hummus bi tahina (a creamy, garlic-laced puree of chickpeas and tahini), baba ghanoush (roasted eggplant dip), and tabbouleh (a lemon-infused salad of bulgur wheat, onions, tomatoes, and lots of parsley). Another staple of the meze platter is falafel: deep-fried chickpea and fava bean balls seasoned with onions, cilantro, garlic, and cumin. Pita sandwiches stuffed with falafel, some sort of salad, and tahini are popular not only in the United States, but also in Israel, where they are jokingly referred to as "Israeli hot dogs."

If you make it to a Moroccan restaurant, be sure to try vegetarian couscous. But again, check to see that the grain is not cooked in a chicken or lamb stock or rolled with butter.

INDIAN

Thanks to the influence of the Hindu and Jain religious traditions—which regard ahimsa, or nonviolence, as a major virtue—Indian cuisine is very vegetarian-friendly. More than 50 percent of all South Asians eschew meat and eggs but do eat dairy products, often in abundance. If you are on a low-fat or vegan diet, ask about the preparation of sauces and breads; many contain cheese, yogurt, or ghee (clarified butter). A good example is nan, a North Indian bread that's flash-baked in a clay tandoor oven. Nan is often vegan (though some cooks add milk or yogurt to the dough) but is frequently topped with butter just before being brought to the table. And in America, mulligatawny—a spicy lentil soup—often contains pieces of chicken and a meat broth. Ask your server to be sure.

ITALIAN

An old standby for healthful dining, Italian restaurants do warrant a mention here, particularly for diners who avoid eggs and dairy. Traditional hard or dried pastas, made with semolina (durum wheat flour) and water, are 100 percent vegan, but many hand- or house-made fresh pastas—ravioli, fettucine, and others—are made with eggs instead of water. Another staple on Italian menus is minestrone, a thick vegetable soup that typically contains pasta and sometimes peas or beans, and often chicken or beef stock. It's also frequently served topped with freshly grated Parmesan or pecorino Romano cheese.

Richly flavored stock—but not always one derived from meat—is a key ingredient in risotto, an Italian rice specialty, as well. Another warning for vegans: The arborio rice used in risotto is traditionally sautéed in butter before simmering in cup after cup of stock or wine. Polenta, an Italian cornmeal mush similar to grits, was a daily staple of the Roman legions. It's been rediscovered by vegetarians looking for a flavorful, hearty main course, in combination with roasted vegetables and topped with butter, oil, or cheese.

JAPANESE

As with Southeast Asian cuisine (see below), the primary bugaboo for vegetarians interested in traditional Japanese cooking is dashi, a broth that's usually based on flakes made from the flesh of the bonito tuna. Dashi provides flavor for a number of concoctions, including otherwise vegetarian delicacies like hijiki—a mild black seaweed dish, often prepared with carrots and tofu—and miso soup, a staple of Japanese breakfasts. Dashi and other broths made with fish are rampant in Japanese restaurants—from miso soup to teriyaki sauce and sometimes the sauce for goma-ae or miso eggplant. Fish is such a mainstay in Japanese culture that even the servers don't realize how commonplace it is, so you really need to "interrogate" your waiter if you are dead-set against having any.

Usually it's better to check out the sushi menu. To please American palates, many sushi bars are starting to offer bite-size pieces of vegetable nori maki, the most common of which is kappa maki. Made with sticky rice and cucumber slices, this mild and refreshing sushi is named for Kappa, a water goblin in Japanese mythology.

MEXICAN

The main thing to look out for at Mexican restaurants is rice and beans, often cooked in chicken broth or with lard, respectively. (See Cuban, above.) Your best bet is to steer toward Cal-Mex cuisine, with its emphasis on big burritos stuffed with salad ingredients and rice, as well as more health-conscious versions of classic Mexican favorites. Be warned, however, that the flour tortilla wraps that hold burritos together sometimes contain lard. Corn tortillas typically do not, but they may be deep-fried in lard prior to serving. Be sure to ask your server what kind of cooking fat is being used. Sauces, like mole poblano, often contain chicken, turkey, or other meat stocks.

SOUTHEAST ASIAN (Burmese, Thai, Cambodian, Vietnamese, Filipino, Malaysian)

Generally light and healthful, Southeast Asian food is among the most veg-friendly cuisines, except for one small and very pungent problem: fish sauce. It is used in everything, it seems—at least all things labeled "vegetarian."

Popular throughout Southeast Asia, fish sauce can be any number of mixtures based on the juices from salted and fermented fish. This distinct, strongly flavored condiment and seasoning is as ubiquitous in Southeast Asian cooking as soy sauce is in Japanese. To compound the problem, fish sauce goes by a variety of names, including nam pla (Thai), nuoc mam (Vietnamese), and patis (Filipino).

Once you manage to steer clear of the nam pla, many Thai dishes, especially curries, are vegan—they're made with coconut milk in place of dairy. The mildest of the vegetarian Thai curries is yellow massaman, followed in BTUs by red curry, and reaching their final gastrothermal glory in the green panang curries: the hottest of the hot, equivalent to Indian vindaloo. The two most common desserts in American

Thai restaurants—sang ka ya, steamed pumpkin custard made with coconut milk, and kha niew mamuang, sticky rice flavored with coconut cream and sugar and topped with sliced mango—are vegan as well.

In Vietnam it's practically a punishable offense to serve a spring roll without a little jar of nuoc cham, the national table condiment. Akin to the classic Indian pairing of onion chutney and sweet tamarind sauce, or Chinese duck sauce and hot mustard, nuoc cham usually contains nuoc mam—an anchovy-based version of fish sauce. Consisting of nuoc mam, vinegar, sugar, chiles, lime juice, and shredded carrot, nuoc cham is utterly delicious—and off limits to strict vegetarians. So when you order cha gio chay (vegetable spring rolls), ask for soy sauce instead. OK, it doesn't have the same *je ne sais quoi*, but it is vegetarian. You'll also want to look out for Vietnamese and Cambodian salads and noodle dishes, which are frequently dressed with fish sauce or peanut sauce (which uses fish sauce as a primary ingredient). Be sure to let your server know ahead of time about your wish to keep your meal fish- and fish-sauce-free.

Perhaps the greatest contribution of Vietnam and Cambodia to the culinary world is a delicacy too often denied vegetarians: the enticing, steaming bowls of white vermicelli noodles and utterly fresh vegetables in broth that the Vietnamese call "pho." Sadly, a bowl of noodles and broth without—yes, you guessed it, fish stock—is unthinkable to most Vietnamese chefs, and the cook who will work with you on this subject is rare indeed. However, the other flavors and textures in a bowl of pho are so yummy, so comforting on a chilly day, so spicy and exhilarating on a baking hot afternoon, that it's certainly worth a try. If you do manage to talk your way into some faux pho, you can bring it closer to the real thing by supplementing a half-hearted vegetable broth with soy sauce to taste, a dash of chili sauce, and a squeeze of lime at the table. It's not exactly authentic, but a decent substitute on the fly.

Once you get past all the piscatory finagling, a Southeast Asian meal can be sublime, with flavors drawing on the fabulous veg cuisines of East Asia—tofu, soy sauce, noodles, stir-frying—and of the Indian subcontinent, with its curries, chilies, rices, and spices. Toss in the sweet, hot sauces of Burma and Malaysia, and you've got a galaxy of flavors that employ veg-friendly practices galore . . . except for all that fish sauce.

If you have a great deal of trouble explaining your avoidance of meat in a Southeast Asian restaurant, one possible solution is to tell your server that you're a Buddhist. Most Vietnamese Buddhists are vegetarian, and certain dishes common to Buddhist kitchens have made their way into the Southeast Asian repertoire. Among the Vietnamese dishes that are usually vegetarian are cari rao kai (curried vegetables), mi don xao chay (tofu, vegetables, and crispy noodles), and rao xao (tofu with mixed vegetables). As always, ask to be certain.

SPANISH

In the United States, Spanish cuisine is frequently confused with Mexican and other Latin American cooking. This is unfortunate, for they have little in common. Spanish dishes are usually mild and closer to the foods of Mediterranean France and Italy. You won't find many tortillas in a traditional Spanish kitchen (unless you count tortilla española, a potato omelette), nor will you find tacos or enchiladas.

There is one major similarity: Spanish rice, like Mexican, is frequently made with a chicken stock base. But other than that, Spanish cuisine, which rarely includes cream or butter, is as low-fat and healthful as the peasant cuisines of Italy and southern France. If you find yourself in a tapas bar or restaurante, be sure to order a cup of gazpacho andaluz: a cold soup of pureed tomatoes, cucumbers, sweet green peppers, garlic, bread crumbs, and olive oil. American chefs often interpret gazpacho as a chunky, fresh tomato and cucumber salsa suspended in its own juices, but it's wonderful in the Andalusian style. Pureed so finely it's almost creamy and reeking of fresh garlic, it's the perfect appetizer on a hot New York summer day.

—SUSAN SHUMAKER AND THAN SAFFEL

Financial District

New York's first district is also its most historic. Lower Manhattan was once the nation's capital, Federal Hall Memorial is where George Washington took his oath as president, and Fraunces Tavern is the spot where he celebrated the end of the Revolutionary War. (Fraunces Tavern, by the way, is one of only eight remaining eighteenth-century buildings in the city.) The heart of downtown is Wall Street, which was once a walled fortress. This tiny corner of the city is the financial capital of the world, with such monoliths as the New York Stock Exchange and the Federal Reserve Bank and several other gleaming and imposing skyscrapers.

Be sure to check out the South Street Seaport for a taste of old New York, with its tall ships, quaint shops, and cobbled streets. At the very tip of Manhattan Island stands Battery Park, with its unparalleled panoramic views of the Statue of Liberty and Ellis Island. The destruction of the World Trade Center has left a visible scar, but as time marches on, this wounded neighborhood is slowly recovering. You'll have to search a bit for great veg eating, but, hey, that's what this guide is for.

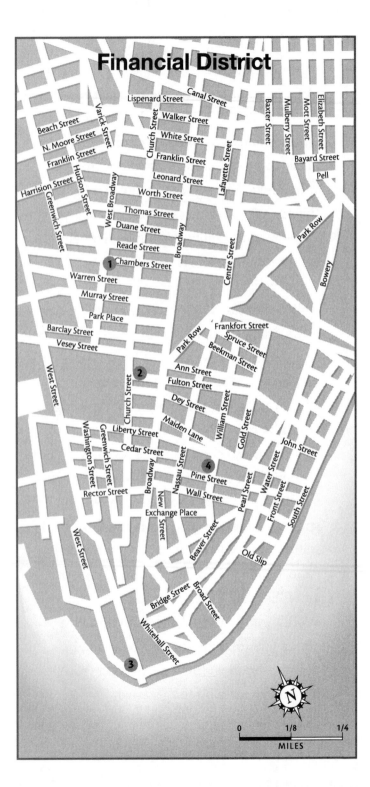

Places to Eat

① Burritoville

144 Chambers Street (at West Broadway)

> **PHONE:** (212) 964–5048
>
> **OTHER LOCATIONS:** 451 Amsterdam Avenue, (212) 787–8181;
> 166 West 72nd Street, (212) 580–7700; 625 Ninth Avenue,
> (212) 333–5352; 352 West 39th Street, (212) 563–9088; 264
> West 23rd Street, (212) 367–9844; 298 Bleecker Street, (212)
> 633–9249; 36 Water Street, (212) 747–1100; 20 John Street,
> (212) 766–2020; 141 Second Avenue, (212) 260–3300; 866
> Third Avenue, (212) 980–4111; 1487 Second Avenue, (212)
> 472–8800
>
> **TYPE OF CUISINE:** Mexican/vegetarian
>
> **DAYS/HOURS:** Varies
>
> **VEGEBILITY:** Excellent
>
> **RESERVATIONS:** Not accepted
>
> **WHEELCHAIR ACCESS:** Yes
>
> **KID-FRIENDLY:** Yes
>
> **TYPE OF SERVICE:** Take-out (seating available but no table serv-
> ice) and delivery (minimum $10)
>
> **PRICING:** Inexpensive
>
> **PAYMENT ACCEPTED:** Major credit cards

Whether you're on the Upper West Side or hanging out in the East Village, you'd be hard-pressed not to stumble upon one of the twelve Burritovilles around Manhattan.

As the name suggests, this is a Mexican-flavored joint. Choose from an extensive menu of tacos, quesadillas, wraps, enchiladas, salads, nachos, soups and chilis, and, of course, burritos. And vegans will appreciate the fact that any item can be made without dairy. (Half the menu is vegan anyway.) Burritoville offers weekly specials, including seven different tortillas, burritos, and wraps (pumpkin, chipolte, or sesame anyone?). The week we were there, they were offering a soy mole burrito and a BBQ tempeh wrap. Try finding something that exotic at another fast-food place. The mandates posted on the wall assure the customers that:

They press all their own tortillas daily.
No lard, pig, or pork.
No preservatives.
No cans in the kitchen.
No prepared products.
Every recipe is made fresh every day.

With Burritoville's exposed brick walls and deep red motif, you feel light-years away from the mass-produced vinyl-and-plastic worlds of other fast-food chains. The posters and paintings on the walls of flamenco dancers and bullfights send you off to faraway Latin locales and the spicy, good-for-you food keeps you coming back for more.

—EILEEN REGAN

If the Spirits Move You: NYC Liquor Laws

As is the case throughout the United States, if you're twenty-one you can purchase the liquor of your choice in New York City. When it comes to dining out, however, you can't always get what you want. While many NYC restaurants have a fully stocked bar with dozens of cocktail choices, plenty of eateries do not have a *full* liquor license, meaning they can offer only beer and wine on their menus. So if you have your heart set on a margarita or Long Island iced tea, it's best to phone ahead.

Some restaurants do not have a liquor license at all—getting one is an expensive and time-consuming process—but often will allow you to bring your own. Some charge you for the privilege, and corkage fees (as they're called) can range from $5.00 to $60.00, depending on the restaurant. (Of course, many places are kind enough to uncork you for free.) Then there are places that serve wine but still allow you to bring your own special bottle; sometimes they will charge a corkage fee only if the wine of your choice cannot also be found on their menu.

Last call for liquor at any restaurant or bar is 4:00 A.M. If you're jonesing for a drink off-hours, you can purchase beer, wine coolers, and hard cider in grocery stores and bodegas around the city twenty-four hours a day, except on Sundays before noon. However, all spirits and wines must be purchased at traditional liquor stores, which are closed on Sunday; check the phone book for listings of New York's extensive roster of excellent spirit shops.

—REBECCA KRASNEY STROPOLI

Places to Stay

2 Fulton Street Suites

110 Fulton Street (between Livingston and Smith Streets)

PHONE: (718) 488–8769
PRICING: Expensive

Luxury doorman building with laundry facilities and spectacular roof garden. Amenities include stereo, TV, VCR, CD player, completely stocked full kitchens, and sheets, towels, and blankets.

3 Oakwood Ocean at 1 West Street

1 West Street

PHONE: (602) 687–3322
PRICING: Moderate

Overlooks Battery Park; some rooms have views of the Statue of Liberty or the water. Small deposit required for pets.

4 Wall Street Inn

9 South William Street (between Broad and William Streets)

PHONE: (212) 747–1500
WEB ADDRESS: www.thewallstinn.com
PRICING: Moderate

For the traveler who wants the downtown location without the corporate blandness.

Chinatown/Little Italy

They used to be separate but equal. But over the past decade, Chinatown has expanded while Little Italy has contracted. Chinatown, sprawling between the north-south borders of Worth and Hester Streets and East Broadway and West Broadway, is not the place for the agoraphobic. Home to the largest Asian population in North America (despite the name, it's not just Chinese here), Chinatown offers visitors everything from traditional herbal medicines to $10 "Rolex"

Chinatown/Little Italy

East Houston Street

Prince Street

④

Elizabeth Street

Mott Street

Bowery

Rivington Street

Spring Street

Broadway

Crosby Street

Mulberry Street

Kenmare Street

Broome Street

Lafayette Street

LITTLE ITALY

Chrystie Street

Forsyth Street

Grand Street

③

Baxter Street

Howard Street

⑦

Canal Street

Centre Street

Hester Street

Walker Street

⑤

White Street

Canal Street

CHINATOWN

Bayard Street

①

Bowery

Mulberry Street

⑥

Pell Street

Division Street

East Broadway

Worth Street

②

Henry Street

Catherine Street

Park Row

Madison Street

N

0   1/8   1/4

MILES

watches to a panoply of restaurants ranging from bargain-priced dim sum to extravagant Mandarin banquets. The swirl of languages, exotic smells and vistas of block after teeming block of exotic produce and pagoda-like buildings might convince you that you've crossed the International Date Line. Be sure to stop by the Eastern States Buddhist Temple on Mott Street—a hidden delight with a hundred golden Buddhas twinkling in the candlelight.

Bordered to the north by Houston Street and to the south by Canal, Little Italy's epicenter is Mulberry Street (*Moonstruck* and *Mean Streets* were both filmed here). A stroll down the cobblestoned streets takes you back in time to the mid-nineteenth century, when the first wave of Italian immigrants was settling into these very tenements. Back then, luxury was a decent meal, a bottle of wine, and maybe a nice cannoli. Funny how little has changed.

Although the number of Italians has dwindled to some 5,000, their presence is very much palpable. Amble past Italian restaurants (thirty-nine in Little Italy, twenty-nine on Mulberry Street alone), espresso cafés, bakeries, and gourmet food shops and window-shop for a place to have dinner. If you want the ultimate Little Italy experience, come in mid-September, when for ten days Mulberry Street hosts the Feast of San Gennaro, patron saint of Italy. Sample zeppoles (fried dough), win a stuffed animal, and pin a dollar bill to the statue of the saint as he's hoisted down the street, just as the locals do. Do anything, in fact, except bring a car into town.

Places to Eat

1 Chinatown Ice Cream Factory

65 Bayard Street (between Mott and Elizabeth Streets)

PHONE: (212) 608–4170

TYPE OF CUISINE: Ice cream and sorbet

DAYS/HOURS: Monday through Sunday from 11:00 A.M. to 11:00 P.M.

VEGEBILITY: Excellent

RESERVATIONS: No

WHEELCHAIR ACCESS: No

KID-FRIENDLY: Very

TYPE OF SERVICE: Take-out

PRICING: Inexpensive

PAYMENT ACCEPTED: Cash only

Feeling a little peckish as you wander around Chinatown? Don't miss the opportunity to sample some of the yummiest sorbets and ice cream in town, in flavors you're unlikely to find elsewhere.

Located between Elizabeth and Mott Streets in the heart of Chi'town, the Chinatown Ice Cream Factory is an NYC institution, jam-packed with locals and savvy *guay low* (a Mandarin term, loosely translated as "gringos"). Since February 1978 owner Sylvia Seid and her family have dished out ice cream "for the adventurous," with flavors like lychee, red bean, almond cookie, and taro listed on the extensive "exotic" menu. Don't miss the delectable green tea version—creamy and smooth, with just a hint of smoky green tea flavor—or the award-winning banana.

Vegans can tuck into a delicious and refreshing true sorbet, made entirely without dairy or egg. Tangerine, pineapple, lychee, blueberry—a total of ten flavors are available. Our favorite is made from longon fruit, sweeter than its sister, the lychee, with a succulent taste reminiscent of pear.

All ice creams are made on the premises and are available in single servings, by the pint, or in gallon-size tubs and even two-and-a-half gallon-size for serious fans. And, in true ice-cream parlor style, all unfamiliar flavors can be sampled before making a final decision.

—SUSAN SHUMAKER

❷ Dim Sum Go Go
5 East Broadway (at Bowery)

> **PHONE:** (212) 732–0796
> **TYPE OF CUISINE:** Chinese dim sum
> **DAYS/HOURS:** Monday through Sunday from 8:30 A.M. to 10:00 P.M.
> **VEGEBILITY:** Good
> **RESERVATIONS:** Suggested
> **WHEELCHAIR ACCESS:** Yes, but restroom is down a flight of stairs
> **KID-FRIENDLY:** Off-hours, yes
> **TYPE OF SERVICE:** Table, take-out, and catering
> **PRICING:** Moderate
> **PAYMENT ACCEPTED:** Major credit cards

It's always a good sign to see locals celebrating in a restaurant. That, we learned, is a common occurrence at Dim Sum Go Go. A combination of fresh food, great location, and hospitable service makes this a regular haunt of Chinatown residents, Lower East Siders, and even government officials. But before we go any further, perhaps we should answer the question, "What, exactly, is dim sum?" The literal translation of the Mandarin phrase is "heart's delight." But that won't help you order. In culinary terms, dim sum consists of a variety of dumplings, steamed dishes, and other goodies such as the famous egg custard tarts.

Dim Sum Go Go is one of the best places for a vegetarian to have his or her heart delighted. At this bustling eatery, with cheerful red walls and waist-high mirrors, we were ushered to a window seat, where we could enjoy the view of busy Chatham Square. After a refreshing cup of jasmine tea, we discussed the difference between Go Go's dim sum and other places' with the manager, Alex. "We steam every dim sum for seven minutes," says Alex. "If you steam more than that, the dim sum is no good."

He was right. Every dumpling is prepared to order, and my selection, the Vegetarian Dim Sum Platter, was amazing: fresh, not sticky or doughy. It arrived in a hot bamboo steamer—no carts here—ten different dumplings circling the centerpiece of white sea fungus, which, trust me, tastes much better than it sounds. It was drizzled with toasted sesame oil and black sesame seeds. Á la carte standouts include the Three Star Dumpling (jicama, cabbage, lotus root), the Green Dumpling (pickled vegetables, fresh black mush-room, white sea fungus), and the Mushroom Dumpling (carrot, wood mushrooms, Chinese mushrooms). All dim sum come with two excellent dipping sauces (a third is made with dried shrimp): a bright and tangy scallion-ginger sauce and a sweet-hot vinegar with chili oil. While there's a vast array of veg options, unfortunately for vegans, wantons, at least here, are made with egg.

Hard as it will be, save room for dessert. The dairy-based Coconut Cake is heaven, flavored with coconut milk, mildly sweet and served cool. The Fresh Mango Pudding is a refreshing tropical end note, especially in warmer months. When it's cooler out, try the warm Tapioca with Egg Yolk (chewy and starchy-sweet but defi-nitely not vegan) or the (also warm) Malaysian Rolls—like an Asian version of the jelly roll, with an egg custard filling. This *must* be a comfort food in Malaysia!

—KATHY AND CARLOS LOPEZ

❸ 18 Arhans
227 Centre Street (between Grand and Broome Streets)

PHONE: (212) 941–8986
WEB ADDRESS: www.18arhans.com
TYPE OF CUISINE: Pan-Asian vegetarian
DAYS/HOURS: Monday through Saturday from noon to 7:00 P.M.; closed on Sunday, but staff is on-site prepping for the coming week and can serve many menu items if you call in advance
VEGEBILITY: Excellent
RESERVATIONS: No
WHEELCHAIR ACCESS: Yes
KID-FRIENDLY: Yes
TYPE OF SERVICE: Table and take-out (order from counter)
PRICING: Inexpensive
PAYMENT ACCEPTED: Cash only
Note: Currently there is no restroom for customers.

Bring your offerings, and your appetite, to Lower Manhattan's only vegetarian cafe/Buddhist shrine. Not only do locals use it as such, one of the three employees is a Buddhist nun. Located near the border of Chinatown and Little Italy, 18 Arhans (the name refers to Buddhist life stages) serves up subtle, made-to-order Pan-Asian food for no more than $7.00 a plate.

An exceptional appetizer is the Curry Spring Roll—the crispy exterior yields to soft, lightly curried vegetables packed with flavor. House Special B is Chinatown's closest cousin to American Southern comfort food. Its mock BBQ pork (smooth-textured wheat gluten and a little dairy) is juicy and savory, well complemented by thick slices of steamed lotus root, broccoli, and bell pepper. The dish also features Arhans' signature tofu, which is made fresh in the neighborhood and acquired by the restaurant daily.

In addition to the three permanent house specials (mock meat dishes with vegetables), the bulk of the menu is comprised of twenty-five Lunch Box dishes (despite the name, they're available all day and do not have to be ordered to carry out) and a range of tofu-vegetable incarnations. The restaurant's many regulars all have their favorites. While the majority of the dishes are vegan, selections containing dairy or egg products are clearly marked on the menu.

Omelettes are available with mock ham or ginger tofu, and there's even an vegan alternative: the substantial Seaweed Bean Curd Crepe. Dumpling fans not put off by a little excess oil will enjoy the Pan-Fried Dumplings, served with a basic Asian vinegar sauce. (House dumplings with mushrooms can be served boiled instead of fried.) The homemade Seaweed Bean Curd Chips have a silky bite and a note of sweetness.

Meals are served with uninspired but filling white rice. Wash them down with the robust and smooth green tea—available iced on warmer days. Bottled soy milk (the owner's favorite brand) and commercial juices are also available.

To fully enjoy the rustic temple decor, choose a seat near the 9-foot shrine to the warrior Guan Gong. Tips can be offered to his memory—or to your memory of a great meal.

—ESTHER JAMES

❹ Ghenet

284 Mulberry Street (between Prince and Houston Streets)

PHONE: (212) 343–1888

TYPE OF CUISINE: Ethiopian

DAYS/HOURS: Tuesday through Thursday from noon to 4:00 P.M. and from 5:00 to 10:30 P.M., Friday and Saturday noon to 4:00 P.M. and from 5:00 to 11:00 P.M., Sunday noon to 3:00 P.M.

VEGEBILITY: Very good

RESERVATIONS: No

WHEELCHAIR ACCESS: Yes

KID-FRIENDLY: Yes

TYPE OF SERVICE: Table

PRICING: Moderate

PAYMENT ACCEPTED: Major credit cards

Wander too far north on Mulberry Street in Little Italy and you'll end up in Africa—or at least that's how it feels when you experience Ghenet, a charming Ethiopian restaurant owned by (Ms.) Yeworkwoha Ephrem. Native art adorns the scarlet walls and handicrafts sit in corners, bringing Ethiopia to a neighborhood that has not only embraced Ghenet but has helped it to thrive over the past five years.

Meals are served family-style, and a soft bread (injera) is used in place of utensils. The meal begins by sharing the injera (in this case, baked crispy) and dipping it in a thin, vinegar-laced chickpea paste similar to hummus. Injera, made from an indigenous gluten-free grain, is not only the smallest grain in existence, but it's also high in iron and packed with protein. The vegetarian menu here is fairly extensive. Most Ethiopians abstain from eating meat 200 days a year (meat is mostly used to celebrate religious holidays). All appetizers on the menu are vegetarian, though vegans should be aware that most contain fried butter. The nine labor-intensive vegetarian entrées, however, are completely dairy-free, and prepared with only the freshest ingredients, including, we are told, love.

Entrées can be ordered individually or as a combination platter. Either way, you'll get injera and a choice of two dipping sauces (mild or spicy) made from lentils. (Note: If the sauce or the dip is red, it's spicy!) Having sampled eight of the nine veggie dishes, we can assure you there isn't a clunker in the bunch. All are made from familiar vegetables (green beans, carrots, collards, beets, potatoes) or lentils. Each has a unique flavor yet is delicately spiced and tastes as though it has simmered for hours. When combined, any two or more dishes are simply heavenly. Ghenet, which means "paradise," is surely where angels eat!

—KATHY AND CARLOS LOPEZ

5 Il Cortile

125 Mulberry Street (between Hester and Canal Streets)

PHONE: (212) 226–6060; Fax: (212) 431–7283
WEB ADDRESS: www.ilcortile.com
TYPE OF CUISINE: Italian
DAYS/HOURS: Sunday through Thursday from noon to midnight, Friday and Saturday noon to 1:00 A.M.
VEGEBILITY: Fair (but happy to accommodate any request)
RESERVATIONS: Recommended on weekends
WHEELCHAIR ACCESS: Yes
KID-FRIENDLY: Yes
TYPE OF SERVICE: Table
PRICING: Expensive
PAYMENT ACCEPTED: All credit cards

The first thing that strikes you as you enter this landmark restaurant in the heart of Little Italy is the grand Roman garden room at the back of the building. Reconstructed from an ancient Roman wall (brought over from Italy piece by piece), the back wall is a gorgeous backdrop for this open and airy dining area. You don't so much feel that you're in Little Italy as you do that somehow, like the wall in reverse, you've been transported to Italy itself. In addition to the atrium, there's a private room for parties and an upstairs lounge area, where patrons sip wine while waiting for their table. But the nicest thing about this lovely and authentic restaurant is that it not only accommodates vegetarians, but welcomes them.

Il Cortile is home to executive chef Michael DeGeorgio, one of Manhattan's premier Italian chefs. Italian cooking is very adaptable to the vegetarian palate, but even though there aren't many veg dishes listed on the menu, the chef and the owner are working to change that and are happy to oblige any requests.

Don't overlook simple delights in search of the exotic. For example, the string bean salad (fagiolini) is just super-fresh beans bathed in balsamic vinegar. It's refreshing and crunchy, and the vinegar has a nice tartness without being too acidic. Or try that Italian favorite, the stuffed artichoke, which is extremely textured in flavor without being overwhelming. Parmesan (Reggiano, of course), bread crumbs, and garlic complete the dish. We also sampled the fried zucchini and battered artichoke leaves. Hearty and satisfying, these are not for those scared of fried food.

Our main course was a pasta dish: orecchiette with zucchini, artichoke, asparagus, bell pepper, fennel, and basil liberally cooked in garlic, onion, and olive oil (the holy trinity of Mediterranean cooking). We decided this dish is the perfect universal comfort meal.

Finish on a sweet note, with a tasting of cheesecake or tiramisu. The former is light and spongy, like true Italian cheesecake, with the perfect note of lemon. The tiramisu was creamy and sweet, ideal for a serious sweet tooth.

The attentive staff is friendly and knowledgeable, and they speak of each dish so proudly, you'd think they made it themselves. This is also the place to go for your birthday. The waiters join together to sing "Happy Birthday" in Italian, and, after the second or third time in an evening, you might find yourself singing along. You come away with the feeling that Il Cortile truly wants you to feel like part of *la famiglia*.

—EILEEN REGAN

⑥ Vegetarian Dim Sum House

24 Pell Street (between Bowery and Mott Street)

PHONE: (212) 577–7176
TYPE OF CUISINE: Chinese vegan
DAYS/HOURS: Monday through Sunday from 10:30 A.M. to 10:30 P.M.
VEGEBILITY: Excellent
RESERVATIONS: Suggested
WHEELCHAIR ACCESS: Yes
KID-FRIENDLY: Yes
TYPE OF SERVICE: Table, take-out, and delivery
PRICING: Inexpensive
PAYMENT ACCEPTED: Cash only

At Vegetarian Dim Sum House, hidden away on Pell Street in Chinatown, the chefs have perfected the art of making mock meat. Among the many options you will find here are the delectable vegetarian "roast pork" buns. Steamed to perfection, the buns are light and airy, the mock pork savory and tender. The fried turnip cakes, which sound like something you would never order, are actually delicious and not to be missed.

Dim sum can be a terrifying experience for those of us who are picky about what we put in our mouths, even for the carnivores among us. Thankfully, everything at Vegetarian Dim Sum House is 100 percent vegan. Translation: You don't need to worry about biting into a steamed bun only to find twelve tiny sets of eyes staring back at you. Best of all, most of the dim sum plates are way cheap—only $2.25 apiece.

There's also a full menu of inexpensively priced appetizers, soups, and entrées, featuring vegetarian facsimiles of Chinese restaurant standards like sweet-and-sour "chicken," Peking "spare ribs," and "beef" with barbecue sauce. And if you're not in the mood for flesh—fake or otherwise—there are plenty of straightforward veggie dishes. Our favorite is Straw Mushrooms and Bean Curd, tossed in a deliciously smoky black bean sauce. For dessert, don't miss the mango pudding, made without eggs. Chinese beer is sold here; you may also BYO wine.

—SUSAN SHUMAKER

Places to Shop

7 VegeCyber
210 Centre Street (between Canal and Grand Streets)

PHONE: (212) 625–3980; Fax (212) 625–8893
WEB ADDRESS: www.vegecyber.com
DAYS/HOURS: Monday through Sunday from 9:30 A.M. to
7:00 P.M.
OVERALL: Very good

Though vegetarian food is not a new concept for Chinatown, health food stores certainly are. Just around the corner from the well-known but mostly wholesale May Wah Healthy Vegetarian Food (lots of frozen items like veggie dumplings) is VegeCyber, which bills itself as Chinatown's first and only organic grocery. The inviting store, with an extensive and intriguing frozen-food section—veggie prawns, anyone?—also has a wide selection of curative teas and a small book section, as well as the standard Chinese sauces, rice and noodles and Western products (Annie's, Tom's of Maine). But the real reason to visit is for the Chinese specialty items and the MSG-free veggie lunchbox.

Don't "Mock" It Till You Try It

Veggie burgers and tofu dogs were the first of the faux meats to hit the American veg scene, but today diners can find everything from mock chicken nuggets to fake ribs and ersatz caviar. Some people can't get enough of this stuff, others run from it, but one thing's for sure: It's a food trend that here's to stay.

Actually, the tradition of fake meat has a long history, stemming back to the Buddhist monks of China, who followed the Buddha's edict against killing sentient beings. Even nonvegetarians in China partake of occasional vegetarian meals, which are said to promote clarity and spiritual wellness. Mock duck—a deliciously sweet concoction of rice-wine-soaked ribbons of tofu skin stuffed with minced mushrooms—is a specialty in Shanghai, where a sophisticated vegetarian cuisine has developed as a result of the great concentration of monks, and can be found at many traditional Chinese restaurants throughout the city.

But leave it to NYC chefs to take the faux frenzy to new heights. There's an actual "New York" fusion-based style, and it prevails at the trendier joints. Many of these spots are Chinese owned and operated but frequently offer much more than the standard Chinese menu fare: Mex/Asian fusion dishes at Zen Palate, for example, or soul food at Red Bamboo. But it's not limited to expensive places. At Mei Ju Vege Gourmet, for example, you can get an excellent full meal for under $10.

So what's in this mystery mock meat? The ingredient of choice at many places is that humble chameleon, the soybean. But wheat gluten and seitan (another wheat product) are also used to make everything from cornmeal-crusted "calamari" to mock steak. A few other surprising ingredients used to fake it include taro (Chinese yam), mushrooms, and arrowroot.

While mock meat can be found at virtually all vegetarian restaurants these days, this section highlights those eateries devoted to this new and immensely popular cuisine.

—EMILY PARK

House of Vegetarian

68 Mott Street, Chinatown (between Bayard and Canal Streets)

PHONE: (212) 226–6572
DAYS/HOURS: Monday through Sunday from 11:00 A.M. to 11:00 P.M.
VEGEBILITY: Excellent
RESERVATIONS: No
WHEELCHAIR ACCESS: No
KID-FRIENDLY: Yes
TYPE OF SERVICE: Table, take-out
PRICING: Inexpensive
PAYMENT ACCEPTED: Cash only

The massive book-of-a-menu is filled with mock duck, pork, chicken, seafood, and beef. House of Vegetarian's food is so amazing and inexpensive that it's become a haven for vegetarian and nonvegetarians alike. I loved the veggie dumplings and the mock duck, roast pork, and lemon chicken, but anything you choose will fill your belly to the brim. The portions are huge, and the food is flavorful, not greasy.

Mei Ju Vege Gourmet

154 Mott Street, Chinatown (between Broome and Grand Streets)

> **PHONE:** (646) 613–0643
> **DAYS/HOURS:** Monday through Sunday from 8:00 A.M. to 8:00 P.M.
> **VEGEBILITY:** Excellent
> **RESERVATIONS:** No
> **WHEELCHAIR ACCESS:** Yes
> **KID-FRIENDLY:** Yes
> **TYPE OF SERVICE:** Take-out plus one table that seats three to four
> **PRICING:** Inexpensive
> **PAYMENT ACCEPTED:** Cash only

It's hard to spend more than $5.00 at Mei Ju Vege Gourmet, a hole-in-the-wall buffet style spot with some twenty different Chinese vegan dishes plus small snack items like spring rolls and fake chicken tenders. A quarter will buy you a good-size portion of white rice, and two quarters will get you perfectly cooked brown rice. While it's hard to draw the staff out about what all the different items are, you really can't go wrong tasting a little of everything: The roast pork, sesame chicken, string beans, bok choy, and veggie curry are all uniformly superb.

Vegetarian Palate

258 Flatbush Avenue, Park Slope, Brooklyn (between Prospect Street and St. Marks)

> **PHONE:** (718) 623–8808 or 8809
> **DAYS/HOURS:** Monday through Thursday from 11:30 A.M. to 11:00 P.M., Friday and Saturday 11:30 A.M. to midnight, Sunday noon to 11:00 P.M.
> **VEGEBILITY:** Excellent
> **RESERVATIONS:** No
> **WHEELCHAIR ACCESS:** Yes
> **KID-FRIENDLY:** Yes
> **TYPE OF SERVICE:** Table, take-out, and delivery
> **PRICING:** Inexpensive
> **PAYMENT ACCEPTED:** Major credit cards

In February 2003 Park Slope gained its first mock-meat joint. The dishes are largely based on soy protein and include crispy nuggets with an addictive sweet-and-smoky sauce, General Tso's chicken and orange beef, and seeming idiosyncrasies such as faux turkey with mashed potatoes. Good news for vegans: The only dishes to avoid are the two fried noodle dishes, which contain eggs.

Vegetarian Paradise 3

33–35 Mott Street, Chinatown (between Park Row and Pell Street)

PHONE: (212) 406–6988 or (212) 406–2896

DAYS/HOURS: Monday through Thursday from 11:00 A.M. to 10:00 P.M., Friday through Sunday 11:00 A.M. to 11:00 P.M.

VEGEBILITY: Excellent

RESERVATIONS: Not necessary

WHEELCHAIR ACCESS: Yes

KID-FRIENDLY: Yes

TYPE OF SERVICE: Table, take-out, and delivery

PRICING: Inexpensive

PAYMENT ACCEPTED: MC/V

Vegetarian Paradise 3, on a bustling strip of Chinatown's Mott Street, offers one of the more "authentic" Chinese dining experiences. Here you can feast on traditional fare like salt-and-pepper prawns, with a texture, flavor, and color eerily reminiscent of the real thing. A resident "nutritional consultant" has developed a tribean soy milk, made from sprouted soy and red and black beans for maximum health benefits. The milk—quite different from grocery brands, with a fresher, nuttier flavor—is made on the premises every couple of days and is available sweetened or unsweetened. The crowd is part of the enjoyment: Chinese families enjoying their big weekend meal next to a dreadlocked guy who hopped off his bike for a solo lunch of sesame chicken.

Also Notable:

Vege Vege II brings mock meat to Manhattan's Murray Hill, with entrées ranging from customary Chinese stir-fry and tofu dishes to elaborate concoctions like Sutra Bundles (zucchini, asparagus, basil, black mushrooms, and water chestnuts wrapped with vegetarian meat) and Golden Boat (steamed pumpkin stuffed with minced mock ham, baby corn, water chestnuts, lotus root, red peppers, and snow peas). Wine, beer, and fresh juices are also available.

Zen Palate, which opened in 1991, was one of the pioneers of the mock meat dining revolution in New York City. Hardly able to keep the doors back then, the ZP empire has new branches sprouting up left and right. In contrast to the other mock-meat palaces, Zen Palate (and its new, more upscale sibling, Gobo) offers a more refined dining experience. The philosophy of the three women who own ZP, all Buddhist vegetarians, also differs in that they don't intend for their dishes to imitate meat; rather, items like the popular Sesame Medallions and Sweet-and-Sour Sensation are delicious in their own right.

And there's . . .

Buddha Bodhai, 18 Arhans, Gobo, The Greens, Happy Buddha, House of Vegetarian, Red Bamboo, Tiengarden, Vegetarian Dim Sum House, Zenith Vegetarian Cuisine (see reviews)

Soho/Tribeca

Within the blocks SOuth of HOuston Street (pronounced Howston) and north of Canal Street are some of the most beautiful cast-iron-fronted buildings in the world. What was once a warehouse wasteland has become the city's leading center of art galleries and designer boutiques. Artists discovered the lofts and huge spaces in the 1980s, and the yuppies weren't far behind. With impossibly trendy shops (so trendy we probably need to spell it "shoppes") and chic restaurants, those same artists sought refuge in Tribeca (TRiangle BElow CAnal). This neighborhood, with the coolest etimology this side of DUMBO, is best known for its large, elegant restaurants. From Nobu to Tribeca Grill (and Robert DeNiro's Tribeca Films company), it is just beginning to feel overrun by hipsters and strollers. The desolate vibe is a favorite among the fashionistas, making it real easy to spot a celeb sipping a coffee or chowing down. Restaurants here are on the upscale side, but there's plenty of affordable healthy eating for a vegetarian in all black.

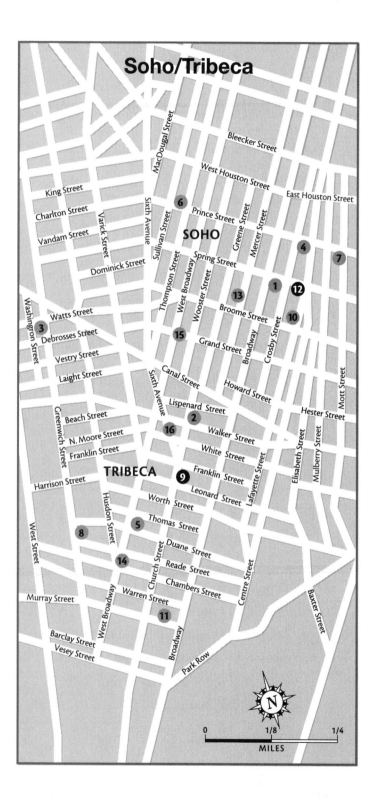

Soho/Tribeca

MacDougal Street
Bleecker Street
West Houston Street
East Houston Street
King Street
Charlton Street
Vandam Street
Varick Street
Sixth Avenue
Sullivan Street
Prince Street
6
Greene Street
Mercer Street
SOHO
4
7
Dominick Street
Thompson Street
West Broadway
Spring Street
Wooster Street
1
12
Washington Street
3
Watts Street
13
Broome Street
Broadway
Crosby Street
10
Debrosses Street
Vestry Street
15
Grand Street
Laight Street
Canal Street
Howard Street
Mott Street
Sixth Avenue
Lispenard Street
2
Hester Street
Greenwich Street
Beach Street
16
Walker Street
Elisabeth Street
Mulberry Street
N. Moore Street
White Street
Lafayette Street
Franklin Street
TRIBECA
9
Franklin Street
Harrison Street
Leonard Street
Hudson Street
Worth Street
West Street
8
5
Thomas Street
Duane Street
Church Street
14
Reade Street
Centre Street
Chambers Street
Murray Street
West Broadway
Warren Street
11
Barclay Street
Broadway
Vesey Street
Park Row
Baxter Street

N

0   1/8   1/4
MILES

Places to Eat

❶ Balthazar

80 Spring Street (between Broadway and Lafayette Street)

PHONE: (212) 965–1414; Fax: (212) 965–9590

TYPE OF CUISINE: French bistro

DAYS/HOURS: Monday through Thursday from 7:30 A.M. to 1:00 A.M., Friday and Saturday 7:30 A.M. to 2:00 A.M., Sunday 7:30 A.M. to midnight (closed for brief intervals each day)

VEGEBILITY: Good

RESERVATIONS: Recommended

WHEELCHAIR ACCESS: Yes

KID-FRIENDLY: Yes (they provide crayons, too!)

TYPE OF SERVICE: Table, take-out, and delivery

PRICING: Expensive

PAYMENT ACCEPTED: Major credit cards

This is a must-do for any saavy tourist coming to New York. In fact, it's a must-do for New Yorkers as well. Not only is Balthazar still one of the hottest places in Manhattan after nearly a decade (and still great for celeb-watching), but the food is simply out of this world.

Balthazar is a bustling Parisian brasserie, complete with the requisite red leather seating, brass mirrors, antique lighting, and raw bar, which we'll skip right over. We highly recommend the Warm Goat Cheese and Carmelized Onion Tart for starters. Decidedly not vegan, it somehow manages to be rich and light at the same time. There are also numerous veg salads and sandwiches, including the Soba with Tamari-Lime Dressing and Smoked Mozzarella (with roasted squash and fennel and marinated olives on grilled levain). Balthazar Bakery is located right next door, and thankfully, the artesan bread and delectable desserts arrive at your table fresh out of the oven. Some of us who prefer to remain nameless could make an entire meal out of one of those crusty loafs and a bottle of French *vin rouge* from the extensive (and expensive) wine list.

Saturday and Sunday brunch offers outstanding egg and waffle dishes, as well as a $10 bread basket, which features some of the finest selections from the bakery. Sounds a bit pricey, but the basket is so popular they usually run out by midafternoon. So don't equivocate:

You could easily miss out. We recommend this gastronomic heaven for any meal—you simply cannot go wrong.

—EILEEN REGAN

2 Burrito Bar

305 Church Street (at Walker Street)

PHONE: (212) 219–9200

TYPE OF CUISINE: Mex-Cal

DAYS/HOURS: Sunday through Thursday from 11:30 A.M. to midnight, Friday and Saturday 11:30 A.M. to 2:00 A.M.

VEGEBILITY: Very good

RESERVATIONS: Necessary for parties of eight or more

WHEELCHAIR ACCESS: Yes

KID-FRIENDLY: Yes

TYPE OF SERVICE: Table, delivery, and bar

PRICING: Inexpensive

PAYMENT ACCEPTED: Major credit cards

Walking up to this Mexican restaurant is half the fun—on the corner it conspicuously stands with a pink "hippie van" parked over the door. Enter, and it's almost like going back in time to the late-'60s era of purple velour seating, lava lamps, Jimi Hendrix posters, and tie-dye everything. Burrito Bar has been tuning in, turning on, and dropping out for more than twenty years.

But cool out, man, and kill your munchies with chips and mellow salsa while looking over the extensive drink menu with everything from Tie-Dye Margaritas to a selection of cervezas from all over the world. There are plenty vegetarian entrées on the menu, which can easily be made vegan. The owner, Greg, is vegetarian, so there's no hidden lard in the beans—or anywhere else. But be careful of the rice: The Mexican version is cooked in chicken broth, but the brown rice is safe. Entrées lean more toward Californian cuisine, with dishes like the Wrap-a-Rito: broccoli, cauliflower, carrots, sprouts, avocado, and cabbage wrapped in a spinach tortilla and topped with vinaigrette. For a slightly more Mexican taste, try the quesadillas or fajitas. Either way, you'll get plenty of food that's a nice balance of real Mexican and healthy dining.

If you can't take the heat, no problemo! Most of the veggie dishes are quite mild in terms of spice, but if you're up for the challenge, ask your server to kick it up a notch. And do look around. Word has it, if you're here at the right time, you may just run into some of the local celebrities.

—CHRISTINA MASSEY

3 Capsouto Frères

451 Washington Street (enter on Watts Street)

PHONE: (212) 966–4900

TYPE OF CUISINE: Contemporary French bistro

DAYS/HOURS: Lunch (every day except Monday): noon to 3:00 P.M., dinner (every day): 6:00 to 11:00 P.M.

VEGEBILITY: Fair

RESERVATIONS: Recommended

WHEELCHAIR ACCESS: A few steps at entrance, but staff are happy to assist

KID-FRIENDLY: More romantic than kid-friendly

TYPE OF SERVICE: Table

PRICING: Expensive

PAYMENT ACCEPTED: All credit cards

Located on the corner of Watts and Washington one block below Canal Street, Capsouto Frères has the kind of understated uptown elegance you might not expect from a cavernous space in a far corner of Tribeca. But from the bow-tied waiters to the rustic wood beams and old-fashioned light fixtures in the open dining room, Capsouto is refined yet cozy. Among the first to colonize Tribeca, the Capsouto brothers (*les frères*) have a lot of experience under their belts, and it shows in everything from the quality of the food to the attentiveness of the waitstaff to the extensive wine list.

Unfortunately for vegetarians, though, the moderately priced prix fixe dinner—including appetizer, entrée, and dessert—has no veggie option, save for a salad. The à la carte menu fares better, with several unusual appetizers and an innovative take on the humble but ubiquitous vegetable plate. A seasonal appetizer consists of spring asparagus and Reggiano cheese, with truffle oil perfectly balancing its strong flavors. The artichoke à la maison, an owner's favorite, features two large hearts with tender potatoes, carrots, and tomatoes;

the whole thing is cooked in a lemon broth, creating a delicate, melded taste. A beautifully layered terrine, roasted vegetable ravioli, and several bright salads are also available.

For dinner, Capsouto Frères offers both a vegetable plate and a vegetable pot-au-feu; the latter is an assortment of everything from snap peas to fiddleheads in a fragrant green broth redolent of truffle oil. It's a dish with very mild flavors, so you can gear up for one of Capsouto's stunning soufflés. This trademark dessert should not be missed. The soufflés must be ordered ahead of time, but they're assuredly worth the wait: Our special fig soufflé arrived with a flawlessly bubbling brown crust, which the server punctured with a spoon to ladle in a rich vanilla sauce. And if that wasn't sumptuous enough, he topped the whole thing with a dollop of whipped cream. It's the opulent finishing flourish for a meal that's the very definition of finesse.

—MELENA Z. RYZIK

4 Hampton Chutney

68 Prince Street (between Lafayette and Crosby Streets)

PHONE: (212) 226–9996

WEB ADDRESS: www.hamptonchutney.com

TYPE OF CUISINE: Healthy Indian

DAYS/HOURS: Monday through Sunday from 11:00 A.M. to 8:00 P.M.

VEGEBILITY: Very good

RESERVATIONS: No

WHEELCHAIR ACCESS: Yes

KID-FRIENDLY: Yes

TYPE OF SERVICE: Counter plus seating

PRICING: Moderate

PAYMENT ACCEPTED: Major credit cards

An ashram in Soho? Well, sort of. Chef and co-owner Gary MacGurn spent a decade as chef-in-residence at an ashram south of Bombay. This restaurant, he says, is an extension of that spiritual lifestyle. Indeed, the cafeteria-style place (a 2000 spinoff of the Amagansett, Long Island, original) is infused with soft chants and decorated with palms and photographs of spiritual leaders. It might not be an actual ashram, but it's a healthy and pure oasis at the edge of tragically hip Soho.

The highlights here are the fourteen variations of the classic South Indian dosa and uttapa, which share the menu with Western-style sandwiches (like the grilled portobello with goat cheese, onion, and arugula on whole-grain bread). Western diners are probably more familiar with the heavy, creamier cuisine of North India. But at Hampton Chutney, dosas rule, and they are authentic. (I spent eighteen months in South India, so I know a good dosa when I taste one.)

The enormous crepe is made of white lentil and rice flour, yielding a crisp yet tender wrapping to fresh roasted vegetables, marinated onions and olives, and homemade chutneys. First I sampled the #1 Classic masala dosa—"the hamburger of South India." I ordered it with the uttapa wrapping, which uses the same basic batter but is thicker and lusher. The roasted red-skin potatoes, with a perfect blend of cumin and onion, was the real thing. Most of the dosa combinations are nontraditional, except the first. The #14, for example, with roasted beets and butternut squash, arugula, and goat cheese, transported me out of Bombay and into a nouvelle-cuisine India.

The chalkboard menu gives Hampton Chutney a friendly and casual air. Mixing and matching your own combos is encouraged—there are fourteen dosas and five different chutneys—*and* it's a real kid-pleaser, Gary notes. Copper-covered tables with stools and a bar along the walls provide seating and room for eating, but it's not exactly a place to linger.

A menu of otherworldly beverages complements your slightly exotic meal. Never underestimate the delight of a rich, smooth cardamom coffee. The restaurant is full of delights and surprises—all so wonderful you'll try to replicate them at home. But why bother, when Hampton Chutney is open seven days a week?

—ANTRIM CASKEY

5 The Odeon

145 West Broadway (between Thomas and Duane Streets)

PHONE: (212) 233–0507

TYPE OF CUISINE: French/American bistro

DAYS/HOURS: Monday through Thursday from noon to midnight, Friday noon to 3:00 A.M., Saturday 11:30 A.M. to 3:00 A.M., Sunday 11:30 A.M. to 2:00 A.M.

VEGEBILITY: Fair

RESERVATIONS: Suggested

WHEELCHAIR ACCESS: Yes

KID-FRIENDLY: Yes (children receive balloons and crayons to write on the paper tablecloths)

TYPE OF SERVICE: Table, take-out, and bar

PRICING: Expensive

PAYMENT ACCEPTED: All credit cards

Right up there with the Chrysler Building and Wall Street, the Odeon is classic New York. Even after two decades—a veritable lifetime by NYC restaurant standards—this timeless art deco French bistro, which put Tribeca on the map, is still one of the elite few places to be seen.

The brasserie's atmosphere is chic and noisy, with tycoons making deals and moving and shaking. The lighting soft and subtle. Come here to pretend you're in Paris or to people-watch, but don't come expecting a mind-blowing veg meal. There aren't many dishes on the classic American and French menu for vegetarians—a few salads and side dishes is about it. But like many fine establishments, the Odeon is happy to accommodate requests. How about a grilled French ham and Gruyère cheese sandwich without the ham? Or a country frisée salad sans bacon lardens? Not only can they do it, they are more than happy to. A few veggie dishes are available from off-menu (like a vegetable plate), so don't be shy about asking.

The Odeon serves lunch and dinner, late-night supper, and Saturday and Sunday brunch, probably an ovo-lacto's best bet. The eggs Sardou (poached eggs, artichoke hearts, spinach, tomato-hollandaise sauce) and the Valrhona chocolate French toast (with ice cream) are real winners. Though the selection for vegetarians is slim, the Odeon is not to be missed. It really is more about the experience of classic New York, even if you just sit at the stylish bar and see why their martinis are so famous.

—EILEEN REGAN

Peep

177 Prince Street (between Sullivan and Thompson Streets)

> **PHONE:** (212) 254–7337
>
> **TYPE OF CUISINE:** Thai
>
> **DAYS/HOURS:** Sunday through Thursday from 11:00 A.M. to midnight, Friday and Saturday 11:00 A.M. to 1:00 A.M.
>
> **VEGEBILITY:** Fair
>
> **RESERVATIONS:** Accepted for parties of five or more only, 7:00 P.M. or 9:00 P.M.
>
> **WHEELCHAIR ACCESS:** Yes
>
> **KID-FRIENDLY:** Not really
>
> **TYPE OF SERVICE:** Table, take-out, delivery, and bar
>
> **PRICING:** Moderate
>
> **PAYMENT ACCEPTED:** MC/V

Located on a bustling Soho street, Peep dishes up traditional Thai cuisine in an eye-catching setting. The interior is bright and splashy: Elaborate light fixtures hang from above; and the chairs by the bar, the light over the bar's mirror, and the flowery-patterned benches by each table are all variations in pink. The restaurant was even a deserved recipient of a Best Bathroom Award. (One-way mirrors allow you to view diners as they enjoy their meals, and a mini-screen on the mirror runs a nonstop reel of vintage cinema clips.)

Back in the dining room, the menu offers several options for vegetarians, but as is almost universal with Thai cooking, many dishes are prepared with fish or shrimp paste. But the good news is that the chef is happy to prepare a fish-paste-free meal (though it will take longer).

Start with a Caesar salad. It's such a treat to find one made without anchovy paste or eggs. And this light and tasty plate is a wonderful specimen, composed of fresh greens with crispy smoked tofu croutons, a flavorful miso-ginger dressing, and a sprinkling of rice chips. The fresh summer rolls are another delightful appetizer—stuffed with light angel hair, firm tofu, sprouts, and smoked soy-tamarind reduction, these rolls are hearty yet not filling enough to spoil your appetite.

Your best bet for a main vegetarian meal is to choose from the sautéed-plate section. Each dish here can be prepared with tofu as the protein source. How about a lemongrass-chili tofu plate with mung bean vermicelli and chili-tamarind paste? Or a green curry tofu, served with bamboo and sweet basil? The Rama Dish includes tofu with curried peanut paste. You can also order a hearty vegetarian pad thai, but it does contain egg.

Complement your meal with a choice from the extensive wine list or one of the house's specialty cocktails. Top it all off with a selection from the dessert menu, which includes Thai ice cream, apple fritters, chocolate mousse, and banana strudel.

—REBECCA KRASNEY STROPOLI

7 Rice

227 Mott Street (between Prince and Spring Streets)

PHONE: (212) 226–5775

OTHER LOCATION: 81 Washington Street (between Front and York), Brooklyn, (718) 222–9880

WEB ADDRESS: www.riceny.com

TYPE OF CUISINE: International eclectic

DAYS/HOURS: Soho: Monday through Sunday from noon to midnight, Brooklyn: Monday through Sunday from noon to 10:00 P.M.

VEGEBILITY: Very good

RESERVATIONS: No

WHEELCHAIR ACCESS: Yes

KID-FRIENDLY: Yes (families tend to come during the earlier hours)

TYPE OF SERVICE: Table, take-out, delivery, and bar

PRICE: Moderate

PAYMENT ACCEPTED: Cash and checks

The owner of Rice, David Selig, has a simple philosophy: Food should be high-quality and appeal to a range of diners. And considering the eclectic menu that caters to carnivores, vegetarians, and vegans alike, it's fair to say Rice lives up to its owner's ideals.

Rice has two locations: one in Soho and the other in Brooklyn's DUMBO section. The former is the flagship location, a smaller venue with a brisk take-out business and a usually jam-packed dining room. Brooklyn is more spacious and mellow, conducive to lingering over meals and having lengthy chats. Both spots have a funky, candlelit decor, with walls splattered with colorful grains, or artfully stacked sacks of rice, to remind you where you are. The menus are identical, though Manhattan's prices are 50 cents higher per item.

The cuisine at Rice is a mishmash of Indian, Thai, Caribbean, Japanese, and South American that somehow seem to belong together. Much of the food is vegan-friendly: There are no chicken stocks or hidden fish or shrimp pastes in any of the homemade sauces, soups, or dressings. Grilled tofu steak, tofu pad thai, eggplant maki, veggie meatballs, and Asian slaw salad should please all appetites. The only no-no is the veggie tamale dish, which is made with chicken stock. One other warning: The sweet and spicy chili sauces served with the veggie meatballs are not made on-site, so the owner can't promise that there isn't a bit of fish paste in the mix.

A great starter is the butternut squash chowder, flavored with thyme and nutmeg. You may want to add a dash of salt for flavor, as the owner caters to customers concerned about sodium. But even without it, the thyme releases a burst of flavor on your tongue that fully complements the rich orange broth. If you do dairy, indulge in the accompanying sour cream.

The grilled tofu steak, with its hearty consistency, is served with mesclun greens and rice. The Thai black rice with edamame is a terrific side choice—the chewy texture of the rice and flavorsome edamame sure beats plain white.

After-meal sweets include kheer, gelato, and the vegan Thai banana leaf wrap. But perhaps the best time to come is for Sunday brunch (Brooklyn only), when Rice departs from the grain theme and offers baked eggs on ratatouille, yogurt with fresh fruit, coconut French toast, and hot cream-of-rice porridge with dried fruit, nuts, and warm maple cream.

—REBECCA KRASNEY STROPOLI

No Ifs, Ands, or Butts

Claiming a strong interest in employee health, New York City mayor Michael Bloomberg signed a law banning smoking that went into effect on March 30, 2003. Some 14,000 establishments—including bars, restaurants, and nightclubs—are covered under the new law and face a maximum fine of $1,000 for infractions.

As with any public policy, there are loopholes, and a quick look at reactions to the law thus far shows that establishment owners are planning to take advantage of their options. A "smoking room" with separate ventilation and guidelines stating when employees can enter is a popular but expensive option. More convenient and immediate seems to be opening outdoor dining patios for the warmer months, as up to 25 percent of an outdoor area can be designated for smoking patrons. A somewhat extreme measure being considered by a few nightclubs is to give employees partial (and slight) ownership in the company, since fraternal organizations and other employee-free buildings are exempt under this law.

In the meantime, it seems that depending on where you go, requests to extinguish flames can go largely unheeded. Some places may induce high school flashbacks, as clouds of smoke emerge from behind the swinging rest room door. One downtown bar has gone so far as to hang a metal bucket filled with sand from its doors with a sign above it reading BLOOMBERG'S BUCKET.

—KATHY AND CARLOS LOPEZ

 Salaam Bombay

317 Greenwich Street (between Duane and Reade Streets)

PHONE: (212) 226–9400

TYPE OF CUISINE: Indian

DAYS/HOURS: Monday through Sunday from 11:30 A.M. to 3:00 P.M. and from 5:30 to 11:00 P.M.

VEGEBILITY: Very good

RESERVATIONS: Suggested

WHEELCHAIR ACCESS: Yes

KID-FRIENDLY: Yes

TYPE OF SERVICE: Table and take-out

PRICING: Reasonable

PAYMENT ACCEPTED: All credit cards

From the outside, Salaam Bombay looks like just another standard-issue Indian restaurant in an off-the-beaten-path section of Tribeca. However, this unassuming spot proves an excellent place to linger over a weekend lunch buffet and offers not only top-notch food, but truly attentive and efficient service.

Besides familiar but well-rendered dishes like palak aloo (spinach and potatoes) and bhindi masala (okra cooked with tomatoes, onions, and spices), Salaam Bombay offers vegetarians a few dishes they might not encounter elsewhere. Kadhi—a soothing, slightly sour porridge of chickpea flour cooked with yogurt, turmeric, and cumin—is a specialty of the owner's native Gujarat (considered to have the most sophisticated veg cuisine in all of India), as is undhiyu, a concoction of sweet potatoes, beans, eggplant, and other vegetables cooked in a coconut and lentil sauce. Pani puri, tiny crispy pockets of poori bread that you stuff with black chickpeas and idly sambar, are as fun to assemble as they are to eat. Finish off by pouring mint water on the dish, creating a bite-size treat exploding with flavor.

The de rigueur mango lassi is refreshingly thick, creamy, and cold, and the nan is prepared to perfection—fluffy, crisp, and not at all greasy (though vegans take note: the nan contains milk). The cardamom-scented kheer offered at the end of the meal is tasty, but the dessert special of the day—carrot halwah studded with pistachios—was the clear winner.

As at other Indian restaurants, vegan diners will be rather limited, as much of the food is cream based. But they'll be pleased to learn that vegetable oil, rather than ghee, is used.

—EMILY PARK

 66

241 Church Street / 66 Leonard Street

> **PHONE:** (212) 925–0202
> **TYPE OF CUISINE:** Haute Chinese
> **DAYS/HOURS:** Monday through Saturday from noon to 3:00 P.M. and from 6:00 P.M. to midnight, Sunday noon to 3:00 P.M. and 5:30 P.M. to midnight
> **VEGEBILITY:** Good
> **RESERVATIONS:** Required except at communal table
> **WHEELCHAIR ACCESS:** Yes
> **KID-FRIENDLY:** Yes
> **TYPE OF SERVICE:** Table
> **PRICING:** Expensive
> **PAYMENT ACCEPTED:** Major credit cards

Don't look for this latest gem from star chef Jean-Georges Vongerichten (his other destination NYC restaurants are Vong and Jean Georges) on Church Street. Turn right on Leonard Street and hunt for an understated red "66" on the door and two beautiful people standing at attention inside it. Land in a minimalist vision of Shanghai courtesy of star architect Richard Meier.

If *haute* and *Chinese* don't usually share space in your lexicon—and if delicate, refined veggie versions of Chinese food is a fantasy of yours—book a reservation now. (Or plan to eat with thirty-nine gourmet strangers at the large communal table.) The decor is postmodern industrial chic, the cutlery (forks and chopsticks) is custom-designed and rests on little stones, and the handsome waitstaff knows what's lurking in every dish. ("That's key," our waitress tells us.) Lunch and dinner menus (similar except for prices) are divided into four categories; there's a core menu with seasonal changes. Chef Josh Eden (who must be good because his mother was dining just behind us) says he wanted to do something different, so he decided to enhance the old classics. "I tried hard to get vegetables right from the beginning because I've noticed more and more people are ordering more and more vegetables."

Skip the soups—all are made with either fish or chicken broth. Of the thirteen dim sum offerings, only the steamed mushroom and pea shoot and tofu dumplings are safe (vegan, in fact), and both are excellent. There are eleven Small Plates, three of which are vegetarian. The cold sesame glass noodles, with julienned apple, cucumber, peanuts, crystallized ginger, wasabi, and a sweet vinegar, is a blast of flavors and raises the old standby to a new height. The scallion pancake is lightly fried and good—but not on a par with the noodles. A green salad that comes with a creamy orange-carrot dressing is way above average. We tasted the Snap Pea, Water Chestnut, Shiitake, and Cloud Ear Mushroom dish—very light and complex. The Eggplant with Spice Marinade was good but didn't touch the amazing Asparagus, Lily Bulb, and Lotus dish, which prompted my dining companion to proclaim, "This is the only Chinese food I want to eat!" She also adored the fresh ginger ale, with fresh lime, ginger puree, and mildly carbonated club soda. Chef Eden tells us the base also makes a mean margarita, and I believe him.

Don't leave without at least sharing a dessert. With options like the Tapioca & Coconut Parfait with Tropical Fruit, Drunken Lotus Cake with Plum & Black Sesame Ice Cream, and Almond Tofu, Kumquat & Grand-Marnier Sugar Roll, you'll never settle for green tea ice cream again. But if you do have a craving for green tea, order it or the passion fruit iced, or wait for the green tea (or chocolate) fortune cookies—the best anywhere. Good fortune to those who dine at 66!

—SUZANNE GERBER

10 Soho Eastanah

212 Lafayette Street (between Spring and Broome Streets)

PHONE: (212) 625–9633

TYPE OF CUISINE: Indonesian/Malaysian

DAYS/HOURS: Monday through Thursday from 11:00 A.M. to
1:00 P.M., Friday and Saturday 11:00 A.M. to 11:30 P.M., Sunday
noon to midnight

VEGEBILITY: Good

RESERVATIONS: Recommended for parties of 6 or more on
weekends

WHEELCHAIR ACCESS: Yes

KID-FRIENDLY: Yes

TYPE OF SERVICE: Table, take-out, and bar

PRICING: Moderate

PAYMENT ACCEPTED: All credit cards

Though Asian restaurants abound in the city—there's no short-age of Chinese, Indian, or Japanese—Indonesia is tragically underrepresented. And that's a real shame, because it's the birth-place of tempeh and gado-gado. Fortunately, we have this restaurant, a good emissary. Complete with carved masks on the dark wood-paneled walls and a tiki bar at the entrance, Soho Eastanah delivers laid-back island ambience and high-quality food with culinary ties to Thailand, India, and China.

A good place to start is the steamed vegetarian rolls. They look similar to their Thai and Vietnamese cousins, but jicama replaces rice noodles on the inside, giving the rolls a satisfying heft. The accompanying homemade plum sauce lends an unexpected sweet dimension to a familiar favorite. The tempeh has a smoother texture than your typical American-made version but packs all the nutty fla-vor you'd expect. Tempeh Vegetarian comes with carrots, snow peas, and shiitake mushrooms on a bed of mixed greens. Lightly sautéed with a garlic sauce, the dish resembles Vietnamese fare with a tempeh twist. You also get a choice of rice, which includes not just white and brown but a tasty coconut alternative. You might also try the Sayur Kari: A pretty covered clay pot hides this devilishly addic-tive rich red coconut curry (made without fish sauce). It was so good, I couldn't stop eating despite protests from my overstuffed belly. Full of tofu, okra, and other veggies, the curry goes great with the coconut rice.

The best thing about Soho Eastanah is that almost every dish can be made vegetarian if you ask (vegetables will be substituted for the meat). So go ahead and peruse the meat entrées with abandon and bring them on over to the veggie team—it's a great feeling.

—JULIE HOLLAR

11 Spice Grill

18 Murray Street (between Church Street and Broadway)

PHONE: (212) 791–3510
TYPE OF CUISINE: Innovative Indian
DAYS/HOURS: Monday through Friday from noon to 10:00 P.M., Saturday and Sunday 5:00 to 10:00 P.M.
VEGEBILITY: Good
RESERVATIONS: Suggested
WHEELCHAIR ACCESS: Yes
KID-FRIENDLY: Yes
TYPE OF SERVICE: Table
PRICING: Moderate
PAYMENT ACCEPTED: Major credit cards

The owners of Spice Grill are justified in calling their restaurant innovative. In addition to familiar favorites like samosas, the menu features appetizers such as mumbai crepes (made of corn and chickpeas and served with tangy cream cheese filling) and uttapam, mini pancakes made from rice and dal, to which you can add such toppings as asparagus, mushrooms, or olives. If you prefer, you can order crepes as an entrée, with four fillings to choose from. Only in a downtown Manhattan Indian restaurant would you find a dish like the New York Wrap, a tomato wrap with portobello mushrooms and eggplant spiced with basil pesto—but it works! The Kandahari Nan, stuffed with coconut, cashews, almonds, and raisins, is an essential accompaniment to your dish and a creative way to serve good old nan bread. All told, there are five different vegetarian entrées. For the dishes with panir (cubes of homemade cheese), you can ask the kitchen to substitute tofu. The restaurant appreciates its vegetarian and vegan customers and is glad to make adjustments to accommodate them.

—SEZIN CAVUSOGLU

⑫ Spring Street Natural

62 Spring Street (at Lafayette Street)

PHONE: (212) 966–0290

TYPE OF CUISINE: Healthy/Organic American

DAYS/HOURS: Monday through Thursday from 11:30 A.M. to midnight, Friday and Saturday 11:30 A.M. to 12:30 A.M., Sunday 11:30 A.M. to 11:30 P.M.

VEGEBILITY: Excellent

RESERVATIONS: Yes

WHEELCHAIR ACCESS: Yes

KID-FRIENDLY: Yes

TYPE OF SERVICE: Table; bar

PRICING: Moderate

PAYMENT ACCEPTED: Major credit cards

It's not strictly a vegetarian restaurant—one glance at the number of poultry and seafood dishes on the menu makes that clear. Yet the number of organic dishes will leave any skeptical vegetarian feeling as if he or she has entered a homey garden, minus the chirping birds and sunshine, of course. Despite its large size, Spring Street Natural is warm and inviting, leading you to almost believe you've stepped into someone's (OK, huge) dining room. How do they do it? They decked it out with dark wooden tables and lush green plants that create an earthy Zen-like backdrop. It's perfect for conversation, perfect for solo diners to catch up on reading the *Times,* and, of course, perfect to nosh on veg-friendly fare.

Spring Street Natural presents inventive spins on simple but comforting meals made from fresh and natural ingredients. Broiled tofu is a great starter for vegetarians. Its slightly charred, smoky flavor is enhanced by an Asian-style spicy peanut sauce. Tricolored corn chips complement a hearty black bean hummus. Like any standout veggie burger, the one here is homemade and uniquely prepared with almonds. It's tasty with or without a slab of Vermont white cheddar on top. Organic vegetables also play an integral part on the menu. Seasonal veggies are the backbone of several entrées, including a stir-fry that—tossed with tamari, ginger, and garlic over a bed of organic brown rice—is one stir-fry worth ordering.

Lighter fan includes a bounty of salad offerings, such as the grilled portobello salad flecked with toasted pine nuts, and the warm goat cheese salad with croutons made of challah bread. A roster of feel-good desserts that changes daily, like peach pie and buttermilk pannacotta, offers a decadent way to say good night. The setting, plus a good selection of beers and wines, make for the rare marriage of elegant and healthy dining.

—ALIA AKKAM

Places to Stay

13 Bevy's SoHo Loft

70 Mercer Street (between Spring and Broome Streets)

> **PHONE:** (212) 431–8214
> **PRICING:** Moderate

This industrial loft with a fireplace is the only bed-and-breakfast in Soho. Complimentary breakfast and kitchen privileges are included.

14 Cosmopolitan Hotel

95 West Broadway (at Chambers Street)

> **PHONE:** (888) 895–9400
> **PRICING:** Moderate

Longest continuously operating hotel in New York City. Feels more like a bed-and-breakfast than a hotel.

15 The SoHo Grand

310 West Broadway (near Grand Street)

> **PHONE:** (212) 965–3000
> **WEB ADDRESS:** www.sohogrand.com
> **PRICING:** Very expensive

Old New York grandeur mixed with downtown edge. Small rooms, but Frette linens and Veuve Clicquot in the minibar make you forget the cramped quarters. If those names don't mean anything to you, don't waste your money staying here. Pet-friendly.

16 The Tribeca Grand

2 Sixth Avenue (near White Street)

> **PHONE:** (212) 519–6600
> **WEB ADDRESS:** www.tribecagrand.com
> **PRICING:** Very expensive

This downtown boutique hotel has small rooms but mini-TVs and Kiehl's beauty products in all of them.

Lower East Side

One of the oldest settled neighborhoods in the city, the Lower East Side is tucked away between the hip East Village to the north and bustling Chinatown to the south. In the nineteenth century it was the most densely populated area in the entire world, packing some 240,000 people into a 16-block radius. Today its borders are typically defined as Houston to the north, Canal to the south, Bowery to the west, and as far east as the East River. Orchard Street, the original home of old Jewish pushcart merchants (until the gentrification of the 1980s), and Ludlow Street are the heart of this surprisingly laid-back neighborhood.

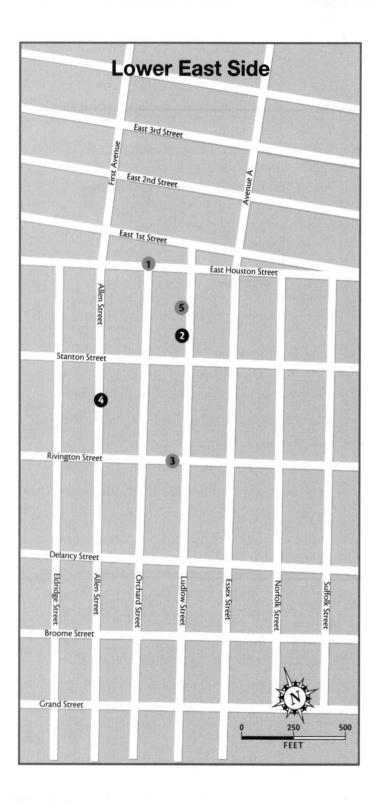

Lower East Side

East 3rd Street

First Avenue

East 2nd Street

Avenue A

East 1st Street

East Houston Street

Allen Street

Stanton Street

Rivington Street

Delancy Street

Eldridge Street

Allen Street

Orchard Street

Ludlow Street

Essex Street

Norfolk Street

Suffolk Street

Broome Street

Grand Street

N

0   250   500

FEET

Half a century ago the Lower East Side was the nation's lead-ing supplier of underwear; today it's a haven for radical politics, chic boutiques, and vegetarian food. Fortunately, gentrification has not entirely taken over. There is still a sizable immigrant population. In fact, 60 percent of Lower East Side residents over the age of five speak a language other than English at home.

Our favorite hangout is Bluestockings Bookstore, at 172 Allen Street, between Stanton and Rivington. Bluestockings is much more than a bookstore. It is a community center, café, and a venue for liter-ary readings, political rallies, and knitting circles. Originally conceived with a feminist mission, Bluestockings has recently undergone a change in ownership and now stocks books focusing more on global injustice.

The Visitors Center, at 261 Broome Street, provides maps, din-ing discounts, free parking and information on walking tours. Con-veniently catercorner is the Tenement Museum, at 92 Orchard Street, a reconstructed tenement of the type in which many immi-grants had their first taste of the New World. The price of admission to the museum includes a tour, in which a guide tells the story of one of the families who lived there more than a century ago.

But the best way to get to know the Lower East Side is by get-ting lost in it. The neighborhood eludes those who enter it with a specific destination. This is a place to commune with the heteroge-neous roots of America. The streets are open for you to wander through. Bring a good book, or a friend, and start walking!

Places to Eat

1 Bereket

187 East Houston Street (at Orchard Street)

> **PHONE:** (212) 475–7700
> **TYPE OF CUISINE:** Turkish/Middle Eastern
> **DAYS/HOURS:** Daily, twenty-four hours
> **VEGEBILITY:** Good
> **RESERVATIONS:** Not necessary
> **WHEELCHAIR ACCESS:** No
> **KID-FRIENDLY:** Yes
> **TYPE OF SERVICE:** Table and take-out
> **PRICING:** Inexpensive
> **PAYMENT ACCEPTED:** Cash only

In less than eight years of existence, Bereket, an affordable, round-the-clock provider of Turkish delights, has become a Lower East Side fixture. It offers an intriguing selection of vegetarian delicacies, such as baba ghanoush, fried eggplant, leek stew and, of course, the familiar staples hummus and falafel, both of which are served with a generous helping of freshly baked pita bread.

The $3.00 falafel sandwich is one of the best deals in the city. The stuffed grape leaves, chockablock with raisins, peanuts, and herbs, are meant to be savored slowly. For a complete meal, order a combination platter that gives a choice of four vegetarian soups, side dishes, and salads. Complete your authentic Turkish experience with aryan, a refreshing yogurt drink. But if you desire something stronger, you'll have to bring it yourself, as Bereket doesn't have a liquor license (for wine, bring your own corkscrew).

The luscious dessert menu offers familiar items (baklava, rice pudding) as well as more exotic ones, such as kadayif, a sweet bread soaked in honey and sprinkled with walnuts, and kazan dibi, baked with rose petals. All desserts are affordably priced at $2.50. And no meal would be complete without a cup of strong Turkish coffee, which is served on a silver tray in miniature hand-painted china.

A tip for ordering: Choose something from the bottom row of the display case. Everything on that level is vegetarian, whereas the food on the top row contains meat. Bereket's atmosphere can be hectic, but the food is worth a little physical discomfort. Since seating is limited, try to come at an off-hour time—but only if you care more about food than ambiance.

—REBECCA GOULD

2 The Pink Pony
178 Ludlow Street (between Stanton and East Houston Street)

PHONE: (212) 253–1922
TYPE OF CUISINE: French café
DAYS/HOURS: Daily from 10:00 A.M. to 2:00 A.M.
VEGEBILITY: Fair
RESERVATIONS: Recommended for parties of five or more and on weekends
WHEELCHAIR ACCESS: Yes
KID-FRIENDLY: Yes
TYPE OF SERVICE: Table
PRICING: Moderate
PAYMENT ACCEPTED: Cash and travelers' checks only

Looking for fine, filling, French-inspired food in a hip Lower East Side setting? Are you tempted by a vegan eggplant Napoleon set on a delicately sweet curry sauce? How about a peanut butter, honey, and banana sandwich? Though his favorite sandwich is indeed on the menu, Elvis is one of the few celebrities you're guaranteed not to see at the Pink Pony. According to owner Lucien Bahaj, Björk and Michael Stipe have been known to stop by, and the restaurant is a bona fide hangout of many neighborhood artists and writers.

The decor is classic French bistro, with a buttery yellow and wine red color scheme. The restaurant is stocked with books and magazines. Occasional film screenings and literary readings are held in the back room, graced by a glammed-up portrait of Emily Dickinson painted directly on the wall.

Like its customers, the Pink Pony's carefully crafted, affordable food has presence and a sense of drama. The vegan carrot-ginger soup is smooth and savory, dominated by neither ingredient. Dig into the smoky vegan lasagna, made with roasted eggplant and meltingly rich ricotta-like tofu. These soft elements are held together with strong, boldly flavored tomato sauce and pasta with a pleasingly firm bite. The eggplant Napoleon (also vegan), with its delicate flavors and stylish presentation, has created a buzz here. A bed of moist, perfectly cooked barley holds up a tower of well-salted steamed vegetables and pan-fried eggplant, and a generous helping of dressed greens comes on the side. The slight sweetness of the sauce paired with the barley made me feel like I was eating a grown-up version of rice pudding. The vegetarian burger, made on-site, is a delicious mix of grains and vegetables. Another good option, beautifully presented, is the roasted beet salad, served with chèvre cheese on baguette toast.

If you come early in the day, order the high-quality coffee and check out the brunch menu, heavy on vegetarian egg dishes. Granola with milk or soy milk and whole-grain toast is also available.

—ESTHER JAMES

3   Teany's

90 Rivington Street (between Ludlow and Orchard Streets)

PHONE: (212) 475–9190

WEB ADDRESS: www.teanys.com

TYPE OF CUISINE: American vegetarian

DAYS/HOURS: Daily from 9:00 A.M. to 1:00 A.M.

VEGEBILITY: Excellent

RESERVATIONS: No

WHEELCHAIR ACCESS: No

KID-FRIENDLY: Yes

TYPE OF SERVICE: Table

PRICING: Moderate

PAYMENT ACCEPTED: Major credit cards

Housed in a former hair salon, bright and sunny Teany's has two claims to fame. First, as its name implies, it stocks almost a hundred varieties of teas for your culinary, medicinal and even spiritual appetites. A five-dollar bill gets you a pot of tea from almost any country in the world—as well as background information on its history and uses. The second draw of this comfy, coffee-shop-like restaurant is that it's owned by the musician Moby and his friend Kelly Tisdale.

Moby is almost as well known for his veganism as his techno-pop music. Not surprisingly, everyone who works here considers vegetarianism not just a healthy way of eating, but a way of life. The

food is strictly vegetarian, and many of the meals can be made vegan. Soy yogurt, for example, can be substituted for the dairy vanilla yogurt in the granola—which is a work of art, by the way, served with fresh strawberries, blueberries, and strawberry sauce on top. The food menu seems limited compared with the tea selections, but all of the dishes are winners. A favorite is the Welsh rarebit, a sandwich with melted cheese, beer, and mustard. For those who get crave a "meatier" plate, there's a scrumptious turkey club, three thick layers of vegan bacon and turkey, mayo and tomato. And if you can't decide, you can order a platter of up to twenty different bite-size sandwiches for $12, including my favorite, the peanut-cashew butter.

At Teany's, atmosphere is as important as food. As soon as you walk in, you are greeted with a friendly smile, and you get the feeling that the waitress is being polite not because that is her job, but

Next Stop: Organic Avenue

The brainchild of Denise Mari, a longtime vegetarian and recent convert to raw-food veganism, Organic Avenue is intended to be a stepping stone for people looking to convert to a fully organic lifestyle. Denise calls her organization a "collective," and at press time she was still looking for a retail space. Organic Avenue offers prepared raw-food and gourmet dinners, classes, hemp parties—even membership in a raw cooperative to make organic produce more affordable by purchasing in larger volume. "It's our goal to make your transitioning easy and enjoyable," says Denise. For more info, check out www.organicavenue.com or e-mail denise@vegucate.com.

—MELENA Z. RYZIK

out of a genuine interest in making customers feel welcome. This is an excellent place to hang out and snack. Don't come famished, however, as the one downside is that the portions are not large.

—REBECCA GOULD

④ Tiengarden
170 Allen Street (1½ blocks south of East Houston Street)

PHONE: (212) 388–1364

TYPE OF CUISINE: Home-style Chinese vegan

DAYS/HOURS: Monday through Saturday from noon to 10:00 P.M.

VEGEBILITY: Excellent

RESERVATIONS: Recommended for parties of five or more

WHEELCHAIR ACCESS: One small (approximately 3-inch) ledge

KID-FRIENDLY: Yes, but no highchairs

TYPE OF SERVICE: Table, take-out, delivery, and catering

PRICING: Inexpensive

PAYMENT ACCEPTED: Major credit cards

This tiny restaurant—with a clean, natural decor and the background sounds of a busy kitchen—will make you feel as if you're eating at some healthy friend's home. The atmosphere, as well as the food, reflects the philosophy on which Tiengarden is based: that of the ancient Chinese five-element theory. Meals are made without any of the five "impurities"—onions, garlic, shallots, leeks, and (of course) tobacco, which are said to damage one's qi (vital life force).

Though most of the food is *not* organic, all dishes are completely vegan, and everything tastes distinctively fresh. The ingredients are carefully picked to complement one another and create balance in flavors and textures. The Seaweed Rolls, a house specialty, are perfect starters. Tofu with the texture of potato and a hint of lemon is rolled in nori and bean curd sheets, crisped lightly, and served warm. Heaven!

Having too many choices is a nice (if infrequent) problem for a vegetarian. Many of the entrées are stir-fries, served with mounds of fluffy brown rice, though there are also plenty of well-prepared sandwiches and rice and noodle dishes. Zesty Gluten is particularly popular, made of sautéed wheat gluten, mushrooms, bell peppers, snow peas and orange slices in a spicy brown sauce. If you prefer your food milder, try the Bok Choy Lover, in which that green is sautéed with bundles of juro (a starchy, spaghetti-like vegetable), shiitake mushrooms, julienned carrot, and baby corn and served with either a black bean or ginger sauce. The unique flavor of each vegetable stands out with a fresh, clean taste.

A nice accompaniment to any dish is one of the eight or so homemade iced teas. Desserts here—from vegan cookies to cakes—are famous. But the best part of a meal at Tiengarden is that no matter how much you eat, you're sure to leave feeling healthier and far more energized than when you came in.

—CHRISTINA MASSEY

A Planet Worth Saving

It took a while, but New York City finally got its own chapter of EarthSave, the international organization dedicated to educating the public about how food choices affect the environment, the economy and everyone's health. Founded by *Diet for a New America* author and activist John Robbins, EarthSave offers a monthly vegetarian dinner and lecture series, where experts speak about the benefits of plant-based diets and discuss genetically modified foods, mad cow disease, and other important issues. Since 2002, EarthSave has also sponsored "Taste of Health," a daylong event in Damrosch Park (near Lincoln Center), with demonstrations, speeches, and booths with eco-friendly products.

To get involved, sign up for their newsletter or become a volunteer—it's a quick way to engage your mind and your body and to meet likeminded neighbors. Visit http://nyc.earthsave.org or call (212) 696–7986.

—MELENA Z. RYZIK

Places to Shop

5 Earth Matters
177 Ludlow Street (between Stanton and East Houston Street)

PHONE: (212) 475–4180
WEB ADDRESS: www.earthmatters.com
DAYS/HOURS: Monday through Saturday from 8:00 A.M. to midnight, Sunday 8:00 A.M. to 11:00 P.M.
OVERALL: Very good

Earth Matters is that rare place that tries to be everything to everyone and actually succeeds. A multistory grocery/health store/juice bar/café, it even has a lovely covered rooftop garden with a dozen tables and a bar serving organic wine and beer. The second floor is an inviting dining room/lounge and library, complete with Internet access. Downstairs, the store stocks a better-than-standard selection of bulk foods, produce, and health products. The café serves breakfast until 4:00 P.M., and co-owner and chef Siggy Sollitto says future plans include a new salad and sandwich menu and table service.

East Village

Artists and students have gentrified this once poor, multiethnic neighborhood, but the native spirit is still very much in evidence. That imprint is evident today with the numerous experimental music clubs and theaters, urban gardens, used book and CD shops, craft shops, tattoo parlors—and the esteemed New York University. Cutting-edge fashion and body piercing is alive and well, with perhaps the largest concentration of punk and funk in all of Manhattan. The East Village probably boasts more vegetarian and ethnic restaurants than any other 'hood. There's fine dining to be sure, but mostly it's healthier and less expensive than you'll find in other, less fun parts of town. (Oh, sorry, is our bias showing?) For the adventurous, head east to Alphabet City (Avenues A, B, C, and D), where it's still a bit rough around the edges, but the eats, drinks, and shopping—and definitely the people-watching—are reasonably priced and lots of fun. Shirts and shoes are usually mandatory, but nose rings are optional.

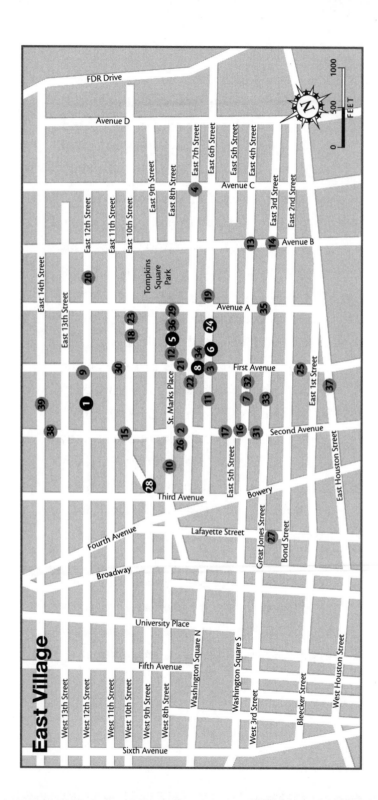

Places to Eat

① Angelica Kitchen

300 East 12th Street (between First and Second Avenues)

PHONE: (212) 228–2909

TYPE OF CUISINE: Organic whole-food vegan

DAYS/HOURS: Monday through Sunday from 11:30 A.M. to 10:30 P.M.

VEGEBILITY: Excellent

RESERVATIONS: No

WHEELCHAIR ACCESS: Yes

KID-FRIENDLY: Yes

TYPE OF SERVICE: Table and take-out (from next door: same menu, same hours)

PRICING: Moderate

PAYMENT ACCEPTED: Cash only

It's probably fair to say that vegan restaurant extraordinaire Angelica Kitchen, which has been around longer than Britney Spears, has launched a thousand imitators. But the AK, with its templelike ambiance and clean, delicious food, is a true original. Much of the credit belongs to owner Leslie McEachern (see sidebar, pages 79 and 80), but she'll deflect a lot of the glory back to her staff, her growers, and her suppliers. Hey, as long as the food doesn't change, we're happy to namaste 'em all.

In at least one sense, this is the gold standard for whole-foods restaurants. As the menu says, "At Angelica Kitchen, fresh and delicious food is served in an atmosphere where sustainable agriculture and responsible business practices are the main ingredients." The promise here is that a minimum of 95 percent of the food is grown organically and served within forty-eight hours of being picked.

The menu is vast and best experienced by sampling a little of everything. But be warned: "Everything" includes three soups, nine appetizers, four breads, four spreads, five salads (and a sampler plate), seven entrées, five soy-based sandwiches, and four signature Dragon Bowls, which are combinations of house basics (tempeh, tofu, grains, beans, and veggies). There are also teas, juices, and desserts, some made with wheat, many with spelt, but only natural sweeteners (maple or rice syrup or barley malt). And once a month when the moon is full, a chocolate dessert is offered—"to really wig them out," says Leslie.

If those are not enough options for you, turn to the daily specials, whose bad-pun names are a house tradition: Sorrel Vaughn (portobello, turnip, squash, and bean stew), Charlie's Triangles (polenta with eggplant-olive tapenade over kidney bean sauce), or Hil-arame Clinton (strudel with tofu cheese, spinach, and arame). Fortunately, their taste is as wonderful as their names are painful. At Angelica no alcohol is served, but you are welcome to BYOB.

You wouldn't know it by looking, but every element in the place has a personal association for Leslie: The menu is adapted from a friend's artwork, and other friends made the tabletops, walls, and artwork (Leslie did the stenciling herself). The food is purchased and prepared with much consciousness. Their tofu is made for them out of nonhybridized local organic soybeans, their tempeh is produced by a local craftsman, and their whole-grain phyllo comes from the oldest Greek pastry maker in New York City. Because he doesn't work with organic flour, Angelica has it shipped from their miller directly to him.

Angelica is favorite spot for small celebrations, but solo diners are common and often sit at the "family table," where, Leslie surmises, plenty of relationships have taken root. Health-minded celebs regularly pop in, favoring the restaurant because no one ever stares or bothers them. The reason for that is simple: At Angelica Kitchen the food is always the star.

—SUZANNE GERBER

Angel of Angelica's: Leslie McEachern

"I've always felt nature was my religion," says Leslie McEachern, owner of NYC's famous vegan restaurant. "And running Angelica Kitchen has given me the opportunity to put my beliefs into practice." The longtime vegetarian (who now eats a little meat for her health) has the résumé of someone who could only have grown up in the '60s. In the '70s she spent six years alone in the North Carolina woods without electricity, during which time she was a U.S. representative of the Scottish spiritual community Findhorn. All the while she was "obnoxiously vocal" about vegetarianism, lecturing anyone who would (or, more likely, wouldn't) listen.

In 1978, while visiting friends in NYC, she came to the original Angelica—then a hole-in-the-wall on St. Marks Place—and had a visceral response. "Total connection," she recalls—"almost an out-of-body experience." Not looking for a life change, she went home and tried to forget about it. But on a return trip a few years later, the feeling was just as strong, and she and the then-owner became romantically involved. Never let it be said the gods don't move in mysterious ways, because within two years he died a tragic premature death and Leslie bought the place from his family. The next six years entailed 100-hour workweeks, with Leslie donning every hat from cook to dishwasher to waitress to plumber. "But it gave me the chance to get on my soapbox, and I was happy," she says.

Sourcing organic food back then was a very different game than it is today. Leslie teamed up with the local health food store (Prana; see review in East Village) to double their buying power. Even then she had a deep commitment to supporting the organic farmers and manufacturers. "We can't let the malls pave over them," she says. Preserving the farm culture is a big part of this South

Carolina girl's mission. "Ironically," she notes, "I'm doing it from NYC."

More than two decades after taking over, Leslie says she's still in love with the place and the people who work there. "One of my greatest joys over twenty-two years has been the contact with people who used to work here and seeing how having been here has influenced their lives. The energy of this place is amazing: the mutual respect of the people, their self-respect, and above all, everyone's respect for the food."

As a result, she feels a tremendous responsibility to keep getting better. That, to her, means finding new ways to work with the ingredients, nurturing the staff, offering the best-quality items, and staying on top of industry developments. For instance, when she learned that the filtering of canola oil was a questionable practice, she stopped using it. When she realized her chopsticks came from a nonrenewable source, she went from wood to disposable bamboo. And after a staffer discovered that their source for sea salt had been bought by ConAgra, Leslie changed suppliers rather than support Big Agriculture.

"The more money we can make at the restaurant means the more money I can give to small growers of fresh, clean food," Leslie says. So why, then, has she resisted opening a second location, something she's been urged to do for years? "I love the sense of place here. And it's hard enough to keep one place operating at this level. Besides, I wouldn't want to be torn between two of them."

Which isn't to say Angelica Kitchen isn't involved in the community. For years the restaurant has supported the Lower East Side Girls Club, and the chef and Leslie have taught vegan cooking at the Rykers Island prison. "I take community involvement very seriously," says Leslie. "It's a way to stay close to home, and a way to use vegetarianism to do good." Guess some things will never change.

—SUZANNE GERBER

② B&H Dairy

127 Second Avenue (between East 7th Street and St. Marks Place)

PHONE: (212) 505–8065

TYPE OF CUISINE: Kosher dairy vegetarian

DAYS/HOURS: Monday through Sunday from 7:00 A.M. to 10:00 P.M.

RESERVATIONS: Not necessary

VEGEBILITY: Excellent

WHEELCHAIR ACCESS: No

KID-FRIENDLY: Yes

TYPE OF SERVICE: Table, take-out, and counter

PRICING: Inexpensive

PAYMENT ACCEPTED: Cash only

Walking into B&H Dairy is like stepping through a time warp, back to the days when Jewish delis dotted the landscape of the East Village, then still considered the Lower East Side. B&H is one of the few remaining Jewish delis in the area (along with the famous Second Avenue Deli), and its spartan lunch counter looks like it hasn't changed much since the joint opened in 1938. Here, handwritten laminated signs announce the multitude of daily specials, regulars crack jokes with the grill man, and the challah bread is made fresh daily in the back.

Unlike Second Avenue Deli, however, B&H is both affordable and vegetarian-friendly. Though it's not certified kosher, everything is prepared according to kosher rules, so you'll find no meat in the entire place (except for a few easily avoided fish dishes). Dairy abounds, and while vegans won't go hungry, they will miss out on some of B&H's signature offerings.

Nearly all of the soups are vegan, and the hot borscht with a touch of dill will please beet lovers. Vegans can also nosh on kasha or stuffed cabbage, which is packed with a mix of rice and mushrooms. But the pièce de résistance is the blintz. It's big, browned to perfection, and oozes such soft, sweet cheese (or berries) that you'll find yourself eating it long after your stomach has told you to stop. The pierogis can hold their own against any restaurant around and are cheaper than most other places to boot. But don't forget the latkes (potato pancakes), which nicely round out the "huge, cheap, greasy, and addictive" section of the menu (otherwise known as

"Our Specials"). At less than $5.00 an order for any of the above, you won't go home hungry—or broke.

If you're feeling adventurous, you might try the vegetarian liver, which comes either in a sandwich or a salad platter. It looks vaguely like cookie dough and has a slightly peanut-buttery taste, but it's made from soybeans, eggs, onions and "a lot of love."

—JULIE HOLLAR

3 Banjara
97 First Avenue (at East 6th Street)

PHONE: (212) 477–5956 or (212) 473–1540
TYPE OF CUISINE: Indian
DAYS/HOURS: Monday through Sunday from noon to midnight
VEGEBILITY: Very good
RESERVATIONS: Not necessary
WHEELCHAIR ACCESS: Yes
KID-FRIENDLY: Yes
TYPE OF SERVICE: Table and take-out
PRICING: Moderate
PAYMENT ACCEPTED: Major credit cards

Where to sit is the biggest dilemma you will face at Banjara. Outside, T-shirts and shorts rule as Village locals do some choice people-watching at this heavily trafficked intersection of First Avenue and Sixth Street. Inside, relaxing music, mint green tablecloths, and a bejeweled waitstaff facilitate your passage to India. Regardless of your decision, the traditional Indian dishes will leave you longing for your next adventure at Banjara.

One of the cheeky upstarts that have moved away from greasy, overcooked food that East 6th Street used to be known for, Banjara turns out well-prepared "upscale" cuisine. The food here is several notches above its neighbors, old-school stalwarts of this famous Indian neighborhood. The menu is shorter and doesn't offer a lengthy list of traditional favorites, but what you do find here is delectable Indian food, where freshness and the purity of seasoning rule.

Start off with a tangy serving of alo chop, made of chickpeas, potato cakes, and onions in a tamarind sauce. The dumpakht is a fascinating creation—the cooking plate is sealed with pastry so that the aroma and taste of the vegetables are locked in. It is one of the pricier dishes at $12, but worth it because it's not something you can find in most Indian restaurants. The bay goon ka goon, featuring a whole eggplant roasted, peeled, and pureed with onion and tomatoes, is the ultimate eggplant lover's dream dinner. With nan, rice, and raita on the side, you will experience a true flavor explosion of tastes and traditions at Banjara.

—MARIANNE SEMCHUK

4 Bao 111

111 Avenue C (at East 7th Street)

PHONE: (212) 254–7773

TYPE OF CUISINE: Vietnamese fusion

DAYS/HOURS: Monday through Saturday from 6:00 P.M. to 2:00 A.M., Sunday 6:00 P.M. to midnight

VEGEBILITY: Fair

RESERVATIONS: Suggested

WHEELCHAIR ACCESS: Yes

KID-FRIENDLY: No

TYPE OF SERVICE: Table and bar

PRICING: Expensive

PAYMENT ACCEPTED: Major credit cards

Late-night Alphabet City denizens, this is your place! This very friendly, very hip Vietnamese-fusion hot spot is open for dinner only, so it's usually packed. The joint—with its dark wood tables, carved wood screens, and large oil paintings by Leo Xuan Tinh—is definitely jumping. Opened by a group of GenX friends to rectify the dearth of anything but greasy pizza when the after-hours munchies hit, 111 is the place for hot noodles and cold sake.

Technically, 111 (you will not see the word "Bao" on the door or the menu) is not a vegetarian restaurant, but it takes its veg customers seriously, and the management is planning more meatless dishes. At press time all of the vegetarian offerings were strictly vegan (no dairy, poultry or meat stocks, or animal fats used). Appetizers include summer rolls, which are listed with beef or shrimp but may be ordered vegetarian with daikon and bok choy, and vegetarian spring rolls (yummy, and loaded with tofu, shiitake mushrooms, and taro root).

For your entrée, feast on stir-fried noodles with market vegetables and tofu, always featuring wild mushrooms. There is also a platter composed of taro root fries, poached baby bok choy, and addictively crunchy spicy yucca fritters, served with a sweet-and-smoky dip and sticky rice.

Ovo-lacto dessert lovers are in for a treat. The ice creams are homemade and to swoon over. We sampled pandan (a juicy leaf, the essence of which is green as pistachio and tastes of nuts, mint, and coconut), a very intense Vietnamese coffee, and anise, with lively licorice and pepper notes playing seductively with the sugar and cream. We leave it to you to try the Vietnamese crème brûlée.

Special features here include a full bar, as well as a dizzying variety of sakes and a very decent small wine list, with at least one organic selection and lots of boutique vintages you won't find at your local store. Jazz aficionados should try to catch the live sessions on Sundays from 8:30 P.M. to midnight.

—EUREKA FREEMAN

❺ Café Mogador
101 St. Marks Place (between First Avenue and Avenue A)

PHONE: (212) 677–2226
TYPE OF CUISINE: Moroccan
DAYS/HOURS: Sunday through Thursday from 9:00 A.M. to 1:00 A.M., Friday and Saturday 9:00 A.M. to 2:00 A.M.
VEGEBILITY: Good
RESERVATIONS: No
WHEELCHAIR ACCESS: No
KID-FRIENDLY: Yes
TYPE OF SERVICE: Table
PRICING: Inexpensive
PAYMENT ACCEPTED: Major credit cards

So does Café Mogador really churn out the "best couscous in town," as its menu boasts, or does this low-key Moroccan eatery pack 'em in because of the choice sidewalk tables offering unparalleled views of funky East Village passersbys? Dark but decked-out with flashy artwork, the two inside rooms (formerly segregating smokers from nonsmokers) manage to capture the spirit of North Africa, evoking a sort of mystical Mediterranean allure. More important, the food is just as authentic—and it's extremely easy on the wallet.

Left on Lexington, Right into Delhi...

They say there's something for everyone in New York City, and that's true right down to your Indian-food dining experience. You'll find Indian joints scattered here and there around the city, but New York boasts three popular neighborhoods that are all Indian food, all the time: Lexington Avenue and 28th Street, East Sixth Street between First and Second Avenues, and 74th Street in Jackson Heights, Queens.

The area surrounding Lexington and 28th—aka Curry Hill—tends to be a lunchtime magnet for the thousands of nearby office workers, so there's a heavy midday rush. It also means that service is quick and the food is fairly cheap, usually with a well-stocked buffet option or lunch specials. Pongal and Vatan (reviews pages 210 and 211; 223) are good choices in this crowd, with their meatless menu and South Indian specialties.

Jackson Heights is the real deal: It's a bit of a schlep, but it's the way to go if you want the full cultural experience (plus you can amaze your friends by saying you've been to Queens). Also known as Little India, the neighborhood is reached from the 74th Street/Roosevelt Avenue subway stop (F, E, G, R, V, or 7 trains), which drops you smack into a carnival of Indian restaurants, sari shops, gold jewelry dealers, and Bollywood (Indian films) rental stores. Jackson Diner, just a block from the station, is perhaps the most famous of the Jackson Heights Indian restaurants (and one of the largest), while Anand Bhavan (review page 365) caters specifically to herbivores.

Finally, if you like to be cajoled into your dining experience, there's East Sixth Street, where eager employees work the sidewalks to lure pedestrians into their restaurants. Best known for the innumerable strings of Christmas lights that flash madly from the restaurants' ceilings, this little cluster of (mostly) BYOB eateries is a fun and frenzied affair—and a great launching point for a night out in the East Village. Though the food at most of these places is only average, the experience is festive, cheap, and truly unique. Over the past few years, however, a string of newer, more upscale places has emerged. Three standouts here include the all-veg Guru and postmodern Banjara (review page 82) and the kosher veg South Indian favorite Madras Café (review page 99).

—JULIE HOLLAR

All the Moroccan staples are on the menu, which means a lot of meat-heavy dishes. Yet vegetarians will find plenty to satisfy. Soups, changing daily, run the gamut from tomato ginger to pumpkin cilantro, and paired with one of the healthy meze, such as spicy carrots, make a light meal in themselves. The cucumber yogurt is tangy, and before you know it, you'll run out of pita wedges in the addicting rush to sop it up. And don't miss the vegan-safe smoky roasted eggplant blended with tahini—one of the best mezes anywhere.

Although vegetarians will be happy with a number of fresh sandwiches—such as falafel, hummus, and a colorful focaccia concoction of goat cheese, roasted red peppers, arugula, and black olive pesto—with a side of parsley-dominant tabouli, it would be sad to come to Mogador and not experience the couscous. After all, it is the national dish of Morocco. The vegetarian version comes laden with plump chunks of turnips, carrots, cabbage, zucchini, and pumpkin, evoking images of a get-well stew Mom would make (if Mom's name happens to be Fatima). Yes, Mogador's fluffy grains may just take the cake for being number one after all. Raisins add a nice textural touch, and if your palate desires something on the spicy side, make sure to get your couscous spiked with fiery harissa, a mix of hot red peppers, olive oil, and garlic. You can always cool off your mouth with one of the refreshing iced green teas with mint. (Beer and wine are also available.)

—ALIA AKKAM

⑥ Caravan of Dreams

405 East 6th Street (between First Avenue and Avenue A)

PHONE: (212) 254–1613

TYPE OF CUISINE: Organic vegan

DAYS/HOURS: Monday from 5:00 to 11:00 P.M., Tuesday through Thursday 11:00 A.M. to 11:00 P.M., Friday and Saturday 11:00 A.M. to midnight, Sunday 11:00 A.M. to 11:00 P.M.

VEGEBILITY: Excellent

RESERVATIONS: No

WHEELCHAIR ACCESS: A few steps down to entrance

KID-FRIENDLY: Yes

TYPE OF SERVICE: Table

PRICING: Moderate

PAYMENT ACCEPTED: All credit cards

Caravan of Dreams is one of those rare restaurants that manage to transcend the label of eatery and slither their way into being branded as a concept. With a totally vegan menu, it should come as no surprise that New York vegetarians have tenderly called the mostly organic Caravan home for more than a decade now. The *très* hip staff is laid-back and pleasant (some might add slow, but you're not really in a rush, are you?). The music alternates between world music and reggae to country and folk, and seating includes tables with comfy pillows strewn about. As you're handed the extensive menu (everything from organic salads to veggie Reubens to hearty "protein" or "carb" platters), you look around at the retro atmosphere, circa 1973 Berkeley, and notice a mix of true granola types and healthy hipsters hanging out in this small, subdued space that's perfect for soul dining.

In recent years raw food has become such an integral part of the Caravan culture that the place now has its own live-food chef, Lucas Rockwood, on board to prepare dishes so tasty, it's hard to believe they have been neither cooked nor processed. For example, the Rainbow Platter marries a refreshing guacamole-topped salad with live almond-butter-filled celery sticks. Even a raw dessert like Creamy Carob Mousse shines without sugar—live raspberry sauce, nuts, and fresh fruit infuse this ethereal confection with their own natural sweetness.

In addition to the raw line, the well-executed offerings at Caravan include a robust tahini-marinated tempeh veggie burger paired with sugar-free ketchup and vegan nayonnaise, and a whole-wheat chapati burrito brimming with grilled seitan and black beans. Innovative and generously portioned (you might have to save one of the delectable fresh fruit smoothies for another visit), all entrées come with energy-packed side salads of raw greens. Those who shun semolina pasta can opt for a wheat- and gluten-free meal and order sea-vegetable kombu noodles instead. From the triple-filtered water (and line-up of organic beers and wines) to the hands-on cooking lectures Caravan offers on their tranquil premises, this East Village veg haven invites you to partake in its unique community.

—ALIA AKKAM

7 Cicciolino

108 East 4th Street (between First and Second Avenues)

PHONE: (212) 260–3105
TYPE OF CUISINE: Italian
DAYS/HOURS: Monday through Sunday from 6:00 P.M. to midnight
RESERVATIONS: Recommended
VEGEBILITY: Good
WHEELCHAIR ACCESS: Yes
KID-FRIENDLY: Yes
TYPE OF SERVICE: Table
PRICING: Moderate
PAYMENT ACCEPTED: Cash only

"Buona sera" is the greeting when you walk into this charming Italian newcomer to the East Village dining scene. But with its welcoming staff and ambience as rich as its entrées, Cicciolino (which loosely translates to "cute little things") isn't likely to get lost in the crowd.

The inviting decor has a whimsical feel. There's a giant abacus at the back of the main space, and the light fixtures are covered with brightly colored plastic baskets. In between courses, amuse yourself by searching for toy figurines in unexpected places.

The menu is separated into four categories: Little Good Things (appetizers), Bigger, Even Better Things (entrées), Tiny Things (sides), and Sweet Things (you guessed it—desserts). If you're in the mood to start with alcoholic things, don't miss the homemade sangria, delicately spiced with clove. A basket of bread and basil-peppercorn olive oil for dipping will keep you occupied while you wait for little good things like eggplant rolls or the portobellos with pesto, a wonderful dish filled with a garlicky, fragrant pesto and topped with toasted bread crumbs and a drizzle of olive oil.

Ciocciolino has several exciting vegetarian pastas (like the pappardelle with roasted pine nuts, cherry tomatoes, and pesto), and the Risotto del Giorno can be made with vegetable stock. (Mine was unbelievably rich and creamy, loaded with mushrooms and a hint of pecorino cheese.) The vegan entrée, a variation on the standard grilled vegetable dish, is anything but. Served with a few squares of grilled polenta, smoky fennel, zucchini, and the ever-present portobellos in a balsamic reduction, it's a good bet, as are many of the sides.

Cicciolino's portions are just the right size to leave you room for dessert, and as you indulge, you can sit back and contemplate what a "buona sera" it's been after all.

—MELENA Z. RYZIK

8 Counter
105 First Avenue (6th and 7th Streets)

PHONE: (212) 982–5870
TYPE OF CUISINE: American eclectic vegan
DAYS/HOURS: Monday through Thursday from 5:00 P.M. to midnight, Friday 5:00 P.M. to 1:00 A.M., Saturday 11:00 A.M. to 1:00 A.M., Sunday 11:00 A.M. to midnight.
VEGEBILITY: Excellent
RESERVATIONS: Not necessary
WHEELCHAIR ACCESS: Yes
KID-FRIENDLY: Very
TYPE OF SERVICE: Table, take-out, and bar
PRICING: Moderate
PAYMENT ACCEPTED: Major credit cards

Welcome to the diner of the twenty-first century. The food is familiar, filling and affordable, and the comfy decor invites you to linger. But here's the twist: It's all vegan and 85 percent organic; the all-organic wine list competes with four-star restaurants'; the music segues from classic rock to lounge to world beat; and it has dishes like Cape Cod cakes, a barbecued mesquite burger, and a smoked-tofu po' boy that would send Emeril Lagasse back to the drawing board.

Partners Deborah Gavito (whose vision was a place she'd want to hang out at) and Donna Binder (DJ/sommelier) hired vegan chef extraordinaire Richard Pierce to create the kind of stunning, textured food that earned him a cult following at Angelica Kitchen in the late '80s. So was born Counter, in March 2003.

There's not a drop of animal anything here, so you can order with confidence. Every dish has tremendous merits, so our suggestions are highly subjective. (The best solution to indecision is to come with a gang and share, or return time and again and work your way through the menu.) In addition to dinner, on Saturday and Sunday, Counter serves brunch, which includes some mean eggless dishes and waffles to die for. The best way to start dinner is with a combo plate of all three appetizers: Mushrooms New Orleans, with an incredible creamy sauce and just enough kick; those Cape Cod cakes (convincing imitations, I'm told); and the Cashew-Kalamata Pâté, served on fresh Amy's bread and which you'll attempt to horde. Counter mixes all its own seasonings, so playing Deconstruct the Dish is extra challenging.

There are so many pleasing entrée options: a sea-vegetable gumbo, an anasazi-chipotle chili, burgers and sandwiches, a Blue Plate Special of French lentil loaf and garlic mashed potatoes, and four varieties of salad (including a roasted beet one that will sway the beet-hater, and my favorite, the "very composed" Asian salad of perfect tofu bundles, tempeh, soba noodles with peanut sauce, broccoli, and more terrific beets).

The wine list is not to be disregarded. Each entry is researched and sampled by Binder and in the aggregate form incontrovertible proof of how sophisticated organic (and sustainable/biodynamic) wine-making has become. A good way to get to know some of these unfamiliar labels to order a "flight"—a tasting of three wines, either red or white—with your meal for a bargain $7.00. Teas, real cappuccinos, beer, and juices are also available. But the best surprise is yet to come: the dessert list. No chalky puddings or dry granola cakes in this house. Go with your gut, but for my money, it's the Hazelnut Mocha Mousse, topped with coconut mousse. Desserts like these are rare in vegan restaurants. But then again, in the words of one anonymous diner, "This place is too cool to be vegan!" Finally, the world is catching on.

—SUZANNE GERBER

9 Cyclo

203 First Avenue (at East 12th Street)

PHONE: (212) 673–3957

TYPE OF CUISINE: Vietnamese

DAYS/HOURS: Sunday through Thursday from 5:00 to 10:30 P.M.,
Friday and Saturday 5:00 to 11:30 P.M.

VEGEBILITY: Fair

RESERVATIONS: No

WHEELCHAIR ACCESS: Yes

KID-FRIENDLY: Yes

TYPE OF SERVICE: Table

PRICING: Moderate

PAYMENT ACCEPTED: Major credit cards

The first clue suggesting the authenticity of the dishes prepared inside is the presence outside the restaurant of a cyclo, an old-fashioned pedicab that transports passengers through the winding streets of Vietnam. Besides serving zesty homespun Vietnamese fare with panache, Cyclo also manages to do it with a simple but stylish ambience. The mint green walls have a soothing effect (to counteract the pumping techno music, no doubt) and so does the effusive waitstaff. Glasses are constantly refreshed with water, and Vietnamese iced teas are made-to-order. The only downside is that vegetarians, and vegans in particular, are going to have to be careful when selecting their food from a meat-heavy menu.

Seafood seems to dominate Cyclo's dishes, but the Bo Bia is a safe—and delightful—way to begin. Interesting flavors merge when sautéed carrots, green chayote, Asian flower mushrooms, snow peas, crushed peanuts, and fresh basil are wrapped in a soft rice paper, accompanied by an irresistible sweet bean sauce. Another vegan-friendly choice is the Ca Tim Nuon, grilled Asian eggplant with a ginger-lime sauce.

Though vegetarian options are slim at Cyclo, the Ca Ri Chay, a mixture of veggies simmered in a light coconut curry sauce with tofu, and the Mi Xao, sautéed mixed vegetables over a bed of crispy noodles, are so tasty you won't mind the narrow selection. Feasting on appetizers is another option. Cyclo's menu may not be designed with the vegetarian palate in mind, but it's still an inviting place to down a few Saigon beers and eat your veggies with a little Asian flair.

—ALIA AKKAM

⑩ Dojo

Dojo East: 24–26 St. Marks Place (between Third and Second Avenues)

PHONE: (212) 674–9821

OTHER LOCATION: Dojo West: 14 West Fourth Street (at Mercer Street), (212) 505–8934

TYPE OF CUISINE: Asian/Japanese and American

DAYS/HOURS: Sunday through Thursday from 11:00 A.M. to 1:00 A.M., Friday and Saturday 11:00 A.M. to 2:00 A.M.

VEGEBILITY: Fair—not as good as you'd think

RESERVATIONS: No

WHEELCHAIR ACCESS: No

KID-FRIENDLY: Fair

TYPE OF SERVICE: Table

PRICING: Inexpensive

PAYMENT ACCEPTED: Cash only

This celebrated East Village haunt is a staple for the young and the hungry. Known as the place to go for simple, cheap, and dependable food, students and starving artists alike keep this cash-only operation alive. However, the convenience and low prices do come at a cost: The truly vegetarian offerings are slim, and you will have to be specific with your server—and very careful. Most fried foods are cooked with animal products, and even some sauces (like the Japanese BBQ sauce on the hijiki salad and platter) are not vegetarian. Nor is the waitstaff very knowledgeable about which dishes contain "animal products," and almost no one in the kitchen who might know speaks English. Safe bets are any of the salad selections. The tofu salad is a mix of lettuce, spinach, tomatoes, carrots, alfalfa sprouts, and cucumbers topped with one of the biggest slabs of fresh tofu this writer has ever seen. Topped off with the Dojo tahini dressing, this is a great selection for a huge, healthy meal.

The soy burger and veggie burger platters come with a patty lightly fried in soybean oil atop a well-cooked plate of steamed brown rice. A simple side salad adorns the meal and makes for an unfussy classic. Other options are hidden on the menu. Make-your-own omelettes are served all day, and the Japanese don menu boasts vegetable don, yakisoba, and yakimesha (just be sure to ask that your meal is cooked in a separate pan). Both locations are great for casual and inexpensive food: Dojo will make you and your wallet much more comfortable.

—JEWEL ELIZABETH PARTRIDGE

11 Guru

338 East 6th Street (between First and Second Avenues)

PHONE: (212) 979–2135
TYPE OF CUISINE: South Indian
DAYS/HOURS: Monday through Sunday from 11:00 A.M. to midnight
RESERVATIONS: Not necessary
VEGEBILITY: Excellent
WHEELCHAIR ACCESS: No
KID-FRIENDLY: Yes
PRICING: Inexpensive
TYPE OF SERVICE: Table and take-out
PAYMENT ACCEPTED: Major credit cards

If you're looking for something different on East 6th Street, try Guru. The menu at this affordable and slightly eccentric eatery is familiar enough to please your less adventurous meat-eating friends, yet offers some exciting options for vegetarians, going beyond the standard saag panir and alu motor gobi (both of which are very good, by the way—heady with the aromas of curry leaves and ginger).

There are six vegetarian dosas on Guru's menu. An excellent choice is the dosa filled with tofu, spinach, and mushrooms. The tofu in this dish is not relegated simply to bland filler, but plays a starring role with its vibrant seasonings. Other dishes you won't find at Guru's many neighbors on the block include avial, a traditional South Indian dish of vegetables cooked with coconut and yogurt, and sautéed korolla, or bitter melon. Tofu works its way into other entrées as well (like the tofu masala), and the menu actually encourages customers to "ask for vegan curry."

You'll know you've left the cookie-cutter restaurants of Curry Row not only because of Guru's fresh and inventive menu, but because of the quirky music it plays: Where else can you hear Enya and the soundtrack to *Twin Peaks* while you enjoy scrumptious vegan curry?

—EMILY PARK

12 Jenny's Café

113 St. Marks Place (between First Avenue and Avenue A)

PHONE: (212) 674–4739

TYPE OF CUISINE: Tea/snacks

DAYS/HOURS: Sunday through Thursday from 1:00 P.M. to midnight, Friday and Saturday 1:00 P.M. to 2:00 A.M.

VEGEBILITY: Good

RESERVATIONS: Not necessary

WHEELCHAIR ACCESS: Yes

KID-FRIENDLY: Yes

TYPE OF SERVICE: Table

PRICING: Inexpensive

PAYMENT ACCEPTED: MC/V

Bubble tea, tapioca tea, pearl tea, that weird tea with chewy balls in it—call it what you will, the latest liquid trend from Taiwan seems to be here to stay. You can find bubble tea places springing up all over Chinatown, but for the best tapioca treat in the city, head up to Jenny's in the East Village. This little café is cute and welcoming, the staff is ever-cheerful, and you can substitute soy milk for dairy in any tea. The hot teas arrive at your table frothed to perfection, and the iced teas refresh like nothing else on a hot summer day. Jenny's also serves up scrumptious snacks like edamame, soba noodles, and a curious assortment of toast with various toppings.

—JULIE HOLLAR

13 Kate's Joint

58 Avenue B (corner of East 4th Street)

PHONE: (212) 777–7059

TYPE OF CUISINE: Vegan diner/comfort food

DAYS/HOURS: Sunday through Thursday from 9:00 A.M. to midnight, Friday through Saturday 9:00 A.M. to 2:00 A.M.

VEGEBILITY: Excellent

RESERVATIONS: No

WHEELCHAIR ACCESS: Yes

KID-FRIENDLY: Yes

TYPE OF SERVICE: Table, bar, and delivery

PRICING: Moderate

PAYMENT ACCEPTED: Major credit cards

Since 1996 Kate's Joint has been pleasing a fiercely loyal Lower East Side crowd with superb, all-vegetarian, faux meat entrées and sides. No rabbit food here—owner Kate Halpern has created diner- and comfort-food dishes that don't shy away from deep-frying, sautéeing, or rich sauces.

A favorite, the Southern Fried Unchicken Cutlets, consists of generous spiced strips of deep-fried tofu, nearly indistinguishable from the original. It comes with a heaping of creamy mashed potatoes and rich vegan gravy. Another hit is the Shepherd's Pie, with mock ground beef so convincing, it's scary. The "meat" is sautéed tofu with an appealing mix of seasonings, and the stew is sealed with a dab of mashed potatoes, baked until lightly toasted. Some regulars swear by the Unturkey Club, a picture-perfect remake, chewy and moist with vegan mayo. The Fettuccine Forestier is tossed with sautéed yet still-crispy spinach and ample portobello mushroom strips and is topped with a rich nondairy garlic cream sauce. Chewy tofu marinated in maple syrup served well as mock pancetta, but we found the big garlic pieces a bit too chunky.

Kate's also offers seven veggie burgers, all doused in sauce, with a choice of dairy or nondairy cheese and chili. We tried Karin's Burger, a huge patty smothered in sautéed spinach, portobellos, nondairy cheese, and fake bacon. It's a glorious greasy treat, made guiltier with a side of potatoes—go for the rich mashed potatoes or crispy fries. Filling as the entrées are, don't skip the appetizers, especially the red-hot Unchicken Wings, hunks of deep-fried tofu with a

hot and seasoned crust. The hummus passed our standards with enough garlic and tahini, if a little light on lemon.

On weekends, be prepared to jostle for space with the hip, hungover crowd, queued up for the bountiful fixed-price brunch that includes drinks (juices and alcohol) with unlimited coffee. We had huevos rancheros, crispy tortillas heaped with better-than-eggs tofu scramble, warm black beans, cheese, and salsa. Add in the salad and choice of potato, and it's a meal that lasts all day.

Yet save room for the terrific vegan desserts made with Kate's signature tofu whip. The creamy, rich chocolate mousse cake and the luscious vanilla-bean cheesecake were our favorites. Just like the ample no-nonsense dishes, the decor is simple and tends toward the artsy, punk-rock ethic of the neighborhood. The corner restaurant also offers plenty of elbow room and great big windows for fabulous people-watching.

—PHIL ANDREWS

14 Le Souk
47 Avenue B (at 3rd Street)

> **PHONE:** (212) 777–5454
> **TYPE OF CUISINE:** Moroccan
> **DAYS/HOURS:** Sunday through Thursday from 6:00 P.M. to midnight, Friday and Saturday 6:00 P.M. to 1:00 A.M.
> **VEGEBILITY:** Good (but it's all about the ambiance)
> **RESERVATIONS:** Required
> **WHEELCHAIR ACCESS:** Yes
> **KID-FRIENDLY:** No
> **TYPE OF SERVICE:** Table
> **PRICING:** Expensive
> **PAYMENT ACCEPTED:** Major credit cards

Step into the cool world of Le Souk, and you will be surrounded by a sense of serenity and mystique at the same time. That this gem of a restaurant serves top-notch vegetarian fare is icing on the cake. The Le Souk salad, a nice blend of watercress, pine nuts, and beets tossed with rose water, or the salata khadra, with cucumbers, tomatoes, peppers, watercress, olives, and feta cheese, are good options to start your meal. (Vegans can order the salata khadra without the feta cheese.)

Unfortunately, the hot appetizers don't offer too many vegetarian choices, but the Moroccan "cigars" will quickly soothe your sorrow as their creamy filling inside the perfectly fried phyllo-dough crust melts in your mouth. The main course is a tough choice between the vegetable tagine and the vegetarian couscous, but go with the tagine and you won't regret it. This signature dish features sautéed vegetables in a thick tomato sauce mixed with the crunchy Moroccan pasta, couscous. Le Souk also features an impressive wine list, some of which come from Morocco. To add to your dining experience, there's delightful outdoor seating in the summer months and, of course, the hookahs come out after dinner along with the belly dancers.

—SEZIN CAVUSOGLU

15 Liquiteria at Lucky's

170 Second Avenue (between East 10th and East 11th Streets)

PHONE: (212) 358–0300

TYPE OF CUISINE: Juice bar

DAYS/HOURS: Monday through Saturday 8:00 A.M. to 9:00 P.M., Sunday 9:00 A.M. to 9:00 P.M.

VEGEBILITY: Excellent

RESERVATIONS: Not necessary

WHEELCHAIR ACCESS: Yes

KID-FRIENDLY: Yes

TYPE OF SERVICE: Ten stools and take-out

PRICING: Inexpensive

PAYMENT ACCEPTED: Cash; MC/V ($15 minimum)

If Liquiteria at Lucky's had a theme song, it would have to be "Don't Worry, Be Happy." This corner shop oozes good vibrations out onto the sidewalk of Second Avenue. The brightly colored tile work is reminiscent of a Jamaican cruise ship, and the silver cubbies full of fresh veggies look like Martha Stewart redecorated Emeril's set.

Mostly all-organic juices, shakes, smoothies, protein additives, and all kinds of diet aids are to be expected at a place like this, but back by the register you'll also find seven kinds of premade sandwiches and four different soups. But a word to the wise: Come here for the juices.

—MARIANNE SEMCHUK

16 Madras Café

79 Second Avenue (between East 4th and East 5th Streets)

PHONE: (212) 254–8002

TYPE OF CUISINE: South Indian kosher vegetarian

DAYS/HOURS: Monday through Sunday from noon to 10:30 P.M.

VEGEBILITY: Excellent

RESERVATIONS: Recommended for parties of more than four on weekends

WHEELCHAIR ACCESS: Yes

KID-FRIENDLY: Yes

TYPE OF SERVICE: Table

PRICING: Moderate

PAYMENT ACCEPTED: MC/V

This all-veg café is named for the owner's hometown of Madras, a South Indian city renowned for its skilled chefs and vivid spices. The ethic shows in the fresh ingredients and homemade sauces and seasonings. The menu is completely vegetarian and kosher, and the few nonvegan dishes are clearly indicated. Since each dish is made to order, both delicate stomachs and fire eaters can have it their way. A word of warning, however: An order of "moderately spicy" was a bit much for our relatively brave tastes.

We started with the idli appetizer, steamed lentil cakes, perfect for dipping in Madras's two signature sauces. Both the sambar sauce and the coconut chutney (featured in many dishes) are subtle, flavorful delights that stand on their own with plainer dishes and accent more heavily spiced items as well. The vegetable uttapam (Indian-style pizza) needed the two sauces' help. It was good, but we preferred the visually impressive marsala dosa, a huge crisp crepe with a pile of lightly curried potatoes in the center.

But the best reason to go to Madras is the thali, a full traditional meal that includes lentil soup, rice, roti bread, riatha, two entrées, and dessert for $10.95. We sampled the curried TVP (textured vegetable protein), perfect chewy pieces soaked in hot curry sauce that did a convincing meat imitation. The spice interplay in the curried vegetables was divine. No generic curry flavor—each element was distinct, with cinnamon, nutmeg, and cumin playing lead roles. We also liked the kofta curry for its two substantial vegetable dumplings doused in rich tomato and butter sauce. But the highlight of the meal was the spinach and red lentil mash, a wonderfully pungent blend of sautéed spinach and mashed lentils, slightly hot and seasoned with garlic, tomato, and a mysterious blend of aromatic spices.

Madras also has a full beverage menu with rich Indian coffee, freshly made fruit and yogurt blends, beer, and several dozen wines.

—PHIL ANDREWS

17 Mary Ann's Mexican Restaurant
86 Second Avenue (at East 5th Street)

PHONE: (212) 475–5939

OTHER LOCATIONS: 2454 Broadway and 90th Street, (212) 877–0132; 1803 Second Avenue and 93rd Street, (212) 426–8350; 116 Eighth Avenue and West 16th Street, (212) 633–0877; 1503 Second Avenue and 78th Street, (212) 249–6165

TYPE OF CUISINE: Mexican

DAYS/HOURS: Monday and Tuesday from 5:00 to 10:30 P.M., Wednesday from 5:00 to 11:00 P.M., Thursday from 5:00 to 11:30 P.M., Friday from 5:00 to midnight, Saturday and Sunday noon to 4:00 P.M. (brunch) and 4:00 to 10:00 P.M. (dinner)

VEGEBILITY: Very good

RESERVATIONS: Not necessary

WHEELCHAIR ACCESS: No

KID-FRIENDLY: Yes

TYPE OF SERVICE: Table, take-out, and bar

PRICING: Moderate

PAYMENT ACCEPTED: Cash only

Mary Ann's is the kind of place that makes you want to get up and party! From the loud Mexican music to the brightly colored walls and tables, this is a spot that will have you tapping your feet and grinning ear to ear—even if you don't indulge in any of the margaritas the chain is famous for. Each of the five restaurants has its own personality, and all are equally pleasing to the vegetarian palate.

Every day at 5:00 P.M. sharp, the doors open to an eager crowd of happy-hour drinkers who promptly belly up to the bar. Here these attitude-adjusted souls munch on chips, salsa, and sometimes hefty platos of nachos, made with vegetable oil and topped with red beans and tofu jack cheese.

Dinner choices are extensive: One whole page of the menu is filled with vegetarian plates. Goat cheese, mushroom, and black bean wraps just melt in your mouth; roasted eggplant quesadillas are a true delight; and you can't go wrong with any of the veggie burritos, tostadas, or gorditas. Lard is never used in the beans, and the rice has never even heard of chicken.

If you've got a group of people and splurge on a pitcher of drinks, Mary Ann's Mexican is a party waiting to happen, both in atmosphere and in taste.

—MARIANNE SEMCHUK

18 Moustache

265 East 10th Street (between First Avenue and Avenue A)

> **PHONE:** (212) 228–2022
> **OTHER LOCATION:** Greenwich Village: 90 Bedford Street
> (between Grove and Barrow), (212) 229–2220
> **TYPE OF CUISINE:** Middle Eastern
> **DAYS/HOURS:** Monday through Sunday from noon to midnight
> **VEGEBILITY:** Good
> **RESERVATIONS:** Not necessary
> **WHEELCHAIR ACCESS:** Yes
> **KID-FRIENDLY:** No
> **TYPE OF SERVICE:** Table, take-out, and delivery
> **PRICING:** Inexpensive to moderate
> **PAYMENT ACCEPTED:** Cash only

At this delicious Middle Eastern restaurant, nearly everything is made fresh to order, from the fluffy warm pita bread to the cheese, parsley, and egg phyllo roll. Ovo-lactos should definitely try that dish, which is a soft homemade dough filled with a creamy cheese mixture. Its fresh cheesy taste makes it hard to put down. Vegans and vegetarians alike should indulge in the baba ghanoush, a smoky roasted eggplant puree with tahini, garlic, and lemon. Its clean, tart, garlicky taste is perfect for the warm pita bread. Moustache also offers an assortment of "pitzas" (pizzas made on pita bread), veggie highlights being the Moustache Pitza and the Sun Pitza. Since everything is made to order, vegans can just ask for one without cheese.

Both of Moustache's locations have the same menu, and they offer free delivery on take-out orders ($10 minimum, within 5 blocks).

—JESSICA WURWARG

19 **O.G.**

507 East 6th Street (between Avenues A and B)

> **PHONE:** (212) 477–4649
> **TYPE OF CUISINE:** Pan-Asian
> **DAYS/HOURS:** Sunday through Thursday from 6:00 to 11:30 P.M., Friday and Saturday 6:00 P.M. to 12:30 A.M.
> **VEGEBILITY:** Fair
> **RESERVATIONS:** Recommended for parties of four or more
> **WHEELCHAIR ACCESS:** Yes
> **KID-FRIENDLY:** No
> **TYPE OF SERVICE:** Table
> **PRICING:** Moderate
> **PAYMENT ACCEPTED:** MC/V

This is a gentle little refuge in an otherwise pulsing neighborhood, with pumpkin-colored walls and rich banquettes that make it feel cozy but not cramped, inviting but not overbearing. O.G. stands for Oriental Grill, and chef Greg Wang's Pan-Asian menu selections back it up. While vegetarians may find the fish-centered menu a little shorter on choices than they're used to, the kitchen is happy to create dishes to your liking.

For starters, there is one terrific veg option, the East/West Green Salad with Miso Viniagrette, and one easily modified, the Cool Sesame Noodles (hold the chicken). For main courses, try the Vegetarian Wheat Noodles with Sesame Soy Sauce and Citrus Essence or the Wheat Noodles (minus the shrimp), a hearty delight. Side orders of Bamboo Steamed Vegetables with Ginger Miso Dressing; Wok Vegetables Sautéed with Ginger, Soy and Garlic; and Brown or White 5 Vegetable Stir Fry Rice can be had in full or half portions.

Chef Wang hooked us up with a special half-serving (still enormous) of a mixed-greens and grilled portobello mushroom salad; the dressing had hints of hoisin and low-heat chili pepper. The dish was the best I've ever had: perfectly charred, moist enough, and just a little salty. As a side, I was presented with two steamed vegetable dumplings: very good unto themselves, but the real treat was the dipping sauce, a wall of sweet-tangy-garlicky flavor and absolutely addictive.

As we sat and tried to absorb more of the Zen-like tranquility that enveloped us, our server explained the secret of O.G.'s success: Chef Wang and owner Chris Geneversa both give a damn. Wang buys everything fresh from purveyors he trusts, and the end result is obvious—plus it breeds loyalty. One German customer makes a pilgrimage to O.G. every time she's in the city; in fact, it's become the *only* restaurant she visits in New York. You'll be wise to follow her example.

Impressive wine list.

—KATHY AND CARLOS LOPEZ

20 Old Devil Moon

511 East 12th Street (between Avenues A and B)

PHONE: (212) 475–4357
TYPE OF CUISINE: American/Southern/Soul
DAYS/HOURS: Monday through Thursday from 5:00 to 11:00
P.M., Friday 5:00 P.M. to midnight, Saturday and Sunday 10:00
A.M. to 4:00 P.M. and 5:00 P.M. to midnight
VEGEBILITY: Good
RESERVATIONS: No
WHEELCHAIR ACCESS: Yes
KID-FRIENDLY: Yes
TYPE OF SERVICE: Table
PRICING: Moderate
PAYMENT ACCEPTED: Major credit cards

No, you haven't accidentally walked into a garage sale, though you may feel like it when you enter Old Devil Moon. From a Lionel train set to old maps and twinkling lights, this cluttered East Village soul food joint feels like one of those places you might stumble upon while driving through Mississippi. But this isn't the Deep South. It's New York, and that means even normally meat-heavy Southern dishes are available in succulent vegetarian versions.

First, you won't want to miss an appetizer of pecan cakes. You'll need to salt these little corn cakes, but the accompanying blackberry dip bursts with fresh fruit flavor. Old Devil Moon offers a large selection of innovative organic tofu dishes, but ration your water carefully if you go for the Jerk Tofu. (The waitstaff is a few notches below attentive.) Extremely spicy, it comes with yams and a refreshing no-mayo slaw. The Pepper Crust Tofu Steak is excellent, but note that the accompanying mashed potatoes are made with dairy. The homemade BBQ Tofu and Portobello Ribs are another safe way to indulge in Southern food, with or without the mac and cheese. If you don't want to succumb to the ever-changing daily array of decadent desserts (but why deprive yourself, sugah?), fill up on something a little healthier, like a spinach, green apple, and red onion salad (have or hold the blue cheese). You won't find a Southern belle calling you sweetie here as you're handed your corn bread, but remember: This isn't *really* the South—just a wonderful Yankee imitation.

—ALIA AKKAM

21 The Organic Grill
123 First Avenue (between East 7th Street and St. Marks Place)

PHONE: (212) 477–7177
WEB ADDRESS: www.theorganicgrill.com
TYPE OF CUISINE: Organic vegetarian café
DAYS/HOURS: Monday through Thursday from noon to 10:00 P.M., Friday noon to 11:00 P.M., Saturday 10:00 A.M. to 11:00 P.M., Sunday 10:00 A.M. to 10:00 P.M.
VEGEBILITY: Excellent
RESERVATIONS: Recommended for parties of six or more
WHEELCHAIR ACCESS: Small step at entrance
KID-FRIENDLY: Yes
TYPE OF SERVICE: Table, "lunch box," and other carryout
PRICING: Moderate
PAYMENT ACCEPTED: Major credit cards

The Organic Grill is like your really cool aunt's kitchen—if you're lucky enough to have a really cool aunt. The Scandinavian-style cherry-wood tables are bathed in sunlight and the glow of stained-glass light fixtures, and glass jars of teas rest in cubbyholes around the bar. In reality, your way-cool aunt is Russian émigré Vladimir Grinberg, who opened the restaurant in 2000 to give his East Village neighbors a home base for consistently good and affordable organic food.

The kitchen does splendid things with soy. The vegan Caesar salad—complete with toasted multigrain croutons—is a light, tangy twin to the real thing, with a rich soy dressing (no eggs, anchovies, or mayo, of course). The vegan tofu omelette—billed as an Organic Grill exclusive—should impress even those who have ventured far and wide for vegan home-cooking. Juicy portobellos with spinach, onion, and a remarkably melty soy cheese come encased in a tofu shell made by grating and shaping the tofu into a crepelike pocket.

Among other savory options is the BBQ seitan sandwich, on a substantial sprouted-wheat roll. The garlic sautéed greens are a joy: Coarsely chopped and glimmering with flavor, the collards and kale are served in their strong, brothy cooking oil with lightly toasted garlic. Two great sides accompany many sandwiches: A springy coleslaw highlights seasonal vegetables, and the home fries are chunky, herby, and prepared with minimal oil. (Even the ketchup you'll dip them in is organic.) Beyond that, there are a dozen specials featuring staples like adzuki beans and millet. The restaurant is sensitive to vegans, macrobiotics, and those who don't eat wheat. In fact, every dessert is vegan and wheat-free.

Do sample the teas—you have some fifty choices. As an alternative to cappuccino, our server suggested a chai latte made with Mayan chai and a mix of soy and rice milks. There are also organic coffees and a good selection of organic beers and wines.

—ESTHER JAMES

㉒ Planet One Café

76 East 7th Street (near First Avenue)

> **PHONE:** (212) 475–0112
>
> **TYPE OF CUISINE:** Inventive Asian/Jamaican
>
> **DAYS/HOURS:** Monday through Saturday from 6:00 P.M. to midnight
>
> **VEGEBILITY:** Excellent
>
> **RESERVATIONS:** Not necessary
>
> **WHEELCHAIR ACCESS:** Yes
>
> **KID-FRIENDLY:** Yes
>
> **TYPE OF SERVICE:** Table and take-out
>
> **PRICING:** Inexpensive
>
> **PAYMENT ACCEPTED:** Cash only

Planet One bills itself as having "exotic whole foods of the world"—and they're not kidding. Though the menu appears to be primarily inspired by Asian and Jamaican cuisines, a deeper look will show that Planet One's offerings are truly original in nature, like Cauliflower Peanut Soup, Planet Eggplant (steamed in a rich tomato-ginger sauce), African Okra (simmered with tomatoes and spinach), and Sweet Potato Pecan Pie. There are juices, sprout-filled sandwiches, and veggie burgers for those less adventurous. Even more striking than the menu are the prices: Everything is under $8.00, and a combination of three sides will only set you back $7.50. The music and decor are as remarkable as the food: dim, calming, and personal (except for the counter-style ordering). Special events like Caribbean Sunday Brunch and International Night Fridays and even the delightful daily specials make Planet One a great place at which to become a regular.

—MARIANNE SEMCHUK

23 Quintessence

263 East 10th Street (between First Avenue and Avenue A)

PHONE: (212) 654–1823

OTHER LOCATIONS: 353 East 78th Street (between First and Second Avenues), (212) 734–0888; 566 Amsterdam Avenue (between 87th and 88th Streets), (212) 501–9700

WEB ADDRESS: www.quintessencerestaurant.com

TYPE OF CUISINE: Raw vegan

DAYS/HOURS: Daily from 11:30 A.M. to 11:00 P.M.

VEGEBILITY: Excellent

RESERVATIONS: No

WHEELCHAIR ACCESS: Yes

KID-FRIENDLY: Yes (if they're raw-friendly)

TYPE OF SERVICE: Table, take-out, and catering

PRICING: Moderate

PAYMENT ACCEPTED: Major credit cards

This tiny vegan East Village restaurant (with newer, larger uptown outposts) is a sanctuary for the healthiest of the healthy, but the food is so scrumptious, you almost can't tell it's good for you. The unique experience of eating only "live" food has been a way of life for owners Tolentin Chan and Dan Hoyt since 2000. Quintessence has a mission: to provide the purest food that you can eat. Raw foods, so the theory goes, are the richest in nutrients, "packed with minerals, vitamins, essential oils, and most importantly, the fountain of youth, enzymes!"

All ingredients are organic, and nothing is processed (except manually). But first you must cast aside any expectations of crunchy carrots or celery sticks with Nayonnaise. For an appetizer, try the black olive and cream dim sum: a spicy, creamy filling of avocado and black olives presented in a seaweed pouch. Alternatively, have a mini-burrito: a tangy combination of vegetables with guacamole, tomatoes, onions, and cayenne vinegar rolled in a crisp lettuce leaf. Slim, dehydrated root-vegetable chips are dense with flavor, and colors are intact, rendering an exciting visual element to something as simple as chips and guacamole.

Peter's Pot is a rich, luxurious soup of blended tomato, yellow pepper, and cucumber; the smoky, subtle flavor is derived from dulse, basil, propolis, and spices. Juliano's Livioli, a live version of ravioli created by a top raw chef, is a tasty embrace; the thinnest slice of turnip envelops a creamy, nutty basil filling and is topped with a marinara sauce. Divine! The breads and tabouli are sprouted, and flax seeds pressed together and then dehydrated make little crackers. Refined, blended sauces using nuts instead of dairy are velvety and rich.

The not-too-sweet favorite dessert is a distinctly textured coconut cream pie, made with silky young coconuts and a crunchy carob crust. Ask your server to set aside a slice (or two—you won't want to share) as soon as you sit down to avoid grave disappointment later.

From start to finish, all the presentations are beautiful and delicate. The atmosphere is cozy, and an air of mindfulness pervades to respect your food, your body, and your mind.

—LARA OLCHANETZKY

24 Raga

433 East 6th Street (between First Avenue and Avenue A)

PHONE: (212) 388–0957

TYPE OF CUISINE: Indian fusion

DAYS/HOURS: Tuesday through Friday from 6:00 to 11:00 P.M., Saturday 6:00 P.M. to midnight, Sunday 6:00 to 11:00 P.M.

VEGEBILITY: Fair (but worth it)

RESERVATIONS: Suggested on weekends

WHEELCHAIR ACCESS: Yes

KID-FRIENDLY: Yes

TYPE OF SERVICE: Table

PRICING: Moderate

PAYMENT ACCEPTED: All credit cards

You know Asian fusion—why not Indian fusion? But don't come to Raga looking for traditional dishes like malai kafta or chana sag. At this hip East Village eatery, with warm brick walls, sleek black banquettes, and good wines and draft beers, you won't even hear tabla music (more like Stevie Wonder or Kid Loco). You will find nan, though it comes with a tangy eggplant dip instead of the usual trio of Indian dipping sauces.

Besides stumbling upon a cozy new haunt you'll want to keep coming back to—as so many regulars do—you'll find aromatic and inventive dishes that turn classic Indian cuisine on its head. The meat-studded menu may not be packed with a wide variety of veg-friendly options, but the few listed are stellar, a result of chef Lee Farrington's flair for food both delicate and exquisitely spiced, as well as her desire for variety. (Plus she's clamoring for more distinct vegetarian offerings for her customers.)

Breathing new life into that favorite Indian appetizer, the tomato and goat cheese samosas are a sublime starter for vegetarians. An artfully arranged plate, the samosas are drizzled with mint-cilantro sauce and tamarind coulis for a spicy kick. You can also dig into a refreshing Anjou pear and watercress salad, but vegans will have to ask for it without the creamy goat cheese. Basically, there are two vegetarian entrées, a curry and a wonderful mixed plate, and the kitchen will modify either to your liking. The latter is, at heart, a simple plate of mixed vegetables, tofu, potato curry, and rice or couscous, but the addition of flavorful dried and curried patra (incredible crisp, spicy lotus leaves) really makes this dairy-free dish shine. But save room for dessert: The lemongrass crème brûlée is the house specialty and shouldn't be missed.

Six-year old Raga is the brainchild of the charismatic Dutchman Hendrik Brussen. It is one of those intimate spots that make a date memorable and after taking one look around, has you wishing you had been the only one to discover it.

—ALIA AKKAM

25 The Sanctuary

25 First Avenue (between East 1st and East 2nd Streets)

PHONE: (212) 780–9786

TYPE OF CUISINE: International vegetarian

DAYS/HOURS: Tuesday through Friday from 4:00 to 10:00 P.M.,
Saturday 11:30 A.M. to 10:00 P.M., Sunday 11:30 A.M. to 9:00 P.M.

VEGEBILITY: Excellent

RESERVATIONS: Not necessary

WHEELCHAIR ACCESS: Yes

KID-FRIENDLY: Yes

TYPE OF SERVICE: Table, take-out, and delivery

PRICING: Moderate

PAYMENT ACCEPTED: Major credit cards

You get a lot more than well-prepared healthy food when you dine at the Sanctuary. You also get a sense of well-being, perhaps because it's all "karma-free food," as anyone who works there will inform you. Owner Susan Bauer and her chef/husband are part of a spiritual community called the League of Devotees, and they believe the best way to reach people is through what they eat.

Mounted on the exposed-brick walls of this serene, simply decorated restaurant are symbols of all the world's religions: a cruficix, Star of David, yin-yang, and crescent moon, as well as less familiar ones of Native American tribes, Sikhs, and others. The menu is similarly inclusive, featuring an array of culinary delights from the four corners of the globe. Begin with something from the bar—the juice bar, that is. Fruit and veggie juices are available, as are smoothies and shots of wheat-grass juice.

Whatever your fancy, you'll find some version of it here. Barbecued veggie ribs, coconut curry, aloo gobi, an "unturkey" dinner (with mashed potatoes and gravy), avocado burritos, and Taiwanese eggplant peacefully coexist on a menu that announces, "We believe in & honor the sanctity of all living forms." It also advises that "about 90 percent" of the menu is vegan, but any dish can be adjusted.

On your way out, pick up a slice of vegan cheesecake or maybe just a take-out menu. If you have the good fortune of living (or staying) within a 10-block radius, Sanctuary will deliver its culinary message of love to your door, free of charge.

—SUZANNE GERBER

26 Shangrila

129 Second Avenue (between East 7th Street and St. Marks Place)

PHONE: (212) 387–7908

TYPE OF CUISINE: Tibetan

DAYS/HOURS: Monday through Thursday from 4:00 to 10:30 P.M., Friday from 4:00 to 11:30 P.M., Saturday from 1:00 to 11:30 P.M., Sunday from 1:00 to 10:00 P.M.

VEGEBILITY: Very good

RESERVATIONS: Suggested

WHEELCHAIR ACCESS: Yes

KID-FRIENDLY: Yes

TYPE OR SERVICE: Table and take-out

PRICING: Inexpensive

PAYMENT ACCEPTED: Major credit cards

From the soothing music to the earth-tone mural of the Dali Lama's temple to the monk dining next to you, Shangrila is an authentic Tibetan experience. And there's tradition behind it: When the Yangzom siblings opened their restaurant in 1999, they were following in the footsteps of their mother, who's had a Tibetan restaurant in India for more than three decades.

Peaceful ambiance and healthful cooking are equally important in this family-run business. The kitchen is located in the basement to ensure calm and quiet while patrons linger upstairs, absorbing the details of the etheral decor: background chanting, prayer flags, and, most important, the frightening mask facing the entrance to ward off evil spirits.

When it comes to the cuisine, manager Tsering ensures there are no compromises. Almost all ingredients are organic and always fresh. Start with the Tibetan national dish shogo momos in a variety of options, including spinach, and potato and scallion dumplings. Served with a chili-garlic dipping sauce, are Tibetan comfort food with a kick. You'll also want to try the tsel nezom, twelve seasonal vegetables (including broccoli, celery, carrots, spinach, and potato) sautéed in a light ginger-garlic sauce and served with a plate of brown rice. Don't forget to sample the steamed bread—safe even for vegans. But save room for a real Tibetan dessert, such as the hand-rolled pasta in toasted barley flour with butter and brown sugar. Not vegan, but mmm-mmm!

While weekends can get rather busy, most weeknights are quiet. Shangrila offers beer and wine and a nightly early-bird dinner special from 4:00 to 7:30 P.M. weekdays, to 7:00 P.M. weekends. It includes an appetizer, soup or salad, and entrée for $12.95. That's a bargain to any culture. The staff is sweet, and the attention to detail is impeccable—conducive to a truly transcendental experience.

—LAURA DISIENA

27 Time Café (east)

380 Lafayette Street (at Great Jones Street)

PHONE: (212) 533–7000

OTHER LOCATIONS: Time Café (north), 2330 Broadway (corner of 85th Street), (212) 579–5100

TYPE OF CUISINE: New American

DAYS/HOURS: Monday through Thursday from 8:00 A.M. to midnight, Friday 8:00 A.M. to 1:00 A.M., Saturday 10:30 A.M. to 1:00 A.M., Sunday 10:30 A.M. to midnight. Wednesday through Saturday from 11:00 P.M. to 4:00 A.M., Time Café becomes the Rehab Lounge.

VEGEBILITY: Good

RESERVATIONS: Recommended

WHEELCHAIR ACCESS: East (Yes), North (No)

KID-FRIENDLY: Yes

TYPE OF SERVICE: Table, bar, take-out, and delivery (local only, 8:00 A.M. to 10:00 P.M. weekdays, 5:30 to 10:00 P.M. weekends)

PRICE RANGE: Moderate

PAYMENT ACCEPTED: Major credit cards

This trendy spot is the place to be seen on a weekend afternoon, brunching among hipsters, young local families, and well-informed tourists. Once inside you'll be whisked off to an oasis-like Southwestern café, where the ceiling fans lull you into a state of total relaxation. Thanks, in part, to the wall-size black-and-white photo of the barren desert, you can't help but shed a little of that New York bravada.

Time was born in 1990 with a California style of cooking and an organic vegetarian aesthetic. Sadly, over the years, it's become meatier to placate the palates of the changing locals (artsy types have given way to yuppie couples and their jogger-strollers). The café serves lunch and dinner every day and a leisurely brunch on weekends. The brunch menu is most impressive, with eleven egg specialties, three griddle delights, ten salads and sandwiches, and five breakfast basics. There is also a prix fixe menu with 6 entrées to choose from. The buttermilk blueberry pancakes are thick, moist, and loaded with real blueberries.

Even though the original vegetarian/healthful focus has changed over the years, Time is still a great choice for a vegetarian lost in Noho (North of Houston). The garden burger is served at every meal, and all sides are veg, as are about half the appetizers and pizzas. All of the salads can be made vegetarian, and there are always a few veg entrées on the specials menu. Choose from the steamed globe artichoke with garlic-mustard sauce, vine-ripened tomatoes with Montrachet goat cheese and cilantro pesto oil, and a shiitake, cremini, and portobello pizza with kalamata olives, sun-dried tomatoes, and fresh mozzarella. There's also a tempting black bean quesadilla with roasted onion, jalapeños, jack cheese, salsa cruda, and guacamole and a spinach salad with gingered carrots, red cabbage, cucumber, and miso-tamari vinaigrette.

Time carries an extensive wine and cocktail menu, offering thirty wines, five champagnes, fifteen beers, and ten specialty cocktails. How about a Sex in the Village or a Berry White? Max out the pleasure principle by sipping your beverage outdoors, where seventy can be seated comfortably.

There are two Time locations: East is the flagship; north opened in 1998. Each has its own chefs, but the menus are quite similar. North is smaller and darker (gray slate decor) but also has outdoor seating. On Wednesday through Saturday from 11:00 P.M. to 4:00 A.M., Time (east) morphs into the Rehab Lounge. In fact, the restaurant closes at 10:30 P.M. on those nights so the staff can rearrange the tables and chairs to accommodate the drinking and mingling that abounds.

There's a whole other level of fun at the Noho Time—literally. Down a narrow flight of stairs beneath the dining room is Fez, a Moroccan-themed performance space. Here you can see established artists and witness emerging talent in music, poetry, theater, and film.

—EILEEN REGAN

28 Tsampa

212 East 9th Street (between Second and Third Avenues)

PHONE: (212) 614–3226

TYPE OF CUISINE: Tibetan

DAYS/HOURS: Monday through Sunday from 5:00 to 11:30 P.M.

VEGEBILITY: Very good

RESERVATIONS: Recommended

WHEELCHAIR ACCESS: Yes

KID-FRIENDLY: Yes

TYPE OF SERVICE: Table and take-out

PRICING: Moderate

PAYMENT ACCEPTED: Major credit cards

In spacious, candlelit Tsampa, surrounded by pictures of Tibetan mountains and soothed by the low sounds of chanting monks, I found myself swept unwittingly into a love affair with the humblest of vegetables.

Cabbage, potatoes, collards, and various common greens form the foundation of most of Tsampa's vegetarian options, which are, across the board, so full of flavor you'll have a hard time believing that few spices are used besides garlic, ginger, salt, and pepper. It's the simplicity of the spices that brings the flavor of the mostly organic vegetables to the forefront. The sautéed greens entrée is merely kale, collards, onions, and shiitake mushrooms (with a broccoli floret here and there), but it's one of the best plates of greens I've ever tasted.

But don't be in such a rush to try the entrées that you skip the appetizers. Momos, traditional Tibetan dumplings, are reserved for special occasions in Tibet, but you can have them every day of the week at Tsampa. Vegetarians choose between potato and vegetable momos, both of which use whole-wheat dough and come with spicy red and green sauces. The shiitake pancakes, also made with whole wheat, are worth a try for the accompanying tahini sauce alone. Vegans take note: Tibetan cooking uses very little dairy and egg, so you'll find few dishes off-limits.

Finish up with the Tsampa dessert. *Tsampa* is Tibetan for roasted barley, the staple food of that country, and Tsampa the restaurant has invented a dessert to bring its namesake to the American masses. Mixed with yogurt and topped with honey and dried cranberries, this dessert is surprisingly satisfying without weighing you down. After an evening here, you might even leave feeling enlightened.

—JULIE HOLLAR

29 Yaffa Café

97 St. Marks Place (between First Avenue and Avenue A)

PHONE: (212) 677–9001 or (212) 674–9302

TYPE OF CUISINE: Healthy continental

DAYS/HOURS: Monday through Sunday, twenty-four hours

VEGEBILITY: Very good

RESERVATIONS: No

WHEELCHAIR ACCESS: Outdoor seating only

KID-FRIENDLY: Yes

TYPE OF SERVICE: Table, take-out, delivery ($10 minimum; no credit cards), and bar

PRICE RANGE: Moderate

PAYMENT ACCEPTED: Major credit cards

The decor of Yaffa Café warrants a review unto itself. With black-and-white leopard-print tabletops set against flower-print wallpaper, heavy gold-gilded frames, and randomly placed statues of cherubs and colonial pageboys and African busts, I challenge anyone to put a label on it.

This East Village institution has seen it all over the past twenty years, and its patrons run the gamut from punks and goths to yuppies and tourists. The menu is equally diverse. Because it's one of the few restaurants to stay open twenty-four hours a day, it serves breakfast, lunch, dinner, and everything in between. The food is best described as healthy diner fare. There's the usual array of soups and appetizers, salads, sandwiches, and pastas, as well as a separate veg entrée section, ranging from your typical garden burger to a savory mushroom and onion crepe. There are even a few vegan platters (sunshine burger platter, avocado salad), and the chef is happy to modify any dish that contains dairy.

The sunshine burger platter is a vegan favorite. Even though forewarned that the patty is quite grainy and hence an acquired taste, we took our chances and were pleasantly surprised. The burger was a juicy and chunky delight; the hot sauce was incendiary but worth the pain. The veggie stir-fry was much kinder to our senses—the tofu was soft and light, and the zucchini, carrots, and broccoli were vibrantly crunchy. The light but tangy ginger-soy sauce drizzled over the dish saved it from blandness.

Rounding out the menu are fresh juices, coffees, teas, and rich desserts, such as a French apple-peach tart and strawberry-rhubarb pie, as lip-puckery as they are sweet. Yaffa also satisfies night owls with a bar, serving wine, champagne cocktails, and beer every night until 4:00 A.M. Sip your cocktail in one of their two outdoor sections: out front on the sidewalk and out back in the spacious garden, open when Mother Nature permits.

—EILEEN REGAN

Places to Shop

30 Commodities East

165 First Avenue (between East 10th and East 11th Streets)

PHONE: (212) 254–1613
DAYS/HOURS: Sunday through Friday from 9:00 A.M. to 11:00
P.M., Saturday 9:00 A.M. to midnight
OVERALL: Very good

Visit this hip East Village store for a wide variety of fresh organic produce, familiar and hard-to-find pantry items (from flour to spices), and snack items. You can almost lose yourself in their huge selection of bulk items, including twenty-three (!) types of granola. It's a bit crowded with overflowing stacks in the aisles, so go during off-peak hours. The staff is fittingly hip and helpful, but the prices are a bit on the high end. There's a small selection of free-range eggs (and chicken for the not-quite vegetarian), as well as many pseudo meats and dairy products made from soy. In short: something for every appetite.

31 4th Street Co-Op

58 East 4th Street (at Bowery)

PHONE: (212) 674–3623
DAYS/HOURS: Monday from 9:00 A.M. to 9:00 P.M.; Tuesday,
Thursday, and Sunday 1:00 to 9:00 P.M.; Wednesday, Friday,
and Saturday 11:00 A.M. to 9:00 P.M.
OVERALL: Very good

This tiny shop has a huge amount of bulk options: rice, seeds, nuts, dried fruits, honey, soaps, even locally made tofu. All produce is 100 percent organic, but there's little in the way of shelf goods, breads, and frozen items. Anyone can shop here, but members' discounts make the average prices quite affordable. Nonworking members, seniors, people using EBTs (electronic benefit cards), and those with disabilities get 10 percent off; working members get 25 percent off. Memberships cost just $10 for the first year and $35 a year after that.

32 Healthfully

98 East 4th Street (between First and Second Avenues)

PHONE: (212) 598–0777; Fax: (212) 598–1879

DAYS/HOURS: Monday through Friday from 9:00 A.M. to 10:00 P.M., Saturday 10:00 A.M. to 9:00 P.M., Sunday 10:00 A.M. to 8:00 P.M.

OVERALL: Good

Healthfully feels like a suburban health food store in the heart of the East Village. While not nearly as big as a Whole Foods, it's clean, bright, and well organized, with a helpful and knowledgeable staff. According to an owner, Healthfully stocks only top-of-the-line products, including herbs, organic coffees, and supplements. The juice bar is an inviting place to sit for a mixed-green smoothie, and the store also offers discounts on bulk purchases, free delivery, and wellness consultations.

33 High Vibe Health & Healing

138 East 3rd Street (between First Avenue and Avenue A)

PHONE: (212) 777–6645 or (888) 554–6645

WEB ADDRESS: www.highvibe.com

DAYS/HOURS: Monday through Friday from 11:00 A.M. to 7:00 P.M., Saturday noon to 6:00 P.M.

OVERALL: Good/fills a niche

A hop, skip, and jump from the Hell's Angels' headquarters you will find earthy, health-conscious people beelining it to one very special East Village building. Follow them and you'll feel as if you're crashing someone's basement, but do check it out. High Vibe is a hidden treasure for super-high-quality beauty products, recipe and health books, vitamins and minerals, home appliances, and prepared and raw foods. There's an extensive collection of products for colon health, liver cleansing, immunity health, rejuvenation, and parasite elimination. Other notable things about High Vibe are the free classes by resident and guest speakers and their booming mail-order business.

34 Prana Natural Foods

125 First Avenue (between East 6th and East 7th Streets)

PHONE: (212) 982–7306

DAYS/HOURS: Monday through Saturday from 9:00 A.M. to 9:00 P.M., Sunday from 10:00 A.M. to 7:00 P.M.

OVERALL: Very good

The quintessential health food nook, this dimly lit, no-frills Village joint is so laid-back, a cat greets you as you peruse the extensive frozen-food section. Despite its small size, Prana manages to pack in quite a bit, from a selection of mixed nuts to soy milk to a chalkboard boasting a list of varied produce. Can't decide between spinach and kale? No worries. The dreadlocked help will be more than happy to throw in their two cents. While it may not be the most attractive health food store in town, the organic pickings can't be beat, and there's a certain charm about this funky mom-and-pop shop that recycles its own batteries.

35 Urban Roots

51 Avenue A (between East 3rd and East 4th Streets)

PHONE: (212) 780–0288

DAYS/HOURS: Monday through Friday from 9:00 A.M. to 10:00 P.M., Saturday and Sunday 10:00 A.M. to 10:00 P.M.

OVERALL: Fair to good

Urban Roots is a health food store that puts equal emphasis on "health" and "food." It is divided down the middle by a juice bar, which offers "memory jogger" and antioxidant drinks. On one side of the juice bar is a broad health/beauty/vitamin section; on the other is the grocery area, with a nice supply of dry goods, a few shelves of frozen foods, and an average selection of organic produce. Look for the occasional specialty item, like veggie caviar.

36 Whole Earth Bakery and Kitchen

130 St. Marks Place (between First Avenue and Avenue A)

PHONE: (212) 677–7597

DAYS/HOURS: Monday through Friday from 8:00 A.M. to midnight, Saturday and Sunday 10:30 A.M. to midnight

OVERALL: Excellent

Featuring an ever-changing menu of cookies, breads, muffins, and kitchen specialties (mmm-mmm: Tofu Date-Nut Sandwich), Whole Earth Bakery may be the biggest little store of its kind. Everything is completely vegan and prepared with no processed sugar—yet irresistibly delicious. Favorites among regulars include the luscious peanut butter truffles and the sticky rolls. Custom-made cakes for weddings and other special events can be ordered. There's also an organic juice bar and a large selection of exotic teas and coffee. The only shortcoming is that there's limited seating, so there's no chance to linger. But that may be in our best interests.

Places to Stay

③⑦ Howard Johnson Express Inn
135 East Houston Street (between First and Second Avenues)

> **PHONE:** (212) 358–8844
> **WEB ADDRESS:** www.hojo.com
> **PRICING:** Inexpensive

Clean beds in clean rooms for budget-conscious travelers who don't plan to spend much time in their rooms.

③⑧ Second Home on Second Avenue
221 Second Avenue (between East 13th and East 14th Streets)

> **PHONE:** (212) 677–3161
> **PRICING:** Inexpensive to moderate

No elevator and an unimpressive exterior, but luxuriously executed guest rooms in different themes (tribal, modern, Caribbean) and a fully furnished kitchen are to be found at this bed-and-breakfast.

③⑨ The Union Square Inn
209 East 14th Street (between Second and Third Avenues)

> **PHONE:** (212) 614–0500
> **WEB ADDRESS:** www.unionsquareinn.com
> **PRICING:** Moderate

Small boutique hotel with charming rooms and daily continental breakfast.

Greenwich Village

New Yorkers call this neck of the woods just "the Village." With its nineteenth-century row houses and tiny gardens, it's more upscale than its east side cousin, but don't let the circumstances of its pomp fool you. This prime neighborhood's claim to fame—firmly and staunchly—is as the birthplace of cool.

From 14th Street to Houston and bordered by the Hudson River and Broadway, this area is a symbol for all things bohemian, artistic, and socialist. The village is home to a large gay community, and its hub, Christopher Street,

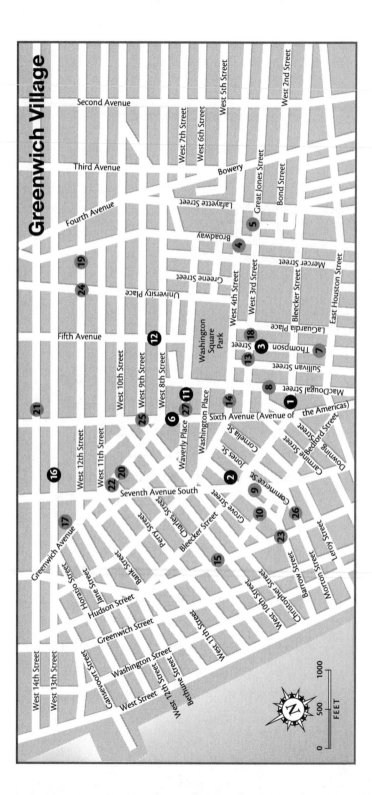

Greenwich Village

is the site of the historic Stonewall Riots of 1969 (named after the Stonewall Bar), which marked the beginning of the gay rights movement.

The heart of the Village is Washington Square Park. The scene of much movie exposure (Sally famously left Harry here when they first arrived in New York), it is both an ode to the past, with its fabled, imposing arch and rows of town houses, and a nod to the present, with its eclectic mix of strollers, sweethearts, students, skateboarders, and stand-up comics. Where else can you start a pick-up game of chess or watch rock stars get busted? (Iggy Pop and David Lee Roth, to name just two.)

From the dawn of the twentieth century, Greenwich Village has been a magnet for free spirits and creative luminaries, including Edna St. Vincent Millay, Eugene O'Neill, Jack Kerouac, Allen Ginsberg, Jimi Hendrix, and Bob Dylan. MacDougal Street, Astor Place, Bleecker Street, and positively Fourth Street are the shopping districts of this neighborhood, chockablock with hipster boutiques and eclectic trinket shops.

Music clubs, experimental theaters, and coffeehouses bring Greenwich Village to life after dark. It probably runs a close second to the East Village for the highest concentration of vegetarian and healthy restaurants. From the rowdy bars and hopping nightclubs to the cabarets and piano bars to the all-night shops and cafés, this area makes a good case for the city that never sleeps.

Places to Eat

❶ Al Gallo Nero

192 Bleecker Street (between Sixth Avenue and MacDougal Street)

PHONE: (212) 475–2355

WEB ADDRESS: www.gallonero.nyc.com

TYPE OF CUISINE: Modern Sicilian

DAYS/HOURS: Sunday through Friday from 5:00 P.M. to midnight, Saturday from 5:00 P.M. to 1:00 A.M.

VEGEBILITY: Good

RESERVATIONS: Recommended weekdays; required weekends

WHEELCHAIR ACCESS: Yes

KID-FRIENDLY: Yes

TYPE OF SERVICE: Table

PRICING: Expensive

PAYMENT ACCEPTED: Major credit cards

And I thought I knew all the great veg-friendly Italian places in town. So how could I have possibly missed Al Gallo Nero? It's been around since November 2001, and it shines like a beacon in the touristy epicenter of the West Village, with its outdoor wooden deck framed by potted and hanging plants. But I'm grateful for the discovery, and you will be, too.

Inside looks—and smells—like a real Tuscan trattoria. I'd call it "rustic" and "charming" if that weren't so cliché: heavy wooden furniture against light stucco walls, terra-cotta vases with dried flowers, copper pots and painted ceramics, walls sconces that bathe the room in a pale yellow light, and, of course, roosters (*gallos*) everywhere. Our waitress was a recent Italian export, and the chef, Piero Minnicucci, is equally authentic. A meal here will transport you to Siena without the benefit of the Italian rail system.

The reason everything is so authentic is the owner, the surprisingly young Melissa Muller. The surname is courtesy of her German dad—but the spirit comes from her Sicilian herbalist/homeopath mother. Melissa was a bit of a prodigy: By age ten she was setting up little restaurants in the backyard for her friends, complete with menus. Every year she summered in Sicily, and she studied at the French Culinary Institute. But it was her year in Florence that gave her the inspiration for Al Gallo Nero ("the black rooster," from a Tuscan legend). She describes the food as modern Sicilian with French technique. We say *delicioso*.

Unless you're vegan, you can't go wrong here. The menu changes regularly, but there are always stand-out salads, appetizers, bruschettas, an all-veg antipasto, a cheese plate, plus a number of pastas and risottos. Many of them are listed with meat or seafood, but Muller says almost any dish can be made veg, so be sure to ask. Not listed but always available is the Pomodoro Ripieno Riso (tomato stuffed with rice), prepared with roasted eggplant and peppers, fingerling potatoes, and pine nuts. We loved the fried artichokes and the asparagus soup, served with a dollop of fresh-from-Italy buffalo ricotta and dill. Entrées provide a tough choice between creamy risottos (asparagus or porcini), the Strozzapeti Ortoloae (cherry tomatoes, peas, eggplant, mushrooms, and asparagus over long, twisted ribbon pasta, with a delectable pesto sauce), and the Butternut Squash Gnocchi. (Maybe the pasta, if only for the translation: "strangle the priest.")

The wine list is good but not cheap; desserts are rich but worth the calories; and, of course, espresso and cappuccino are offered. The entire experience is so wonderful, you'll hate to finally say *buona sera*.

—SUZANNE GERBER

② Anissa

13 Barrow Street (at Seventh Avenue)

PHONE: (718) 741–6699
WEB ADDRESS: www.anissarestaurant.com
TYPE OF CUISINE: Contemporary American
DAYS/HOURS: Monday through Saturday from 5:30 to 10:30 P.M.,
Sunday 5:30 to 9:30 P.M.
VEGEBILITY: Good
RESERVATIONS: Required
WHEELCHAIR ACCESS: No
KID-FRIENDLY: No
TYPE OF SERVICE: Table
PRICING: Very expensive
PAYMENT ACCEPTED: Major credit cards

Worlds collide at the small but *très* haute Anissa, in the heart of Greenwich Village. The owners are two women, American-born chef Anita Lo, whose parents are Chinese-Malaysian and who studied savory and pastry in France, and Jennifer Scism, also a trained chef who worked for architects and designed (and runs) the front room. In Anissa, which means "woman" in Arabic, the two have created an elegant, serene shrine to refined dining and drinking. Done in earth tones and designed with the diner's comfort in mind, Anissa has a feminine vibe, but Dad would be as comfortable here as daughter.

Anissa may mean woman, but it doesn't mean vegetarian. However, call in advance (especially if you're vegan) and Chef Lo will create a truly stunning meal for you. She'll even have your dinner in mind when she shops for veggies at the market that day. One of the things she loves to do is create "parallel tasting menus" for you and your non-veg companion. At least half the menu changes seasonally, and nothing ever repeats. One of the eight appetizers is always veg, and there's a regular field-greens salad with fresh herbs, as well as an off-menu delicate silken tofu, crisped with Chinese black bean sauce. Lo truly enjoys the challenge of cooking à la minute—for my visit, she wasn't even sure what she'd serve till I arrived, and everything was write-home-about impressive.

Normally she draws veg inspiration from what's on the meat side, because, as she puts it, "a good restaurateur is a good janitor." Lo credits her mother for teaching her about cooking: "It's part of the Chinese culture, which always features fresh vegetables."

My meal—a five-course tasting menu that sadly will never be repeated—began with twice-stuffed baby new potatoes and a composed frisée salad with black truffles, pistachios, and a sherry-mustard vinaigrette. Presented on simple white dishes, each course is so attractive that you almost hate to dig in. Next came roasted kabocha squash and shiitakes, with a bitter-chocolate mole sauce and ringed by more mushrooms and pumpkin seeds, then French blue cheese and croutons stuffed in grape leaves, served with green grapes and paper-thin radish and scallion curls. (Note to self: Grape leaves should always contain blue cheese.) The crisped tofu with bean sauce is coated in cornstarch and served with greens (could be spinach, could be mustard). Order this and be warned: You'll never order Chinese take-out again.

Dessert was a quartet that played in bowls on a rectangular plate. This evening it was sesame mochi (sweet rice gluten), one of Lo's signature popsicles (berry, tamarind, coconut), candied ginger, and a house-made chocolate-mint truffle. The wine list is a story unto itself. The hundred-plus terrific offerings are ever-changing, but one thing remains constant: They all come from women vintners or vineyard owners.

The space is designed for maximum comfort—Scism personally measured the space between each table to allow for a sense of privacy and walking room. Her favorite overheard comment, which sums up the Anissa dining experience, is "This is so Zen, I want to stay forever." You can't, of course, but you can always come back.

—SUZANNE GERBER

❸ Chez Moha

230 Thompson Street (between West 3rd and Bleecker Streets)

PHONE: (212) 477–6562

WEB ADDRESS: www.chezmoha.com

TYPE OF CUISINE: Moroccan

DAYS/HOURS: Sunday through Saturday from 4:00 to 11:00 P.M.

VEGEBILITY: Good

RESERVATIONS: Required for parties of six or more

WHEELCHAIR ACCESS: One step at entrance

KID-FRIENDLY: Yes

TYPE OF SERVICE: Table and take-out

PRICING: Moderate

PAYMENT ACCEPTED: Cash only

This five-year-old Moroccan restaurant spent the first four years of its life known as Cookies & Couscous, but in the summer of 2003, the owner went more "politically correct" and changed the name—to his. Despite its former name, Chez Moha is about more than pastries and grains; still, you'd be remiss if you didn't try the dishes that originally lent their name to this cozy Moroccan place. The restaurant, with yellow walls and tile floors, is run by chef Moha Orchid, a Berber from southern Morocco who regales his customers with tales of his home and history between forays into the kitchen. (He'll also tell you Moroccan cuisine is one of the most important in the world, along with French and Chinese.)

With its romantically dim lighting and sheer sari-like curtains, the restaurant feels like a Berber outpost somewhere in Paris, and Orchid admits that Moroccan cooking is inspired by French cuisine. But his must-try organic Union Square Pumpkin Soup breaks with culinary tradition: Served with ginger and a drizzle of honey, the rich soup has no cream, though you would never guess it from the velvety texture. There's also a traditional Moroccan soup—full of lentils, barley, and cilantro—a hearty companion to an anise-flecked roll.

Another appetizer standout is the Mélange of Salads, which combines the tender roasted eggplant, potato, white bean, and carrot salads and is large enough to serve as a main dish. And, of course, there's a vegetarian couscous, served with seven vegetables and a spicy harissa sauce, and a veggie pizza. But don't let your evening end without dessert: Orchid makes all of his own pastries— the chocolate mousse and strawberry-apple frangipane are prepared

Viennese style—and offers some of the most unforgettable sorbets this side of the Seine. Made with fresh fruit and very little sugar, the sorbets and ice creams—including Red Plum with Anise, Mango Lavender, and Lychee with Jalapeño!—are explosions of flavor. On a warm summer night, there's little more you can ask for.

—MELENA Z. RYZIK

Don't Be Cowed into Wearing Leather

"Stylish" and "affordable" are not the words that first come to mind when you think of vegan (non-leather) footwear. But that's probably because you've never been to MooShoes. Founded by a pair of vegan siblings, MooShoes (212–481–5792) offers well-designed, top-quality shoes, sandals, boots, and sneakers from a variety of companies in its retail store at 207 East 26th Street or on-line at www.mooshoes.com. Bored with being a heel whore? Check out their selection of accessories (bags, wallets, belts, and gloves), T-shirts, and jackets. And MooShoes doesn't discriminate: There's just as much stuff for guys as there is for girls. Who says you can't be hip *and* humane?

—MELENA Z. RYZIK

4 Dojo (see East Village)

14 West 4th Street (at Mercer Street)

PHONE: (212) 505–8934

5 The Emerald Planet

2 Great Jones Street (between Broadway and Lafayette Street)

PHONE: (212) 353–9727; Fax: (212) 529–5480
OTHER LOCATION: 30 Rockefeller Plaza Concourse, (212) 218–1133; Fax: (212) 218–1138
TYPE OF CUISINE: Wraps and sandwiches
DAYS/HOURS: Monday through Friday from 9:00 A.M. to 10:00 P.M., Saturday noon to 10:00 P.M., Sunday noon to 8:00 P.M.
VEGEBILITY: Very good
RESERVATIONS: Not necessary
WHEELCHAIR ACCESS: Yes
KID-FRIENDLY: Fair
TYPE OF SERVICE: Cafeteria-style and take-out
PRICING: Inexpensive
PAYMENT ACCEPTED: Major credit cards

The trademark green flag and Eastern-inspired decor invite you into this fast-paced restaurant in both Cooper Square and Rockefeller Center. While mostly a take-out joint, Emerald Planet's bounty of wraps, sandwiches, and fruit smoothies make it a great spot for lunch—or breakfast or dinner—on the go. Folks who like variety will be in heaven here. Since everything on the menu is made-to-order, you can substitute any meat or dairy product with tofu, vegetables, or beans. The twenty-one wrap choices range from whole-wheat to spinach to tomato; rice can be either Spanish or jasmine; fillings include tofu and veggies; and you can always leave off dairy products like goat cheese and garlic-yogurt dressing.

House specialties include the Burlington (portobello mushrooms, bean sprouts, jasmine rice, and a sweet tomato-basil salsa) and the Berkeley—sautéed tofu with toasted sesame seeds and a syrupy teriyaki sauce that brings out the sweet zest of caramelized onions, steamed broccoli, and mushrooms, which is actually worth writing home about. The New Delhi is exactly what you'd expect: an

Indian-inspired wrap with curried carrots, lentils, and cauliflower and a fat-free garlic-yogurt sauce.

The smoothies are made with juice and nonfat frozen yogurt or sorbet (all can be made vegan upon request). Sip the Bali, with bananas, coconut, pineapple juice, and yogurt, and you feel like you're on a tropical isle. Berry lovers will prefer the Fiji, a tart concoction of raspberries, strawberries, bananas, apple juice, and a very tangy raspberry sorbet.

The plentiful dessert and beverage selections includes homemade sangria and baked goods (alas, none is vegan). Breakfast, served until noon, is basically omelettes and egg wraps, so vegans must make do with a black bean wrap. There are also five fresh salads that come without meat (or can be served meat-free), as well as two daily soups. And if all else fails, use your imagination and make something up.

—JEWEL ELIZABETH PARTRIDGE

❻ Gobo

401 Avenue of the Americas (Sixth Avenue) (between 8th Street and Waverly Place)

PHONE: (212) 255–3242
TYPE OF CUISINE: Asian vegan
DAYS/HOURS: Sunday through Saturday from 11:30 A.M. to 11:30 P.M.
VEGEBILITY: Excellent
RESERVATIONS: Recommended on weekends
WHEELCHAIR ACCESS: Yes
KID-FRIENDLY: No
TYPE OF SERVICE: Table, take-out, and bar
PRICING: Moderate
PAYMENT ACCEPTED: Major credit cards

Gobo's wonders start as soon as you walk in the door. A peaceful ambiance of low lights and candlelit tables makes this a wonderful setting for any special dinner. At this offshoot of the NYC chain Zen Palate, you'll find the same tasty food, doting service—and a full bar.

Completely vegan except for a few dishes prepared with honey, Gobo offers a long dinner menu divided into sections: Quick Bites, Small Plates, Large Plates, Salads & Soups, and Side Dishes. The lunch menu is shorter but still impressive. One of the most popular dishes is the pulpy Avocado Tartare with Wasabi Lime Sauce, a pâté-like roll that's half sweet, half crispy. At the top of the not-to-be-missed list is the meaty, smoky flavor of the Grilled Oyster Mushrooms & Asparagus with Fresh Lily. Another delicious plate is the Soy Protein & Spinach Roll with Jade Mushrooms. But really, with their extensive and inventive menu, you can't go wrong with any of the selections.

Dessert options change regularly, but if it's available, definitely try the Hazelnut Napoleon, phyllo squares filled with dates and hazelnut-soy cream and topped with cranberry sauce. Besides an extensive list of smoothies, juices, teas, and seltzer tonics, Gobo has an inviting list of organic wines and beers, established by Herve Pennequin, 2003 U.S. candidate for Best Sommelier of the World.

—DIANA BOCCO

7 Lupa

170 Thompson Street (between East Houston and Bleecker Streets)

PHONE: (212) 982–5089

WEB ADDRESS: www.luparestaurant.com

TYPE OF CUISINE: Italian trattoria

DAYS/HOURS: Monday through Sunday from noon to 2:30 P.M. and from 5:00 to 11:30 P.M.

VEGEBILITY: Good

RESERVATIONS: Recommended

WHEELCHAIR ACCESS: Yes

KID-FRIENDLY: Yes, but the place is busy and loud

TYPE OF SERVICE: Table and bar

PRICING: Expensive

PAYMENT ACCEPTED: Major credit cards

If you can overlook the cluttered space, the incessant noise, and the fact that Lupa is Italian for "she-wolf," you'll find this downtown hot spot worth the minor inconveniences. The brainchild of telechef Mario Batali (the Food Network's "Molto Mario") is in the able hands of executive chef Ken Ladner, who composes an authentic

Roman menu from which vegetarians have plenty to choose. In case of confusion, the back page includes a *glossario* to guide you to the rucola (wild arugula), ceci (chickpea), and bavette (thin linguini), while steering you clear of the guanciale (cured pig jowl) and saltimbocca (literally "meat that jumps into the mouth").

The menu's Primi section includes "verdura," concoctions of perfectly ripe seasonal vegetables. Ladner admits to being obsessive about the bookends of seasons for herbs and greens—never too soon or too late. He spent a year cooking at the (now defunct) macrobiotic restaurant Luna, but because of volume, his menu cannot cater to vegans, who will have a tough time avoiding butter and cheese. In summer Lupa usually has five raw and five cooked verdura choices. We sampled a few that made us look differently at oft-overlooked vegetables. Don't write off beets until you've had them graced with ginger at Lupa. The citrus and fennel was more sweet than bitter. And you knew Lupa could make a zesty eggplant parmigiana.

There are usually at least two vegetarian pastas available at Lupa, where al dente means al dente. Linguini with herba primavera sounds plain enough, but, oh, those herba: dandelion, wild cherry leaves, mustard greens, mint, garlic chives, raddichio. The formaggi, or cheese plate, trumped the dolci, or dessert, in our eyes. Batali's in-laws own the Upstate Coach Farm, which produces a smooth, cool goat curd. The ricotta with honey was a sweet treat and a good balance for the salty gift of Emilia Romagna, the parmigiano-reggiano that Batali likes to call the king of cheeses.

—BRIAN CAZENEUVE

8 Meskerem

124 MacDougal Street (between West 3rd Street and Minetta Lane)

PHONE: (212) 777–8111

OTHER LOCATIONS: 468 West 47th Street, (212) 664–0520

WEB ADDRESS: www.meskeremrestaurant.com

TYPE OF CUISINE: Ethiopian

DAYS/HOURS: Monday through Sunday from 11:30 A.M. to 11:30 P.M.

VEGEBILITY: Very good

RESERVATIONS: Suggested at midtown location

WHEELCHAIR ACCESS: Yes

KID-FRIENDLY: What kid doesn't like to eat with his or her hands?

TYPE OF SERVICE: Table and take-out

PRICING: Inexpensive

PAYMENT ACCEPTED: Major credit cards ($20 minimum)

Ethiopian food has always been a welcoming cuisine for vegetarians, and Meskerem is no exception. The popular restaurant—which started in Hell's Kitchen (the Theater District) in 1993 and expanded to another location in the West Village a few years ago—offers good food in portions perfect for sharing.

The dishes are based around injera, the traditional spongy Ethiopian bread that's used as both plate and utensil. Meskerem's version is not as sour as some can be, which will please picky palates. The vegetarian section of the menu offers several types of lentils and chickpeas, but it's the azefa appetizer, a green lentil salad with a nose-tickling mustard kick, that's especially notable.

Fans of milder food should try the string beans, one of the most popular veggie choices. A faintly sweet dish that mixes green beans and carrots in a tomato base, it's a nice complement to the shiro wat (a spicy chickpea mixture) or one of the lentil stews, which come either mild (scoop up with injera) or spicy (chunkier, with a middle-of-the-throat heat). Samosa lovers can sample the sambosa, a similar fried dumpling stuffed with lentils and served with a hot red pepper sauce. And if you long for the crispness of a salad, try the timatim, with fresh tomatoes, onions, and green peppers.

A new addition to Meskerem's menu is a house wine, also called Meskerem. It's a traditional honey wine, but unlike the blackberry- and cranberry-flavored versions, this one is both sweet and clean-tasting. Ending your meal with a pot of Ethiopian coffee is a must for purists: Served in a jebena, an elegant long-necked pot, it's the perfect pick-me-up after a dense dinner.

—MELENA Z. RYZIK

⑨ Mirchi
29 Seventh Avenue South (between Morton and Bedford streets)

> **PHONE:** (212) 414–0931; Fax: (212) 414–0932
> **WEB ADDRESS:** www.mirchiny.com
> **TYPE OF CUISINE:** Indian
> **DAYS/HOURS:** Sunday through Thursday from noon to 11:00 P.M., Friday and Saturday noon to midnight
> **VEGEBILITY:** Very good
> **RESERVATIONS:** Suggested
> **WHEELCHAIR ACCESS:** Yes
> **KID-FRIENDLY:** Fair
> **TYPE OF SERVICE:** Table
> **PRICING:** Inexpensive
> **PAYMENT ACCEPTED:** Major credit cards

Your first clue that this Indian restaurant is different from the pack comes before you even take your first bite. The atmosphere is a radical departure from standard-issue Indian: Earthy cherry woods and purples are accented with vibrant shades of green, metallic accessories, and larger-than-life black-and-white photos of Hollywood icons. Then the trifold menu opens your eyes to a new kind of Indian, one with freshly cut vegetables, Southwestern-infused spices, and multigrain breads. And visually, the authentic cuisine is transformed with toppings of ripe tomatoes, cilantro, and green onion.

Most of the meat-free dishes are listed under bread and rice, as well as a vast assortment of lentil and potato. Fans of Indian breads will savor the uncommon selection of whole-wheat, multigrain, and white ingredients, but vegans should note that several are prepared with egg washes. The ragda pattice, a large potato cake topped with white peas and sautéed onions, is sugary and satisfying. A more robust choice is the dahi batata poori, puffed whole-wheat balls stuffed with cold potatoes and served with mango chutney and a creamy cucumber yogurt. Skip the dal of the day, a bland daily offering of soupy mashed lentils. Instead, opt for the khicheree, a flavorful rice-and-lentil mix, or go straight to one of the six vegetarian entrées, including hyderbadi baingain (stuffed baby eggplant) and malai kofta (vegetable and panir croquettes).

Another distinguishing characteristic is the lunch deal. Fill up on a chutney sandwich, vegetable box, or vegetable wrap (all served with salad) for $5.00 to $7.00. A weekend brunch menu boasts plenty of vegetable-and-egg omelettes for even less.

—JEWEL ELIZABETH PARTRIDGE

🔟 Moustache (see East Village)
90 Bedford Street (between Grove and Barrow Streets)

PHONE: (212) 229–2220

⑪ North Square

103 Waverly Place (at MacDougal Street)

PHONE: (212) 254–1200

WEB ADDRESS: www.northsquareny.com

TYPE OF CUISINE: New American

DAYS/HOURS: Monday through Friday: breakfast, 7:30 A.M. to 11:00 A.M.; lunch, noon to 3:30 P.M.; dinner, 5:30 to 10:30 P.M. Bar, daily 4:00 P.M. to 12:00 A.M.; Saturday brunch, noon to 3:30 P.M.; Sunday brunch 11:30 A.M. to 4:00 P.M.; Saturday and Sunday dinner from 5:30 to 10:30 P.M.

VEGEBILITY: Good

RESERVATIONS: Recommended

WHEELCHAIR ACCESS: Yes

KID-FRIENDLY: More romantic than kid-friendly

TYPE OF SERVICE: Table and take-out

PRICING: Expensive

PAYMENT ACCEPTED: Major credit cards

Occupying the northwest corner of Washington Square Park, North Square is a neighborhood restaurant for the kind of neighbors who can afford a West Village town house. The subterranean setting is genteel yet casual, with plush purple booths and warm wooden tables that give off a romantic glow.

The food is a similar blend of homey and rich; North Square is equally popular with NYU professors and downtown ladies who lunch. Because the restaurant is attached to the Washington Square Hotel, it serves nearly every meal imaginable: breakfast, lunch, afternoon tea, dinner—even a weekend jazz brunch in the spacious back room. For lunch, don't miss the lentil veggie burger, a scrumptious blend of lentils, carrots, celery, and pistachios that's pan-seared and served open-faced (and butterless) on a roll. Sides of crispy plantain and malanga (Japanese potato) chips are tasty with the accompanying chive aoli, and a small dish of Asian coleslaw is a vinegary counterpart to the meaty burger. For dinner, try the chopped or cobb salads (with exotic purple potatoes) or the wild mushroom ravioli—with goat cheese *and* Gouda—as either an appetizer or an entrée (just ask to double the portion size).

Though the main dishes are mostly meat, there is a rotating pasta option, and chef Yoel Cruz puts together a mean veggie plate, available for lunch or dinner. An artfully presented seasonal ensemble, it may include quinoa, seaweed salad, and expertly grilled portobellos and asparagus. Keep your eye out for the veggie tamale special, or create your own plate of side dishes. And if you're a wine buff, expect to be pleasantly surprised: North Square boasts a 1,500-bottle cellar and has twice been given the Award of Excellence by *Wine Spectator* magazine.

—MELENA Z. RYZIK

⑫ Otto Enoteca Pizzeria

One Fifth Avenue (entrance on East Eighth Street)

PHONE: (212) 995–9559
WEB ADDRESS: www.ottopizzeria.com
TYPE OF CUISINE: Italian
DAYS/HOURS: Monday through Sunday from 9:00 to 11:00 A.M. and from 11:30 A.M. to 11:30 P.M.
VEGEBILITY: Very good
RESERVATIONS: Accepted for parties of six or more
WHEELCHAIR ACCESS: Yes
KID-FRIENDLY: Very
TYPE OF SERVICE: Table, bar, and delivery
PRICING: Inexpensive/Moderate
PAYMENT ACCEPTED: Major credit cards

"We don't look at any food as vegetarian," proclaims Überchef Mario Batali, the force behind landmark NYC Italian restaurants Babbo and Lupa. "We love vegetables by themselves, so we just think of ways to use beautiful vegetables."

Though he doesn't abandon animal products (lard-topped pizza, anyone?), the newest jewel in Batali's toque, Otto, represents a lot of thought about beautiful vegetables. As you chomp on rustic bread that comes delivered bakery-style wrapped in wax paper, let the incredibly knowledgeable waitstaff guide you through the menu —which is divided into sections for antipasti, fritti (fried food), pizza, dessert, and cheese—and the novella-size list of reasonable-to-expensive wines. Be sure to start with a sampling of appetizers—even vegans can make a meal out of Otto's antipasti. Several little dishes, like the marinated artichokes, the thinly sliced beet salad with walnuts and horseradish, and, especially, a phenomenal caponata (roasted eggplant) with homemade raisins, would serve as a filling lunch or dinner, even without the pizza.

And pizza à la Molto Mario is nothing like Famous Ray's. The thin-crusted, grilled version at Otto is perhaps best described as a postmodern translation: Batali has distilled the pizza to its most rudimentary form, basically just dough and olive oil. Not all the pizzas have cheese, and not all of them have sauce. Pies range from the standard Margherita (buffalo mozzarella, tomato sauce, and basil) to tempting experimental toppings, like fennel and bottarga. Most of the daily pizza specials are not vegetarian, but funghi lovers should definitely try the taleggio and mushroom, and the garlic, olive oil, and fresh chile pizza packs powerful flavors. Just one word to the wise: Otto's pizza is best when it's hot; otherwise, the crispy edges cool to a crackerlike state.

Don't feel bad if you want to skip the pie and head straight for the ice cream. The gelatos and sorbettos are not to be missed—the olive oil gelato, sprinkled with sea salt and macerated strawberries, is astounding, and the vegan lemon-basil sorbet is another surprising gem. Ovo-lactos without a sweet tooth might opt for a cheese course. The selections are paired with unusual—and amazing—fruity sauces, like sour cherry with Gorgonzola.

Though Otto's terra-cotta-hued dining room is quite large, the buzz of a new Batali restaurant often means long lines. But the charming bar area, reminiscent of an Italian train station, is a great place to sample a quartino (quarter-bottle) of wine and wait for your table. The staff takes the train station motif one step further by giving you a ticket with your "destination" on it. Since Otto is a place to see and be seen, perch on a bar stool and pose—your train will arrive before you know it.

—MELENA Z. RYZIK

⑬ Quantum Leap

88 West 3rd Street (between Sullivan and Thompson Streets)

PHONE: (212) 677–8050

TYPE OF CUISINE: International vegetarian

DAYS/HOURS: Monday through Friday from 11:30 A.M. to 11:00 P.M., Saturday and Sunday 11:00 A.M. to 11:00 P.M.

VEGEBILITY: Excellent

RESERVATIONS: No

WHEELCHAIR ACCESS: Yes

KID-FRIENDLY: Yes

TYPE OF SERVICE: Table

PRICING: Inexpensive

PAYMENT ACCEPTED: Major credit cards

SPECIAL NOTE: Not affiliated with the Quantum Leap in Queens

Quantum Leap opens its arms wide to veggie lovers with a menu of favorites from around the globe. At this quaint, New-Agey eatery with thick wooden tables and chairs and local art on the walls, you can choose from nine varieties of vegetarian burgers (three vegan), including the Black Bean with BBQ sauce, the Grilled Thai with lemongrass-peanut sauce, and the Baked Walnut-Lentil. The Veggie Cutlet Parmigiana is a hearty take on the classic, served with spaghetti, grilled zucchini, and mushrooms and so authentic-tasting, it should be served by your Sicilian grandmother. The Baja Fajita features grilled strips of seitan under a mix of sautéed onions and peppers, salsa, guacamole, and sour cream (optional). The Fried Wasabi Tofu—breaded in wasabi "crumbs," fried and topped with a miso-wasabi sauce—leaves a kick long after you've stopped eating.

A weekend brunch menu offers whole-grain pancakes and waffles, scrambled eggs, and tofu omelettes, as well as soy breakfast meats. Quantum Leap is sure to please even the most finicky of vegetarians and vegans, which is precisely why it's become an underground favorite.

—JEWEL ELIZABETH PARTRIDGE

14 Red Bamboo

140 West 4th Street (between the Avenue of the Americas and MacDougal Street)

PHONE: (212) 260–7049 or (212) 260–1212

TYPE OF CUISINE: Mock-meat vegetarian

DAYS/HOURS: Monday through Friday from 12:30 P.M. to midnight, Saturday and Sunday noon to midnight

VEGEBILITY: Excellent

RESERVATIONS: Suggested

WHEELCHAIR ACCESS: No

KID-FRIENDLY: No

TYPE OF SERVICE: Table and take-out

PRICING: Moderate

PAYMENT ACCEPTED: Major credit cards

Red Bamboo is the perfect compromise for a vegetarian and a meat-eating friend. But do be warned: Some of the mock-meat dishes look and taste awfully real. And with dishes like the Philly cheese steak and grilled bourbon chicken, the untrained eye (and palate) needs to do a double take to realize the menu is 99 percent vegan. The owner told me that many people bring carnivorous friends without ever telling them, and they never realize it.

If seafood was your thing, try the crispy Cajun shrimp, deep-fried and seasoned with paprika and thyme and served with BBQ sauce on the side. One of the star entrées is the grilled chicken salad, strips of tender soy chicken marinated in a spicy ginger dressing and grilled over open coals, served with a mixed-green salad. Then there's the sticky-sweet BBQ buffalo wings, the stuffed codfish cakes with mango salsa, and the chunky eggplant parmesan hero, made with your choice of dairy or vegan (soy cheese with or without casein) mozzarella.

Wash down your meal with a glass of organic wine or beer, or pick from a traditional list of fresh juices and sodas. After dinner linger over a cup of coffee and some dessert—Red Bamboo may have some of the best vegan versions in the city. A taste of their chocolate-covered strawberry shortcake will give any skeptic new regard for healthy desserts. As Red Bamboo's regulars testify, this place is addictive.

—DIANA BOCCO

15 Sacred Chow

522 Hudson Street (between West 10th and Charles Streets)

PHONE: (212) 337–0863

TYPE OF CUISINE: Asian vegan

DAYS/HOURS: Monday through Friday from 7:30 A.M. to 9:30 P.M., Saturday and Sunday 8:30 A.M. to 9:30 P.M.

VEGEBILITY: Excellent

RESERVATIONS: No

WHEELCHAIR ACCESS: Yes

KID-FRIENDLY: Yes

TYPE OF SERVICE: Seats twelve; mostly take-out

PRICING: Inexpensive

PAYMENT ACCEPTED: Major credit cards

This little West Village vegan carryout draws in a constant stream of people who (mostly) take away anything from fresh salads and tangy soy dishes to baked goods of all kinds. A warm and close-knit team of cooks, including owner Cliff Preefer and head chef Yossi Zur, fashion the food and ambiance into something inviting and healthy. Almost everything is organic, and only price considera-tion may deter the team from buying certain organic ingredients.

The eclectic fare is priced at $7.00 to $8.00 a pound and is an excellent idea for catering a vegetarian party. Zur's primary concern is making good food for all people while embracing a philosophy of nonviolence. Favorites are juicy, marinated-then-grilled chunks of Southwestern-style tofu; black-olive-roasted seitan; and rosemary-roasted tempeh. For a slightly Asian twist, try something like a sweet, smoky dulse salad (served warm) or a spicy peanut udon. Enjoy an unusual and flavorful carrot pâté with a sweet potato scone. Sacred Chow's steamed red cabbage is simply tossed with apple juice, keeping intact the taste and goodness of the vegetable.

For dessert, there's a plethora of treats: cookies, muffins, bars, carrot cakes, a gorgeous fruit cobbler, halvah and chocolate pie, soy milk rice pudding, and, my favorite, a vanilla-tofu and pear pie with a wheat-free crust. No hydrogenated oils are used.

—LARA OLCHANETZKY

⑯ Salam Café

104 West 13th Street (between Sixth and Senventh Avenues)

PHONE: (212) 741–0277

TYPE OF CUISINE: Middle Eastern

DAYS/HOURS: Monday through Thursday from 5:00 to 11:00
P.M., Friday and Saturday 5:00 to 11:30 P.M.

VEGEBILITY: Good

RESERVATIONS: Yes

WHEELCHAIR ACCESS: No

KID-FRIENDLY: Yes

TYPE OF SERVICE: Table

PRICING: Moderate

PAYMENT ACCEPTED: Major credit cards

Salam has three dimly lit rooms, and in any of them you half expect a gyrating belly dancer to magically appear. The tasseled pillows and jingly music create a mystical backdrop, perfect for dining on the restaurant's authentic specialties. Though the front room's loungey vibe is ideal for appetizers and drinks with your friends, it's the dark middle room with convivial tables that will make you want to feast in a more intimate environment.

As Middle Eastern cooking dictates, dishes normally rely upon meat—a lot of meat. Luckily, at Salam you'll find fresh vegetable versions of most of the Lebanese, Moroccan, and Syrian preparations, such as a casserole-like macloubee with such fresh veggies as eggplant and squash and a zesty coriander-infused mixture of vegetables. Start with a terrific rendition of baba ghanoush, a smoky blend of grilled eggplant, sesame paste, and garlic, served with warm slices of pita bread. Or try the sfeeha, a traditional Syrian pizza laden with so many chunky vegetables, you'll need a fork to dig into it. (Both are vegan.) You can't go wrong with a bowl of veggie couscous (prepared with an all-vegetable stock), but the real standout is the vegetable ouzi. The distinctive flavors of squash, spinach, carrots, rice, raisins, peas, and beans meld together when baked in a crisp, flaky phyllo dough. Integral to Middle Eastern cookery, curried spices, such as cumin, are unleashed in the ouzi. Bite after bite is aromatic bliss.

So are the desserts. Classics like baklava and the shredded-wheat-topped knafeh are on the menu, as well as Syrian chocolates that can be leisurely washed down with thick Middle Eastern coffee, evoking feelings of unwinding after a culinary feast at someone's home. But perhaps that's because the restaurant occupies the ground level of an elegant brownstone on a tree-lined West Village street.

—ALIA AKKAM

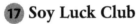 **Soy Luck Club**

115 Greenwich Avenue (at Jane Street)

PHONE: (212) 229–9191

WEB ADDRESS: www.soyluckclub.com

TYPE OF CUISINE: Smoothies, coffee, snacks

DAYS/HOURS: Monday through Friday from 8:30 A.M. to 9:30 P.M., Saturday and Sunday 9:30 A.M. to 9:30 P.M.

VEGEBILITY: Very good

RESERVATIONS: No

WHEELCHAIR ACCESS: Yes

KID-FRIENDLY: No

TYPE OF SERVICE: Counter

PRICING: Inexpensive

PAYMENT ACCEPTED: Major credit cards

Started as the Starbucks of soy, this hip West Village café has expanded its soy milkshake and coffee drink menu to include brunch staples like soups, salads, and sandwiches. The tofu salad sandwich is summery and snackable, a New Wave version of egg salad made more memorable with hearty walnut-raisin bread, avocado slices, and crunchy celery and onions. The artichoke heart, roasted pepper, spinach, and goat cheese panini has a serious bite, and the Zen salad is a protein powerhouse with edamame, black soy, garbanzo beans, and soy nuts. Stop in for a signature drink: soy milk with added ingredients (the vanilla and caramel is a sweet, velvety dream) or a Soyafrost, soy milk blended with ice and fresh fruit, coffee, or chocolate. Dessert takes the form of soy ice creams and vegan cakes and cookies from local bakeries.

Eating is just half the pleasure at Soy Luck Club—customers enjoy their health-promoting choice while reading the menu for soy factoids, perusing the walls of local art, or checking their e-mail on the complimentary DSL lines.

—JEWEL ELIZABETH PARTRIDGE

18 The Temple in the Village

74 West 3rd Street (between Thompson Street and LaGuardia Place)

PHONE: (212) 475–5670

TYPE OF CUISINE: Asian (mostly) vegan

DAYS/HOURS: Monday through Saturday from 11:00 A.M. to 9:30 P.M.

VEGEBILITY: Excellent

RESERVATIONS: No

WHEELCHAIR ACCESS: No

KID-FRIENDLY: No

TYPE OF SERVICE: Self-serve / Take-out

PRICING: Inexpensive

PAYMENT ACCEPTED: Cash only

Small and simply decorated, the Temple in the Village has been a haven for vegetarians since 1986. Joseph Lee, the owner and manager, confirms what you sense when you walk in: Not only do the customers know one another, they're on a first-name basis with the staff.

Instead of a menu, Temple offers a deli-style arrangement of food. For $5.59 a pound, you can choose from a salad bar with steamed and raw seasonal vegetables, hot and cold dishes, and four different types of rice. Included are toasted bread rolls and your choice of homemade dressings, from sweet-and-sour mustard to duck sauce. For an extra $1.00 you can add a gigantic cup of miso soup. Everything is vegan, except for the egg-battered eggplant and one dish of cod that has to be specially ordered. Small cards over every dish indicate if it's appropriate for raw, macrobiotic, high-fiber, or diabetic diets. The restaurant also specifies whether oil was used and if so, which kind (sesame, olive, or soybean). Everything is sugar-free, low in fat, and cooked from scratch. In fact, Rae Lee, the owner's wife and Temple's chef, prides herself on not owning a can opener.

One of the most popular dishes is Tofu Jim, chunks of firm tofu marinated in soy sauce and sautéed with Chinese vegetables. Other standouts are the steaklike seitan sautéed with shiitakes and onions, tofu in a chili pepper sauce, and spicy buckwheat noodles. The crispy whole-wheat tempura, one of only two deep-fried dishes (the other being the spring rolls), is heavenly.

There is a variety of teas and coffees but only a limited number of sweet treats, so Temple is not the best place for dessert lovers. If what you want, however, is a satisfying, inexpensive, and healthy meal, it's hard to beat.

—DIANA BOCCO

19 Terra 47

47 East 12th Street (between University Place and Broadway)

PHONE: (212) 358–0103

TYPE OF CUISINE: Mostly organic New American

DAYS/HOURS: Monday through Friday from 7:30 A.M. to 10:00 P.M. (closed 10:00 to 11:00 A.M. and 3:00 to 5:00 P.M.), Saturday 11:00 A.M. to 10:30 P.M. (closed 4:00 to 5:00 P.M.), Sunday 11:00 A.M. to 10:00 P.M. (closed 4:00 to 5:00 P.M.)

VEGEBILITY: Very good

RESERVATIONS: Recommended for parties of six or more

WHEELCHAIR ACCESS: No (two steps to front door; restrooms downstairs)

KID-FRIENDLY: Yes

TYPE OF SERVICE: Table, take-out, delivery (breakfast and lunch), and catering

PRICING: Moderate

PAYMENT ACCEPTED: Major credit cards

After fours years, the popular organic restaurant Other Foods closed its doors, only to reopen in March 2003 as Terra 47. The ownership and kitchen staff remained the same, but the space and the ambitions of the menu (still more than 90 percent organic) expanded. The restaurant's co-owners, two women who met at the Natural Gourmet Cookery School, were lucky enough to fall in love with the first space they saw, and no wonder: Ornate tiles line the floor, and a tremendous curved panel of stained glass is inset in the ceiling. But the room was small and cramped, with only thirty seats; the redesigned space fits forty far more comfortably, plus five at the bar. The open kitchen was closed off with specially made Moroccan tile to dampen noise, and the whole place was painted a soothing shade of celadon green. A similarly hued painting graces almost an entire wall.

The cuisine at Terra 47 is eclectic, but an Asian theme dominates, in both flavor and presentation. Dishes like crispy spring rolls, filled with marinated portobello and tempeh and wrapped in flaky fried tofu skin, are offset by intriguing sauces: cashew-leek, with a pool of infused chili oil at one end, for example. Spices play a similar role. An outstanding appetizer of sautéed spinach with almonds and sun-dried cherries is dusted with just enough cinnamon to give a sweet kick. Though Terra 47's menu changes every four weeks or so, the spinach is so popular, it's been granted permanent residence.

The restaurant does serve meat, but with the generous appetizers, salads, and several veggie entrées, there's plenty to choose from. Curry, a menu staple, often comes with a tofu option, and a special roasted eggplant and zucchini lasagna makes ingenious use of crisp rice paper instead of noodles. The "cheese" is actually a tofu-olive tapenade, making it an ideal dish for vegans. Wine, sake, and beer—with many organic selections—are also available.

Leah Devde, a co-owner, talks about Terra's desserts with pride: All are vegan, and many are wheat-free. The spelt carrot cake is light and fluffy, with coconut icing in place of the usual dense cream cheese. "Every dish we have on the new menu is something *we* want to eat," says Devde. Her customers would agree.

—MELENA Z. RYZIK

⓴ Thali

28 Greenwich Avenue (between West 10th and Charles Streets)

PHONE: (212) 367–7411

TYPE OF CUISINE: Indian vegetarian

DAYS/HOURS: Monday through Sunday from noon to 3:00 P.M. and from 5:30 to 10:30 P.M.

VEGEBILITY: Excellent

RESERVATIONS: No, but parties of more than four should call ahead

KID-FRIENDLY: Yes

WHEELCHAIR ACCESS: Yes

TYPE OF SERVICE: Table

PRICING: Inexpensive

PAYMENT ACCEPTED: Cash only

There's no written menu at Thali, a tiny Indian restaurant with cheerful yellow walls and barely a dozen tables. But don't let that scare you—it's the main reason you should visit. The lack of a set menu allows the chef, Kusum Pandey, to vary her routine, and since the pocket-size kitchen is too small for a storage area, all the ingredients are fresh every day.

The lone waiter—who serves triple-duty as attentive host, manager, and walking menu—puts waiters who grumble about serving groups to shame. His prompt, attentive, and exceedingly friendly service is largely responsible for Thali's warmth. Every dish here is strictly vegetarian, and many are vegan as well. (There's no butter used in cooking, so with the exception of things made with cheese, milk, or yogurt, there are no hidden "traps.")

When you arrive, the waiter will immediately offer you a choice of tea or mango lassi (Thali doesn't have a liquor license, but welcomes you to BYOB). Served in a chilled glass, the yogurt-based lassi is a good way to start your meal. It's thick and sweet with the perfect hint of piquant mango. From there, you choose from a handful of appetizers, such as dosas, stuffed with one of several savory fillings, including spicy potatoes, green chiles, and spinach with cheese (which resembles an exotic spinach pie). The dosas—served in generous portions with two dipping sauces, a spicy pale green coconut and a mild lentil flecked with cilantro—are a staple of Thali's cuisine and surface again in a more ambitious appetizer, a mango crepe with pineapple and creamy cheese. The slightly salty dosa dough balances out the sweet filling, and the accompanying mango chutney is appropriately tangy.

Thali's signature—in fact, its only—entrée is also its namesake. A thali is a traditional Indian way of eating, with many small portions to sample. Presented on a large metal tray, also called a thali, are a medley of main dishes: cauliflower and potato curry, sag paneer, and an exceptionally good dal, for example. Served with rice, salad, yogurt sauce, bread, and even a small dessert, the thali is perfect for sharing or as a complete meal for one—and with two new options every day, there's plenty of variety.

Round out your meal with a cup of sweet milky tea, and wait for the best part of your time at Thali—the check! Meals at this corridor-size gem are prix fixe: Lunch is $6.99 and dinner is $10.99 (beverages and appetizers are not included).

—MELENA Z. RYZIK

21 Veg City Diner
55 West 14th Street (at Sixth Avenue)

PHONE: (646) 336–7822
TYPE OF CUISINE: American vegetarian diner
DAYS/HOURS: Monday through Sunday, open twenty-four hours
VEGEBILITY: Excellent
RESERVATIONS: No
WHEELCHAIR ACCESS: Yes to restaurant; not to restroom
KID-FRIENDLY: Yes
TYPE OF SERVICE: Table, delivery, take-out
PRICING: Moderate
PAYMENT ACCEPTED: Major credit cards

Veg City Diner, established in 2001 by the geniuses behind the Mexican fast-food success story called Burritoville, is a meat-free greasy spoon that took over space vacated by a Greek diner between a wig shop and nail joint on West 14th Street. Its walls are a testament to how well-loved the place is: All artwork is customer-made, including sweet crayon drawings on paper menus paying homage to the chef and friendly staff.

Veg City offers breakfast any time of day and specializes in standard American fare made from such meat substitutes as wheat gluten and TVP. While some items sport names like Phony Island Corn Dog and FauxPhilly Cheesesteak, others carry the traditional names (Meatloaf, Chicken Parmesan) of their meat-dish counterparts.

The diner offers four to five soups daily, plus a range of special appetizers and entrées. It also has a complete burger menu with a vegan quarter-pounder and a chili cheeseburger that shouldn't be missed. Selections from Burritoville's menu and an assortment of down-home entrées—including shepherd's pie and lentil loaf—round out the eclectic assortment of tastes and textures. The lentil loaf itself comes served as two slices over a generous portion of amazingly chunky garlic mashed potatoes with mushroom gravy and a side of delectable green beans sautéed with walnuts.

While it's possible to have a diner meal without dessert, it's not recommended. Besides your basic ice cream, there's a revolving selection of tempting vegan dessert options, including layer cakes, cupcakes, and soy ice creams. And perhaps the best news: All of this fun fare is available upon demand, 24/7.

—KATHY AND CARLOS LOPEZ

22 Village Natural

46 Greenwich Avenue (between Sixth and Seventh Avenues)

PHONE: (212) 727–0968

TYPE OF CUISINE: International natural

DAYS/HOURS: Monday through Friday from 11:00 A.M. to 11:00 P.M., Saturday 10:00 A.M. to 11:00 P.M., Sunday 10:00 A.M. to 10:00 P.M.

VEGEBILITY: Very good

RESERVATIONS: Not necessary

WHEELCHAIR ACCESS: No, three steps down at entrance

KID-FRIENDLY: Yes

TYPE OF SERVICE: Table

PRICING: Inexpensive

PAYMENT ACCEPTED: Major credit cards

In operation for thirteen years, Village Natural is Vietnamese owned and operated—but you'll be hard-pressed to find any Vietnamese dishes here. It serves more Japanese-inspired cuisine, with some Italian, Middle Eastern, and Moroccan dishes thrown in for good measure. A Mexican assistant chef contributes tasty burritos, enchiladas, and tostadas. The interior is bright and airy, and feels more like the cafeteria of a Zen retreat center than a trendy West Village restaurant.

I started with a glass of freshly pressed carrot-beet juice. Sweet, smooth, and jewel-like, the beverage was an excellent tonic. Many fresh juice combinations are available, and the restaurant strives to use as many organic fruits and vegetables as possible. (Your salad greens will generally be organic, too.)

The savory and delicate Veggie Cutlet Parmigiana, available as an appetizer or in a sandwich with salad, comes drenched in home-made tomato sauce and melted Muenster or a vegan soy cheese alternative. (With the exception of cheese, Village Natural does not use eggs or other animal products in its vegetarian dishes.) Other standout vegan dishes include the Amber Wave, an open-faced sandwich with avocados, mushrooms, onions, and tomatoes; the Seitan Club Sandwich; and the Macro Platter (wheat-free and macrobiotic), featuring steamed veggies spiked with hiziki and ginger-burdock sauce. And there's good news for the wheat-sensitive: Many of the pastas are made with artichoke or buckwheat flour.

Daily specials (lunch and dinner) always include a baked pasta dish. The Tofu Lasagne is excellent—nourishing yet light, with steamed plain tofu and the brightly flavored house tomato sauce. You know a restaurant takes whole foods seriously when there's a bean of the day and a grain of the day. All desserts are made on the premises. Dive into the dairy-free and wheat-free pies, available in flavors straight out of the American diner dessert case—banana cream crumb, sweet potato, pumpkin, blueberry, and mocha—and/or indulge in a glass of one of the tasty organic wines hand-selected by the owners.

—ESTHER JAMES

Top 10 Vegan Desserts

In no particular order, here are the ten best arguments for leaving out the eggs and dairy.

- Angelica Kitchen: Often imitated, Angelica is the standard to which all vegan restaurants aspire. They have some of the highest-quality, most inventive whole-food, vegan desserts around. Check for daily specials, but seek them out when the moon is full—it's the only time they use chocolate. However, they are probably best known for their Kanten Parfait, a healthy but decadent wheat-free fresh-fruit kanten layered with nut cream and cookie crumbs.

- Hangawi: This beautiful restaurant has very few desserts, but their vegan chocolate pudding is sublime. Not only does it taste like the real thing, it has the consistency of velvet: The mouth feel is a trip in its own right.

- Quintessence: There are many great desserts here, but the most famous and by far the best-selling is the Live Coconut Cream Pie. It is fluffy and flavorful and packs a tropical coconut punch that is to die for. It also has an amazing carob-nut crumb crust. But the best thing is that this dessert is full of enzymes and good fats, so it's guilt-free.

- Lifethyme Natural Market: This health food store has a traditional bakery counter that is a welcome sight for a vegan. For the most outrageous vegan cookies, look no further. They have about eight different flavors to choose from, but the Snickerdoodle and Tollbooth take the, er, cake.

- Kate's Joint: When you need a good joint, Kate's is the place. They dispense with the health food attitude and serve up decadent, maybe-not-so-good-for-you desserts, so you really feel like you're being naughty. They have a Chocolate Mousse Cake, served with Tofu Whip, that is awesome.

- Caravan of Dreams: This down-home restaurant serves up really good live and cooked desserts, but their standout is the Rice Dream Pie. Made with Rice Dream frozen dessert, crushed cookies, house-made berry sauce, and a hard chocolate shell, it's the kind of dessert someone might invent if he or she were really stoned.

- Candle Café: Among the many outstanding desserts at this fine restaurant, they get high marks for the originality of their creamy and rich pumpkin cheesecake. Made with tofu cream cheese and fresh roasted pumpkin, this may be Charlie Brown's Great Pumpkin.

- Organic Grill: This is the only place in New York City, and perhaps anywhere, that makes vegan rugalach. It is amazing that no one has tried it before. It's just like the Old World recipe and goes great with their impressive tea menu.

- Counter: This latest entry in the vegan whole foods game is delicious soup to nuts, but their Hazelnut Mousse is worth a visit all by itself. It's so creamy and rich (and served with a fat shard of organic vegan chocolate), you are sure to double-check with your server that it's "safe."

- Candle 79: All the vegan desserts here rock, but the Mexican Chocolate Cake is a knockout. A sinfully rich small round cake floats in a soup of tequila and coconut and is topped with a spicy cinnamon–ancho chile ganache that melts all over it. Holy mole!

—PETER A. CERVONI

Places to Shop

23 Health and Harmony

470 Hudson Street (between Commerce and Grove Streets)

PHONE: (212) 691–3036; Fax: (212) 691–0855

DAYS/HOURS: Monday, Tuesday, and Thursday from 9:00 A.M. to 8:30 P.M., Wednesday and Friday 9:00 A.M. to 8:00 P.M., Saturday 10:30 A.M. to 7:30 P.M., Sunday 11:00 A.M. to 7:00 P.M.

OVERALL: Very good

Health and Harmony offers a wide variety of healthful cuisine, vitamins, natural herbs, homeopathic remedies, and beauty aids. The well-stocked deli features tasty mock chicken and turkey salads that you can dig into between slices of hearty whole-grain bread. You can also get a nice-size veggie burger at the counter; they'll heat it up for you if you request it. The organic juice bar sells fruit smoothies that are great refreshers on a sweltering summer day. The frozen-food section features many veggie burger and soy chicken choices, and the fridge is bursting with tofu. The produce selection is fresh and organic. Health and Harmony always has nice sales on food and other products that last for months at a time. They also deliver around the West Village area.

24 Wholesome Market

93 University Place (between West 11th and 12th Streets)

PHONE: (212) 353–3663

OTHER LOCATIONS: 489 Broome Street between Broadway and Wooster, (212) 431–7434

DAYS/HOURS: Monday through Sunday from 7:00 A.M. to 11:00 P.M.; Broome Street, 7:30 A.M. to 10:00 P.M.

OVERALL: Excellent

This pair of health food stores is known for having items you can't find elsewhere. You'll find everything on your shopping list—and then some. An endless row of organic produce, refrigerator and freezer items, dry and bulk goods, kosher and sushi sections, and an impressive supplement and packaged goods make this a healthy shopper's dream come true.

The best feature, however, may be the extra-long salad bar. In addition to salad fixin's, there are between four and eight varieties each of soup, rice, vegetables, main dishes like sweet-and-sour tofu, burgundy mushrooms, pasta, and more. Insiders know that after the dinner "rush hour," the salad bar at all locations becomes half-price. Note to longtime customers: The Uptown store, at Broadway and 93rd Street, closed in December 2003, leaving a gap that will be hard to fill.

25 Lifethyme Natural Market
410 Sixth Avenue (between 8th and 9th Streets)

> **PHONE:** (212) 420–9099
> **DAYS/HOURS:** Monday through Friday from 8:00 A.M. to 10:00 P.M.; Saturday and Sunday from 9:00 A.M. to 10:00 P.M.
> **OVERALL:** Excellent

Lifethyme has a great variety of fresh produce and all types of vegetarian/vegan products, but what makes it so unique are the fresh juice bar and the very impressive vitamin and supplements section. The bakery is so good that even nonvegans shop here for the dairy- and egg-free carob-chip cookies. (Warning: They are huge, fattening, and addictive.) The salad bar always has a nice selection of hot and cold comfort foods. Customers rave about the book selection. Of course, quality comes at a cost, and you will be paying for it at Lifethyme. But remember, the pleasure of your shopping experience and eating organic are priceless.

Places to Stay

26 Morton Street Suites

55 Morton Street (between Hudson and Bedford Streets)

> **PHONE:** (646) 638–2271
> **PRICING:** Expensive

Prewar art deco–style brownstone. Each apartment has a fully stocked kitchen, and pets are welcome.

27 Washington Square Hotel

103 Waverly Place (between Sixth Avenue and MacDougal Street)

> **PHONE:** (212) 777–9515
> **WEB ADDRESS:** www.washingtonsquarehotel.com
> **PRICING:** Expensive

Family-owned hotel with an unbeatable location, on the northwest corner of Washington Square Park.

Chelsea

Only in recent years has Chelsea become a posh address and a place to be seen—and to eat. Because of the skyrocketing rents in Greenwich Village, the vibrant gay community there flocked to this revitalized neighborhood (14th Street to 29th Street, Fifth Avenue to the Hudson River), and others naturally followed. Known for its many nightspots, Chelsea also boasts a burgeoning art scene, the Joyce Theater for dance, and the Chelsea Pier Sports and Entertainment Complex for all things jock. Be sure to check out the plant and gardening district along Sixth Avenue in the mid-20s and the Chelsea Flea Market on Saturdays (on 26th Street). There's no shortage of great veg wining and dining; the list following is, of course, partial but represents the soy crème de la crème.

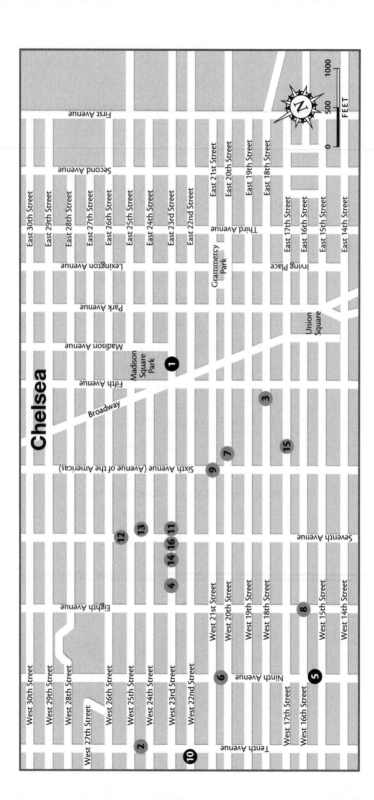

Places to Eat

❶ Bonobo

18 East 23rd Street (between Fifth and Madison Avenues)

> **PHONE:** (212) 505–1200
> **TYPE OF CUISINE:** Live vegetarian
> **DAY/HOURS:** Monday through Saturday from 11:30 A.M. to
> 8:00 P.M. Closed Sunday.
> **VEGEBILITY:** Excellent
> **RESERVATIONS:** Not necesssary
> **WHEELCHAIR ACCESS:** Yes
> **KID-FRIENDLY:** Yes
> **TYPE OF SERVICE:** Cafeteria-style ordering with table seating;
> take-out; delivery except during lunch rush hour; catering
> **PRICING:** Inexpensive
> **PAYMENT ACCEPTED:** All credit cards ($10 minimum)

Less is definitely more at this exciting new addition to New York's vegetarian dining scene. Opened in November 2003, Bonobo's is the culmination of a five-year dream for proprietor David Norman, who may be the healthiest real estate developer in the northeastern grid.

Ironically located on a block of fast-food chains and next door to a bar called Live Bait, Bonobo's looks healthy even from the sidewalk, with its high ceilings, hanging plants, wooden floors and tables, exposed brick walls, and the brightest salad bar in town. The restaurant bills itself merely as vegetarian, but it's actually part of the hottest culinary trend: live (uncooked, unprocessed) food. "We're just celebrating the tastes of fruits, vegetables, nuts, and seeds," says Norman, who's been practicing what he preaches since 1999. "We don't talk about 'raw' or 'vegan'—we're just serving the freshest organic food in a natural setting."

Another way to think of the food is the way Norman does, as salads in a variety of formats: traditional, blended (soups), sandwiches (between nappa cabbage leaves), and exotic (rolled inside nori, for example). But the bottom line is creating phenomenally delicious meals. Norman is so convinced "mainstream taste buds" will enjoy this type of food, he exhorts the staff to hand out an endless stream of free tastes. ("We're Sample City!" he says). The proof is in the mango-banana pudding. In just a few months, many first-time customers have become regulars—if not gushing devotées.

Lunch is the busiest meal. You can custom-order a familiar salad but be prepared for more flavor and energy in your food than you're used to. The organic mixed greens are kept between 30° and 40° F—most salad bars leave them at wilty room temperature—and all the fixings are super fresh and about 80 percent organic. Add-ons include homemade nut and seed pâtés (or spreads) that burst with flavor. They change daily, as well as seasonally, so ask for samples and decide on the spot. Ditto with the salad dressings. I loved the olive oil with garlic, ginger, and lemon, but the creamy tahini ran a close second. Warning: These are not your ordinary bottled dressings, and you could become addicted.

The blended soups need to be experienced firsthand. There's a reason the Sweet Bell Pepper with Coconut is the most popular: It's out of this world. But the others, including the (organic heirloom) Tomato and Basil or the Butternut Squash with Hazelnut, are also knockouts. All are the product of three years of trial-and-error testing, until Norman felt he got it right. He did.

There are also entrées, which change regularly but are likely to include a Vegetable Medley with Herbs and a Veggie Nut Patty Platter. Live desserts may not look tempting, but one bite will change your opinion. Look for the frozen "puddings"—pressed fruits that taste so much like ice cream you'll swear they're cream-based. In your life you may never have ordered a fresh date for dessert, but try it. It's as sweet and chewy as candy, only good-for-ya. And if the carob truffle is available, get one, or maybe several. Like many live concoctions, they're deceptively simple: just carob, date, and walnut. And yet they're so rich and chewy, you may never crave a cupcake again.

So what's the deal with the bonobo (ba-NO-bo)? They're our closest relative in nature, explains Norman, and instinct tells them to eat fruits, vegetables, nuts, and seeds. Unlike humans, they do not get degenerative diseases (heart disease, cancer, diabetes, arthritis, obesity), and they live six to eight times past their age of maturity—an equivalent of well over one hundred in humans. If that's monkey business, sign me up!

—SUZANNE GERBER

2 Bottino

246 10th Avenue (between 24th and 25th Streets)

PHONE: (212) 206–6766

TYPE OF CUISINE: Northern Italian

DAYS/HOURS: Monday from 6:00 to 11:00 P.M., Tuesday
through Friday noon to 3:00 P.M. and 6:00 to 11:00 P.M. (11:30
P.M. Friday), Saturday noon to 3:00 P.M. and 6:00 to 11:30 P.M.,
Sunday 6:00 to 10:30 P.M.

VEGEBILITY: Very good

RESERVATIONS: Suggested

WHEELCHAIR ACCESS: Yes

KID-FRIENDLY: Yes

TYPE OF SERVICE: Table and bar

PRICING: Moderate

PAYMENT ACCEPTED: Major credit cards

This finely designed former hardware store has been serving eclectic Northern Italian food since 1998. The simple decor, full bar, and extensive wine list make Bottino a good place for both drinks and a relaxing dinner. And fortunately for vegetarians, the staff and kitchen at this stylish west Chelsea restaurant are extremely flexible about creating meat-free meals.

Bottino's menu changes seasonally, but with each season there is a number of suitable appetizers and entrées for both vegetarians and vegans alike. To start, the artichoke, radicchio, and frisée salad or the fennel and arugula salad are both light and flavorful, served with a delicate vinaigrette dressing. They both come topped with a delightful shaved Tuscan pecorino cheese, but the chef will happily leave it off upon request.

It is Bottino's fresh homemade pastas that stand out as their forte. The Ravioli Verde is a spinach pasta filled with ricotta and Swiss chard and topped with tomato sauce—a wonderful blend of mild flavors. The Rigatoni with Roasted Eggplant, a chunky pasta with (of course) roasted eggplant, yellow and red peppers, tomato, and basil, can be made with or without the creamy ricotta salata. Chef Prosperi also offers nightly specials, and one is always vegetarian. For us he made a pappardelle with a slightly creamy mushroom sauce. The blend of the thick pasta and the earthy mushrooms was perfect, and a sprinkle of cheese on the top balanced the flavors to make a great dish. An assortment of pies, tarts, and ice creams offers a wonderful ending to an excellent, filling meal.

—JESSICA WURWARG

3 The City Bakery
3 West 18th Street (between Fifth and Sixth Avenues)

PHONE: (212) 366–1414

TYPE OF CUISINE: Nouvelle cafeteria

DAYS/HOURS: Monday through Friday from 7:30 A.M. to 7:00 P.M., Saturday 7:30 A.M. to 6:30 P.M., Sunday 9:00 A.M. to 5:30 P.M.

VEGEBILITY: Very good

RESERVATIONS: No

WHEELCHAIR ACCESS: Yes

KID-FRIENDLY: Yes

TYPE OF SERVICE: Counter with table seating

PRICING: Moderate

PAYMENT ACCEPTED: Major credit cards

The name tells only half the story: The City Bakery isn't just a wonderful destination for sweets, it's also an ideal spot for a veg lunch or early dinner, with arguably the most creative salad bar in town. A soaring, light-filled space with a simple decor and lots of seating on two levels, plus a young, friendly counter staff make it one of the more bustling spots in the hip Flatiron neighborhood, especially at lunchtime. And the regular appearance of exotic ingredients like jicama, black rice, and chayote; a kid-friendly atmosphere; and great weekend brunch food make it worth fighting the crowds.

While it's not cheap ($12 a pound), the salad bar is innovative, and the offerings change daily. On any given day you might find orzo salad with feta, raisins, and capers or grilled pineapple slices. Or try the green burrito filled with queso blanco, pumpkin-seed puree, and greens, available every day. A hot-food station serves oatmeal for breakfast as well as mac and cheese at lunchtime. And there's a seven-seat counter with hot-food specials that change with the seasons.

Tangy lemonade in flavors like blueberry or edible flower are highlights in the summer, while the annual hot chocolate festival each winter offers daily flavors like ginger, in addition to the super-rich regular version.

Oh, yeah, and the baked goods are pretty tasty, too. City Bakery's muffins, corn bread, Danish pastries, and croissants (one is made of pretzel dough) are satisfying fare for breakfast or an afternoon coffee break. And don't miss the sublime tarts (small or large) and oversize cookies, all decadently rich and deeply flavorful. After eating your veggies at City Bakery, it's almost obligatory to have dessert.

—EMILY RUBIN

F&B

269 West 23rd Street (between Seventh and Eighth Avenues)

PHONE: (646) 486–4441

TYPE OF CUISINE: European street food

DAYS/HOURS: Tuesday through Saturday from noon to 11:00 P.M., Monday and Sunday from noon to 10:00 P.M.

VEGEBILITY: Very good

RESERVATIONS: No

WHEELCHAIR ACCESS: One step, but staff is happy to assist

KID-FRIENDLY: Yes

TYPE OF SERVICE: Counter

PRICING: Inexpensive

PAYMENT ACCEPTED: Major credit cards

If you occasionally pine for a good ol' hot dog, this is the place for you. F&B, short for Frites and Beignets (or fries and cream-filled donutlike street food), carries eight types of vegetarian hot dogs, four of which are vegan (and all of which are soy-based). The most popular is the Veggie Great Dane, made of smoked tofu and topped with all sorts of Danish specialties, like remoulade (a sharp-tasting sauce that usually contains mayonnaise, ketchup, parsley, horseradish, and Tabasco), apple ketchup, Danish mustard, crisp roast onions, and pickles. The combination is unusual but tasty and addictive.

F&B, which opened in August 2000, also offers a great assortment of fries, onion rings, and haricots frites (fried string beans), which come with a variety of flavorful and unique dipping sauces. The garlic aioli has a strong, creamy, garlic flavor, and the sweet-tasting (vegan) Thai chili sauce is fantastic with the salty fries.

Don't leave without trying a cup of fresh, perfect lemonade or one of the heavenly ice creams (crème brûlée is their most popular flavor) or sorbets. They also serve beer, wine, and champagne. At press time owners Nicholas Type and Till Horkenbach were looking to convert the counter seating at their hip hot dog house to small booths and hoping to open up two new locations. This is good news for vegetarians, who comprise at least 50 percent of F&B's customers.

—JESSICA WURWARG

❺ The Green Table

Inside Chelsea Market, 75 Ninth Avenue (at 15th Street)

PHONE: (212) 741–6623
WEB ADDRESS: www.cleaverco.com
TYPE OF CUISINE: Sustainable, veg-friendly American
DAYS/HOURS: Tuesday through Saturday from noon to 9:00 P.M.
VEGEBILITY: Very good
RESERVATIONS: Suggested
WHEELCHAIR ACCESS: Yes (restroom in market)
KID-FRIENDLY: Yes
TYPE OF SERVICE: Table, take-out, and bar
PRICING: Expensive
SPECIAL NOTE: Space can be rented for parties
PAYMENT ACCEPTED: Major credit cards

L ike most treasures, the Green Table is secreted away in a place where you'd only find it by accident (happy accident) or if you were a very clever foodie. A recent offshoot of the twenty-five-year-old NYC catering institution Cleaver & Co., this tiny bastion of organic haute cuisine is squirreled away inside the Chelsea Market. Enter on Ninth Avenue and wend your way to the middle to find this tiny French-countryside bistro, with its brick red walls and wooden tables that seat twelve lucky diners.

Its modest size and decor belie the extraordinary dishes turned out by Culinary Institute of America-trained chef Margaret Morse. Almost everything here, including the tremendous wine list (which is not an incidental draw), is organic or grown with sustainable practices. The menu changes daily, though there are revolving staples, and everything is always super fresh.

While you decide what to order (a difficult task, best accomplished by a process of elimination), you'll be treated to a basket of ancho-orange popcorn. (True to the Green Table's principles, even the organic corn was hand-picked in New Jersey.) Of fifteen menu items, ten are vegetarian. All soups are veg-based and can be made vegan. Carrot, chilled pea, and asparagus: all winners. To start, you might overlook the blasé-sounding crudités—but don't! The presentation alone makes them worth ordering. Served in individual lacquer boxes, the baby veggies (hot radishes; orange, yellow, and purple carrots!) are perfection by themselves, but they come with grilled flatbread and a dip that changes. We sampled the hummus—another ho-hum dish one might think. But this is no ordinary hummus. It's so creamy and full of subtle flavors, you'd swear it's dairy-based (it's not). The secret, we learned, is that liquids are poured in slowly, and it's seasoned with a smoky Moroccan pepper called Aleppo.

We lucked out and visited during ramp season ("New Yorkers love their ramps," says Morse) and so tasted a superb ramp and yogurt soup with pansies, served in a demitasse. There's always a meze plate special, and it's usually half-veg. If you see endive with Stilton mousse, pear relish, and candied walnut, be sure to order it. It's only two or three bites, but we are still talking about its texture and blast of flavors and contrasts.

Everything here is presented with artistry. ("Vegetarians need beautiful, delicious food, too," says Morse, who made vegan haute cuisine a personal mission because one of her friends was always left out of the fun.) But the food's just half the thrill. We paired our courses with wine. The tiny staff is all well conversant with the wines and won't steer you wrong. The best deal is Happy Hour (Tuesday through Thursday from 4:00 to 7:00 P.M.), when you get 30 percent off all wines by the glass. Organic and uncommon, they'll win your heart, and you'll likely bring one home.

Do not miss dessert, especially if the rhubarb soup is in season. I know what you're thinking because I thought it, too: Right, I'm going to waste a dessert on rhubarb. Trust me on this. Served with real vanilla-bean ice cream, candied ginger, and shortbread, this soup will change your mind about that maligned green. Of course, if the chocolate-rosemary pots de crême, the ultimate rich chocolate dessert, is available, you'll need to order both and share them. Or go back and have an order of each all by yourself. Just remember, the Green Table is our little secret.

—SUZANNE GERBER

The Natural Gourmet Cookery School

Something's cooking on West 21st Street. In fact, something's always cooking on West 21st Street, because it's home to the first and arguably most influential whole-foods cooking school in the world. The Natural Gourmet Cookery School (48 West 21st, 212–645–5170), founded in 1977 by Annemarie Colbin, teacher and author (*Food and Healing,* Ballantine, 1996), is a small space that's had a disproportionately large impact on healthy eating. It's best known as a professional chef's training school, with five programs running at any given time. A highly qualified, eclectic staff annually teaches some 150 students, 85 percent of whom find careers in the food industry. Graduates have gone on to work in some of NYC's best kitchens, including Gramercy Tavern, Heartbeat, Angelica Kitchen, Candle Café, and Quintessence. What's unique about this school is its emphasis on whole foods and its commitment to inculcating a real understanding of healthful principles in its students. For example, beyond traditional techniques, students learn about meal balance from both a Western and an Eastern perspective. Colbin's personal insistence on fresh, organic whole foods is the school's hallmark. "I am not interested in imitation food," she says.

But the Natural Gourmet is a valuable resource for everyone. Public classes are offered throughout the year by the Natural Gourmet Institute for Food and Health in the West 21st Street school. Every year more than 1,500 students are taught everything you ever wanted to know about healthy cooking—from knife techniques to principles of balance to new ways to cook tofu or sea vegetables. The school also offers cooking retreats, in conjunction with "Conscious Gourmet" Diane Carlson.

Participants are immersed in cooking intensives in locations like Italy, Hawaii, and Sedona, Arizona.

Another school function is placing chefs in restaurants, spas, and even private homes. Before September 11, 2001, says director of placement Rosemary Serviss, they couldn't keep up with the demand for in-home chefs. That has fallen off a bit, but a big part of Serviss's job still is matching trained chefs with individuals seeking healthier meals, hospital patients eager for better food, people with diseases or allergies needing assistance preparing health-supportive meals, or just people wanting onetime catering for a party or a cooking demonstration. Chefs charge $25 to $40 an hour, and there's typically a four-hour minimum.

We've saved the best for last. Almost every Friday night at 6:30 sharp, two of the classrooms are transformed into candlelit dining rooms, where students serve an elaborate veggie meal (often all-vegan) to the public. Just $27.50 buys you a gourmet four-course meal. A recent dinner included butternut squash and sweet potato fritters served with a creamy horseradish sauce, wild rice pilaf in baby pumpkin, and a Thai mushroom sauté, followed by a chocolate-almond and raspberry sorbet. Bring your own bottle to make it really festive. (Reservations are required: 212–645–5170, ext. 0.) Because they sometimes close for maintenance, check far enough in advance if it's a special occasion.

"When I started this school back in 1977," says Colbin, "it was considered weird and totally off the wall. My vision wasn't that everyone be vegetarian or vegan but that those dietary choices should be as acceptable as Italian or Chinese. Over the years vegetarianism has lost its stigma, and I'm pleased to have been a part of that trend. My main goal has been to train others to do this kind of cooking, because the vegetarian option has to be there, it has to be part of our culture, and it has to be done well."

—SUZANNE GERBER

6 O Mai

158 Ninth Avenue (at 20th Street)

> **PHONE:** (212) 633–0550
> **TYPE OF CUISINE:** Vietnamese
> **DAYS/HOURS:** Monday through Sunday from 5:30 to 10:00 P.M.
> **VEGEBILITY:** Fair
> **RESERVATIONS:** Suggested
> **WHEELCHAIR ACCESS:** Yes
> **KID-FRIENDLY:** No
> **TYPE OF SERVICE:** Table
> **PRICING:** Moderate
> **PAYMENT ACCEPTED:** Major credit cards

O Mai is a Chelsea offshoot of the very popular and tragically hip Nam; those who have been to the original will find O Mai similar in tone, but less intimidating. Still, the place is of the square-white-box, grass-plants-not-flowers, Zen-with-artesian-spring-water genre. Black clothing is optional, but advised.

Begin with a bottle of that artesian spring water and some Bo Bia (veggie soft-rice-paper rolls), featuring crunchy bean sprouts, peanuts, and a few bracing mint leaves and served with a chile-bean sauce (this sauce is more sweet than hot). As an appetizer it's large and satisfying; add an order of Ca Tim Nuong (grilled eggplant with a ginger-lime sauce), and you have a light dinner. An intriguing vegan starter is Banh Cuon, steamed mushroom ravioli tops—open-faced ravioli, as it were—with fried shallots and basil. Only vegetable oil is used.

Alas, the menu's Soups and Noodles section contains no vegetarian offerings at all; you must also skip the entrées and proceed directly to Rice and Vegetables. Here, however, you will find the makings of a hearty dinner. The mixed vegetables are presented in a lovely coconut-curry sauce, with just a trace of heat. Several different kinds of mushrooms—as well as carrots, snow peas, and bok choy—appear, along with wheat gluten. It's advisable to order the jasmine rice as an accompaniment, to soak up the sauce. A real disappointment, though, is the spicy lemongrass-crusted tofu. The excellent (homemade) soft tofu, sadly, was coated with a blackened rice flour that tasted much more of burnt charcoal than anything else. Desserts, which we did not sample, include a chocolate mousse with orange marmalade and chilled coconut cream with tapioca sauce (both ovo-lacto).

The vegetarian choices here are not extensive, but O Mai is worth a trip just for the freshness and high quality of the ingredients. This is not cookie-cutter Asian fare, which is to say they make their own tofu and rice-paper pasta. The waitstaff is knowledgeable and friendly. There is a respectable wine list but very few wines available by the glass—try beer instead.

—EUREKA FREEMAN

7 Periyali

35 West 20th Street (between Fifth and Sixth Avenues)

PHONE: (212) 463–7890
WEB ADDRESS: www.periyali.com
TYPE OF CUISINE: Greek
DAYS/HOURS: Monday through Friday from noon to 3:00 P.M. and from 5:30 to 11:00 P.M., Saturday 5:30 to 11:00 P.M.
VEGEBILITY: Fair
RESERVATIONS: Strongly recommended
WHEELCHAIR ACCESS: Four steps at entrance
KID-FRIENDLY: No
TYPE OF SERVICE: Table
PRICING: Expensive
PAYMENT ACCEPTED: Major credit cards

If the Oracle didn't predict a cruise through the Greek isles in your future, come to Periyali for the next best thing. It's decidedly not a vegetarian place, but if you're clear with your server from the get-go, you'll be rewarded with a sensational meal in a charming old-world setting. You might even spot a celeb or two.

Chef Thomas Xanthopoulous is—surprise!—a Greek native, and his food is wonderful evidence of the simplicity of the cuisine and its brilliant use of fresh, quality ingredients. Lunch and dinner feature the same foods (but different prices), and it's easy to fill up on slightly exotic delicacies.

Appetizers can and probably should be the bulk of your meal—order several and share with your group, who won't miss the meat. There are five equally great options: the horlatiki salad (big chunks of tomato, feta, cukes, red onion, and olives); the spanokopita, served with zucchini fritters; the fava beans with red onion, lemon, and olive oil; the gigandes skordalia (giant white beans in a very garlicky sauce); and the melintzano (eggplant puree) and Tzatzila (cuke, yogurt, and dill) salads but make sure they leave out the Taramosalata (caviar) that come with the plates. Not on the menu but always available—and always fabulous—is a (safely) char-grilled portobello salad. Vegetarians can make a meal out of these, especially when you use the marvelous bread to soak up the dips, but vegans will feel shortchanged and may feel like invading a Turk-ish restaurant.

On the entrée side you will find nothing. But no worries: Just ask for the grilled vegetable plate and discover how great that hum-ble dish can be when the veggies are super fresh and grilled to per-fection with quality Greek olive oil. It really is head and shoulders above most places' eponymous dish.

The wine list offers ten Greek bottles. Try the Kouros, a light and dry wine from Patras that tastes like Pinot Grigio. If your taste runs a little sweeter, order the Cretan Boutari. Or consider the Greek national beer, Hellas, which has a mild bite of hops.

If you're trying to be moderate, beware of Greeks bearing dessert trays. All are made on-site by Periyali's Greek pastry chef, so the (huge) baklava, orange semolina cake, and fried-dough diples are richly authentic. We loved the walnut cake, syrupy and moist and served with honey, powdered sugar and berries. There's also Greek coffee and cappuccino to end your meal. But take your time—the screening of Zorba on the cruise ship doesn't start for hours.

—SUZANNE GERBER

8 Rue des Crepes

104 Eighth Avenue (between 15th and 16th Streets)

PHONE: (212) 242–9900

TYPE OF CUISINE: French

DAYS/HOURS: Sunday through Thursday from 11:00 A.M. to 11:00 P.M., Friday and Saturday 11:00 A.M. to 1:00 A.M.

RESERVATIONS: Not necessary

VEGEBILITY: Fair

WHEELCHAIR ACCESS: No

KID-FRIENDLY: No

TYPE OF SERVICE: Table, take-out, and delivery

PRICING: Moderate

PAYMENT ACCEPTED: Major credit cards

For a true French experience in the heart of Chelsea, head to Rue. The decor and the food will remind Francophiles of their favorite outdoor Parisian café. And if you fell in love with crepes on the Ile de la Cité, you must come here to relive that heady experience.

Few dishes are vegan at Rue des Crepes, but you can still find something to take with you to one of the outdoor tables. Try the Veggie Wrap, a spinach tortilla with a thin layer of hummus and filled with sun-dried tomatoes, lettuce, cucumber, and sprouts. The dish is served with a cup of homemade soup. *Mais oui*—you came for the crepes! The options are all delightful, though I would heartily recommend the wild mushroom, sautéed with shallots, tarragon, and white wine.

For a truly unique experience, enjoy a Bowl of Five Onion, a homemade soup made from a puree of potato and five different onions. Completely vegan, it's made with no cheese or cream. *Mon Dieu!*

—DIANA BOCCO

9 The Tomato Restaurant

676 Sixth Avenue (at West 21st Street)

PHONE: (212) 645–6225; (212) 645–5305 (take-out and delivery)
TYPE OF CUISINE: American / continental
DAYS/HOURS: Monday through Friday from noon to 10:00 P.M.,
Saturday and Sunday 10:00 A.M. to 10:00 P.M.
VEGEBILITY: Good
RESERVATIONS: Required for dinner
WHEELCHAIR ACCESS: Yes
KID-FRIENDLY: So-so
TYPE OF SERVICE: Table, bar, take-out, and delivery
PRICING: Moderate
PAYMENT ACCEPTED: Major credit cards

When you first enter this Chelsea restaurant, it looks like a typical sports bar, with several big-screen TVs, a large bar, and a lively atmosphere. But appearances in this case are deceiving. Tomato is a very pleasant spot for a quick bite or a more leisurely meal, chosen from a surprisingly veg-friendly menu. To its roster of assets add a cozy dining room in the back, featuring dramatic over-size photos on the walls and comfortable banquette seating, outdoor café seating in good weather, a long wine list, and genial service.

Tomato is a place that will satisfy almost anyone's palate. There are numerous vegetarian options on the menu—just know that most have a touch of butter added at the end (which can be omitted). Though the restaurant generally caters to business types and hipsters, the Vegetarian Tofu Meatballs is a kid-friendly dish. Other favorites include the Vegetarian Tempeh Reuben, BBQ Tofu, and Fried Green Tomato Sandwich.

The produce is mostly organic, and soy substitutes are readily available for most dishes. Even the Veggie Wrap's hummus is made from soybeans (not the usual chickpeas). Don't miss the highly recommended Tomato Soup as an appetizer. Thick, hearty, and redolent with the flavor of fresh basil, it will warm you instantly on cold winter days.

Tomato does a brisk delivery and take-out service and offers a daily lunch special. Catering is also available.

—CHRISTINA MASSEY

⑩ Wild Lily

511 West 22nd Street (between Tenth and Eleventh Avenues)

PHONE: (212) 691–2258
TYPE OF CUISINE: Asian
DAYS/HOURS: Tuesday through Sunday from 11:00 A.M. to 10:00 P.M.
VEGEBILITY: Very good
RESERVATIONS: Recommended on weekends
WHEELCHAIR ACCESS: No
KID-FRIENDLY: No
TYPE OF SERVICE: Table and take-out
PRICING: Moderate
PAYMENT ACCEPTED: MC/V

Almost invisible from the street, Wild Lily opens into a fresh oasis once you step in. The serene sight of a modern, minimalist interior awash with paintings and sculptures is just one of the many perks of eating here. A lot of people come for the fish—the live ones, that is—who reside in a tiny pond built into the center of the restaurant. When they're in the right mood, it seems they might almost let you pet them.

Vegetarians will find many tempting dishes on the menu, like the Tofu Salad, served with seaweed and walnuts and a ginger dressing, or the Steamed Vegetables and Tofu Basket with Sesame Sauce. But many customers come here just for the tea. Loose, always fresh, and served at the proper temperature, tea here is an authentic treat. Favorites include Darjeeling, with a golden nutty flavor; Tong Tin Oolong, flowery and fragrant; and the custom-made mixes such as Yang Guay Fay, a Chinese black tea brewed with lichee fruit, perfect for dessert.

If tea's not your cup of, well, you know, try the sake. Pick any four from the menu for a $20 tasting price. A special selection is the Japanese Judas Tree, a creamy fruity-flowery mix that resembles a sparkling wine.

—DIANA BOCCO

Places to Shop

11 Garden of Eden

162 West 23rd Street (between Sixth and Seventh Avenues)

PHONE: (212) 675–6300

OTHER LOCATIONS: 7 East 14th Street, (212) 255–4200; Monday through Sunday from 7:00 A.M. to 10:00 P.M.; 180 Montague Street, Brooklyn Heights, (212) 222–1515, Monday through Saturday from 7:00 A.M. to 9:00 P.M.; Sunday from 7:00 A.M. to 8:30 P.M.

DAYS/HOURS: Monday through Saturday from 7:00 A.M. to 10:00 P.M.; Sunday from 7:00 A.M. to 9:30 P.M.

OVERALL: Excellent

A well-stocked salad bar complete with goodies that actually look fresh and appealing, like cool jicama and white tofu salad, may be the real draw at this inviting gourmet market—there's actually four of them—but the produce section can't be missed for its array of hard-to-find veggies and fruits, from parsley root to sunchokes to cranberry beans. You'll want to bring a camera—or perhaps a picnic table. An innovative selection of hot meat-free soups and prepared foods also breathe new life into meals-to-go. Clean and well-lit, the aisles are neatly arranged and if you're lucky, the site of a few tasty free samples. Here you'll find everything you could ever hope for: breads, desserts, cold and pantry items, and things you've never even heard of.

12 Organic Market

275 Seventh Avenue (between West 25th and West 26th Streets)

PHONE: (212) 243–9927

DAYS/HOURS: Monday through Friday from 8:00 A.M. to 9:00 P.M.; Saturday 10:00 A.M. to 9:00 P.M., Sunday from noon to 7:00 P.M.

OVERALL: Very good

Organic Market's high ceilings and wide aisles are immediately inviting, as are its almost medicinal cleanliness and the layout of the floor plan. There's limited produce, but it's all organic and very fresh, with preference given to seasonal vegetables. The bulk bins and frozen foods more than make up for the limited supply of fresh veggies, and you'll be happy with the fresh pitas and sandwiches, which are wrapped and ready to go.

For health and beauty, there is a separate section with a marvelous department for vitamins and supplements. Just like the groceries, they are organized logically and with a clinical atmosphere. Don't leave without sampling a very frothy and reasonably priced juice drink. The aroma of wheat grass permeates your surroundings and energizes your body.

 Whole Foods
250 Seventh Avenue (at West 24th Street)

> **PHONE:** (212) 924–5969
> **DAYS/HOURS:** Monday through Sunday from 8:00 A.M. to 10:00 P.M.
> **OVERALL:** Excellent
> **OTHER LOCATIONS:** In Time-Warner Center, 10 Columbus Circle, Suite 101, (212) 823–9600. Monday through Sunday from 8:00 A.M. to 10:00 P.M.
>
> **WHOLE BODY AT WHOLE FOODS MARKET**
> 260 Seventh Avenue (at 25th Street), (212) 924–9972
> **DAYS/HOURS:** Monday through Sunday from 8:00 A.M. to 10:00 P.M.
> **OVERALL:** Excellent

How did Manhattanites survive without a Whole Foods for so long? This national chain of organic and natural foods (not to mention an entire seperate bath and beauty department) opened its first New York outpost in Chelsea just a couple of years ago, and there's been a buzz around the place ever since. From its wide packaged goods and produce selections to its excellent bakery and deli to its prepared-foods area that rivals some restaurants, Whole Foods is one-stop shopping for, well, everything. It's so popular, in fact, that the store has to employ special "line expediters" for the checkout; keep your eye out for the one who's been written up in *The New Yorker*.

Places to Stay

14 The Chelsea Hotel

222 West 23rd Street (between Seventh and Eighth Avenues)

PHONE: (212) 243–3700
WEB ADDRESS: www.hotelchelsea.com
PRICING: Expensive

Stay at this notorious hotel that Sid and Nancy made famous—and where Dylan penned "Sad-Eyed Lady of the Lowlands."

15 Chelsea Inn

46 West 17th Street (between Fifth and Sixth Avenues)

PHONE: (800) 640–6469; (212) 645–8989
PRICING: Moderate

This bed-and-breakfast in a nineteenth-century town house has expansive rooms with flea-market-style furnishings. Lower-priced rooms share a bathroom.

16 Chelsea Savoy Hotel

204 West 23rd Street (at Seventh Avenue)

PHONE: (212) 929–9353
WEB ADDRESS: www.chelseasavoynyc.com
PRICING: Moderate

The rooms are bare bones, but the address and the price are perfect.

Gramercy/
Union Square East/
Midtown East

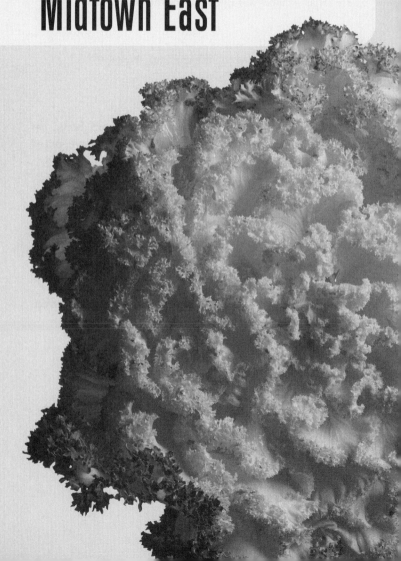

Technically we're mixing apples and oranges here, but for convenience's sake, we've lumped everything from the iconic Flatiron Building to the East River into one big neighborhood. (To paraphrase Steven Wright, it's not *that* big, but I wouldn't want to paint it.) Into that group we've dumped two architectural landmarks, the Empire State and the Chrysler Buildings; the (majestically restored) Grand Central Terminal; Union Square; the United Nations complex; Rockefeller Center; and St. Patrick's Cathedral. The boundaries we've invented start with Broadway and 23rd Street (Flatiron) in the west but mostly we're focusing on points north of 14th Street and sprawling northeastward to the Upper East Side. Some of Manhattan's trendiest restaurants call Park Avenue South home; aside from them, you might have to walk a mile for a good veg meal. After that dinner, check out historic Pete's Tavern, where O. Henry penned *The Gift of the Magi*, for a hearty pint and a taste of classic New York. Or if teetotaling in winter, head for Rock Center, where you can rent ice skates and make like Michelle Kwan.

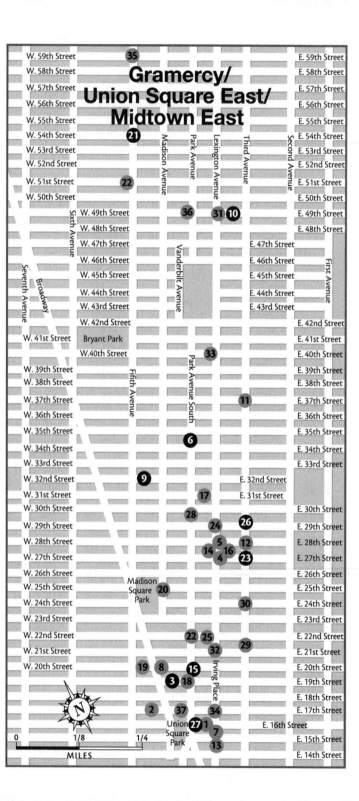

Gramercy/
Union Square East/
Midtown East

Places to Eat

Candela

116 East 16th Street (between Park Avenue South and Irving Place)

PHONE: (212) 254–1600

TYPE OF CUISINE: New American-Asian

DAYS/HOURS: Sunday and Monday from 5:30 to 10:00 P.M., Tuesday and Wednesday 5:30 to 11:00 P.M., Thursday 5:30 to 11:30 P.M., Friday and Saturday 5:30 P.M. to midnight

VEGEBILITY: Very good

RESERVATIONS: Recommended for Friday and Saturday

WHEELCHAIR ACCESS: Yes

KID-FRIENDLY: Yes

TYPE OF SERVICE: Table and bar

PRICING: Moderate

PAYMENT ACCEPTED: Major credit cards

With its high ceilings, velvet curtains, full bar (exotic martinis, great wines), outdoor seating in warm weather, and some dimly lit rear seating year-round, Candela is perfect for a date or an intimate meal. Candles provide most of the lighting, and there's even space between tables. Opened in 1996, owners Mario and Sergio Riva transformed this former wine storage warehouse into its present romantic incarnation.

Although the menu revolves around seafood, chef Joseph Macri is happy to adapt dishes for vegetarians and vegans at this eclectic restaurant, which features both pasta and sushi on its seasonally changing menu. There are mixed-green salads and pasta dishes (all cheeses can be omitted), as well as an avocado sushi roll. The side of spinach with sesame seeds and soy sauce does contain a bit of butter, but ovo-lactos shouldn't hesitate to order this garlicky delight. They will also have no trouble choosing among the numerous pasta and risotto dishes. In the summer the risotto (made with vegetable broth) with fava beans, sweet corn, and pecorino Romano cheese is a real treat. The corn adds a fresh flavor to the intense and delicious garlic and cheese combination that melds smoothly into the risotto. All the side dishes are vegetarian—some are even vegan—and put together, they make a great meal. The chef is also happy to serve any combination of sides that accompany seafood or meat dishes.

For dessert, ovo-lactos will love the warm chocolate cake, served with malted milk-ball ice cream and dark and milk chocolate malt sauces, or the vanilla crème brûlée, which speaks for itself.

—JESSICA WURWARG

2 Chop't

24 East 17th Street (between Fifth Avenue and Broadway)

PHONE: (646) 336–5523

TYPE OF CUISINE: Salads, sandwiches, and soups

DAYS/HOURS: Monday through Thursday from 11:00 A.M. to 8:00 P.M., Friday and Saturday 11:00 A.M. to 5:00 P.M.

VEGEBILITY: Very good

RESERVATIONS: No

WHEELCHAIR ACCESS: Yes

KID-FRIENDLY: Yes

TYPE OF SERVICE: Take-out, counter, delivery, and catering

PRICING: Inexpensive

PAYMENT ACCEPTED: Major credit cards

The impressive throng of hungry New Yorkers winding its way in and out of the front door on any given weekday around noon makes it clear that this is one popular lunch spot. When it opened in January 2001, Chop't owners Colin McCabe and Tony Shure were hoping to "bring something creative, fresh and healthy to the lunchtime scene in New York City," as they say in their mission statement. The bustling joint's lime green walls are decorated with photographs of fresh vegetables, and the place exudes a vibrant and healthy energy, making Chop't a perfect place for an upbeat lunch, though it seems a bit high-energy for a relaxing dinner. (More like, grab a salad to bring home.)

Chop't has a system. Walk up to the counter, pick a lettuce, and design your own salad by choosing from a long list of vegetarian, vegan (and non-veg) ingredients. The worker behind the counter will assemble your dish for you—and chop it up as well. Chop't has a good assortment of protein sources for vegans and vegetarians, including smoked tofu, eggs, and a variety of cheeses, and

A Dose of Dosa

You might not have heard of them until just a few years ago, but dosas, a South Indian specialty, are all the rage in New York City. And what a great—and spicy—way to get your veggies in. Always on the scent for creative and exotic cuisine, New Yorkers are packing into both the no-frills take-out joints and exquisite white-tablecloth South Indian eateries across town to sample crispy, crepelike dosas.

Looking like nothing you've ever seen (except, perhaps, in a Cheech and Chong movie), these labor intensive pancakes are sometimes 18-inch-long eye-popping logs, sometimes crispy delectable tepees. Whether yours comes horizontally or vertically, its blend of soft filling (traditionally potato-based) and crackling paper-thin exterior boasting a spicy flavor that is never too much to eat. Made of fermented parboiled rice and lentils, the healthy dosa, teeming with fillings like chunky potatoes and peas (or more exotic offerings, such as one served downtown with roasted beets, butternut squash, arugula, and goat cheese), is a South Indian staple that begs to be shared. Two chutneys (one tangy, one coconut) usually come on the side for an even bigger wow.

—ALIA AKKAM

the help is happy to substitute ingredients in set salads and sandwiches. Though the salads are large and served with grilled tortillas, I was disappointed that some of the ingredients tasted canned or frozen.

Chop't also offers two soups daily, one of which, Grandma Evelyn's Vegetarian Vegetable, is vegan. The salads come in disposable plastic containers, so they are easy to take away. As we went to press, the owners, who also do catering and offer free deliveries, were looking to open a second location.

—JESSICA WURWARG

❸ Craft

43 East 19th Street (between Park Avenue and Broadway)

PHONE: (212) 780–0880

WEB ADDRESS: www.craftrestaurant.com

TYPE OF CUISINE: New American

DAYS/HOURS: Monday through Friday from noon to 2:00 P.M. and from 5:30 to 10:00 P.M. (11:00 P.M. Friday), Saturday 5:30 to 11:00 P.M., Sunday 5:30 to 10:00 P.M.

VEGEBILITY: Very good

RESERVATIONS: Required

KID-FRIENDLY: Yes

WHEELCHAIR ACCESS: Yes

TYPE OF SERVICE: Table and bar

PRICING: Very expensive

PAYMENT ACCEPTED: Major credit cards

When you arrive at Craft, you know you've arrived. Twenty-foot ceilings with rows of drop lights on thin wires, a leather-paneled curved wall to the left and an impressive bar (which was the work table during construction) to the right, and all around what appears to be thousands of bottles of vintage wine chilling at just the right temperature (and, in fact, are). The restaurant, which opened in March 2001, is the brainchild of owner/chef Tom Colicchio (of Gramercy Tavern fame; see review page 199), and the kitchen is helmed by chef William Knapp. The idea behind Craft is simple, yet not so simple to pull off. Colicchio, as both chef and diner, was growing tired of overly fussy food and decided to create basic dishes that glorified locally grown, high-quality ingredients. "Less art and more craft" is the driving principle here. Even the architecture reflects this: simplicity, but to the max.

The whole ordering approach is unique at Craft. You won't find complex dishes with Capitalized Titles. Rather, the menu is a simple sheet of paper, with foods organized by "subject matter." With the exception of Salads, the left side lists just meats and fish, so you can fold the menu in half and focus on the right side. Here you'll find Side Dishes, which are divided into four categories: Vegetables, Mushrooms, Potatoes, and Grains & Beans. Vegetables are sub-divided into Roasted, Sautéed, and Braised. Menus are printed daily to reflect availability and seasonal changes. (Much of the produce is bought around the corner at the Union Square Greenmarket. Buying from farmers they know and trust is more important than chasing down organic.)

Vegetarians' biggest problem will be deciding what *not* to order. Vegans will be thrilled, too—as most of the food is prepared à la minute, so leaving out the dairy is no problem. Food is served family-style, the way Colicchio ate growing up in his Italian-American home. Let your server know straightaway what you do and don't eat, and he or she will guide you through your options. Most items can be made vegetarian or vegan, but not all of them (chicken broth or bacon being the main offenders). Since the menu changes often, it's hard to make specific suggestions, but in the case of Craft, that's not really necessary. Anything you order will wow you. So here's our recommendation: Bring a friend who also likes to eat veg and come very hungry (and without your credit card maxed out), then order with abandon.

But to whet the appetite, here are a few random samples of what you might find (or if you truly can't decide, let the kitchen create a tasting menu for you). Salads might be white dandelion, fava and pecorino, or shaved fennel; roasted veggies often involve Jerusalem artichokes, eggplant, and salisfy. In spring, definitely sample the braised ramps or white asparagus. Mushrooms include roasted hen-of-the-woods, roasted bluefoots, and a dish of truffle vinaigrette. For more stick-to-your-ribs grub, order the polenta, farro, chick peas, risotto, or various potato dishes. The gnocchi (always made with egg) literally melt in your mouth. I was about to put down my fork to rave to the chef but was cut off. "Don't talk," he said. "Eat."

When you come to Craft, order up a storm, have a lengthy discussion with the sommelier, and have a dessert or two (preorder the donuts)—but mostly just follow the chef's advice and eat.

—SUZANNE GERBER

④ Curry Leaf

99 Lexington Avenue (at East 27th Street)

PHONE: (212) 725–5558

TYPE OF CUISINE: Indian

DAYS/HOURS: Monday through Sunday from 11:30 A.M. to 3:00 P.M. and from 5:00 to 11:00 P.M.

VEGEBILITY: Very good

RESERVATIONS: Suggested

WHEELCHAIR ACCESS: No

KID-FRIENDLY: No

TYPE OF SERVICE: Table and take-out

PRICING: Inexpensive

PAYMENT ACCEPTED: All credit cards

Located next to the old New York neighborhood Murray Hill, dubbed "Curry Hill," Curry Leaf stands out from the dozens of other Indian restaurants for its rather upscale food. Its best asset may be its relationship with Kalustyan, the city's best spice market. Not only are they owned by the same family, but Kalustyan's extensive spice offerings and proficiency with exotic combinations is evident in every single dish.

Although not entirely vegetarian, Curry Leaf offers an impressive array of veg dishes. Start with the zesty vegetable samosa, a fried mix of seasoned potatoes and ground peas wrapped in a light pastry. Spicy, chewy, and simple (just peas and potatoes), it's a stand-out. Most appetizers are vegan—cooked in vegetable oil, not ghee—and there's a large section of vegetable specialties, only two of which are made with paneer (Indian cottage cheese). The aloo gobi, a spicy dish of cauliflower and potatoes seasoned with a special blend of seven herbs, is a knockout. If you're feeling adventurous, ask for your food to be prepared vindaloo, or spicy; otherwise, it will be cooked mild. All dishes are served with pullau rice, a savory blend of basmati rice and green peas seasoned with saffron.

Unfortunately, all desserts are made with milk, but even vegans will want to linger after dinner with a cup of homemade spicy tea. The dining experience is completed with a walk to Kalustyan (open till 9:00 P.M.), just a block away, for a chance to bring home some of the spices you just tasted.

—DIANA BOCCO

⑤ Dosa Hut

102 Lexington Avenue (between 27th and 28th Streets)

PHONE: (212) 725–7466

TYPE OF CUISINE: South Indian kosher vegetarian

DAYS/HOURS: Monday through Friday from 11:00 A.M. to 3:00 P.M. and from 5:00 to 10:00 P.M., Saturday and Sunday 11:00 A.M. to 10:00 P.M.

VEGEBILITY: Excellent

RESERVATIONS: Suggested

WHEELCHAIR ACCESS: Yes

KID-FRIENDLY: Yes

TYPE OF SERVICE: Table, counter, take-out, and delivery

PRICING: Inexpensive

PAYMENT ACCEPTED: Major credit cards ($15 minimum)

Besides being completely vegetarian (no to meat and eggs, yes to dairy), this authentic South Indian restaurant is also kosher. A rabbi comes in twice a week, inspects and blesses the food, then presents an official Kashrut certificate. Indian, Jewish, and nondenominational dosa fans make pilgrimages from Long Island and New Jersey to dine on the delectable specialties dished out at this minimally decorated restaurant.

The menu offers no less than sixteen varieties of dosas—some soft, some crispy. A spiced potato or savory bean filling may be wrapped up inside the dosa, or the dosa may be used to scoop up a flavorful sauce. We tried the paper masala, the presentation of which was an experience in itself. The crispy, tepee-shaped monolith was about 18 inches in diameter and came with sides of potatoes, coconut chutney, and sambhar, a spicy bean sauce. This was a truly memorable dining experience.

In addition to dosas, the restaurant offers an assortment of appetizers, rice dishes, breads, and curries. An unusual vegan appetizer is iddly, two steamed lentil and rice puffy cakes that come with coconut chutney and sambhar for dipping. The iddly itself is very mild, light, and absorbs flavor wonderfully. The rasam, a traditional South Indian tamarind-lentil soup, is spicy and refreshing—eaten after a big meal to aid in digestion. Dosa Hut also serves homemade samosas, which are the most popular appetizer (and vegan to boot).

As a main-course alternative to a dosa, ovo-lacto vegetarians should try the Indian classic palak paneer, homemade cottage cheese cubes cooked in a puree of cream, spinach, and spices. The cheese and cream make this dish rich, but the spinach adds a nice freshness to the combination of tastes, and I found it hard to stop eating long after I was full. Beer and wine are available.

—JESSICA WURWARG

6 Franchia

12 Park Avenue South (between 34th and 35th Streets)

PHONE: (212) 213–1001

WEB ADDRESS: www.franchia.com

TYPE OF CUISINE: Tea and Asian vegan

DAYS/HOURS: Monday through Saturday from 11:00 A.M. to 10:00 P.M., Sunday noon to 10:00 P.M.

VEGEBILITY: Excellent

RESERVATIONS: Suggested

WHEELCHAIR ACCESS: Yes

KID-FRIENDLY: Yes

TYPE OF SERVICE: Table

PRICING: Expensive

PAYMENT ACCEPTED: Major credit cards

Franchia, a new restaurant from the people behind Hangawi (see review, page 200), calls itself a "tea shrine in another space and time." Its kitchen, the menu tells us, is committed to creating dishes that are tasty, nutritious, and vegetarian—"the healthiest way of eating." But as with Hangawi, the greatest joys here are ones not easily put into words.

After three solid years of planning, Terry and William Choi opened Franchia (fran-CHEE-a) in the spring of 2003 as a place to celebrate the art of tea. "Tea is a very important part of our lives," says Terry ("Tea is Zen," is inscribed on one of the serving plates). Everything else—the fabulous light meals that blend Korean, other Asian, and Western influences; the decor that truly does transport you to another space and time—is designed to complement the tea, not the other way around. Open and airy with an extraordinary tiled ceiling that is a replica of a ceiling in a famous Korean palace, the front room invites you to linger. Upstairs is additional seating as well as a traditional tearoom, which can be used for dining but is usually reserved for tea ceremonies and workshops (and the Chois' daily private teatime).

The couple's lifestyle changed about a decade ago, when William asked his spiritual master how he could deepen his meditation practice. He was told he needed to break the karmic chain by giving up meat. "And tea completes the idea of being vegetarian and the spiritual idea of Zen," William explains. His master taught them tea ceremony and how to use tea to discover peace of mind. And so, adds Terry, "Franchia is primarily a teahouse, then a restaurant, where you can enjoy food with tea and experience peace of mind."

The menu at Franchia is more Westernized than at Hangawi, though just as delicious and exquisitely presented. (There's a full-time staffer whose only job is to make vegetable garnishes for the plates: daikons butterflies, carrot flowers, radish blossoms, etc.). Trips to Korea—as well as around the U.S.—give the New Jersey–based Korean couple ideas for new dishes, and Terry is always asking, "How can we 'Koreanize' this?" Besides its emphasis on tea, Franchia's biggest deviation from Hangawi is the use of a soy-grain meat substitute the Chois created. I'm no fan of meat analogs, but this is delightful—not at all reminiscent of meat. It's used in a few appetizers ("meat" sticks with peanut sauce, mini patties), burgers, and a couple sautéed entrées but only represents a small portion of the menu. Another distinction is the use of tea in several of the dishes: There are pancakes, noodles, and salads made with green tea, for example.

Now, the Chois may tell you this is a teahouse, but trust me, it's also a first-rate vegan restaurant, though the options are so creative and wide-ranging, you tend not to label it vegan. The menu includes six appetizers, with dumplings, two kinds of pancakes, and patties; six salads, all light and unique; six different soups; four wraps and burgers (lunch only); five rice dishes, including bibimbap and stone bowls; and six noodle dishes, with noodle options like green tea, pumpkin, and spinach. And then you come to the main dishes, served only at dinner. The meat substitute and mushrooms are the workhorses here. All are superb, but the Tofu Steak, served with sweet-potato glass noodles, is a standout. I asked the Chois how they accomplished the perfectly light but substantive texture of the noodles, and they said candidly, "We don't know." Whatever those Korean chefs are doing in the kitchen, it works.

Of course, when you come to Franchia, you must drink tea. The tea menu alone runs four pages and is hard to summarize. Five varieties of green tea range from 1st Picked Royal Green Tea from Mt. Jilee to Mt. Guhwa 2nd Picked, but there are also oolongs, black teas, flavored teas, and even eight herbal "teas," such as date paste and persimmon. Ten varieties of iced teas are also available, as are delicious desserts made from soy and grains.

All the food is exciting and filling but never heavy. Part of the reason for that is how William works with his chefs. "Stay conscious," he tells them, "Be happy." And just as you will benefit from the nutrients in the food, so will you absorb that.

—SUZANNE GERBER

7 Galaxy Global Eatery
15 Irving Place (at 15th Street)

PHONE: (212) 777–3631
TYPE OF CUISINE: International
DAYS/HOURS: Monday through Saturday from 8:00 to 4:00 A.M., Sunday from 8:00 to 3:00 A.M. Kitchen closes well before restaurant.
VEGEBILITY: Excellent
RESERVATIONS: Suggested
WHEELCHAIR ACCESS: Yes
KID-FRIENDLY: Yes
TYPE OF SERVICE: Table and bar
PRICING: Moderate
PAYMENT ACCEPTED: MC/V

"Innovative foods for progressive palates" is the motto at Galaxy Global Eatery, the postmodern bar/restaurant next to Irving Plaza that draws a hip young crowd. This place is so veg-friendly, the menu signifies which dishes are vegan and vegetarian. Galaxy Global pulls flavors from all corners of the Earth: poppy-seed oil from Europe, (vegan) seaweed caviar from Asia, za'atar (a spice) from the Middle East. Chef Batya Goldstein, who trained at the Natural Gourmet Cookery School, utilizes all forms of hemp in her cooking, which adds not just a nutty rich flavor, but all the essential amino acids and a wealth of minerals and vitamins, including A, C, E, and beta carotene.

Without a doubt, ovo-lactos should start with the Hempnut Edamame Cakes, an unusual combination of ground hemp nuts and edamame (soy beans) formed into little mounds and served with a hot-sweet-creamy mango aioli. Another wonderful appetizer is the Star Rocket Salad, composed of baby arugula, star fruit, avocado, and mandarin oranges, lightly tossed in the rare poppy-seed oil vinaigrette. The gentle kick of the arugula paired with the creamy avocado and the sweet-tart taste of the star fruit is a stroke of brilliance.

The Sea Square, so named because it is a perfectly square, well-balanced meal, is another must. It includes lemon-tahini grilled tofu, seaweed caviar, bamboo rice (specially ordered from China), and toasted seaweed salad and is topped with ginger-shoyu dressing. The tofu is firm and fresh-tasting, with a hint of lemon. The seaweed caviar bursts in your mouth, covering your tongue with a delicious salty sea flavor. And the ginger-shoyu dressing's deep, almost grainy, ginger-vinegary flavor seeps into all parts of the meal, infusing a bold tanginess.

And it gets better: This innovative restaurant actually remembered vegans when planning its dessert menu. The vegan carrot cake—not on the menu when I visited—is supposed to be outrageous. I did try the out-of this-world Hempnut Crusted Key Lime Pie. And the Beggar's Purse, a crunchy, not-too-sweet dough filled with melting bittersweet chocolate, served with creamy ice cream, is another decadent way to finish the meal.

—JESSICA WURWARG

Moveable Midtown Feasts

We all know it's a jungle out there, but midtown can be a desert for vegetarians—a never-ending stream of steak houses, tourist traps, and overpriced (and underserviced) steam tables. But there is an oasis, at least where the noontime crowd is concerned: the lunch cart.

Everyone knows you can grab a falafel on nearly any street corner between Times Square and Grand Central--along with a hot dog, pretzel, or your name on a grain of rice. But if you're not street-food squeamish, there are several outstanding stands worth stepping up to. One caveat: Lunch carts are mobile, after all, so locations and hours may vary.

- Mohammed Rahman's Kwik Meal cart is plastered in favorable notices from newspapers and TV stations alike. Don't be put off by the references to his lamb or tiger shrimp. Rahman, a former chef at the Russian Tea Room who wears a chef's toque at his outsize stand, also offers several veg options. There's the standard falafel, of course—available as a sandwich or in a platter with rice—and a more interesting veggie polaw—a mix of mushrooms, peppers, onions, and tomatoes topped with a tsatziki-like sauce. Served in a pita ($3.00) or with rice ($4.00), it deserves its own fanfare. 45th Street at Sixth Avenue; Monday through Friday from 10:30 A.M. to 9:00 P.M.

- The selection at Ruben's Empanadas changes often, and the options are always good. At the mobile outpost of the downtown storefront, broccoli and cheese, corn, mushroom, and spicy spinach and tofu empanadas beckon. It's easy to see why: The crusts are flaky, the sizing just right, and the price ($3.25 each) is pocket change. For an even better deal, try one of the soups ($3.25), such as the refreshing gazpacho (served in a 16-ounce plastic cup) or the vegetarian chili. 39th Street and Broadway; Monday through Friday from 10:30 A.M. to 3:30 P.M.

- The Baked Potato King serves giant spuds with a wide variety of toppings: sour cream, of course, but also spinach and cottage cheese or mixed vegetables. The beatific king of the cart keeps your tater warm inside a special oven, then slits it open and stuffs it with your choice of filling ($3.95, includes filling). 39th Street and Broadway; Monday through Friday from 11:00 A.M. to 3:45 P.M.

- If it's sweet stuff you're after, bypass the Mr. Softee truck (what *is* that stuff, anyway?) and head for the Crepe Café, a bastion of Francophilia near the Museum of Modern Art. Though they also offer savory varieties, you can't go wrong with a Nutella-smothered crepe ($4.00). 53rd Street between Fifth and Sixth Avenues; Monday through Friday from noon to 6:00 P.M.

—MELENA Z. RYZIK

8 Gramercy Tavern

42 East 20th Street (between Park Avenue South and Broadway)

PHONE: (212) 477–0777; Fax: (212) 477–1160
WEB ADDRESS: www.gramercytavern.com
TYPE OF CUISINE: American bistro
DAYS/HOURS: Monday through Thursday from noon to 11:00
P.M., Friday and Saturday noon to 11:30 P.M., Sunday 5:00 to
11:00 P.M.
VEGEBILITY: Fair
RESERVATIONS: Recommended
WHEELCHAIR ACCESS: Yes
KID-FRIENDLY: Yes
TYPE OF SERVICE: Table and bar
PRICING: Very expensive
PAYMENT ACCEPTED: Major credit cards

Every morning at 8:00 A.M., before their stands officially open, farmers at the sprawling Union Square Greenmarket await their moment of reckoning. "We're the market mafia," jokes John Schaefer, executive chef at Gramercy Tavern, six blocks north. Within minutes, bushels and baskets arrive at the front door of Gramercy, where fresh produce brightens even meat dishes, and one can savor an haute vegetarian tasting menu, six courses of proof that vegetables are the restaurant's signature rather than its afterthought.

Everything about the dining experience at Gramercy is unrushed and uncramped: tall arched ceilings, ample space between tables—there are even wide spaces between listings on the menu. The message: You want your space in New York? Come to Gramercy. You will be pampered.

The spring tasting menu includes a tangy eggplant napoleon, in which an eggplant puree is set against breaded, silver-dollar egg-plant chips for a pleasant contrast of textures and topped with a light, lemon-rosemary vinaigrette. A potato risotto with morels and asparagus highlights crunchy treats that should never be missed in spring. The colorful roasted spring vegetables with pea puree and truffle vinaigrette looks like a painting you'd rather not disturb. Oh, but disturb. The puree is smooth, and the vinaigrette has a classy tartness to match the caramelization of the vegetables.

Schaefer changes his menus seasonally, adding root vegetables and roasted beets during the winter. He plays to the simple strengths of his fresh ingredients and only occasionally steps near the edge with a mushroom tarte Tatin—a trio of flaky tart, salad, and mushroom cappuccino, a foamy, slightly bitter reduced stock. Though most dishes are not vegan, the kitchen will adapt to such requests.

Desserts are excellent. The warm banana tart with caramel sauce and candied cashew ice cream is luscious, and the chocolate-caramel tart with caramel ice cream will remind you of a Belgian café. If you have a yen to stretch, linger, and de-stress but can't find a good spa, Gramercy Tavern will rejuvenate you just fine.

—BRIAN CAZENEUVE

❾ Hangawi

12 East 32nd Street (between Fifth and Madison Avenues)

PHONE: (212) 213–0077
TYPE OF CUISINE: Korean vegan
DAYS/HOURS: Monday through Friday from noon to 3:00 P.M. and from 5:00 to 10:30 P.M., Saturday 1:00 to 11:00 P.M., Sunday 1:00 to 10:00 P.M.
VEGEBILITY: Excellent
RESERVATIONS: Recommended
WHEELCHAIR ACCESS: Yes, but two steps to restroom
KID-FRIENDLY: No
TYPE OF SERVICE: Table and take-out
PRICING: Expensive
PAYMENT ACCEPTED: Major credit cards

It calls itself "a vegetarian shrine in another space and time," and after one visit to this most extraordinary restaurant in Little Korea, you will agree. Hangawi is a complete dining experience, which can last several hours. Step in and you're asked to remove your shoes, coat, and shoulder bag before being escorted to a sunken table, where you sit on cushions on the hardwood floor. The soft lighting, placid music, and lack of windows turn the place into a true sanctuary, completely isolated from the bustle of city life.

Hangawi's food is traditional Asian vegan cuisine, and many of the dishes consist of mountain roots, raw greens, veggies and grains. Don't let that discourage you—master hands are at work here, transforming the simplest ingredients into astonishing pieces of art. We've dined here with canny carnivores and Midwesterners, and every last one of them always insists on return visits.

Start with the Stuffed Shiitake Mushrooms, an astounding dish of mushrooms in a slightly sweet cinnamon sauce. Move on to the meaty Grilled Todok (aka lanceolata), mountain-root strips grilled in a spicy ginger soy sauce and served on a stick. You can't explain the taste because nothing else on the planet tastes like it—to coin a phrase, it's indescribably delicious. We also adore the mixed pancakes (kimchee, mung bean, scallion). It's hard to believe they can create that texture without eggs. The Tofu Stone Bowl Rice with Sesame Leaves is just what the name implies: sautéed tofu served over rice in a piping-hot stone bowl with sesame leaves and vegetables. Or try our favorite, the crispy mushrooms. Lightly sautéed in a vegan batter and coated with an orange sauce, you'll never think of mushrooms the same way. Each meal is served with six complementary side dishes that vary daily and include options like marinated vegetables, shiitake mushrooms, kimchee, and seaweed.

Desserts, which you probably won't have room for, are traditional Asian confectionery. We love the Korean mochi (sticky rice and white bean cakes), and the ice creams are so rich and creamy, you will be tempted to ask if they are truly soy. There's also a tiny area in the center of the restaurant that sells delicate teacups, candles with the Heart Sutra, books, and small accessories, so you can take a little bit of Hangawi's magic home with you.

—DIANA BOCCO

⓾ Heartbeat

W Hotel New York, 149 East 49th Street (between Lexington and Third Avenues) or through hotel: 541 Lexington Avenue

PHONE: (212) 407–2900

TYPE OF CUISINE: American eclectic

RESERVATIONS: Suggested; required for parties of six or more

DAYS/HOURS: Monday through Friday from 7:00 A.M. to 10:30 P.M. (closed 11:00 A.M. to noon and 2:30 to 6:00 P.M.), Saturday 8:00 A.M. to 10:30 P.M. (closed 2:00 to 6:00 P.M.), Sunday 8:00 A.M. to 9:30 P.M. (closed 2:00 to 6:00 P.M.).

VEGEBILITY: Good

WHEELCHAIR ACCESS: Yes

KID-FRIENDLY: Yes

TYPE OF SERVICE: Table and bar

PRICING: Moderate

PAYMENT ACCEPTED: All credit cards

Remember when hotel restaurants were dreary rooms serving up mediocre food to travelers willing to sacrifice quality for the convenience of eating and sleeping under the same roof? Well, Heartbeat, at the hip W New York Hotel, has set out to change all that. Walk into the airy space and you're immediately seduced by a warm fireplace, mosaic-studded columns and a mix of red banquettes and earthy wooden chairs. But as the large jars of preserved veggies atop the bar suggest, Heartbeat isn't just another trendy backdrop for a power meeting (although the prime Midtown East location makes it a perfect place to have one). It's a destination for health-conscious diners to sit back and sample flavorful dishes prepared with fresh and wholesome ingredients by chef John Mooney.

Since Heartbeat's inception in 1998 off the lobby of the W, Mooney has been at the helm of the kitchen, first as chef de cuisine, now as chef. Health is a cornerstone of the restaurant. Mooney strives to make exciting vegetarian dishes, and he succeeds. Vegans will rave over his velvety asparagus-chunk soup blended with onions, garlic, anise and toasted Sicilian pistachio—just be sure to request it without the cream. (Mooney's soup creations vary from season to season, but there are always good choices for vegans.) The Asian pear salad, looking rather ethereal with its delicate slices of fresh fruit, with or without the Maytag blue cheese, is another masterpiece, prepared with currants and reduced pear syrup. And instead of just sliding over a boring vegetable plate, Mooney marries the different smoky flavors and textures of seasonal veggies, from celery and parsley root to grilled broccoli rabe and kabocha squash, and serves it alongside exotic helpings of crispy shallots and red chili chutney covered raisins.

Prepared simply but attractively, the dishes at Heartbeat are clearly crafted with an artistic touch and, shall we say?, a lot of heart. There's nothing healthy about those scrumptious desserts, however, but you won't really care when choosing from delights such as a poached pear with sherry compote and lemon-berry gelato.

—ALIA AKKAM

11 Josie's

565 Third Avenue (at 37th Street)

> **PHONE:** (212) 490–1558
> **OTHER LOCATIONS:** 300 Amsterdam Avenue (at 74th Street),
> (212) 769–1212
> **WEB ADDRESS:** www.josiesnyc.com
> **TYPE OF CUISINE:** Healthy New American
> **DAYS/HOURS:** Monday through Thursday from noon to 11:00
> P.M., Friday noon to midnight, Saturday 11:30 A.M. to mid-
> night, Sunday 11:00 A.M. to 10:00 P.M.
> **VEGEBILITY:** Very good
> **RESERVATIONS:** Recommended
> **WHEELCHAIR ACCESS:** Yes
> **KID-FRIENDLY:** Yes
> **TYPE OF SERVICE:** Table, bar, and take-out
> **PRICING:** Moderate
> **PAYMENT ACCEPTED:** Major credit cards

Sleeker and hipper than its older sister on the Upper West Side, this newer Josie's, which opened in May 2001, serves an eclectic mix of healthy food with something for all culinary proclivities. And the hip, comfy setting provides a perfect backdrop for leisurely meals. The staff color-coordinates with the reds, greens and yellows of the nouveau diner decor, and the zinc-and-zebrawood bar bumps the chic factor up another notch.

As with all of owner Louis Lanza's restaurants, the cuisine here is consciously healthful, and they use only expeller-pressed oils, triple-filtered water, and organic ingredients "when available and economical." All dishes are dairy-free, but some have honey or egg, so be sure to ask. Also in the works is a food-allergy manual, which will help the conscientious waitstaff to know at a glance all the options for your specific needs.

Juice could be Josie's middle name, and even the cocktails are made with fresh-squeezed juice. Only fruit-juice sweeteners are used, so whether you've ordered lemonade or sangria, your drink has a refreshingly natural taste. Chow-wise, Josie's serves everything from stir-fry to pasta to veggie meat loaf, but as a Texas transplant, I was especially eager to try the portobello fajitas with chipotle-corn salsa. Though I will never quite understand the wheat tortilla phenomenon, I wasn't disappointed with the fresh salsa (which contains honey) or the lightly marinated mushrooms. A rainbow of grilled bell peppers adds a splash of color to the plate, and it comes with guacamole on the side. The butternut squash soup balances delicately between sweet and salty and comes topped with roasted seeds that liven up the texture. The salads are winners, too; every bite tastes fresh from the garden, and the dressings are fittingly light and let the veggies do the talking.

If you've still got room after your meal, don't pass up the apple pie. The macadamia nuts are such a brilliant touch, you won't even care that à la mode is actually soy.

—JULIE HOLLAR

12 L'annam

393 Third Avenue (at 28th Street)

PHONE: (212) 686–5168

OTHER LOCATION: 121 University Place (at East 13th Street),
(212) 420–1414

TYPE OF CUISINE: Vietnamese

DAYS/HOURS: Sunday through Thursday from 11:30 A.M. to
11:30 P.M., Friday and Saturday 11:30 A.M. to 12:30 P.M.

VEGEBILITY: Very good

RESERVATIONS: Suggested

WHEELCHAIR ACCESS: Yes

KID-FRIENDLY: No

TYPE OF SERVICE: Table and bar

PRICING: Inexpensive

PAYMENT ACCEPTED: Major credit cards

L'annam is the sort of relaxing, no-fuss restaurant you dream of after a long day at work. Open since 1997 and decorated with a little Asian flair, this pair of Vietnamese restaurants definitely kept vegetarians in mind when planning the menu. The staff is highly aware of the omnipresence of fish broth and fish sauce in Vietnamese food, so we took their word when they assured us that "vegetarian means no fish."

Start with the combination vegetarian platter, which comes with a spring roll, vegetable dumpling (there's egg in the dough), grilled skewered vegetables (with a chili-soy dipping sauce), a soft salad roll, and some lettuce. (Veggies are cooked on the same grill as meat, but it's wiped in between.) The spring rolls are a delightful blend of rice noodles and basil, served crispy and light, but my favorite (sorry, vegans) is definitely the dumplings. The bright green baby bok choy dough, stuffed with a delicate blend of carrots and onions, explodes with flavor.

The tofu steak, a vegan main course, is served with lemongrass, bell peppers, steamed fresh spinach, and soft brown rice. The dish is simple and good: The tofu is firm and grilled with care, giving it a thin crispy skin. The deep, earthy taste of the spinach plays off the fresh, lemony flavor of the tofu. Ovo-lactos should try the bun xao (a Vietnamese pad thai), stir-fried rice noodles served with bean sprouts, egg, roasted peanuts, tofu, onions, and bell peppers. The dish has the soothing appeal of pasta, with the added dimension of eggs (which can be left out), peanuts and a soy-vinegar sauce to lighten things up.

To make any residual stress disappear, order yourself something from the full bar or (reasonably priced) wine list. For dessert, consider something from their nice selection of ice creams, including that Asian favorite, green tea.

—JESSICA WURWARG

13 Link

120 East 15th Street (at Irving Place)

PHONE: (212) 995–1010

TYPE OF CUISINE: New American

DAYS/HOURS: Monday through Friday from 11:30 A.M. to 3:00 P.M. and from 5:30 to 10:30 P.M. (11:00 P.M. Friday), Saturday 5:30 to 11:30 P.M., Sunday 10:30 A.M. to 4:00 P.M. and 5:30 to 9:00 P.M.

VEGEBILITY: Good

RESERVATIONS: Recommended

WHEELCHAIR ACCESS: Yes

KID-FRIENDLY: Yes

TYPE OF SERVICE: Table

PRICING: Moderate

PAYMENT ACCEPTED: Major credit cards

Another downtown eatery with a strange name, Link serves up New American cuisine amid a decor of sleek geometric shapes and contrasting comfy benches. On Friday and Saturday nights, go to be fed *and* entertained. From 10:30 P.M. until about 3:00 A.M., a DJ spins for the young and groovy at this restaurant/lounge/bar.

Chef Julian Clauss-Ehlers's starters, such as the Spiced Carrot and Ginger Soup with Whipped Orange Yogurt and the Link Green Salad, cater and pay homage to the vegetarian and vegan (just hold the yogurt) palate. The carrot soup is a blend of sweet, tangy, and bitter ingredients that delights the taste buds with different sensations; it is an excellent start to a delicious meal. The Link Salad is a great combination of fresh, light mesclun and tantalizing herbs topped with crunchy vegetable chips.

For the main course, the fettuccini primavera is a great option for vegans (the Parmesan cheese that's sprinkled on top can be omitted). If you're more adventurous, go for the intensely garlicky, creamy, Middle Eastern–style crispy strudel made with spinach, feta cheese, and pine nuts, served with a salad of tomatoes and kalamata olives. The combination of all these fresh ingredients and the strong garlic and cheese flavors provides a wonderful balance of salty and creamy tastes to make the perfect entrée.

The Link Pot Pie is the ovo-lacto version of comfort food—simply cooked vegetables covered with smooth, melted cheese. Link's desserts, like the warm chocolate cake served with melting ice cream, provide a heavenly finale to the meal.

—JESSICA WURWARG

14 Madras Mahal

104 Lexington Avenue (between 27th and 28th Streets)

PHONE: (212) 684–4010
WEB ADDRESS: www.madrasmahal.com
TYPE OF CUISINE: Indian kosher vegetarian
DAYS/HOURS: Monday through Friday from 11:30 A.M. to 3:00 P.M. and 5:00 to 10:00 P.M. (10:30 P.M. Friday), Saturday noon to 10:30 P.M., Sunday noon to 10:00 P.M.
VEGEBILITY: Excellent
RESERVATIONS: Required for dinner
WHEELCHAIR ACCESS: Yes
KID-FRIENDLY: Yes
TYPE OF SERVICE: Table
PRICING: Moderate
PAYMENT ACCEPTED: Major credit cards

An exciting food trend, evidenced by many top NYC chefs, is all about vegetables: insisting on the freshest ones available, relocating them from the side of the plate to the center, even sweetening them for desserts. These chefs might look to Madras Mahal for an advanced lesson in glorifying the vegetable.

This mainstay of Lexington Avenue takes its classic Indian cuisine, as well as its kosher vegetarian identity, seriously. Its dishes are vibrant veggie-centric creations—but without the high prices and pretension you may find elsewhere. Kosher accoutrements include an area with bowls filled with water for hand-washing as you enter. The deep interior allows for plenty of room between tables. Walls bedecked with painted greenery, good lighting, and streamlined wood benches will make you feel like you're eating in a garden.

In operation since the mid-1980s, Madras Mahal takes pride in its longevity in a neighborhood loaded with Indian restaurants. Another point of pride is its emphasis on freshness. All food is prepared from scratch the day it is served, which can mean waiting ten to fifteen minutes for your food to be cooked to order—but no one ever seems to mind. Of course, if you need instant gratification, go for the lunch buffet. A bargain at $6.95, it's available weekdays from 11:30 A.M. to 3:00 P.M. When I visited, the majority of the dozen buffet items were vegan. (The well-trained staff can easily point out the few nonvegan items.) The lineup changes daily, but there are always two appetizers, two rice dishes (usually lemon or tomato rice), and three entrées. The dessert of the day was a sweetened green squash dish, with a pleasant grainy texture.

On the main menu, don't miss the dosa. These crepes—made with rice, lentil flour, or wheat, and served with coconut chutney—are house specialties, with more than ten varieties to choose from. Many come with heavenly pureed potatoes. The mixed-vegetable biryani—rice paired with peas, carrots, and cauliflower and topped with lightly caramelized onions—is as moist and rich as Spanish paella. Those craving flavorful spinach should order the classic palak paneer, which features the house-made Indian cheese, the freshest I've ever had.

Madras Mahal does not use eggs, but cheese and creamy yogurt sauces do star in a few dishes. These nonvegan dishes are clearly marked on the menu. The only difficulty vegans may have is in ordering drinks and dessert: There's nary a dairy-free option on the eight-item dessert menu. Beverages, too, often contain yogurt and milk, though there is a vegan homemade mango juice. Wine is not served, but customers may BYOB. The small beer menu includes Taj Mahal, a favorite of Indian customers.

—ESTHER JAMES

⑮ Patria

250 Park Avenue South (at 20th Street)

PHONE: (212) 777–6211; Fax: (212) 533–9633

WEB ADDRESS: www.patrianyc.com

TYPE OF CUISINE: Nuevo Latino

DAYS/HOURS: Monday through Saturday from noon to 3:30 P.M. and from 5:30 to 11:00 P.M. (5:00 P.M. to midnight Friday and Saturday) Sunday 5:30 to 10:30 P.M.

VEGEBILITY: Fair

RESERVATIONS: Recommended

WHEELCHAIR ACCESS: Yes

KID-FRIENDLY: Yes

TYPE OF SERVICE: Table and bar

PRICING: Very expensive

PAYMENT ACCEPTED: Major credit cards

I f you're in a serious, no-frills, eat-for-sustenance mood, then save Patria for another day. This burst of Nuevo Latino inspiration on Park Avenue South is a place to gaze at the pretty people and prettier food; to wonder what you might see, smell, and taste next; to let your senses play. It's what you get when you cross vibrant cuisine with the energy of a Latin dance. And the menu is really only an approximation for Miami-trained executive chef Andrew DiCataldo, who creates on the fly with an imaginative whim.

Vegetarians shouldn't be dismayed by the fact that on a given day there may be no more than sides and an empanada de queso on the regular menu for them. Patria offers three- and five-course tasting menus, *todos sin carne,* and can adapt them to individual tastes. Fancy a mojo sauce or vegetarian ceviche? Like your dishes spicy? Not a fan of peppers? No problemo. DiCataldo will do his best to cater the tasting menu to your preferences. (Better yet: Call ahead or e-mail from the icon at www.patrianyc.com that says "special requests.")

On our visit, DiCataldo's dishes evolved from lighter to more robust. The chilled cantaloupe consommé with jicama and lemongrass, infused with red chili and Thai basil, was sweet at first sip but had a lingering bite. Then came yucca, surrounded by crusted hearts of palm, fresh from Costa Rica, with a mojo of cumin, onion, chive, and cilantro. DiCataldo rued the crust's failure to adhere, but the inspiration had only come to him an hour earlier. Our favorite was the roasted hen-of-the-woods mushrooms over black-truffle butter, surrounded by sautéed peppers, chilis, and huitlacoche, the large Mexican mushroom corn whose distinctive nutty, woodsy flavor will leave you guessing if, and where, you've ever had anything like it.

A place that combines influences of a dozen Latin cultures should make a tasty flan, and Patria serves three good ones—vanilla, pineapple, and corn—in one sampler. Another winner is the Choco-late Bonbone, an accented, elevated bonbon laced with caramel and folded over sour cherries.

With so many adaptations to choose from, it is nearly impossible to match every face with each culinary specification, but don't be surprised if, before you leave, either DiCataldo or another staffer stops to ask your name. They want you satisfied, entertained, ready to hit the dance floor, and eager to return.

—BRIAN CAZENEUVE

16 Pongal

110 Lexington Avenue (between 27th and 28th Streets)

PHONE: (212) 696–9458
TYPE OF CUISINE: Indian kosher vegetarian
DAYS/HOURS: Monday through Friday from noon to 3:00 P.M. and from 5:00 to 10:00 P.M., Saturday and Sunday noon to 10:00 P.M.
VEGEBILITY: Excellent
RESERVATIONS: No
WHEELCHAIR ACCESS: Yes
KID-FRIENDLY: Yes
TYPE OF SERVICE: Table and take-out
PRICING: Inexpensive
PAYMENT ACCEPTED: Major credit cards

If dosas are your thing, don't miss Pongal; if you don't know what a dosa is, go immediately to Pongal and find out. It offers these huge, crisp South Indian crepes in fourteen different varieties, made of rice and either wheat or lentil flour. The fillings are substantial and fresh (a generous helping of sautéed onions makes the onion and potato masala particularly tasty). The crepes are light and nicely browned and come with coconut chutney and a spicy lentil sambhar on the side. They're not fancy, but with all fresh ingredients and some skilled chefs, Pongal manages to make them the highlight of the menu.

But that's not because the rest of the menu is lackluster. South Indian appetizers like iddly (steamed rice and lentil flour patties) and medu vadam (fried lentil flour donuts) shine here. They're not greasy or tasteless, like you'll often find them at mediocre restaurants, and the accompanying chutneys—one spicy (made with mint) and one sweet (dates and tamarind)—are a real treat. Pongal also offers good curries and other rice dishes, though they're not quite the same caliber as the outstanding South Indian offerings.

As an added bonus, the dosas and all appetizers are served in the traditional South Indian style, on a banana leaf. The manager tells me banana leaf infuses the food with vitamin E. I have no idea if that's true or not, but it sure looks cool.

Because there are so many nearby office buildings, the little restaurant tends to be packed during lunch hours. Pongal doesn't serve up a buffet like most of its competitors because it emphasizes freshness; instead, it offers three popular lunch special combination plates. Things can get crowded at dinner too, so either come early or be prepared to wait.

—JULIE HOLLAR

17 The Pump Energy Food

113 East 31st Street (between Park and Lexington Avenues)

PHONE: (212) 213–5733

DAYS/HOURS: Monday through Thursday from 9:30 A.M. to 9:30 P.M., Friday 9:30 A.M. to 8:00 P.M., Saturday 11:00 A.M. to 6:30 P.M.

OTHER LOCATION: 40 West 55th Street, (212) 246–6844, Monday through Friday from 8:30 A.M. to 8:30 P.M., Saturday 11:00 A.M. to 6:00 P.M.

TYPE OF CUISINE: Healthy American

VEGEBILITY: Very good

RESERVATIONS: No

WHEELCHAIR ACCESS: Yes

KID-FRIENDLY: No

TYPE OF SERVICE: Table and take-out

PRICING: Inexpensive

PAYMENT ACCEPTED: Major credit cards

Calling itself "the Physical Fitness Restaurant," Pump is a destination for customers who want to keep a slim waistline while still enjoying amazing food. The menu is free of salt, oils, and preservatives, and nothing is fried. In fact, everything is prepared on the spot—no prepackaged salads or sandwiches here.

Another nice thing about Pump, for vegetarians, is the fact that all food is prepared separately. Pancakes are never cooked on the same grill as meat, for example. And because each dish is made individually, there's no risk of "contamination." Although the menu does offer meat dishes, vegetarians will find plenty of exciting choices here. The falafel, which Pump claims is the only nonfried one in New York, is spiced just right and very light. The smoky baked tofu, grilled in low-sodium soy, is a favorite among regulars.

The zesty High Tide, a jumbo dish consisting of a homemade veggie burger served over brown rice and topped with lentil soup, is a meal unto itself. Bring a friend and share the enormous Dynamite Pita Sandwich, prepared with your choice of a veggie burger, baked falafel, or baked tofu and grilled with tomatoes, onions, peppers, and low-sodium tomato sauce. As if that weren't enough, it comes with a side of hummus and whole-wheat pita. For dessert, try the apple pie, a vegan delight so rich and sweet, you won't believe it's made without dairy and sweetened only with fruit juice.

—DIANA BOCCO

18 SushiSamba

245 Park Avenue South (between 19th and 20th Street)

> **PHONE:** (212) 475–9377
>
> **OTHER LOCATIONS:** 87 Seventh Avenue South, (212) 691–7885
>
> **TYPE OF CUISINE:** Japanese / Brazilian
>
> **DAYS/HOURS:** Both locations: Monday through Wednesday from 11:45 to 1:00 A.M. Thursday through Saturday from 11:45 to 2:00 A.M. Park Avenue: Sunday open from 1:00 P.M. to midnight. Seventh Avenue: Brunch served Saturday and Sunday from 11:45 A.M. to 4:00 P.M.
>
> **VEGEBILITY:** Fair
>
> **RESERVATIONS:** Highly recommended (especially evenings and weekends)
>
> **WHEELCHAIR ACCESS:** Yes
>
> **KID-FRIENDLY:** No
>
> **TYPE OF SERVICE:** Table and bar
>
> **PRICING:** Moderate
>
> **PAYMENT ACCEPTED:** Major credit cards

Tired of the same old tofu dishes? SushiSamba may be a meat-and-fish-oriented Brazilian / Japanese place, but the exciting, out-of-the-ordinary options make this adventurous restaurant worth a visit. (Except, perhaps, for vegans.) The atmosphere is a big part of the experience: Pulsating samba music and Carneval-inspired colors set the mood in the dining area. And most nights every one of the rooms—sushi bar, lounge, beverage bar, open-air Japanese roof garden—is packed.

Before the meal, let the waitstaff know your preferences, and they'll guide through the non-menu alternatives. We started with a crunchy green bean tempura, coated in a crispy egg-based batter. (This may not sound like a big deal, but it is to vegetarians who eschew tempura because the veggies are usually cooked in the fish fryer; at SushiSamba fish and veggies are never cooked together!) Next came the Pastel, a fried South American turnover with a rich blue cheese filling, served on a bed of corn and tomato salad. Have them hold the carne on the Stuffed Medjool Dates, a pairing of sweet dates and pungent cabrales cheese soaked in sweet balsamic teriyaki (made without fish sauce). The terrific Samba Salad was a light mix of shredded vegetables wrapped in a crispy paper-thin cucumber, drizzled with tangy citrus dressing. We loved the subtle

Six Seaweeds, a blend of salt- and freshwater seaweeds served on a bed of ice.

The hearty, traditional Brazilian Moqueca, available without meat, resembles a gumbo with its thick and spicy mix of tomatoes, asparagus, and other vegetables. The coconut base dominates the dish, which is served with moist white rice. And on the lengthy sushi menu, don't make the mistake of assuming cucumber and avocado are your only choices. The chefs will create any combination you can think of using the ingredients on the menu. For our visit, head chef Michael Cressotti created a divine all-tempura roll with avocado, heart of palm, shiitake, and asparagus. (Hey, when you wait this long for something, you want to take advantage!)

Finally, don't forget SushiSamba's extensive wine and alcohol menu—no modifications needed here.

—PHIL ANDREWS

19 T Salon and Emporium

11 East 20th Street (between Broadway and Fifth Avenue)

PHONE: (212) 358–0506

WEB ADDRESS: www.tsalon.com

TYPE OF CUISINE: Light American

DAYS/HOURS: Monday through Saturday from 9:00 A.M. to 8:00 P.M., Sunday 11:00 A.M. to 8:00 P.M.

VEGEBILITY: Very good

RESERVATIONS: Not necessary

WHEELCHAIR ACCESS: Yes

KID-FRIENDLY: No

TYPE OF SERVICE: Table

PRICING: Moderate

PAYMENT ACCEPTED: Major credit cards

Created as a refuge from hectic New York City life, this elegant tea salon in the Flatiron district offers an incredible selection of high-quality and unique teas, most of which are blended in-house. Sit on comfy cushions as you choose from more than two dozen green teas, dozens of black teas or unusual offerings like South African red rooibos. T Salon also offers a nice variety of soups, salads, and light fare. The staff is impressively knowledgeable about both teas and food, and the chef is happy to leave the cheese off any salad or sandwich. A tasty choice is the sandwich with goat cheese, cucumber, radish, and arugula on pecan-raisin bread, served with a side salad. Vegans should try the Tea Salad, which comes with dried figs, cashews, and raisins (but have them hold the blue cheese).

T Salon will help you match teas to your food. It's a great spot to decompress after a draining New York afternoon. In fact, bring a little relaxation home with you by visiting the T Emporium upstairs, which offers a huge selection of loose teas and tea products.

—JESSICA WURWARG

20 Tabla

11 Madison Avenue (at 25th Street)

PHONE: (212) 889–0667

TYPE OF CUISINE: Nouvelle Indian

DAYS/HOURS: Monday through Friday from noon to 2:30 P.M. and from 5:30 to 10:30 P.M., Saturday 5:30 to 10:30 P.M.

VEGEBILITY: Good

RESERVATIONS: Necessary

WHEELCHAIR ACCESS: No

KID-FRIENDLY: No

TYPE OF SERVICE: Table and bar

PRICING: Very expensive

PAYMENT ACCEPTED: Major credit cards

Tabla exemplifies the American twist on ethnic food, now familiar to Manhattan sophisticates. In this case, traditional Southwest Indian flavors and spices are delectably woven into a nuanced and rich cuisine—a sweet blend of Goan and Portuguese influences.

Although this is not a vegetarian restaurant, Tabla offers a good range of possibilities for vegetarians and vegans alike. From the moment you arrive, you will be pleasantly surprised with the little amuse-bouches, small pappadams with chickpeas and a coconut-coriander chutney, while you wait at the bar; a light asparagus mousseline as you are seated; and a chilled carrot soup spiced with cumin, coriander, and cardamom (exquisitely subtle and fresh) served between courses. You will dine in a spacious, elegant setting among softly spoken people, where a warm, sophisticated, yet unpretentious ambiance is the product of close attention to detail in the service, the decor, and, of course, the food.

Four prix fixe menus are available, ranging from $54 to $88. The asparagus tasting menu ($65, in spring only) is ideal for vegetarians, offering asparagus in all courses (except dessert). Asparagus soup with chervil, leeks, and toasted spices and Besan linguini with roasted asparagus, morels, and black cumin are just two of the items included. The $54 menu offers a wild mushroom rasam (a light and aromatic bouillon) with leeks, tamarind, tarragon, and chervil, followed by a fricassee of vegetables in a lentil broth. Cap that with a chilled tropical fruit soup or a mango and almond clafoutis with rhubarb compote and coconut ice.

Even the most seasoned diner will leave Tabla feeling excited by the variety and innovation that can be found at this tasteful establishment.

—LARA OLCHANETZKY

㉑ Tea Box Café
693 Fifth Avenue (between 54th and 55th Streets)

PHONE: (212) 350–0100 or (800) 753–2038
TYPE OF CUISINE: Japanese fusion
DAYS/HOURS: Monday through Saturday from 11:45 A.M. to 6:00 P.M.
VEGEBILITY: Good
RESERVATIONS: No
WHEELCHAIR ACCESS: Yes (elevator service)
KID-FRIENDLY: No
TYPE OF SERVICE: Table
PRICING: Expensive (for lunch)
PAYMENT ACCEPTED: All credit cards

The Tea Box is a secret we're loathe to reveal. The sixty-seat café, tucked away on the lower level of Takashimaya, the upscale midtown Japanese department store, is decorated with a palette of stone and sand. Even the pillow-covered banquettes seem to whisper minimalism.

The tearoom is popular with the few shoppers and Midtown workers who know it's there, some ladies who lunch, and the occasional celebrity or regular, so it can get crowded at lunchtime. For a quieter experience, stop by for the late afternoon tea service (3:00 to 6:00 P.M.), which includes sandwiches, fruit, a veggie roll, and, of course, a selection of teas—all of which are beautifully presented in the traditional Japanese style on lacquered footed trays.

For lunch, chef Daniele Kay has created a menu of light Japanese-French fusion cuisine, anchored by seasonal offerings like noodles in curried vegetable broth or a seven-vegetable terrine. A vegetarian bento box is always available. With vegetable tempura on a bed of hijiki, a rice du jour, and rotating items like vegetable dumplings, it's a good choice for most vegetarians (but note: veggies are fried in same fryer as fish). You should also steer clear of the miso soup, as it's made with a fish stock and bonito flakes.

The veggie rolls were a hit, as was the layered terrine, built around some grilled white and green asparagus and topped by out-of-this-world light and greaseless onion rings. Desserts, like black rice pudding and apple spring rolls, all have an Asian theme. Sipping on one of the forty-two varieties of tea—from toasted-rice green tea to orange-cinnamon flavored black tea—is a must, no matter what you're eating. But if you're having trouble deciding on a tea, no worries: Just pick up a small bag of your second choice in the tea shop outside the restaurant.

—MELENA Z. RYZIK

22 Tossed

295 Park Avenue South (between 22nd and 23rd Streets)

PHONE: (212) 674–6700

OTHER LOCATION: 30 Rockefeller Plaza, (212) 218–2525

TYPE OF CUISINE: Salads and sandwiches

DAYS/HOURS: Monday through Friday from 7:00 A.M. to 10:00 P.M., Saturday and Sunday 11:30 A.M. to 10:00 P.M.

VEGEBILITY: Very good

RESERVATIONS: Not necessary

WHEELCHAIR ACCESS: Yes

KID-FRIENDLY: Fair

TYPE OF SERVICE: Table, take-out, and catering

PRICING: Inexpensive

PAYMENT ACCEPTED: Major credit cards

Tossed claims its salads are "worth waiting 45 minutes for," but not to worry—it seldom takes more than five to get one. While you wait, you can watch your salad being made or take in a little art show: Paintings by local artists adorn the walls.

Almost all salads can be made vegan, but soups are prepared with a touch of butter, and the red peppers are sometimes grilled alongside meats. (Oddly, the rest of the grilled items are prepared separately). Produce is about 30 percent organic, and we're told that is due to increase. Choose from their "runway" of options to create a Salad Palette, or go with a predesigned mix. Popular items include the Tri-Color Salad and the Tofu Wrap, and there are always seasonal dishes. The Spring Vegetable Salad, for example, is made with organic lettuce, roasted asparagus, peas, corn, tomatoes, and plantain chips and topped with your choice of twenty-two homemade dressings—all vegetarian (except the Caesar). Nonvegan dressings include buttermilk ranch, blue cheese, black peppercorn Asiago, roasted red pepper, fat-free cucumber dill, and a delightful pesto vinaigrette.

There's plenty of room to kick back and enjoy your well-balanced salads, but large groups should avoid the lunchtime rush. And definitely keep your eyes peeled: We hear a number of celebs frequent the place.

—CHRISTINA MASSEY

23 Turkish Kitchen

386 Third Avenue (27th and 28th Streets)

PHONE: (212) 679–6633

WEB ADDRESS: www.turkishkitchenny.com

TYPE OF CUISINE: Upscale Turkish

DAYS/HOURS: Monday through Friday from noon to 3:00 P.M. and from 5:00 P.M. to midnight, Saturday 5:00 P.M. to midnight, Sunday 11:00 A.M. to 3:00 P.M. and 5:00 P.M. to midnight

VEGEBILITY: Very good

RESERVATIONS: Necessary

WHEELCHAIR ACCESS: No

KID-FRIENDLY: Yes

TYPE OF SERVICE: Table, take-out, and bar

PRICING: Expensive

PAYMENT ACCEPTED: Major credit cards

Whether they admit it or not, Turkish Kitchen is the standard against which every other Turkish restaurant in the city compares itself. In its dozen years of existence, it has ascended to the throne as the king of all Turkish eateries this side of Istanbul, thanks to its consistently remarkable food and warm, inviting ambiance.

Despite the fact that the house specialty is kebabs, this is still a haven for vegetarians. With more than ten different kinds of cold and three hot meze (appetizers), four types of salads, and a daily vegetarian entrée special, there is something on the menu to please even the pickiest of palates—including mine (and I was raised in Istanbul).

The delectable (cold) appetizer sampler is a feast in and of itself. It comes adorned with spinach and onions lightly sautéed in olive oil, and onions and topped with yogurt (which can be excluded upon request); tasty hummus; vine leaves; cabbage leaves; and eggplant stuffed with rice, pine nuts, and black currants. Oh, but there's more: barbunya pilaki (kidney beans tossed with olive oil, lemon juice, and diced carrots and potatoes) and two varieties of eggplant—the traditional salad and eggplant tossed with tomato sauce and garlic. The eggplant salad is the one dish that can't be made vegan, as it contains mayonnaise. The cooking oils are olive or safflower; no lard or other animal by-products are used in the kitchen.

As for the hot appetizers, don't miss the mucver, pan-fried zucchini pancakes served with yogurt atop a bed of lettuce (or hold the yogurt). Fried to perfection, these fluffy rounds are a little taste of heaven. Sigara boregi—fried phyllo scrolls stuffed with feta cheese and parsley—are crunchy on the outside, yet the creamy filling will melt in your mouth. Upon request, the hot meze can be doubled and served with a side of rice for a complete meal, but the appetizers simply paired with Turkish pita bread also make for an exceptional feast. (Vegan alert: The rice is cooked with butter, but chef Ibrahim Kilic is happy to prepare it without; the pita bread, on the other hand, is irrevocably egg-washed.)

Turkish Kitchen serves the same dishes for lunch and dinner. Their veg entrée changes daily, but there are certain staples, including the okra cooked with tomatoes and served with rice and the grilled veggies over pureed eggplant (which contains milk). Another treat is the impressive wine list, with nineteen wines by the glass, including many specialty Turkish varieties. Reliable choices are the Kalecik Karasi (red) and Cankaya (white).

While meat is a big part of the culture, Turkish Kitchen prides itself on being able to accommodate its vegetarian and vegan customers. Long live the king!

—SEZIN CAVUSOGLU

24 Udipi Palace

101 Lexington Avenue (between 27th and 28th Streets)

PHONE: (212) 889–3477
TYPE OF CUISINE: South Indian kosher vegetarian
DAYS/HOURS: Monday through Thursday from noon to 10:00 P.M., Friday and Saturday noon to 10:30 P.M.
VEGEBILITY: Excellent
RESERVATIONS: Recommended on weekends
WHEELCHAIR ACCESS: Yes
KID-FRIENDLY: Yes
TYPE OF SERVICE: Table
PRICING: Inexpensive
PAYMENTS ACCEPTED: Major credit cards

Udipi Palace, one of a handful of Indian places that serve an all vegetarian and kosher menu, is living proof that there are 1,001 ways to cook lentils. As an appetizer you can get your choice of iddlys (steamed lentil and rice cakes) or vadai, fried lentil donuts in seven different variations. Both dishes are served with a variety of chutneys and dips that range in spiciness. Make sure you try the sour chutney: A blend of tamarind, vinegar, and dates creates a sweet contrast to the mint chutney and the sambhar. The samosas are flaky and soft, fried to perfection. Nine different kinds of rice are offered, and each one is big enough to be a main course. If it's more flavor and tradition you're looking for, try a traditional curry. The chef is glad to adjust the spice level to suit your taste. Curries are served with fragrant pullau rice and cooked with tomatoes, onions, and peas.

The vegan selections are not as wide, though more are promised. For now, vegans have their choice of the tomato rice or the kichadi, cream of wheat cooked with onions and cilantro.

For a casual, affordable, and tasty vegetarian dining experience, Udipi is the place to go. Though they don't serve alcohol, they encourage patrons to bring their own beer or wine (no cork charge).

—SEZIN CAVUSOGLU

25 Union Pacific

111 East 22nd Street (between Park and Lexington Avenues)

PHONE: (212) 995–8500; Fax: (212) 460–5081
WEB ADDRESS: www.unionpacificrestaurant.com
TYPE OF CUISINE: French-Asian fusion
DAYS/HOURS: Monday through Friday from noon to 2:00 P.M. and from 5:30 to 10:00 P.M., Saturday 5:15 to 10:30 P.M.
VEGEBILITY: Fair
RESERVATIONS: Recommended for dinner
WHEELCHAIR ACCESS: Yes
KID-FRIENDLY: No
TYPE OF SERVICE: Table
PRICING: Expensive
PAYMENT ACCEPTED: Major credit cards

The first glance inside this splashy, polished three-star restaurant off Park Avenue South hints at its mystery. Peek above the waterfall to the balcony staircase and wonder who might be behind the sliding doors of the private party space upstairs. Or try to focus through the blurry, thick, frosted first-floor glass that lets you make out the pots, pans, and outlines of busy chefs in the kitchen. It is quiet and spacious, and you want to know the details you can't quite see. The same is true for the restaurant's menu, which lists some meatless selections but doesn't foretell what a diverse vegetarian tasting menu Rocco DiSpirito can compose with a little notice. DiSpirito is a celebrity executive chef with movie-star looks, a TV show on the Food Network called *Melting Pot,* and a dynamic culinary hand to confirm the substance behind his style. He entered the Culinary Institute of America at age sixteen and has been flying ever since, mixing flavors with such an innate sense of what works, it's hard to define his culinary expertise or to limit it to one category.

First we enjoyed a cool carpaccio of squash blossom with pickled sweet onion and sancho peppercorn that was unique but simple, as a starter should be. Next we savored two soups, the first cold, the second hot. No complaints with the chilled avocado with cilantro oil and diced watermelon, whose sweetness deftly balanced the bite of the oil, but the carrot soup, with tarragon oil and a pea-tarragon foam, was extraordinary. Union Pacific twice rewarded our passion for morels, first in a salad with jumbo green asparagus and pecorino, then with a pappardelle with smoked ricotta, morels, and walnut oil that added depth to the meatiness of the fungus. Both selections were on the regular menu.

For dessert, we tucked into a molten chocolate cake with a chocolate-hazelnut parfait. The selection is common these days, but this one was uncommonly good and not excessively sweet. A toasted sesame seed crème brûlée added a delightfully light touch with a pink grapefruit sorbet on the side. DiSpirito is esteemed and fancied for more than vegetables, but he has enough panache to make them sparkle.

—BRIAN CAZENEUVE

26 Vatan

409 Third Avenue (at 29th Street)

PHONE: (212) 689–5666

TYPE OF CUISINE: Indian vegetarian

DAYS/HOURS: Sunday and Tuesday through Thursday from 5:00 to 9:30 P.M., Friday and Saturday 5:00 to 10:30 P.M.

VEGEBILITY: Excellent

RESERVATIONS: Suggested

WHEELCHAIR ACCESS: Yes

KID-FRIENDLY: Yes

TYPE OF SERVICE: Table

PRICING: Moderate

PAYMENT ACCEPTED: Major credit cards

In a unique and colorful background of South Indian fantasy, the Vatan vegetarian dining experience is like no other. To enter, you truly think you've been swept up by a monsoon and have landed in a perfectly reconstructed Indian village (definitely not Kansas anymore). Sit in private little gazebo-like rooms and be served by a beautiful, costumed waitstaff. Do kick back, for you're sure to be eating more food than you plan to.

The more-than-reasonable $20 prix fixe dinner comes in a traditional array of small dishes served over three courses. (À la carte options may be preferable for vegans.) A meal at Vatan serves up an enjoyable diversity of tastes. Little vegetable samosas, garbanzo beans in a light yogurt sauce, spicy rice cakes, dal soup, and sticky saffron rice (among others) are accompanied by tamarind, coriander, and yogurt sauces; mango chutney and hot chili concoctions. The spicing is generous but not overwhelming. Choose your fire: mild, medium, or hot (medium being quite sufficient for the average palate). At the end of each course, you will be invited to order more of any of your favorite items—but beware, there is still more to come.

Be prepared for a relaxing, mandatory-shoes-off evening where you can slouch into couches and eat with your hands if you wish. Close the meal with mango ice cream and chai followed by a crunchy digestive pinchful of sesame, fennel, and caraway seeds.

—LARA OLCHANETZKY

27 Zen Palate

34 Union Square East (at 16th Street)

PHONE: (212) 614–9345

DAYS/HOURS: Monday through Saturday from 11:30 A.M. to 10:45 P.M., Sunday noon to 10:45 P.M.

OTHER LOCATIONS: 663 Ninth Avenue, (212) 582–1669, Monday through Saturday from 11:30 A.M. to 10:30 P.M., Sunday 11:30 A.M. to 10:45 P.M.; 2170 Broadway, (212) 501–7768, Monday through Thursday from noon to 10:45 P.M., Friday and Saturday noon to 11:45 P.M., Sunday noon to 10:45 P.M.

TYPE OF CUISINE: Asian-influenced vegetarian

VEGEBILITY: Excellent

RESERVATIONS: Recommended

WHEELCHAIR ACCESS: No

KID-FRIENDLY: No

TYPE OF SERVICE: Table, take-out, and delivery

PRICING: Moderate

PAYMENT ACCEPTED: Major credit cards

Zen Palate is the granddaddy of Pan-Asian vegetarian restaurants in NYC. Though a pioneer (they opened in 1981), it has not lost the edge that made it a New York legend. Zen Palate was the first to fashion mock duck, shrimp, and chicken out of soy protein. They remain at the top of the heap, with dishes like the Mini Vegi-Loaf, crunchy croquettes of tofu, chestnut, and cilantro, served over spaghetti with tomato sauce (which comes with a taro spring roll and a bowl of brown rice).

Although Zen has a clear Asian influence, the dishes have evolved and are now hipper and more contemporary. For a spin on a classic favorite, order the Stir-Fried Fettuccini, cooked with mushrooms, bean sprouts, snow peas, and scallions in a peanut-soy brown sauce. This is not the place to go if you're watching your waistline—meals are rich and made without sparing oils, creams, or starches. A prime example is the Zen Ravioli. One of the restaurant's most popular dishes, comes with a super-rich peanut sauce. Perhaps this is why it's a perennial favorite among nonvegetarians.

Ask the staff to confirm which dishes are vegan before you order. Confusion can set in here, and many a customer has discovered that some dishes (like the Shepherd's Pie Croquets and the Zen Rolls) contain egg after they had ordered them. Dessert options change often, but, if available, get the Pear Pie, sweetened with natural fruit juices and served with a blueberry topping—always a winner.

—DIANA BOCCO

Places to Shop

28 Health 4-U
432 Park Avenue (between 29th and 30th Streets)

> **PHONE:** (212) 532–2644
> **DAYS/HOURS:** Monday through Friday from 8:00 A.M. to 8:00 P.M., Saturday 10:00 A.M. to 7:00 P.M.
> **OVERALL:** Very good

In the morning you will find iced and hot organic tea and coffee; in the afternoon there are two prepared-food stations, offering Indian and Greek macrobiotic dishes, soups, sandwiches, and sushi. In the evening on your way home, you can stop in for a taste from the juice bar, maybe with a little Spirutein to give you a boost at the gym. Where can you go for three meals a day and do all your grocery shopping in clean, wide, wooden-floored aisles? At Health 4-U on Park Avenue between 29th and 30th! In this residential area, where pedestrians are few and far between, you will always find a happy crowd at Health 4-U.

29 Natural Frontier
266 Third Avenue (between 21st and 22nd Streets)

> **PHONE:** (212) 228–9133
> **DAYS/HOURS:** Monday through Sunday 8:00 A.M. to 10:00 P.M.
> **OTHER LOCATIONS:** 424 Third Avenue, (212) 664–0520
> **OVERALL:** Very good

Natural Frontier's large selection of certified organic produce is just one of its many perks. Its prepackaged food options are excellent, ranging from homegrown organic Mac & Cheese to Chili & Garlic Asian Noodles. An entire aisle at the back of the store is devoted to eco-friendly cleaning supplies. There's an extensive selection of bulk foods and an equally large section dedicated to organic teas, vitamins, and natural herbs. The store's best asset, however, is its combination deli counter and juice bar. Generous portions of mouth-watering vegan tofu "egg" salad, eggplant moussaka, and a veggie version of shepherd's pie start at only $4.99.

Places to Stay

30 American Dream Hostel

168 East 24th Street (between Third and Lexington Avenues)

> **PHONE:** (212) 260–9779
> **PRICING:** Inexpensive

Family owned and operated. The owner speaks Spanish, Portuguese, and Italian.

31 Best Western Hospitality House

145 East 49th Street (between Third and Lexington Avenues)

> **PHONE:** (212) 753–8781
> **PRICING:** Moderate

Few points for style but lots for value. Spacious accommodations, well-equipped kitchens, continental breakfast, and other amenities are especially welcome in a neighborhood with few budget-minded hotels.

32 Gramercy Park Hotel

2 Lexington Avenue (at 21st Street)

> **PHONE:** (212) 475–4320
> **WEB ADDRESS:** www.gramercyparkhotel.com
> **PRICING:** Moderate

This hotel has retained its looks since it opened in 1924. The number one perk is access to the exclusive Gramercy Park. Pets are welcome.

33 Hotel Bedford

118 East 40th Street (between Park and Lexington Avenues)

> **PHONE:** (212) 697–4800
> **PRICING:** Moderate

No-frills design but large rooms and a decent number of amenities.

34 Inn at Irving Place

56 Irving Place (between 17th and 18th Streets)

> **PHONE:** (212) 533–4600
> **PRICING:** Very expensive

Working fireplaces and breakfast served to you in bed. Why go out when you can stay Inn?

35 The Plaza Hotel

Fifth Avenue (at Central Park South)

> **PHONE:** (212) 759–3000
> **WEB ADDRESS:** www.plazahotel.com
> **PRICING:** Expensive

The ultimate in gracious luxury, this is classic New York. Afternoon tea is a must, and keep your eyes peeled for Eloise. Pets are welcome.

36 W New York

541 Lexington Avenue (at 49th Street)

> **PHONE:** (212) 755–1200
> **PRICING:** Expensive

What you get in the hipness factor (oh so many points) you make up for in the small (but stylish!) rooms. Pets are allowed.

37 W New York

201 Park Avenue South (at 17th Street)

> **PHONE:** (212) 253–9119
> **PRICING:** Expensive

The first hotel on Union Square, W is Bohemian and opulent at the same time. Pets are allowed.

How Green Is My Market

Manhattan may be the concrete jungle, but for almost three decades, farmers from New Jersey, the Hudson Valley, the Finger Lakes, and even Vermont have been making the trek to New York City to sell their fresh produce and baked goods at Greenmarket.

Greenmarket is a program of the Council on the Environment of New York City that organizes and manages open-air farmers markets at more than thirty locations in all five boroughs of the city. On any given day of the year, you can find farmers selling their goods to appreciative city dwellers. (Some twenty markets in thirteen locations operate year-round.) Greenmarket has about 175 participants, most of them full-time farmers. At the height of the season (late summer to early fall), more than a quarter-million customers cram the markets each week to bring home everything from berries and blankets and bee honey to cheeses and baby organic greens and apples. (Here's a mind-blowing statistic: Greenmarket farmers grow 120 different varieties of apples alone!)

The largest of 'em all, the Union Square Greenmarket, is one of the main produce sources for approximately one hundred of NYC's finest chefs, who shop there regularly. Another nice aspect of the program is that Greenmarket farmers annually donate about 500,000 pounds of food to City Harvest and other hunger-relief organizations.

By providing small family farms with an outlet to sell directly to the public at retail prices, Greenmarket has given many farmers the means to preserve their farmland. And when that happens, everyone's a winner. For more information about Greenmarket, call (212) 477–3220 or e-mail greenmarket@rcn.com.

—JESSICA WURWARG

Here's the definitive list of where and when to find a Greenmarket near you.

MANHATTAN:

Abingdon Square
West 12th Street and Hudson Street
Year-round: Saturday from 8:00 A.M. to 1:00 P.M.

Balsley Park
West 57th Street and Ninth Avenue
Year-round: Wednesday and Saturday from 8:00 A.M. to 6:00 P.M.

Bowling Green
Broadway and Battery Place
Year-round: Tuesday and Thursday from 8:00 A.M. to 5:00 P.M.

Columbia
Broadway between 114th and 115th Streets
Late May through November: Thursday from 8:00 A.M. to 5:00 P.M.

Dag Hammarskjold Plaza
East 47th Street and Second Avenue
Year-round: Wednesday from 8:00 A.M. to 6:00 P.M.

97th Street
West 97th Street and Columbus Avenue
Year-round: Friday from 8:00 A.M. to 2:00 P.M.

175th Street
West 175th Street and Broadway
Late June through November: Thursday from 8:00 A.M. to 6:00 P.M.

Rockefeller Center
Rockefeller Plaza at 50th Street
October through November: Thursday, Friday, Saturday from 8:00 A.M. to 6:00 P.M.

St. Mark's Church
East 10th Street and Second Avenue
Year-round: Tuesday from 8:00 A.M. to 7:00 P.M.

77th Street–I.S. 44
West 77th Street and Columbus Avenue
Year-round: Sunday from 10:00 A.M. to 5:00 P.M.

South Street Seaport
Fulton Street between Water and Pearl Streets
May through November: Tuesday and Thursday from 8:00 A.M. to 5:00 P.M.

Tompkins Square
East Seventh Street and Avenue A
Year-round: Sunday from 10:00 A.M. to 6:00 P.M.

Tribeca
Greenwich Street between Chambers and Duane Streets
Year-round: Wednesday and Saturday from 8:00 A.M. to 3:00 P.M.

Tucker Square
Columbus Avenue and 66th Street
July through December: from Saturday 8:00 A.M. to 5:00 P.M.

Union Square
East 17th Street and Broadway
Year-round: Monday, Wednesday, Friday, and Saturday from 8:00 A.M. to 6:00 P.M.

BROOKLYN:

Bedford–Stuyvesant

Fulton Street between Stuyvesant and Utica Avenues

July through October: Saturday from 8:00 A.M. to 3:00 P.M.

Borough Hall

Court and Remsen Streets

Year-round: Tuesday and Saturday from 8:00 A.M. to 6:00 P.M.; April through December: Thursday from 8:00 A.M. to 6:00 P.M.

Borough Park

14th Avenue between 49th and 50th Streets

July through October: Thursday from 8:00 A.M. to 3:00 P.M.

Fort Greene Park

Washington Park between Dekalb Avenue and Willoughby Street

July 12 through November 22: Saturday from 8:00 A.M. to 5:00 P.M.

Grand Army Plaza

Entrance to Prospect Park

Year-round: Saturday from 8:00 A.M. to 4:00 P.M.

Greenpoint–McCarren Park

Lorimer Street and Driggs Avenue

Year-round: Saturday from 8:00 A.M to 3:00 P.M

Metrotech

Lawrence and Willoughby Streets

May 15 through November 22: Thursday from 8:00 A.M to 5:00 P.M.

Sunset Park
Fourth Avenue between 59th and 60th Streets
July through October: Saturday from 8:00 A.M to 3:00 P.M.

Williamsburg
Havemeyer Street and Broadway
July through October: Thursday from 8:00 A.M to 5:00 P.M.

Windsor Terrace
Prospect Park West and 15th Street, northwest entrance
April through November: Wednesday from 8:00 A.M to 3:00 P.M.

BRONX:
Lincoln Hospital
148th Street and Morris Avenue (south of hospital entrance)
July through November: Tuesday from 8:00 A.M to 3:00 P.M.; July through October: Friday from 8:00 A.M to 3:00 P.M.

Poe Park
Grand Concourse and 192nd Street
July through November: Tuesday from 8:00 A.M to 2:00 P.M.

QUEENS:
Jackson Heights
34th Avenue between 77th and 78th Streets
May through November: Sunday from 8:00 A.M to 3:00 P.M.

STATEN ISLAND:
St. George
St. Mark's and Hyatt Streets (Borough Hall parking lot)
May through November: Saturday from 8:00 A.M to 2:00 P.M.

Nothing in this world can prepare you for your first visit to Times Square. The lights, the billboards, the crowds—it's like nothing else on Earth. The scene of the annual New Year's Eve ball drop, the area is just slightly less crazy all year-round. But unless you're claustrophobic, it's definitely an experience to be had, at least once. Native New Yorkers grumble at the Disneyfication of the area and the conspicuous disappearance of X-rated stores and jiggle joints, but they can't deny that it's a lot safer.

And, of course, this area is most famously home to New York's theater district, where first-run Broadway productions—and live music and actually funny comedy—delight audiences on a nightly basis. A little further west is Hell's Kitchen, which was once a slum but is now on the upswing, with terrific restaurants, shops, and bars. Ninth Avenue in the 40s and 50s is its nexus, with possibly more—and a more eclectic mix of—restaurants than any other 20-block strip in town.

Theater District

W. 59th Street

Central Park South

W. 58th Street **20**

Tenth Avenue

Ninth Avenue

W. 57th Street

Eighth Avenue

Broadway

Seventh Avenue

Sixth Avenue (Avenue of the Americas)

Fifth Avenue

W. 56th Street **1** **23**

W. 55th Street **11**

W. 54th Street

6

W. 53rd Street

W. 52nd Street **19**

W. 51st Street

13

W. 50th Street **3**

Rockefeller Center

W. 49th Street **21**

W. 48th Street **17**

9

W. 47th Street

12

W. 46th Street **18** **15**

5 W. 45th Street

W. 44th Street

22

W. 43rd Street **8**

16 W. 42nd Street

Bryant Park

W. 41st Street

W. 40th Street **14** **4**

W. 39th Street Broadway

W. 38th Street

W. 37th Street

W. 36th Street

W. 35th Street **2**

W. 34th Street

N

W. 33rd Street

0   1/8   1/4

W. 32nd Street **7**

MILES **10**

Places to Eat

1 Baluchi's

240 West 56th Street (between Broadway and Eighth Avenue)

PHONE: (212) 397–0707 (office)

DOWNTOWN LOCATIONS: 193 Spring Street, (212) 226–2828; 275 Greenwich Street, (212) 571–5343; 90 West Third Street, (212) 529–5353; 361 Sixth Avenue, (212) 929–0456; 104 Second Avenue, (212) 780–6000; 8 East 18th Street, (212) 352–1000

MIDTOWN LOCATIONS: 224 East 53rd Street, (212) 750–5515; 1149 First Avenue, (212) 371–3535; 240 West 56th Street, (212) 397–0707; 329 Third Avenue, (212) 679–3434

UPTOWN LOCATIONS: 1431 First Avenue, (212) 396–1400; 1724 Second Avenue, (212) 996–2600; 1565 Second Avenue, (212) 288–4810; 283 Columbus Avenue, (212) 579–3900

QUEENS LOCATION: 113–30 Queens Boulevard, (718) 520–8600

BROOKLYN LOCATION: 263 Smith Street, (718) 797–0707

TYPE OF CUISINE: Northern Indian

DAYS/HOURS: Monday through Sunday from noon to 10:30 P.M. (all locations)

VEGEBILITY: Very good

RESERVATIONS: Suggested for parties of ten or more

WHEELCHAIR ACCESS: Call in advance, as locations vary; most okay

KID-FRIENDLY: Yes

TYPE OF SERVICE: Table, delivery, catering, and take-out

PRICING: Moderate

PAYMENT ACCEPTED: Major credit cards

What began as one very good British-style Indian restaurant on Soho's hopping Spring Street in 1993 has grown into a dynasty of eateries throughout the city—and more are on their way. The formula is simple: great food, nice ambiance, and a good value for your buck. (Especially at lunch, when the entire menu is half-off. Or you can have a huge meal—entrée, rice, nan, cucumber, raita, and mango chutney—delivered to your door for just $12.95.)

In addition to the ten vegetarian appetizers and thirteen vegetarian entrées listed on the menu, you can order off-menu, as your taste or dietary needs dictate. The familiar appetizers like samosas and tikiyas are tasty, but for a real kick, try the ka-choir, with a spicy edge and unique mix of flavors (or, as the menu puts its, "too difficult to describe, but recommended"). For milder tastes, the navrattan curry—assorted vegetables in a cream sauce with nuts and fruits—will suit your tolerance. Heat-seekers should try the mixed-vegetable curry dish or aloo dum (stuffed potato). Saturated with flavor, you won't be disappointed no matter what you choose. A mango yogurt drink is the perfect way to cleanse your palate.

Vegans need to skip the breads—made with dairy and eggs— and go for the long-grain white rice (just tell them no butter). And to ease your taste buds after their ride of intense flavors, order a spice tea or one of Baluchi's many desserts. The ras malai is surprisingly sweet, made from cottage cheese, rose water, and pistachio. The mango ice cream is a recommended sweet and soothing finish.

All locations serve the same menu. West 56th Street, Spring Street, and Queens have the largest rooms for big parties; Columbus Avenue has the most intimate setting. For outdoor seating, visit Sixth Avenue, Columbus, Spring, and 53rd Street; otherwise, enjoy the carved wooden altars on the walls, soft Indian music, wine displays and shinny copper plate settings indoors. Catering is available for large events.

—CHRISTINA MASSEY

❷ Cho Dang Gol

55 West 35th Street (between Fifth and Sixth Avenues)

PHONE: (212) 695–8222

TYPE OF CUISINE: Korean

DAYS/HOURS: Monday through Sunday from 11:30 A.M. to 10:30 P.M.

VEGEBILITY: Very good

RESERVATIONS: Recommended

WHEELCHAIR ACCESS: Yes

KID-FRIENDLY: Yes

TYPE OF SERVICE: Table

PRICING: Moderate

PAYMENT ACCEPTED: Major credit cards

You may feel you've crossed the Pacific instead of Fifth Avenue when you visit Cho Dang Gol. The interior is elegantly decorated in a Korean style, and the waitstaff is decked out in traditional Korean garb. But the highlight is the food, which, like the decor, is authentically Korean. The menu has an extensive list of vegetarian and vegan options, but don't feel limited by them. Some meat dishes—those marked with an asterisk—can be made vegetarian.

To start, try the delicious DooBoo YaChae GamJaJun, a potato pancake mixed with assorted vegetables and the house's special homemade tofu—with a richer flavor than any store-bought version. Also offered is a number of tofu casseroles. The YaChae Cham-DooBoo, a soup with tofu and vegetables, has an earthy mushroom flavor and a nice spicy kick.

A wonderful ovo-lacto entrée is their version of the traditional dish GobDol Bibimbab, a medley of vegetables mixed with steamed rice, homemade tofu, and egg (easily omitted). It is served in a hot stone bowl, and hot pepper paste is mixed into the dish at the table, so it can be as spicy or bland as you like. The JapChae is sticky pan-fried vermicelli mixed with assorted vegetables and perfectly seasoned sauce. Each main course comes with an array of delicious little side dishes, including fresh seaweed and kimchee, a spicy pickled cabbage condiment. But be warned: As at many traditional Korean restaurants, the kimchee is made with fish stock.

The perfect closure to this very enjoyable and healthy dining experience is a lightly sweetened tea, served at the end of the meal.

—JESSICA WURWARG

3 The Emerald Planet (see Greenwich Village)

30 Rockefeller Plaza Concourse

> **PHONE:** (212) 218–1133; Fax: (212) 218–1138

4 Ilo (in the Bryant Park Hotel)

40 West 40th Street (between Fifth and Sixth Avenues)

> **PHONE:** (212) 642–2255; Fax: (212) 642–2256
> **WEB ADDRESS:** www.ilorestaurant.com
> **TYPE OF CUISINE:** International
> **DAYS/HOURS:** Monday through Friday from noon to 2:30 P.M. and from 5:30 to 11:30 P.M., Saturday 5:30 to 11:30 P.M., Sunday 11:30 A.M. to 2:30 P.M. and 5:30 to 10:30 P.M.
> **VEGEBILITY:** Fair
> **RESERVATIONS:** Recommended
> **WHEELCHAIR ACCESS:** Yes (elevator)
> **KID-FRIENDLY:** Not allowed in bar/lounge area
> **TYPE OF SERVICE:** Table and bar
> **PRICING:** Expensive
> **PAYMENT ACCEPTED:** Major credit cards

Food doesn't always play a starring role in boutique-hotel restaurants. The urge to create a *Sex-in-the-City* vibe can lure even the most grounded chef to excess, so too often the food is as overdressed as the clientele it services. Happily, Ilo (Finnish for "unbridled bliss") defies the chic-over-substance mandate. Enter the Bryant Park Hotel (just off Midtown's picnic park for power brokers), navigate the sprawling bar/lounge, walk up the six steps to Ilo's obscured dining area, and you start thinking: Cool place for a drink, wrong place to dine. Ah, but then you feast.

The vegetarian tasting dinner, no longer on the menu but always available for the asking, is the creation of executive chef Rick Laakkonen, an alumnus of River Café, who composes with restrained innovation and a reverence for freshness. Our indulgence unveiled with two starters before a nine-course tasting menu that included two palate cleansers. It was a play with two intermissions that should never have ended.

A starter of white asparagus and cucumber revved our tongues with a red wine vinegar sauce that teased with a hint of anise. Next came a roasted German butterball potato roll with haricots verts, chanterelles, and a deftly enriching sorrel citrus sauce, uncommonly light and sharp for a course with a potato base. The sweetly caramelized roast endive with spinach puree, green-pea shoots, green apple, and carrot was Christmas-colored and equally warming. The highlight of the dandelion and sheep's milk ricotta cannelloni was a grilled tomato coulis, graced with olives, oregano, and preserved lemon that was just tart enough to stand up to the cheese, without getting in its whey.

For dessert, we immersed ourselves in a procession of chocolate selections, many paired with traditional partners: caramel and chocolate tart, chocolate peanut butter bombe, chocolate and banana gâteau. The Mexican hot chocolate would have won *la medalla grande* on either side of the border: smooth and naturally smoky with accents of nutmeg, cinnamon, and a vexing infusion we couldn't get our taste buds around.

The staff at Ilo raves about Laakkonen's sage touch—his measured penchant for elevating flavors, textures, and colors without quite scaling the high wire. So forgive Ilo's misleading entrance that merely begs a passing visit. To its dining room, bring your best company and savor the stay.

—BRIAN CAZENEUVE

5 Jezebel

630 Ninth Avenue (at 45th Street)

> **PHONE:** (212) 582–1045
>
> **TYPE OF CUISINE:** American Southern
>
> **DAYS/HOURS:** Tuesday and Wednesday from 5:30 to 10:00 P.M., Thursday 5:30 to 10:30 P.M., Friday and Saturday 5:30 to 11:30 P.M., Sunday noon to 6:00 P.M.
>
> **VEGEBILITY:** Fair
>
> **RESERVATIONS:** Necessary before 8:00 P.M.
>
> **WHEELCHAIR ACCESS:** Yes
>
> **KID-FRIENDLY:** No
>
> **TYPE OF SERVICE:** Table and bar
>
> **PRICING:** Expensive
>
> **PAYMENT ACCEPTED:** Major credit cards

The daughter of poor Southern sharecroppers, owner/chef Alberta Wright has never been to Louisiana, but she's managed to create the feeling of a New Orleans bordello in her remarkable twenty-year-old Theater District institution, Jezebel. Her own story is a bit of a Cinderella tale, but we're here to talk about the restaurant.

I can't think of another place like it in New York, and that's why—in spite of the meaty Southern menu—it has to be included in this book. Jezebel is the ultimate antidote to the austere blond-wood-and-batik decor of so many veggie restaurants. Your dining options may be limited, but you will come away full—in body and in spirit. (You may also come away with a hankering to go out dancing or canoodling, so be prepared.)

The draped Ninth Avenue side looks like a private club, but don't be fooled: Enter on 45th Street, where the doors are likely to be open. Inside you'll think you crossed the Mason-Dixon line, and you might spontaneously start droppin' your *gs*. The interior of Jezebel is feminine, heated, and erotic. Twenty-foot black ceilings are set off the blood red walls, and everywhere are pillars, hanging porch swings, tall potted plants, elegant veranda furniture, and can-dlelit tables with red cloths—all giving a nineteenth-century planta-tion feel. The clientele is distinctly good-looking, and you suspect some of those faces might be famous.

Vegetarians have to tread a little carefully here, but you will find the waitstaff most willing to work with you. (In the South, veg-etarians are viewed as an intriguing curiosity—like a visitor from

Seoul Survival

Nothing satisfies after a long night out on the town like a huge bowl of bibimbap, and there's only one place to get it. Tucked away among the wig shops and wholesale joints in an unassuming section of southern Midtown lies the heart of Koreatown, home to the best Korean food this side of the Mississippi.

The blocks emanating out from 32nd Street between Broadway and Fifth Avenue are packed with dozens of restaurants, and the choices can be overwhelming. Not to worry: Most are first-rate. Everyone seems to have a different favorite, but just look for crowds and you'll be good to go. Of course, if you want the best Korean meal of your life, head to Hangawi, at 12 East 32nd (see Gramercy/Union Station/Midtown East). It stands out from the pack like a diamond among rhinestones.

Generally speaking, the food in K-town is pretty traditional; though more and more outsiders are discovering the outstanding food available here, the restaurants still cater mostly to the Korean-American community. The people next to you could well be grilling their own raw meat right at the table, but if you can deal, you're in for a treat.

Before your meal, any Korean restaurant worth its kimchee will bring you a bevy of free side dishes, called ban chan. These cold or room-temperature dishes tend to be vegetarian, but do ask your server because the fish dishes can be hard to identify. Spinach, bean sprouts, tofu, and kimchee are regular ban chan offerings, and they range from mild to scorching.

But the ultimate vegetarian Korean dish is bibimbap, a large bowl of rice topped with various vegetables and an optional egg (make sure you specify no beef). The veggies usually include shiitake mushrooms, bean sprouts, carrots, spinach, and seaweed, and you can add red chili sauce to taste. Bibimbap is good in a regular bowl, but it's divine in a hot stone pot. Called dolsot or gopdol bibimbap, this sizzling version toasts the outer layer of rice till it's slightly brown and crunchy, and it keeps your dinner hot until the last bite.

True diehards will also want to take the 7 train out to Flushing, Queens, home to the largest Korean-American population in New York City. It's less user-friendly to those who don't speak Korean, but if you like your culture undiluted, you shouldn't miss it.

—JULIE HOLLAR

Outer Mongolia.) If you happen to appreciate Southern cookin', you will actually come away gloriously sated. (That said, vegans will not have an easy time of it. All that buttah, you know.)

Instead of bread, corn muffins start you off: Light, with a crispy edge, they melt in your mouth. Yes, they're full of butter—as is most everything—but precious little is made with animal fats, so it's a fair trade-off. The green pea soup (made with water, not chicken broth) is thick and velvety and tastes like real peas. The green salad is small but terrific: mixed greens and a rich garlicky dressing (and served with goat cheese upon request). For an entrée, there's a veg plate composed of side dishes, but nothin' wrong with that. Sautéed carrots with onion; creamy mashed potatoes; home fries; yams with butter and candied brown sugar; heavenly baked mac and cheese; broccoli that's delightfully crunchy; spicy, lightly oiled okra: This may not be health food but it is divine. In fact, about the only side you can't eat is the collards (made with turkey wings). Desserts include chocolate fudge cake, strawberry shortcake, and pecan pie. These are not vegan imitations—they are the real thing.

There's live jazz on Friday and Saturday nights, and after the theater crowd evacuates at 7:45 P.M., plan to linger. Check out the back room (with an autographed Steinway) and the restroom. If you get a chance, chat with Alberta; she's a warm and engaging hostess. But good luck—she's also the chef. It's hard to believe there are no recipes and that she measures nothing and just goes by taste. But whatever you do, don't suggest she alter the menu—"you can't change it but so much," she says. After an evening under Jezebel's spell, you wouldn't want to anyway.

—SUZANNE GERBER

6 Julian's Mediterranean Restaurant
802 Ninth Avenue (between 53rd and 54th Streets)

PHONE: (212) 262–4800
TYPE OF CUISINE: Italian
DAYS/HOURS: Monday through Saturday from noon to midnight, Sunday 11:30 A.M. to 11:00 P.M.
VEGEBILITY: Fair to good
RESERVATIONS: Recommended for parties of four or more
WHEELCHAIR ACCESS: Yes
KID-FRIENDLY: Yes
TYPE OF SERVICE: Table
PRICING: Moderate
PAYMENT ACCEPTED: All credit cards

Spacious and sunny, Julian's makes a nice stop for a relaxing snack on the West Side or a romantic pretheater dinner. Two large indoor rooms, a candlelit alcove. brick garden with a Mediterranean mural, and alfresco dining on the roof or the sidewalk offer ambience for any mood.

The highlight here is the vegetarian-friendly antipasti platter: Of eleven different cold appetizers, eight are vegetarian, so you can either ask your waiter to ditch the meat (they'll throw a few more veggies in to even it out) or use it to distract your meat-loving friends while you load up on veggies. From roasted peppers to Rosa's Italian eggplant to tomato-basil bruschetta, the samplings complement one another nicely and encourage hearty face-stuffing. And at $14 for a two-person plate, it's not a bad deal.

Beyond the antipasti, vegetarians have a choice of a handful of salads and pastas. Julian's well-executed fusion of the standard beet and endive salads comes complete with goat cheese (always optional), pear, endive, walnuts, and vinaigrette. The pastas are your customary Italian fare, with vegetarian options like penne pomodoro and linguine with spinach and pine nuts (vegans need only hold the grated cheese).

—JULIE HOLLAR

7 Mandoo Bar

2 West 32nd Street (between Fifth Avenue and Broadway)

PHONE: (212) 279–3075
TYPE OF CUISINE: Korean/dumplings (mostly)
DAYS/HOURS: Monday through Sunday from 11:00 A.M.to 11:00 P.M.
VEGEBILITY: Good
RESERVATIONS: Not necessary
WHEELCHAIR ACCESS: Yes
KID-FRIENDLY: Fair
TYPE OF SERVICE: Table, take-out, and delivery (within 3 blocks)
PRICING: Inexpensive
PAYMENT ACCEPTED: Major credit cards

Mandoo Bar is a small dumpling restaurant tucked into the heart of Koreatown, within walking distance of the Empire State Building, Madison Square Garden, and great retail shopping. The energy of the city is palpable in the restaurant's stylish clientele, the hiply utilitarian interior, and the speedy turnover, especially during lunch.

Like its host city, Mandoo Bar is a bit of a cultural mishmash, offering not only dumplings but Chinese-inspired fried rice, Thai soups, and Japanese noodles. But hey: You can get fried rice in Iowa City. Mandoo Bar is about dumplings, in three stunning varieties: plain wheat, bright green spinach, and fluorescent orange (colored with carrot juice), all filled with an array of ingredients.

The women who crank out the 750 daily dumplings do so in the front window, displaying their trays of plump treasures for all the city to admire. It's the best possible advertisement—and a mesmerizing sight. We suggest you head straight for Vegetables Goon Mandoo, lightly pan-fried dumplings filled with mixed vegetables and served with a sweet soy dipping sauce. A fabulous complement is the Fried Tofu appetizer, plump cakes of light, crispy pan-fried tofu, garnished with a soy-scallion sauce. The sauce is at once salty, spicy, and sweet, a perfect contrast to the mildly creamy, slightly savory interior of the tofu.

As a primarily Korean restaurant (serves beer, wine, and sake), Mandoo Bar offers an obligatory kimchee dumpling that looks terrific, but like many of the restaurant's offerings, it contains pork. If you luck into the right server, you can lobby for a veggie version, but don't hold your breath.

—THAN SAFFEL

8 Manhattan Chili Company

1500 Broadway (near 43rd Street)

PHONE: (212) 246–6555
TYPE OF CUISINE: Mex-Cal
DAYS/HOURS: Monday through Sunday from 11:30 A.M. to 10:00 P.M.
VEGEBILITY: Very good
RESERVATIONS: Suggested for parties of three or more
WHEELCHAIR ACCESS: Yes
KID-FRIENDLY: Yes
TYPE OF SERVICE: Table, delivery, and bar
PRICING: Moderate
PAYMENT ACCEPTED: Major credit cards

Judging from the multiple TV screens, dim red lights, and noisy Midtown crowd, it's easy to think you're going to be stuck ordering greasy nachos hold-the-carne. But don't be fooled: There's actually a ton of fresh and innovative vegetarian options at this family-owned restaurant, which takes great pride in accommodating every diet. Most entrées are served with cheese, but the chilis, which are served with corn bread and rice, are totally vegan. There's the Totally Vegetables (mild), Arthur's Chili Con Lentil (medium hot), Tierra del Fuego 3 Bean (which lights on fire and is medium hot), and Pima City Green (hot-hot).

Despite the restaurant's name, you're not limited to chili. Other tasty options include quesadillas with portobello mushrooms and goat cheese and an avocado salad with black olives, tomatoes, and mixed greens. The various chilis also make cameo appearances in the enchiladas, tacos, and fajitas. Unlike many other popular Mexican restaurants, dishes here come in human proportions, so the tendency to overeat is curbed. Water is served with a hint of lime, but if you're going for the spicy chili, ask ahead of time for refills or a pitcher. Beer, wine, and delicious margaritas (in a variety of flavors) are available at the always-crowded bar or with your meal.

—CHRISTINA MASSEY

9 Meskerem (see Greenwich Village)

468 West 47th Street (between Ninth and Tenth Avenues)

PHONE: (212) 664–0520

10 Pret à Manger

875 Sixth Avenue (at 31st Street)

PHONE: (212) 868–4363

OTHER LOCATIONS: 630 Lexington Avenue, (646) 497–0510, Monday through Friday from 7:00 A.M. to 5:00 P.M.; 30 Rockefeller Center, (212) 246–6944, Monday through Friday from 8:00 A.M. to 6:00 P.M.; 469 Seventh Avenue, (212) 279–5997, Monday through Friday from 7:30 A.M. to 4:30 P.M.; 205 East 42nd Street, (212) 867–1905, Monday through Friday from 7:30 A.M. to 4:00 P.M.; 60 Broad Street, (212) 825–8825, Monday through Friday from 7:30 A.M. to 4:00 P.M.; 287 Madison Avenue, (212) 867–0400, Monday through Friday from 7:30 A.M. to 5:00 P.M.; 530 Seventh Avenue, (646) 728–0750, Monday through Friday from 7:30 A.M. to 5:00 P.M.; 1350 Sixth Avenue, (212) 307–6100, Monday through Friday from 7:00 A.M. to 5:00 P.M.; 135 West 50th Street, (212) 489–6458, Monday through Friday from 7:30 A.M. to 4:00 P.M.; 11 West 42nd Street, (212) 997–5520, Monday through Friday from 7:30 A.M. to 6:00 P.M.; 400 Park Avenue, (212) 207–3725, Monday through Friday from 7:30 A.M. to 5:00 P.M.; 466 Lexington Avenue, (212) 661–9350, Monday through Friday from 7:00 A.M. to 5:00 P.M.

WEB ADDRESS: www.pret.com

TYPE OF CUISINE: Sandwiches, salads, and breakfast foods

DAYS/HOURS: Monday through Friday from 7:30 A.M. to 4:00 P.M.

VEGEBILITY: Good

RESERVATIONS: No

WHEELCHAIR ACCESS: Not at this location (45th and Lexington location only)

KID-FRIENDLY: Yes

TYPE OF SERVICE: Counter (a few bar seats) and take-out

PRICING: Inexpensive

PAYMENT ACCEPTED: Major credit cards

For many years the terms "vegetarian" and "fast food" were mutually exclusive. It had been next to impossible to find decent, healthful vegetarian food that's prepared quickly—if you don't count pizza or eating at home. But the wake-up call for the veg fast-food revolution may have been sounded on the streets of Manhattan with the recent appearance of Pret à Manger—Pret, for short—a British import to rival the Beatles in quality and innovation.

You'd never guess that the chain, which debuted in this country with locations throughout Manhattan, is 33 percent owned by McDonald's, especially after looking at the sandwiches it sells. If you do dairy, how about thickly sliced avocado and Parmesan cheese on whole-grain bread? Or French brie, tomatoes, and basil on a freshly baked baguette? Then there's Eggs Florentine, a mix of egg salad, slices of sharp Parmesan cheese, red onion, tomato, and spinach on granary bread, and More than Mozzarella, fresh cheese, tomato, roasted pine nuts, basil, arugula, and mayonnaise on chewy sourdough bread.

Vegans will *kvell* over the Hummus Salad Wrap, stuffed with garlicky hummus, red onion, spinach, cucumber, and sweet red pepper, all rolled up in a vegan wrapper. The menu also features delicious salads, fresh fruit bowls, breakfast breads, juices, nondairy smoothies, coffees, and our new favorite soft drinks, Pret Cools—premixed bottles of juice and sparkling water, no sugar added, in flavors like Grape & Elderflower or Orange & Passionfruit.

Satisfy your sweet tooth with Pret Pots with Yogurt, with a choice of Honey & Granola, Strawberry & Rhubarb, Blueberry, or Cherry. The massive, always-soft chocolate-chunk cookie is another menu standout, the perfect midafternoon pick-me-up.

Best of all, every morsel of food you'll find at Pret is made from all-natural, preservative-free ingredients. Fresh, non-irradiated, non-genetically modified produce is delivered to each location every morning; breads and sandwiches are made on-site; and everything is appropriately labeled vegan, vegetarian, egg-free, or dairy-free. Just walk in the door, grab a sandwich, pay at the counter, and you're outta there—in substantially less time than it takes to press the water out of a block of tofu at home.

Bonus points to Pret for using all recycled materials in their packaging and promotional materials and for their work with local charities. At the end of the day, all food not sold at a NYC Pret is given to City Harvest to help feed New Yorkers who otherwise would go hungry.

NOTE: According to the folks at Pret, McDonald's does not have any influence over what is sold in Pret restaurants. They have simply "invested in Pret because they like what we do."

—SUSAN SHUMAKER

11 The Pump Energy Food (see Gramercy/ Union Square East/Midtown East)
40 West 55th Street (between Fifth and Sixth Avenue)

> **PHONE:** (212) 246–6844

12 Queen of Sheba
650 10th Avenue (between 45th and 46th Streets)

> **PHONE:** (212) 397–0610; Fax: (212) 397–0611
> **WEB ADDRESS:** www.queenofshebanyc.com
> **TYPE OF CUISINE:** Ethiopian
> **DAYS/HOURS:** Monday through Thursday from 11:00 A.M. to midnight, Friday and Saturday 11:00 A.M. to 1:00 A.M.
> **VEGEBILITY:** Very good
> **RESERVATIONS:** Recommended for dinner
> **WHEELCHAIR ACCESS:** Yes
> **KID-FRIENDLY:** Yes
> **TYPE OF SERVICE:** Table, bar, delivery, and take-out
> **PRICING:** Moderate
> **PAYMENT ACCEPTED:** MC/V

No cuisine is more hands-on than Ethiopian food. Expect bold flavors at Sheba, but nary a fork or spoon to collect them. You scoop up goodies with rolls of injera, the sponge bread made from tiny cereal finely ground into a fermented batter that forms its pocketed surface over a clay plate. And vegetarians have plenty to scoop. The Orthodox Coptic of Ethiopia preaches abstinence from animal products during seasonal fasting periods and on Wednesdays and Fridays throughout the year, and Sheba's menu reflects that mandate.

Go for the vegetarian mesob, colorful dollops of assorted menu items, many in thick purees. Most have a restrained but noticeable bite, with a foundation of berbere, a pepper- and spice-based hot sauce. Ater kik alicha is a mild, smooth puree of split peas cooked in onion, garlic, olive and a trove of spices. Buticha are finely milled chickpeas pan-crusted in olive oil, with lemon, shallots, and jalapeño. They have an egg-salad consistency, with a delayed jolt of mystery. Neither the misir wot (split lentils) nor shiro (creamed split peas) tastes like the other dishes. Only when Sheba embarks on familiar Western cousins, such as gomet wot (chopped collard greens) or atikilt wot (green beans and carrots), does it lose distinction. A couple tips: Ask for an item that isn't on the menu called shimbra asa, a subtle chickpea and onion fritter sautéed with ginger, garlic, and a robust berbere. Better to pass on desserts, since sweets are not their forte.

All dishes are dairy-free but can be prepared with oil instead of clarified butter, upon request, by Philipos Mengistu, the chef and proprietor who insists, "I want you to taste Ethiopia." The son of restaurant owners in the capital city of Addis Ababa, Mengistu drove cabs after he arrived in New York in 1990. He started Meskerem (see Greenwich Village) in 1995, then left to open Queen of Sheba in 2001. His bar and restaurant has thirty-two seats and three traditional basketwork tables for large groups. It sports various paintings, including one of King Solomon, who seems to be eyeing your feast from on high, and features Etheopian music—instrumentals at lunch, modern pop tunes in the native Amharic at dinner, and even a live band in the evenings.

—BRIAN CAZENEUVE

⑬ Rice 'n' Beans

744 Ninth Avenue (between 50th and 51st Streets)

PHONE: (212) 265–4444

TYPE OF CUISINE: Brazilian

DAYS/HOURS: Sunday through Thursday from 11:00 A.M. to 10:00 P.M.; Friday and Saturday from 11:00 A.M. to 11:00 P.M.

VEGEBILITY: Good

RESERVATIONS: Suggested

WHEELCHAIR ACCESS: One step at entrance

KID-FRIENDLY: Yes (but small place)

TYPE OF SERVICE: Table, delivery, and catering

PRICING: Inexpensive

PAYMENT ACCEPTED: Major credit cards

This quaint hole-in-the-wall is ideal for a first date or an anniversary. The little white candles on the tables, photos of the stars who have dined there, ceramic plates hanging from the walls, and Brazilian music create a perfect cozy setting.

There are four entrée choices for vegetarians, which can be made vegan by omitting the dab of butter added just before serving. Fittingly, the dishes are made primarily from rice and beans—you choose red or black beans; plain, yellow, or white rice with a little garlic; and a side of fried sweet plantains, veggies, or both. Served with a warm dinner roll and butter, your meal has a welcoming, homey feeling to it.

If you're not in the mood for rice and beans (but then, why come?), there's a fantastic avocado salad, and the cheese rolls on the appetizer list are a great start. Save room for the amazing desserts: The caramel custard will satisfy the sweetest of sweet-tooth cravings, and the Brazilian herbal tea is the perfect top-off to the evening.

If you're with a large group, or even on a double date, you should call in advance because space is limited. Catering is available, and the restaurant has a weekday lunch special from 11:00 A.M. to 4:00 P.M., with free delivery.

—CHRISTINA MASSEY

⑭ Tagine Dining Gallery
537 Ninth Avenue (at 40th Street)

> **PHONE:** (212) 564–7292; Fax: (212) 564–7280
>
> **WEB ADDRESS:** www.taginenyc.com
>
> **TYPE OF CUISINE:** Moroccan
>
> **DAYS/HOURS:** Monday through Friday from noon to 4:00 A.M.,
> Saturday from 4:30 P.M. to 4:00 A.M., Sunday 4:30 P.M. to mid-
> night
>
> **VEGEBILITY:** Very good
>
> **RESERVATIONS:** Recommended for dinner
>
> **WHEELCHAIR ACCESS:** Upstairs only
>
> **KID-FRIENDLY:** Yes
>
> **TYPE OF SERVICE:** Table and bar
>
> **PRICING:** Moderate
>
> **PAYMENT ACCEPTED:** Major credit cards

Take a 2-block detour from the whining horns outside the Lincoln Tunnel, cross the street from the diesel blanket of the Port Authority bus terminal, slip under an unremarkable canopy along Ninth Avenue to escape the wobbly couple in front of you, and you may think you've gotten hopelessly lost. The good news: You've landed in Casablanca. Actually, you've arrived at Tagine Dining Gallery, a lively Moroccan bistro that's an oasis in a culinary desert.

The decor is the first hint of authenticity. Running along the length of the brick walls are spongy cushions with handmade covers, whose patterns and colors distinguish one tribe of Berbers, living high in the Atlas Mountains, from another. Live music and belly dancing begin at 8:00 P.M. and last until 4:00 A.M., when the hearty regulars reluctantly retire from the incense-scented, dimly lit room downstairs.

It feels like home to executive chef Hamid Idrissi, whose irreverent poetry got him chased from the homeland he has not revisited in twenty years. Idrissi became vegetarian in 1999 and leaves the preparation of meat dishes to his assistants. Today he mixes spices with the passion he once used to marry words. His appetizers satisfy different tastes and are nearly all meat-free. Shekshouka, a dish of eggplant and peppers sautéed in a wine and garlic reduction, is aptly pungent and a good partner for the lighter vegetable borek, seven seasoned vegetables baked in a light phyllo dough.

But the showstopper is the vegetable tagine, a blend of chickpeas, turnips, calabaza, carrots, and zucchini, sweetened with currants and served in the pot for which the dish—and the restaurant—is named. The cone-shaped tagine is made of deep-dug clay from the coastal city of Safi. Its glazed interior is said to be so rich in minerals, pregnant women eat sprinkles of it as a supplement. Bold palates will add dabs of harissa, a fiery condiment of emulsified cayenne, crushed pepper, and wine. All of Idrissi's dishes are made without meat or dairy products; he starts many with a stock from the water in which chickpeas have soaked. You might finish the meal with flaky honey letters, a pâté of grounded blanched almonds rolled in phyllo dough and soaked in honey. Then sit back, sip on the mint tea, enjoy the music, and disappear into Northwest Africa.

—BRIAN CAZENEUVE

⓯ Utsav

1185 Sixth Avenue (Avenue of the Americas) Enter on 46th or 47th Street between Sixth and Seventh Avenues.

> **PHONE:** (212) 575–2525
>
> **TYPE OF CUISINE:** Upscale Indian
>
> **DAYS/HOURS:** Monday through Saturday from noon to 3:00 P.M., Monday through Thursday 5:30 to 11:00 P.M., Friday and Saturday 5:30 to 11:30 P.M.
>
> **VEGEBILITY:** Very good
>
> **RESERVATIONS:** Suggested
>
> **WHEELCHAIR ACCESS:** Yes, but call ahead
>
> **KID-FRIENDLY:** Yes
>
> **TYPE OF SERVICE:** Table
>
> **PRICING:** Moderate
>
> **PAYMENT ACCEPTED:** Major credit cards

U tsav, which means "festival" in Hindi, is aptly named. The elegantly decorated restaurant is unusually large, with cathedral ceilings in the upstairs dining room that give the dining room a grand atmosphere. Its Midtown location attracts theatergoers, businesspeople, and a pretty cheery happy-hour crowd—which is why Utsav offers a variety of meals. There's a daily lunch buffet (with all the veggie offerings on one side) from noon to 3:00 P.M., take-out lunch, happy hour with drink specials and complementary hors d'oeuvres (downstairs at the bar from 4:00 to 7:00 P.M.), the Broadway Special (a three-course prix fixe meal), and, of course, à la carte lunch and dinner menus. And each meal has plenty of terrific vegetarian offerings.

But this is no cheap curry palace. (Nor is it easy to find. It's between 46th and 47th Streets, midway between Sixth and Seventh Avenues.) Chef Walter D'Rozario creates dishes that are heads and shoulders above what passes for Indian food in New York. Samosas are made in-house, which, D'Rozario explains, is similar to the difference between fresh pasta and dried. He's right: Utsav's samosas—with a salty, fried outside and a soft, gently spiced inside—are perfect, especially when dipped in the anise-seed-flavored tomato chutney. Another appetizer, New Delhi Chaat, is a deceptively simple concept but oh so tasty: just a potato, cooked until tender, topped with chutney, and served on top of a simple rice cracker.

The nan is served warm and brushed with ghee, but vegans can request it without. Each veggie entrée is unique and finely spiced. One vegan option, Hyderabadi Mirchi Ka Salan (Anaheim peppers in coconut and sesame sauce) is just spicy enough to bring out the flavor of the pepper-coconut combination, but not so hot that it takes over. Ovo-lactos can't go wrong with the Paneer Masaledar, homemade cheese tossed with pepper and spices. The mild cheese balances the flavorful roasted peppers and onions. Perhaps because the owner is (mostly) veg, Utsav is happy to cater to vegetarians. There's also a full bar, with a wide selection of California wines, and a long list of dessert drinks.

—JESSICA WURWARG

16 West Bank Café

407 West 42nd Street (at Ninth Avenue)

PHONE: (212) 695–6909

TYPE OF CUISINE: Upscale Italian

DAYS/HOURS: Monday through Saturday from 11:45 A.M. to 1:00 A.M., Sunday 11:30 A.M. to midnight

VEGEBILITY: Good

RESERVATIONS: Required 5:00 to 8:00 P.M., recommended other times

WHEELCHAIR ACCESS: Yes

KID-FRIENDLY: Yes

TYPE OF SERVICE: Table and bar

PRICING: Moderate to expensive

PAYMENT ACCEPTED: Major credit cards

At all costs, I try to avoid Times Square, with its bright lights, glacial-speed tourists, and overpriced theme restaurants. But after a visit to West Bank Café, I'd return in a New York minute, if only for another serving of the polenta portobello.

West Bank is not cheap; if you get a drink (they boast a seventeen-page wine list and a full bar) or dessert with your meal, expect to depart at least $30 poorer. But if you're looking for a special treat or a pretheater splurge, West Bank will not disappoint. The large space is candlelit, with fresh-cut flowers on every table, and Miles and Billie waft down soothingly from hidden speakers. The careful presentation of each dish is exquisite, and though the vegetarian options are not extensive, they are excellent—better yet, promises the chef, the veg menu is about to expand.

I'll never look at polenta the same way after trying the aforementioned portobello appetizer. Smooth and creamy, it's an ideal platform for the earthy mushrooms, and the dash of truffle oil and artistic drizzling of sweet reduced balsamic vinegar transform a simple concept into a dazzler. Sadly, for appetizers vegans are limited to the fresh garden salad or a side of broccoli rabe, since the polenta contains cheese and cream.

For a main course, the spinach lasagna is rich and excellent, but the more subtle spaghetti squash gets my vote for first prize. Lightly seasoned tomato sauce surrounds a mound of tender squash, topped with gently cooked vegetables (with pesto for vegetarians, without for vegans). It's a hearty portion, but it feels light and delicate to the palate, and the simplicity of the concoction allows the fresh flavors of the vegetables to shine.

Because it's in the Theater District, you'll need a reservation before 8:00; after that, you'll have the place to yourself as people rush off to their shows.

—JULIE HOLLAR

17 Zenith Vegetarian Cuisine
311 West 48th Street (between Eighth and Ninth Avenues)

PHONE: (212) 262–8080
TYPE OF CUISINE: Asian vegan
DAYS/HOURS: Monday through Friday from 11:30 A.M. to 10:00 P.M., Saturday and Sunday noon to 10:00 P.M.
VEGEBILITY: Excellent
RESERVATIONS: Recommended for parties of six or more
WHEELCHAIR ACCESS: No (a few steps at entrance)
KID-FRIENDLY: No
TYPE OF SERVICE: Table, take-out, delivery, and catering
PRICING: Moderate
PAYMENT ACCEPTED: Major credit cards

In this dimly lit, mellow establishment, you'll find real orchids, live bamboo plants, fish tanks, candlelit tables—and excellent vegan meals for about $20 a person.

Though all the meals are meatless, Zenith aims to please a meat-eating crowd. Almost without exception, dishes look and taste like the various meats they impersonate in an almost theatrical way—appropriate given the restaurant's Theater District location. To start, try the Zenith Rolls, a delightfully unexpected array of textures and flavors rolled up into gorgeous small bites. For entrées, the beautifully composed Purple Moon (fried stuffed eggplant) or Vegetarian Quilt (soy protein in tofu skin) are enough to warrant a trip. The former is lightly fried Chinese eggplant, stuffed with mashed potatoes and topped with black bean sauce. Finish with the Ambrosia Chocolate Cake—it's so smooth and rich, you'll have a hard time believing it's completely vegan.

Zenith has recently relocated, so beware of any old listings reading Eighth Avenue and 52nd Street. Catering for events and lunch delivery are available, as is wine, three kinds of beer, and mixed drinks.

—CHRISTINA MASSEY

Places to Stay

18 Broadway Inn B&B

264 West 46th Street (between Eighth Avenue and Broadway)

> **PHONE:** (212) 997–9200
> **PRICING:** Moderate

A must-do for theater lovers. The decor is simple, but the location is *fabulous*—right on restaurant row. Higher-priced rooms have kitchenettes. An on-site car service is also available.

19 Flatotel

135 West 52nd Street (between Sixth and Seventh Avenues)

> **PHONE:** (212) 887–9400
> **PRICING:** Moderate

Each suite comes with a marble Roman jacuzzi and a fully equipped gourmet kitchen. Popular with families.

20 Hudson Hotel

356 West 58th Street (between Eighth and Ninth Avenues)

> **PHONE:** (212) 554–6000
> **WEB ADDRESS:** www.hudsonhotel.com
> **PRICING:** Expensive

This is where the young, the hip, and the beautiful stay. Just watch out for the attitude and the small rooms.

21 The Mayfair New York

242 West 49th Street (between Eighth Avenue and Broadway)

> **PHONE:** (212) 586–0300
> **PRICING:** Moderate

This European-style boutique hotel is easy on the wallet. There is no bar on-site, and it won't register on the cool radar, but the mattresses are good and the bathrooms clean. Times Square, Fifth Avenue, and the Theater District nearby.

22 The Millennium Broadway New York

145 West 44th Street (between Sixth Avenue and Broadway)

> **PHONE:** (212) 768–4400
> **WEB ADDRESS:** www.millennium-hotels.com
> **PRICING:** Expensive

Not much for style, but you will be well taken care of. Geared to the business traveler but well suited for the leisure set as well.

23 Park Central Hotel

870 Seventh Avenue (at 56th Street)

> **PHONE:** (212) 247–8000
> **PRICING:** Expensive

Built in 1926, it's the quintessential Midtown bright lights, big city hotel. An interesting fact: The hotel was Jackie Gleason's main residence while taping his immensely popular TV show, *The Honeymooners*. Pet-friendly.

Upper East Side

This is where old money and high society meet, dahling. Running from 59th Street to 96th Street between the East River and Fifth Avenue, this neighborhood is considered the city's Gold Coast. Museum Mile, located on Fifth Avenue from 72nd Street to 104th Street, boasts such institutions as the Metropolitan Museum of Art, the Guggenheim, the Frick Collection, and the Whitney. Madison Avenue is synonymous with high-end shopping and super-expensive boutiques. Park Avenue is what the Brits would call a dual carriageway, with awe-inspiring architecture on either side of the median and tulips and statues planted in it. (There's a reason Park Avenue is one of world's most coveted addresses.) Fifth Avenue is the eastern boundary of Central Park, home to a castle, a reservoir, a zoo, a boathouse (where you can rent rowboats), a conservatory garden, and numerous trails for jogging, bicycling, and horseback riding. There's Shakespeare in the Park in the summer and ice-skating in the winter. And all year long there are more restaurants than you could get to if you ate out every single day—and don't think many denizens don't.

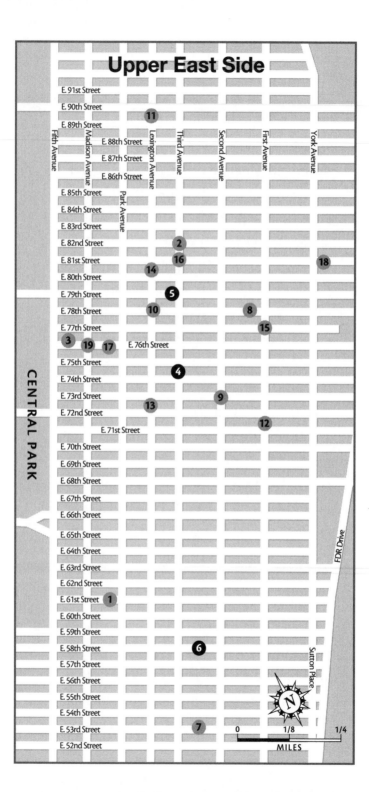

Upper East Side

Places to Eat

Aureole

34 East 61st Street (between Madison and Park Avenues)

> **PHONE:** (212) 319–1660; Fax: (212) 750–8613
>
> **WEB ADDRESS:** www.aureolerestaurant.com
>
> **TYPE OF CUISINE:** Progressive American
>
> **DAYS/HOURS:** Monday through Friday from noon to 2:00 P.M. and from 5:30 to 11:00 P.M. (5:00 to 11:00 P.M. Friday), Saturday 5:00 to 11:00 P.M.
>
> **VEGEBILITY:** Fair
>
> **RESERVATIONS:** Strongly recommended
>
> **WHEELCHAIR ACCESS:** First floor only (restrooms are on basement level; no elevators)
>
> **KID-FRIENDLY:** Not prohibited, but jackets required, decorum expected
>
> **TYPE OF SERVICE:** Table and bar
>
> **PRICING:** Very expensive
>
> **PAYMENT ACCEPTED:** Major credit cards

When Dante Bocuzzi, Aureole's executive chef, began his first tour of kitchen duty here ten years ago, he considered vegetarianism "a boring pain in the neck." After Bocuzzi left Aureole, he worked as a chef for Georgio Armani in Italy, but it was his three years in California, working with the freshest of ingredients, that converted him. In 2001 Charlie Palmer, Aureole's classy founder, brought back Bocuzzi. The result is one of the most thoughtful, innovative vegetarian tasting menus at one of the most elegant restaurants in the city.

Aureole is located in a converted brownstone, with a single pane of glass absorbing the natural light over two stories that seat ninety people. Floral arrangements and honey-colored wood paneling suggest you are in for something special, and the $85 tasting menu is worth the splurge. In each dish, Bocuzzi sets off tart against sweet, sharp against smooth, while still paying homage to seasonal ingredients. The ricotta dumplings with roasted wood ear mushrooms is a destination dish by itself. Bocuzzi uses mushrooms marinated in soy sauce as a bed for the subtler tastes of the dumplings and a ragout of spring peas. Next, savor the saltiness of roasted eggplant blocks with robust toasted quinoa, macadamia nuts, and pencil asparagus. The caramelized spring onions and rhubarb strudel with ginger-infused gastric will make you appreciate the versatility of rhubarb as a balancer between sweet and pungent that need not be relegated to pies.

Only our first course—a salad of baby artichoke, frisée, and oven-roasted tomatoes—was vegan, but the kitchen can make substitutions. It can also make a course of the crisp potato doughnuts or shallot-potato cakes used as bases for the fish dishes on the menu. Aureole has an extensive wine list and can pair wines with the meal, if you choose.

Chocoholics will melt over the caramelized hazelnut pyramid, with bittersweet chocolate and praline sauce poured onto the first chocolate mound. Bocuzzi calls the oozing treasure a "moving dessert," and each bite/sip will leave you yearning for the next intensified chocolate layer. On the lighter side, try the stone fruit sampler, a plate of slow-roasted white peaches, caramelized plums, and a bing cherry tartlet, topped with basil ice cream that could only work with such a tasty, sour base.

—BRIAN CAZENEUVE

2 Beyoglu

1431 Third Avenue (between 82nd and 83rd Streets)

PHONE: (212) 650–0850
TYPE OF CUISINE: Turkish
DAYS/HOURS: Monday through Sunday from noon to midnight
VEGEBILITY: Good
RESERVATIONS: Recommended
WHEELCHAIR ACCESS: Yes
KID-FRIENDLY: Fair
TYPE OF SERVICE: Table
PRICING: Moderate
PAYMENT ACCEPTED: Major credit cards

The ambiance is authentic and vegetarian choices abound at this new Upper East Sider, Beyoglu. The decor is rich with copper and clay, and upstairs you can get a glimpse of what old Istanbul looked like. As with any Turkish restaurant, you can have yourself a feast on the appetizers alone. Ten kinds of mezes on the menu consist of such staples as hummus (seasoned chickpeas with tahini), eggplant salad (charcoaled eggplant puree), sigara boregi (phyllo dough scrolls stuffed with feta cheese), and stuffed grape leaves, but the restaurant also features less common items, such as kisir (Turkish tabouli) and zeytinyagli ispanak (fresh spinach, shallots, and dill sautéed in olive oil). Vegans can enjoy all these items, save for the sigara boregi.

A vegetarian combination platter can serve as your entrée, or you can enjoy one of the deliciously huge salads for an even healthier choice. The truly Turkish shepherd (onions, tomatoes, and cukes with lemon dressing) and Greek salads are pure vegetarian (vegans can ask the chef to hold the feta in the Greek). The Beyoglu Salad is made with chicken but can be prepared without it upon request. Even though the menu is not as extensive as those at most Turkish restaurants, vegetarians dining at Beyoglu will surely find enough to satisfy their appetites.

—SEZIN CAVUSOGLU

③ Café Boulud

20 East 76th Street (between Fifth and Madison Avenues)

PHONE: (212) 772–2600
WEB ADDRESS: www.danielnyc.com
TYPE OF CUISINE: French
DAYS/HOURS: Monday from 5:45 to 11:00 P.M., Tuesday through Friday noon to 2:30 P.M. and 5:45 to 11:00 P.M., Saturday 5:30 to 11:00 P.M., Sunday 5:45 to 10:00 P.M.
VEGEBILITY: Good
RESERVATIONS: Recommended
WHEELCHAIR ACCESS: Yes
KID-FRIENDLY: No
TYPE OF SERVICE: Table and bar
PRICING: Very expensive
PAYMENT ACCEPTED: Major credit cards

A favored haunt of visiting dignitaries, ladies who lunch, and businesspeople on expense accounts, Café Boulud—the more casual eatery of culinary superstar Daniel Boulud—is an essay in understated elegance. From the moment your well-shod feet hit the thick, chocolate brown carpet to when you rise, stuffed, from your leather dining chair, you're surrounded by the best New York City has to offer: efficient service, richly appointed surroundings and, of course, outrageously good food.

If you eat eggs and dairy, that is. CIA-trained executive chef Andrew Carmellini says that while vegans can be accommodated, there simply isn't time to make them a special tasting menu, even with advance notice. Substitutions are happily made, however, affording even the fussiest of diners some measure of sublime happiness. And sublime it is. The restaurant boasts four menus, all of which feature seasonal ingredients and change "as the chef gets bored." Vegetarian dishes can be found on all four but are concentrated on "le Potager," a menu introduced by Carmellini and inspired by his wife, a longtime vegetarian. French for "kitchen garden," le Potager celebrates all-vegetarian cuisine. On a late-February visit, the menu featured squash soup, a frothy winter brew infused with Indian earthy spices and spiked with cilantro. Signature soups in other seasons include Chilled Five Spring Pea Soup, Swiss Chard and Bean Soup with Ricotta Toasts, and Curried Cream of Cauliflower and Apple Soup.

Other appetizer treasures, like the crisp marinated beet salad, are easily made vegan. Decorated with raisins, pumpkin seeds, frisée, and pungent goat cheese, the dish is delicately flavored, beautifully presented, and thoroughly egg- and dairy-free (without the cheese).

Main courses are equally divine. Carmellini's hearty vegetable lazanette is closer to a stew than a lasagna, with roasted eggplant, pine nuts, onions, tomatoes, and grapes (!) in a musky eggplant puree, surrounded by a light tomato broth and a drizzle of basil oil. Another spring menu standout is mascarpone and green pea ravioli. Topped with romaine, sprigs of mint, thinly shaved Parmesan, and barely opened pods revealing pearl-like peas within, it's like eating spring on a plate.

For dessert, vegans would be sad to miss some of the delicious true sorbets or fruit-based "soups" made in-house. A favorite for ovo-lactos is the chocolate-fennel gratin: a molten, dark-chocolate cake scented with fennel and perfectly matched with a slightly gritty pear sorbet, topped with an ultra-thin pear "chip."

The waitstaff seems to intrinsically understand the balance between attentive service and diners' need for privacy. Their knowledge of accompanying wines is thorough, thanks to weekly wine seminars given by Daniel's sommelier Olivier Flosse. In all, the experience at Café Boulud is one not soon forgotten. Now, if we could just do something about those leather chairs . . .

—SUSAN SHUMAKER

❹ Candle Café

1307 Third Avenue (at 75th Street)

PHONE: (212) 472–0970

TYPE OF CUISINE: Gourmet seasonal organic vegan

DAYS/HOURS: Monday through Saturday from noon to 10:30 P.M., Sunday noon to 9:30 P.M.

VEGEBILITY: Excellent

RESERVATIONS: Suggested for parties of four or more

WHEELCHAIR ACCESS: Yes, but restaurant is narrow and cramped for space

KID-FRIENDLY: Yes

TYPE OF SERVICE: Table, take-out, and delivery

PRICING: Moderate

PAYMENT ACCEPTED: Major credit cards

Candle Café is never empty. At lunch and especially dinner, the tiny place is always hopping, but even at 3:00 in the afternoon, there are groups, solo diners, and people dropping in for a juice or take-away. Many of the customers seem to know owners Joy Pierson and Bart Potenza—in fact, in the world of natural foods, it's hard to find anyone who doesn't know them (see sidebar later in this chapter). So when you dine at Candle Café, which is one of the few absolute requirements of any trip to NYC, don't stand on ceremony. Introduce yourself and become one of the in-crowd.

Open for a decade now, Candle has established itself as one of the leading organic whole-foods vegan restaurants in the country. It has found the perfect balance of commitment to fresh organic food and a gourmet, seasonally changing menu that takes those ingredients to new heights. The decor is pleasant, and the vibe is truly one of a small-town restaurant—or social club.

You can start with a juice, smoothie, tea, latte or glass of organic wine or beer. Choosing your meal is decidedly harder. The core menu offers dozens of familiar and exotic dishes, but even the familiar-sounding ones have special twists. There's also a roster of daily specials: usually a ravioli (sweet red pepper, herb tofu, lemon parsley), a soy dish (herb-crusted tempeh, tofu-vegetable phyllo triangle, an unspeakably delicious grilled basil tofu), something ethnic (Indian plate, Mexican wrap), and things beyond categorization (rosemary-walnut-crusted seitan and the stupendous fennel and new potato crepe with a roasted garlic aioli—order these if available).

Of course, if all that's too exciting, stick with a salad (their Greek salad is the best vegan one out there), burger, lasagna, stir-fry, or meze plate. But—as predictable as it sounds—you must save room for dessert. Candle takes vegan baking to a new level: a daily cheesecake with a graham cracker crust, decadent chocolate cake with chocolate frosting, and, my weakness, the chocolate peanut butter terrine.

On my last visit, one of the 4:00 P.M. customers was walking out and waved to Joy and Bart, who know him by face but not by name. They smiled and waved back as he said, "Thanks. You're the best! But I've been saying that for years."

—SUZANNE GERBER

❺ Candle 79

154 East 79th Street (between Lexington and Third Avenues)

PHONE: (212) 537–7179
WEB ADDRESS: www.candlecafe.com
TYPE OF CUISINE: Upscale seasonal vegan
DAYS/HOURS: Monday through Saturday noon to 3:30 P.M. and 5:30 to 10:30 P.M.
VEGEBILITY: Excellent
RESERVATIONS: Suggested on weekends
WHEELCHAIR ACCESS: Yes
KID-FRIENDLY: Yes
TYPE OF SERVICE: Table, take-out, and bar
PRICING: Moderate
PAYMENT ACCEPTED: Major credit cards

Like its older sibling, Candle Café, a few blocks away, Candle 79 offers the winning combination of super-fresh seasonal vegetables and chefs with fertile imaginations. But in a welcome display of sibling rivalry, the newcomer fills a niche that's been gapingly empty in this city where one can indulge any culinary whim. While there's no shortage of terrific vegetarian restaurants, finding one appropriate for your parents' anniversary or a special date has almost always involved compromise. Lucky for us, since September 2003, we no longer must flip a coin to choose between "elegant," "vegan," and Hangawi.

Owners Joy Pierson and Bart Potenza have always wanted a place like this. The two-story townhouse is done up in rich jewel tones and muted gold lighting, with banquettes at almost every table. Real linens cover every table, soft jazz or lounge music wafts down from the ceilings, and food comes perfectly plated on oversize white square and rectangular dishes. The attentive wait staff is very knowledgeable about the menu yet never hovers. (Our server, Brian from Pittsburgh, had never eaten vegan food before, but since working here, he's become a "convert." Even his Midwestern mom raved for weeks about how great she felt after her first exposure.)

The setting is elegant and comfy, but what will make you linger is the menu. Start with a drink—anything from fresh-squeezed juice to a tea from their impressive roster to one of the two-dozen organic wines or half-dozen beers—and spend some time devouring the menu. You can't go wrong with any of the five Teasers, but the seitan chimichurris (marinated cubes that melt in your mouth) and live nori cone rolls alone warrant a visit. Of the ten Starters, not one is a dud. The delicate sesame seed tofu cakes (with shiitakes and bok choy) are light and tender, but if you're only going to have one appetizer and it's listed, you must order the toasted quinoa salad with roasted winter squash. This is the best squash we've ever had anywhere, period. Of course, if the three-beet special with creamy wasabi is being offered, you'll just have to order both. It's only fair to mention that the mini crispy dumplings, served with a balsamic-soy reduction and carrot-miso sauce and resembling little party favors, are indescribably tasty.

What Candle Café does well, Candle 79 takes to new heights. Yes, the veggies are always farm-fresh and sauces all house-made, but it's the combination of flavors and textures that make the food so memorable. Each of the nine menu entrées is a worthy contender and will delight your palette with its mix of crunchy, chewy, and crispy. Many will leave you guessing what that subtle overtone in the sauce is (roasted pepitas? fig reduction?) or what that little curlicue on edge of the plate is (some kind Japanese Jerusalem artichoke; who knew?). The cashew-crusted tempeh is write-home delicious, and the live seasoned vegetable strata with macadamia ricotta will put raw foods in a whole new light. But trust me on this: If your companion orders the rosemary walnut-crusted seitan (with roased garlic potato mash and a spinach sauté) and you don't, you will resent that person all night.

Candle Café Luminaries:
Joy Pierson and Bart Potenza

Talk about a dollar and a dream. Back in early '90s, Bart owned a health food store/juice bar and Joy was the in-house nutritionist. Together they dreamed of expanding into a full-service restaurant. Their vision became a reality, thanks to a lot of hard work and a little bit of luck—in the form of a winning New York State lottery ticket.

Nearly a decade ago Joy and Bart created the Candle Café, and today it's a bona fide NYC institution. Out-of-town chefs, foodies, and just plain folk stop by when they're in town, and plenty of locals come by so often that they don't need a menu to order. The food is the big draw, of course, but Candle wouldn't be the success it is without the passion—and personalities—of its owners.

Tall and lanky, with a full head of graying hair and a N.Y. broadcaster's voice, Bart is the perfect counterpart to petite, brunette Joy. Conversations with them run from chatty and light to serious and political. "My passion is the mission," says Joy, "practicing nonviolence, love, a respect for the earth. And, of course, making excellent food! We work with small farmers, and all our food is delivered within twenty-four hours of being picked. Now that's nutrient-packed food."

Though he's no doubt been issued his "senior card" from AARP, Bart hasn't mellowed with age. "I've only gotten more political," he says. "Veganism and the animal rights movement have taken on a life of their own, and the trend is our friend. It's spreading into powerful, mainstream circles. We can't keep up with the demand for more catering and A-list parties."

Candle is such a successful, smooth operation, it would be easy for Joy and Bart to kick back and rest on their laurels. But for them, that would be missing the point. Both are involved in day-to-day operations: Bart manages staff and records the day's specials on the voice message, for example, and Joy helps fine-tune dishes and holiday menus and researches sources and suppliers. They keep a log of customers' comments and act on anything that could be improved. And both meet and greet customers as if entertaining at home. Today, for example, a man at the juice counter is eyeing one of our fabulous-looking plates. "Sir, come try it!" insists Joy. The man demurs, a bit embarrassed. "You really don't mind?" he asks. "Are you kidding?" says Bart, shoveling a large forkful toward the man. When he takes a few bites and raves, Joy turns to me and says quietly, "This is what it's all about for me."

In between overseeing Candle and Candle 79—and finishing the long-anticipated *Candle Café Cookbook* (Clarkson Potter, 2003)—Joy and Bart are very active in local and national projects, from Farm Sanctuary and PETA to EarthSave and the Social Venture Network. But they don't see this kind of work as optional. Explains Bart, "We have a planet to save, one meal at a time."

—SUZANNE GERBER

Because this is Candle, there are two things to remember. First, any dish can modified to suit your mood or accommodate allergies (they even make adjustments for people on Atkins). Second: Save room for dessert! The chocolate peanut butter terrine is even better than it sounds, the Mexican chocolate cake is so decadent no one believes it's vegan, the cider doughnut is light but filling, and the poached seckel pears with vanilla jasmine rice pudding is heavenly. But my money is on the live dessert, the shockingly tart and fresh and yummy lime parfait, with macadamia nut crème and pecans.

Head chef Jonathan Grumbles left Candle Café in 2000 to move west with his family, but when he got a call from Joy and Bart inviting him back to run 79, he jumped. His goal: "To be to NYC what Millennium is to San Francisco." With food like this in a setting like that, it's fair to say they're almost there.

—SUZANNE GERBER

6 Dawat

210 East 58th Street (between Second and Third Avenues)

PHONE: (212) 355–7555
TYPE OF CUISINE: Upscale Indian
DAYS/HOURS: Monday through Saturday from noon to 3:00 P.M. and from 5:00 to 11:00 P.M., Sunday 5:00 to 11:00 P.M.
VEGEBILITY: Very good
RESERVATIONS: Recommended
WHEELCHAIR ACCESS: Yes
KID-FRIENDLY: Yes
TYPE OF SERVICE: Table and bar
PRICING: Expensive for Indian
PAYMENT ACCEPTED: All credit cards

Dawat is often referred to as the Holy Grail of Indian restaurants in New York (in the world, some say), and despite challenges from newcomers, its reputation is intact. Here you will find nothing fusion or trendy—just classic Indian food, from the simplest home-style stews to the richest Mughlai dishes—and the staff greets you warmly, with the spiritual graciousness of the Indian people.

If you are vegan, you need ask your server only one question: "Is this dish garnished with ghee?" Dawat's food is not cooked in ghee, but many veggie dishes are given a final spoonful as a flavor enhancer. About a third of the menu is devoted to the vegetarian foods of India, from elaborately spiced curries and lush biryanis to simple home-style dishes.

Start with a vegan plate of pappadams and cilantro chutney—the chutney will startle you with its freshness and clarity of flavor. Continue with two appetizers from "Madhur's snack cart," a nod to the seaside vendors of Mumbai: bhel poori, a plate of sweet-sour crisps and noodles tasting of tamarind (vegan), and dahi aloo poori, larger crisps, chunks of potato, yogurt, and chickpeas, also in a tamarind sauce (ovo-lacto). Next up, the vegetarian thali (presented on a silver tray), a mound of basmati rice surrounded by seven little dishes of delicacies like green beans with coconut and split peas, flavored with asafetida; potato chunks in a gingery tomato sauce; and sindhi karhi, a veggie stew thickened with chickpea flour and seasoned with fenugreek.

Dawat's menu does not change much, and specials are not usually offered; however, we urge you to consider the many dishes that bear the name of the famed Indian chef Madhur Jaffrey. They are unique to this restaurant and truly representative of the excellent food made by the great cooks of India.

Although this is very much a "special occasion" restaurant, you need not wait for a birthday or an engagement. We have spent many happy moments at the U-shaped bar, enjoying an expertly made Bombay gin and tonic or a Kingfisher beer. Dawat has a well-priced lunch menu, and though dinner can certainly be expensive, it is by no means stuffy. The service is expert and unobtrusive, and questions are answered respectfully. The ambience is not overwhelmingly Raj, but tailored, soothing and even playful, with Dawat's trademark puppet masks on the walls and fresh flowers everywhere.

—EUREKA FREEMAN

7 Organic Harvest Café

235 East 53rd Street (between Second and Third Avenues)

PHONE: (212) 421–6444

TYPE OF CUISINE: Organic eclectic

DAYS/HOURS: Monday through Friday from 11:00 A.M. to 10:00 P.M., Saturday and Sunday 10:00 A.M. to 9:00 P.M.

VEGEBILITY: Excellent

RESERVATIONS: Not necessary

WHEELCHAIR ACCESS: No

KID-FRIENDLY: Yes (but shelves are easily accessible to little ones)

TYPE OF SERVICE: Table and take-out

PRICING: Inexpensive

PAYMENT ACCEPTED: Major credit cards

Up a short flight of stairs in the heart of vegetarian-challenged Midtown lies a hidden treat: mouth-watering entrées, sandwiches, and shakes made from all-organic ingredients. Five-year-old Harvest does a brisk take-out and catering business, which isn't surprising given its eclectic, tasty selection of Greek, Asian, Mexican, Indian, and standard veggie dishes. At lunchtime the three tiny tables are always packed, as the local workforce ebbs and flows through the doors to slurp down a nutritional shake or grab a fresh juice and a wrap to eat outdoors or take back to the grind.

Obviously, owner/chef Mark Mager, who trained at the Natural Gourmet Cookery School, has a sense of humor, with dish names like Hop Along Casserole (polenta, black beans, and sweet potatoes with miso) and Big Daddy Seitan Steak. The Quinoa Conqueror Salad—with carrots, kombu, arame, scallions, and sesame and pumpkin seeds over mesclun lettuce—is the perfect antidote to midafternoon fatigue. And talk about having it your way: A choice of seven homemade dressings guarantees that every order will be to your liking.

If you luck out and score a prime window seat, take advantage and linger over the seitan enchiladas with tomato-coriander sauce. Who needs salsa when a dish is this robust? There's a reason the vegetarian dumplings appetizer is so popular: The tangy green morsels just melt in your mouth. And paired with ginger shoyu sauce, they're filling enough for a meal.

—MARIANNE SEMCHUK

8 Quintessence (see East Village)
353 East 78th Street (between First and Second Avenues)

PHONE: (212) 734–0888

9 Üsküdar
1405 Second Avenue (between 73rd and 74th Streets)

PHONE: (212) 988–2641
TYPE OF CUISINE: Turkish
DAYS/HOURS: Monday through Sunday from noon to 11:00 P.M.
VEGEBILITY: Very good
RESERVATIONS: Suggested
WHEELCHAIR ACCESS: No
KID-FRIENDLY: No
TYPE OF SERVICE: Table, delivery, and catering
PRICING: Moderate
PAYMENT ACCEPTED: All credit cards

Üsküdar is a neighborhood in Istanbul, and, to the good fortune of Manhattanites, it is also a small neighborhood restaurant on the Upper East Side. With just twenty-eight seats and walls covered with photographs of Turkey and Turkish good luck charms, the fifteen-year-old eatery has a relaxed, comfortable feeling. The customers appear to be regulars, which is always a good sign.

It's easy to eat well at Üsküdar, despite the preponderance of meat dishes. The key to eating well at Turkish restaurants is always to focus on appetizers, most of which are vegetarian, if not vegan. Üsküdar does offer one vegan entrée, the vegetable casserole, a tomato-based dish chockablock with artichokes, squash, carrots, and spinach and served over perfectly moist Turkish rice. But for a more exciting dining experience, vegetarians should order a combination of appetizers and soups. Dips, eaten with pita bread, are an important part of Turkish cuisine. The zesty hummus and smoky patlican (similar to baba ghanoush) are classic (vegan) Turkish dishes and fun to share with your dining companions. One of Üsküdar's specialties is mucver, a fried zucchini pancake; its heavy rich flavor is balanced out by a fresh yogurt sauce that's delicately flavored with dill and cucumber.

Though Üsküdar's wine list is not extensive, there are a few interesting Turkish choices, some available by the glass. Other authentic beverages include Turkish soda, apricot juice, cherry juice, and ayran, made with yogurt. For dessert, ovo-lactos should try the buttery baklava or the coconut pudding. There's even a healthy vegan dessert, kayis: apricots stuffed with almonds (usually ordered with whipped cream).

—JESSICA WURWARG

10 Wrap-n-Run Grill

1125 Lexington Avenue (between 78th and 79th Streets)

PHONE: (212) 744–1588

OTHER LOCATION: 788 Lexington Avenue (between 61st and 62nd Streets), (212) 788–7781

TYPE OF CUISINE: Wraps and sandwiches

DAYS/HOURS: Monday through Friday from 11:00 A.M. to 10:00 P.M., Saturday and Sunday 10:00 A.M. to 9:00 P.M.

VEGEBILITY: Good

RESERVATIONS: No

WHEELCHAIR ACCESS: Yes

KID-FRIENDLY: Yes

TYPE OF SERVICE: Take-out (a few tables downtown), delivery (both)

PRICING: Inexpensive

PAYMENT ACCEPTED: Major credit cards

Wrap-n-Run serves the purpose of providing standard lunches and delivery dinners with all the speed and efficiency that New York City is famous for. It is the type of non-diner yet do-it-all place that nearly every company has a corporate account with, and the densely packed tables provide quick pit stops for busy shoppers along Lexington Avenue.

The most appealing dishes at this veg-friendly chain are baked potatoes, make-your-own salads, and the vegetarian wrap. The drink choices are much more diverse, including fresh-squeezed juices, yogurt shakes, and smoothies. As the menu declares, the smoothies are "whipped into a frenzy," and with names like Melons Gone Banana and Caribbean Sunrise, you know you're in for a treat.

—MARIANNE SEMCHUK

Places to Shop

⑪ Food Liberation
1349 Lexington Avenue (between 89th and 90th Streets)

PHONE: (212) 348–2286
DAYS/HOURS: Monday through Friday from 8:00 A.M. to 7:00 P.M.,
Saturday 10:00 A.M. to 6:00 P.M., Sunday 11:00 A.M. to 5:00 P.M.
OVERALL: Excellent

John Miklatek has been running Food Liberation for a dozen
years, having taken it over from his father, who opened it in
1976. Though the location has remained the same, John makes sure
the store is stocked with the most up-to-date vitamins, herbs, magazines, protein bars, and healing products.

Looking to pick up a few groceries on your way home from
work? Snacks, soy treats, frozen foods, soy cheeses, and a full range
of personal-care products are easily accessible. If you want to eat
right now, the mini-kitchen offers up veggie, tempeh, and sunflower
burgers with optional toppings. A refrigerated shelf contains premade sandwiches, cold drinks, and burritos, which can be warmed
for you. Have a cup of vegetarian chili or the soup du jour with your
entrée for a filling combo. And every imaginable juice is available,
with your choice of fruits, vegetables, soy milks, or protein powders.

⑫ Good Earth Natural Food
1330 First Avenue (between 71st and 72nd Streets)

PHONE: (212) 472–9055
DAYS/HOURS: Monday through Friday from 9:00 a.m. to 7:00
P.M., Saturday 9:00 A.M. to 5:30 P.M., Sunday noon to 5:30 P.M.
OVERALL: Fair

Good Earth is a very large store with a limited selection of food.
If you're looking for exotic brands or specialty products, this is
not the place to go. You can still stock your basic pantry here, starting in the organic produce section and going all the way to the sizable selection of cereals and pasta sauces. There's a deli counter
where you can buy prepackaged goodies such as Tofu Nuggets or
order fresh sandwiches, salads, and soups. Good Earth's best asset

may be its impressive selection of vitamins and homeopathic remedies, a must-see for anybody interested in natural medicine.

13 House of Health

1014 Lexington Avenue (between 72nd and 73rd Streets)

> **PHONE:** (212) 772–8422
> **DAYS/HOURS:** Monday through Friday from 8:30 A.M. to 9:30 P.M.,
> Saturday 10:00 A.M. to 9:00 P.M., Sunday 10:00 a.m. to 8:00 P.M.
> **OVERALL:** Good

House of Health looks like any old deli in Manhattan, but don't be fooled by its shabby exterior. Inside is a long, winding gro-cery store redolent with aloe shampoos and berry-scented candles. A deli-style counter offers soups, ready-to-eat sandwiches, shakes, and juices like the Hawaiian Delight, with pineapple, strawberry, and banana. The organic veggies and fresh-ground peanut butter are true delights, and many regulars stop by for their morning cuppa organic joe. The one disappointment is that the aisles are too narrow to fit a grocery cart through.

14 Likitsakos

1174 Lexington Avenue (between 80th and 81st Streets)

> **PHONE:** (212) 535–4300
> **DAYS/HOURS:** Monday through Saturday from 7:30 A.M. to 9:00
> P.M., Sunday 8:00 A.M. to 8:00 P.M.
> **OVERALL:** Excellent

Likitsakos is a one-of-a-kind gourmet store. Rows of organic pro-duce line the sidewalk and give the place an air of times gone by. The theme continues inside, where ceiling-high wood shelves are filled with everything from German pasta to soy bread. Likitsakos has its own gourmet brand that manufactures a variety of products, including freshly packed food like the exquisite Artichoke and Mush-rooms Stew. A deli counter at the back of the store sells a rich stuffed eggplant, or try the vegetable ratatouille, a grilled mix of greens brushed with olive oil and garlic. For a sweet treat, you can't beat Likitsakos's own vegan Apple Crumbs Pie. This is a store you'll have to visit again and again to discover all its hidden treasures.

15 A Matter of Health

1478 First Avenue (at 77th Street)

> **PHONE:** (212) 288–8280
>
> **DAYS/HOURS:** Monday through Friday from 9:00 a.m. to 8:30
> P.M., Saturday 10:00 A.M. to 7:30 P.M., Sunday 11:00 A.M. to
> 7:00 P.M.
>
> **OVERALL:** Excellent

A Matter of Health is a diamond in the rough. Once you make it through the claustrophobic aisles stacked to the ceiling with vitamins and herbs, you will find a full-service grocery store hidden behind. This store has every product that the biggest groceries carry, but with a healthy slant. Way in the back is a tiny "deli" counter offering take-out soups, salads, and sandwiches. Highlights include the organic vegetable soup, the hummus sandwich, and the veggie-mix juice with apple and orange. Be brave and try the vegetarian chicken, turkey, or tofu salads—or the tofu cacciatore that would impress even the most die-hard Italian.

16 Natural Frontier (see Gramercy/Union Square East/Midtown East

424 Third Avenue (between 80th and 81st Streets)

> **PHONE:** (212) 794–0922
>
> **DAYS/HOURS:** Monday through Sunday from 8:00 A.M. to
> 10:00 P.M.
>
> **OVERALL:** Very good

Places to Stay

17 Carlyle Hotel

35 East 76th Street (between Park and Madison Avenues)

> **PHONE:** (212) 744–1600
> **PRICING:** Very expensive

A legendary Manhattan hotel since 1930, the Carlyle's 180 guest rooms and suites are furnished with antiques and original Audubon prints. The preferred choice of presidents, royalty, and old money. Pets are welcome.

18 The Gracie Inn

502 East 81st Street (on York)

> **PHONE:** (212) 628–1700
> **PRICING:** Expensive

Twelve antique-filled apartments on five floors with elevator service and fresh-baked muffins and coffee every morning, compliments of the establishment. The inn is around the corner from Gracie Mansion.

19 Surrey Suites

20 East 76th Street (between Fifth and Madison Avenues)

> **PHONE:** (212) 288–3700
> **PRICING:** Expensive

Distinguished and old-world in its decor—think eighteenth-century English. One block from Central Park and mere steps to Madison Avenue shopping.

Upper West Side

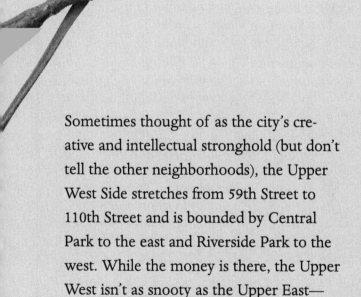

Sometimes thought of as the city's creative and intellectual stronghold (but don't tell the other neighborhoods), the Upper West Side stretches from 59th Street to 110th Street and is bounded by Central Park to the east and Riverside Park to the west. While the money is there, the Upper West isn't as snooty as the Upper East—but not for a lack of trying.

Prewar architecture (neo-Gothic and Victorian) on the boulevards coexist beautifully with the brownstones along the shady streets. On the western spur of Broadway

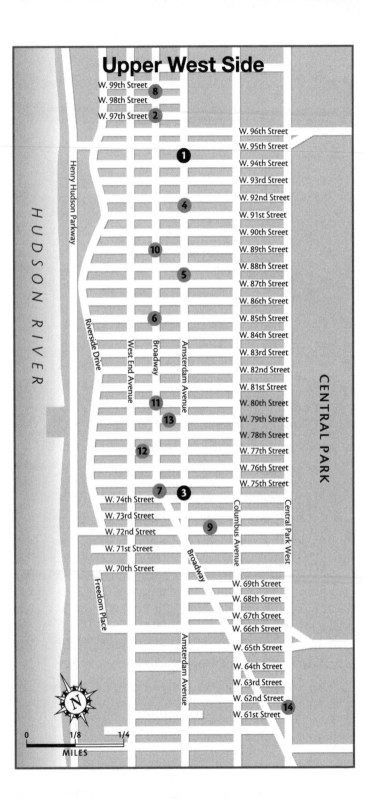

Upper West Side

W. 99th Street **8**
W. 98th Street
W. 97th Street **2**

1

HUDSON RIVER

Henry Hudson Parkway

Riverside Drive

West End Avenue

Broadway

Amsterdam Avenue

Columbus Avenue

Central Park West

Broadway

Freedom Place

Amsterdam Avenue

CENTRAL PARK

W. 96th Street
W. 95th Street
W. 94th Street
W. 93rd Street
W. 92nd Street **4**
W. 91st Street
W. 90th Street
W. 89th Street **10**
W. 88th Street **5**
W. 87th Street
W. 86th Street
W. 85th Street **6**
W. 84th Street
W. 83rd Street
W. 82nd Street
W. 81st Street
W. 80th Street **11**
W. 79th Street **13**
W. 78th Street
W. 77th Street **12**
W. 76th Street
W. 75th Street
W. 74th Street **7** **3**
W. 73rd Street
W. 72nd Street **9**
W. 71st Street
W. 70th Street
W. 69th Street
W. 68th Street
W. 67th Street
W. 66th Street
W. 65th Street
W. 64th Street
W. 63rd Street
W. 62nd Street **14**
W. 61st Street

N

0   1/8   1/4

MILES

between 61st and 66th Streets, you'll find Lincoln Center, Manhattan's cultural mecca. Ballet, theater, jazz, opera, and film (including the annual New York and New Directors festivals) all can be found here. Columbus Avenue is known for its ritzy boutiques and restaurants. Amsterdam Avenue's bars and bodegas cater to the bridge-and-tunnel crowd (the outer-borough residents and New Jerseyites who come in to party on the weekends).

Central Park West supports mammoth co-ops and their notorious boards (Madonna didn't make it into *two* of them). The Dakota is located here, where John Lennon was killed. (But pay your respects across the street, at Central Park's Strawberry Fields memorial.) And talk about great bone structure: Check out the dinosaurs at the American Museum of Natural History. Also in the area are the fantastical Tavern on the Green and, further uptown, the world's largest Gothic cathedral, the Church of St. John the Divine, and the bucolic campuses of Columbia University and Barnard College. There's swilling and noshing aplenty, with loads of New American and ethnic restaurants packed onto all the avenues. But do peek east and west: There's gold in them there side streets.

Places to Eat

❶ Ayurveda Café

716 Amsterdam Avenue (between 94th and 95th Streets)

> **PHONE:** (212) 932–2400
>
> **TYPE OF CUISINE:** Indian vegetarian
>
> **DAYS/HOURS:** Monday through Sunday from 11:30 A.M. to 11:30 P.M.
>
> **VEGEBILITY:** Excellent
>
> **RESERVATIONS:** No
>
> **WHEELCHAIR ACCESS:** Yes
>
> **KID-FRIENDLY:** Yes
>
> **TYPE OF SERVICE:** Table
>
> **PRICING:** Inexpensive
>
> **PAYMENT ACCEPTED:** All credit cards

Ayurveda is made up of two Sanskrit words: ayu (life) and veda (the knowledge of). To Hindus, life is comprised of four parts: mind, body, senses and the soul. Ayurveda Café caters to all four.

Everything about the cozy little restaurant is calming. The soft lighting, Zen chanting, traditional Indian music—even the pale colors and natural woods create the exact opposite effect of the East 6th Street places that assault the senses with psychedelic movie soundtracks, claustrophobic party lights, and foiled wallpaper. Here you'll feel as if you've been invited to share a meal at the house of an old friend, and, as if you were, there is a completely balanced menu that's already chosen for you. You eat what everyone else does.

Since 1999 the café has been serving multiregional Indian cuisine prepared fresh—and with compassion and love—on a daily basis, beginning with a prayer. Not only vegetarian, the food is surprisingly limited in the use of dairy, with no eggs at all. Regional and seasonal vegetables are used to ensure that everything is fresh and at its peak, instead of chasing after exotic demands that might suffer in quality as the seasons change. Every day there's a different menu at lunch and dinnertime; in theory, you could come daily and sample a completely different original creation—and many regulars do.

There is no alcohol served or allowed to be brought in, as it interferes with the healthy agenda and energy. Instead, I began with a very rich and creamy mango-banana lassi, which was both sweet and tart and had the consistency of a well-blended smoothie. When my lunch arrived, I was immediately met with the challenge of more food than I personally could tackle. Every flavor and texture was covered: sweet, salty, spicy, bitter, sour, thick, smooth. All the dishes were served in individual metal containers on a beautiful decorative plate. There was a potato pakora (surprisingly crisp and savory for something without eggs), spicy cauliflower with peas in a mild curry, bell peppers and potatoes in a tomato stew, masoor dal (lentils), tandoori bread, tangy raita, salad, basmati rice, and the traditional mint and plum chutneys.

Upon leaving, which one does only reluctantly, a little box by the door offers you inspirational words of wisdom, a cute take on the fortune cookie. Take one and you'll leave feeling full, physically *and* spiritually.

—BLAIR BARNETTE

2 Café Viva

2578 Broadway (at West 97th Street)

PHONE: (212) 663–VIVA (8482)
TYPE OF CUISINE: Italian kosher vegetarian
DAYS/HOURS: Sunday through Friday from 11:00 A.M. to midnight, Saturday 11:00 A.M. to 2:00 A.M.
VEGEBILITY: Excellent
RESERVATIONS: No
WHEELCHAIR ACCESS: Yes
KID-FRIENDLY: Yes
TYPE OF SERVICE: Table, take-out, and delivery
PRICING: Moderate
PAYMENT ACCEPTED: Major credit cards

Vegetarians will find bliss at Café Viva, where vegan pizza means so much more than a soggy crust with blah marinara sauce, and pasta sprints past flavorless primavera.

Owner/visionary Tony Iracani has been a vegetarian for a quarter century, and he opened Café Viva in 1992 so that he would have a place to eat. Everything at Viva is vegetarian, and much—including the creamy pasta dishes—can be made vegan. The vegan pasta Florentine—with fresh garlic, mushrooms, onions, spinach, and a soy pesto cream sauce—will satisfy any vegan's alfredo nostalgia. The

Pasta Toscana features a bounty of delicious organic vegetables: fresh plum tomatoes, mushrooms, onions, zucchini, delicious whole cloves of roasted garlic, and capers. Viva uses organic vegetables as often as possible, unbleached flour, sea salt, and filtered water, and the restaurant is certified kosher. Those who shun wheat can choose from corn, rice, spelt, and artichoke pasta.

Tofu marinated in miso may sound like a poor man's substitute for pepperoni, but it's actually a fabulous pizza topping. The Naturale is an amazing dairy-free slice that's topped with roasted eggplant, zucchini, red bell peppers, spinach, and that marinated tofu. Iracani loves to experiment with new ingredients and crusts, like those made from cornmeal and spelt. The menu at Café Viva's sibling, Viva Herbal Pizzeria (179 Second Avenue between 11th and 12th Streets) reveals his affection for hemp (an optional pizza crust ingredient) and green tea, both of which are said to possess incredible health benefits. There you will also find pizza choices like the heavenly Zen, loaded with green-tea-seasoned miso tofu, green tea basil pesto, shiitake and maitake mushrooms, caramelized onions, sun-dried tomatoes, and roasted garlic, all on a green-tea-herbed spelt crust. A true culinary iconoclast, Iracani had even been known to churn out vegan hemp and green tea ice creams, until the last of the hemp—which he imported from Canada—was confiscated.

—EMILY PARK

Satisfy Your Yen for Vegetarian Sushi

When your fish-loving friends start raving about the best sushi places in New York City, make a mental note of those names—and a point of not going to those places. We've noticed that the finest sushi restaurants, with the freshest and most exotic fish, tend to have the fewest vegetarian sushi selections. So we've sought out the sushi spots in NYC that seem to have the longest lists of vegetarian rolls. As reviewer Melena Ryzik put it: "Veggie sushi is really a study in contrasting textures: the crunch of a crisp cucumber against a creamy avocado; a smooth shiitake mushroom paired with a chewy oshinko pickle."

We agree. Beyond the standard array of veggie options at Japanese restaurants (vegetable dumplings, tofu teriyaki, seaweed salad), it's these complex combinations that we crave. So we have compiled a list of our eight favorite sushi restaurants in New York City. These restaurants have demonstrated a true understanding of combining textures and flavors for vegetarians to enjoy.

—JESSICA WURWARG

Aki

181 West 4th Street (between Sixth and Seventh Avenues)

PHONE: (212) 989–5440
DAYS/HOURS: Sunday, Tuesday through Thursday from 6:00 to 11:00 P.M., Friday and Saturday from 6:00 P.M. to midnight, closed Monday

Aki is a quaint hole-in-the-wall, with an intimate setting that's great for dates. Entrées are a bit on the expensive end, but if going just for the sushi, you've hit your mark—their vegetarian rolls are amazing! Definitely try the unique and engaging spicy vegetable roll—made inside out (rice on the outside); filled with white rice, spinach, burdock, and avocado; and served with a flavorful spicy sauce. For the spice-intimidated, there is the more typical vegetable roll with your choice of avocado, cucumber, oshinko, kanpyo, or natto. Aki has a charming atmosphere and ideal prices for rolls. They're not open for lunch, so dinners and late-night snacks only.

—CHRISTINA MASSEY

Choshi

77 Irving Place (at 19th Street)

> **PHONE:** (212) 420–1419
> **DAYS/HOURS:** Monday through Friday from noon to 10:15 P.M., Saturday and Sunday 1:00 to 10:00 P.M.

On a warm summer evening, snag an outdoor table at Choshi, located on one of the city's most pleasant blocks for street-side dining. While the sushi—particularly the creative specialty rolls—are fresh and innovative enough to please your "pescatarian" friends, you won't be left munching iceberg lettuce salads and bland cucumber rolls. The healthy tofu salad could be a light meal in itself; it's a refreshing combination of sea vegetables, asparagus, tofu, and greens with a sesame dressing. An asparagus and mayonnaise roll proved rather memorable, but the vegetable roll—with pickled vegetables, avocado, and cucumber—was fresh and refreshingly crisp, and the kampyo (sweet squash) roll had a satisfyingly chewy texture and delightfully sweet taste.

—EMILY PARK

Miyako Sushi

642 Amsterdam Avenue (near 91st Street)

> **PHONE:** (212) 724–3448
> **DAYS/HOURS:** Sunday through Thursday from noon to 11:00 P.M., Friday and Saturday noon to 11:30 P.M.

Miyako Sushi, on the Upper West Side is a wizard when it comes to concocting the distinctly complementary textures that define great vegetarian sushi. A prime example of this is the avocado peanut roll. Filled with roasted peanuts and sliced cukes and topped with slivers of rich avocado, it is crunchy-smooth perfection! More

complex is the flavorful Special Vegetable Roll, packed with shiitakes, cucumbers, oshinko, and kampyo (pickled Japanese squash) and topped with fried tofu skins. Try an appetizer of haru maki (Japanese spring roll), which has a flaky—but not greasy—fried crust surrounding sautéed cabbage, carrots, and mushrooms. And with no fish paste or bonito flakes, the miso soup at Miyako is also veggie-friendly.

—JESSICA WURWARG

Mizu Sushi
29 East 20th Street (between Broadway and Park Avenue South)

PHONE: (212) 505–6688
DAYS/HOURS: Monday through Thursday from noon to 10:45 P.M., Friday noon to 11:30 P.M., Saturday 5:00 to 11:30 P.M.
RESERVATIONS: Required for parties of six or more

This hip spot, where businesspeople and celebrities rub elbows at their trendy lunches, has some interesting vegetarian sushi options. The rice is steamed with water, but keep in mind that the rolls are cut alongside the fish with the same knives, so you take your chances asking for a quick swipe. The veggie roll, with its unique crunchy taste, is made inside out, lightly sprinkled with sesame seeds, and filled with crunchy raw asparagus, cucumber, and avocado. The rolls are served on chic rectangular glass plates, but despite the stylish decor, Mizu's sushi prices stay low. There is also a good, although much more expensive, selection of entirely vegetarian entrées.

—CHRISTINA MASSEY

Mottsu

285 Mott Street (between Houston and Prince Streets)

> **PHONE:** (212) 343–8017
> **DAYS/HOURS:** Monday through Friday from noon to 3:00 P.M. and
> from 5:00 to 11:00 P.M. (11:30 P.M. Friday), Saturday 5:00 to 11:30 P.M.

This hip Nolita (North of Little Italy) Japanese place is owned by two Italian-American cousins who know how to run a restaurant. The well-informed and very pleasant waitstaff is eager to help vegetarians and vegans understand what they can eat here. For example, watch out for the chicken broth in the teriyaki. Also, all deep-fried items on the menu are fried in the same oil as the fish. Don't worry, though—there is a great selection for vegetarians and vegans. The menu changes twice a year: In the winter everyone must try the miso eggplant, a tender baked Asian eggplant topped with a rich almost-chocolate-tasting miso sauce. (Ask for it year-round; sometimes they're willing to oblige.) Mottsu also offers a wide variety of veg sushi rolls, including two "must-tries": the vegetable futomaki (futo means "big") and the Nolita roll, filled with red pepper, garlic, and black olives. When it's warm, grab a table outdoors.

—JESSICA WURWARG

Togi

232 Seventh Avenue (between 23rd and 24th Streets)

> **PHONE:** (917) 606–1415 or –1416
> **WEB ADDRESS:** www.togirestaurant.com
> **DAYS/HOURS:** Monday through Friday from 11:00 A.M. to 11:00 P.M.,
> Saturday noon to 11:00 P.M., Sunday noon to 10:00 P.M.

At this mellow Korean/Japanese hybrid, vegetarians are presented with a lot more than avocado and cucumber options. A shiitake and spinach roll is impeccably flavored with rice vinegar and soy. The Korean influence shows through in a spicy fish-free kimchee and tofu roll, a nod to fusion that succeeds surprisingly well. The sharp and tangy bite of the kimchee is a perfect foil for the tofu, nori, and rice—causing my dining companion and me to wonder why no one had thought of it before. The yasai roll is a messy affair, but well worth it for the explosion of tastes and textures jam-packed in this roll of pickled radish, carrot, avocado, cucumber, and scallion. Often the little details make a restaurant, and at Togi one of those trifles is the complimentary Korean herbal root tea. A finale of intensely flavored, but not too sweet, green tea and red bean ice cream, beautifully served on white plates and garnished with sunflower seeds, was a thoughtful and tasty touch.

—EMILY PARK

Yuki Sushi
656 Amsterdam Avenue (at 92nd Street)

PHONE: (212) 787–8200
DAYS/HOURS: Monday through Sunday from 11:30 A.M. to 11:30 P.M.

Yuki Sushi, a wood-paneled Upper West Side favorite with orchids at each table, has delicious vegetarian options, including umeshiso (plum paste) rolls, vegetable udon noodle soup, and a miso-eggplant appetizer. The Green Dragon roll is a pleasing combination of asparagus, cucumber, and avocado. The innovative, light-as-air soybean seaweed roll, available by request, is white with mottled green veins. Unlike traditional nori, the soy seaweed isn't dense or salty; instead, it practically melts around the roll. Ask the solicitous staff for soy seaweed or any other accommodation you need—they're happy to oblige. And don't leave without indulging in some dessert; in another nod to customers' favorites, Yuki Sushi serves Ciao Bella ice cream.

—MELENA Z. RYZIK

❸ Josie's

300 Amsterdam Avenue (at West 74th Street)

PHONE: (212) 769–1212

TYPE OF CUISINE: Nondairy healthy organic

DAYS/HOURS: Monday through Wednesday from noon to 11:00 P.M., Thursday and Friday noon to midnight, Saturday 11:30 A.M. to midnight, Sunday 11:00 A.M. to midnight

VEGEBILITY: Very good

RESERVATIONS: Recommended

WHEELCHAIR ACCESS: Yes

KID-FRIENDLY: Yes

TYPE OF SERVICE: Table, counter, take-out, and delivery after 5:00 P.M.

PRICING: Moderate

PAYMENT ACCEPTED: Major credit cards

Here at the original Upper West Side outpost of the Josie's minichain, the large, airy dining room is packed with customers eager to sample some of chef Louie Lanza's dairy-free organic cuisine. The restaurant's popularity clearly demands a quick turnover of tables—just a few moments after you sit down, a server with a large basket of bread approaches. Will it be focaccia, seven-grain, or corn bread? Not that it matters, as all go great with Josie's delicious butter substitute, a curried carrot–sweet potato puree.

The harvest-colored walls are a precursor to the menu, which features an "earth friendly" vegetarian section with veggie meatloaf, portobello mushroom fajitas and a chopped salad of tofu, avocado, and chickpeas. Veggie burgers come in several different packages—Lanza is developing a protein-rich version—and pastas are available with veggie ground "beef." Also popular among vegetarians are the make-your-own stir-fry options.

Since Josie's menu features everything from veggie sushi to roasted eggplant–mushroom cakes to couscous, it's easy to find something tasty, no matter what your mood. An appetizer of steamed dumplings, filled with broccoli and Yukon gold potato and served with a tomato coulis, is more like an upscale pierogi than the standard Asian dumpling you might expect. And a spicy tofu salad with diced mangos, cucumbers, and cherry tomatoes has a chili pepper heat that's offset by the bitter greens it's presented on. Josie's doesn't use any dairy products, but you won't feel as though anything's missing.

Don't pass over the specialty drinks, like the infused watermelon lemonade or a rejuvenating iced tea (both sweetened with fruit juice instead of sugar). They'll leave you with a liquid high no milkshake can beat.

—MELENA Z. RYZIK

4 Mana

646 Amsterdam Avenue (between 91st and 92nd Streets)

PHONE: (212) 787–1110

TYPE OF CUISINE: Natural organic

DAYS/HOURS: Monday through Friday from 11:00 A.M. to 11:00 P.M., Saturday and Sunday 11:00 A.M. to 10:00 P.M.

VEGEBILITY: Excellent

RESERVATIONS: Suggested for parties of five or more

WHEELCHAIR ACCESS: Yes

KID-FRIENDLY: Very

TYPE OF SERVICE: Table

PRICING: Moderate

PAYMENT ACCEPTED: Cash only

Step foot in this unassuming neighborhood restaurant and you'll feel as if you've left Manhattan and just entered a small town. Everyone seems to know one another, people drop in just to say hi, and chef/owner Lee might even pop out of the kitchen to offer a little something extra on a spatula. Eating here is like dining at the home of that family member who makes sure you leave stuffed from her fresh and nourishing meals.

Brunch is a popular event on weekends—largely owing to delicious whole-wheat waffles, tofu scramble, and organic vegan pancakes—but the place is packed with locals at all times. Everything here is completely vegan (except the few fish dishes) and cooked with filtered water, and the produce is about 95 percent organic. The vegetables simply melt in your mouth in the vegetable soup and are perfectly firm with a slightly golden edge in the penne salad, and the ripe avocado in the sushi rolls are little bites of heaven. The (seasonal) Brussels sprout dish is amazing, and the carrot cake is not to be missed.

All the dishes are so fresh, it's as if there's a garden out back where produce is picked specifically for your meal. Prices are just right and portions so generous, you're sure to leave with one of their doggie bags that read, "Be happy."

—CHRISTINA MASSEY

❺ Quintessence (see East Village)
566 Amsterdam Avenue (between 87th and 88th Streets)

PHONE: (212) 501–9700

❻ Time Café (north) (see East Village)
2330 Broadway (at 85th Street)

PHONE: (212) 579–5100

Places to Shop

7 Fairway
2127 Broadway (at 75th Street)

> **PHONE:** (212) 595–1888
> **DAYS/HOURS:** Monday through Sunday from 6:00 A.M. to
> 1:00 A.M.
> **OTHER LOCATION:** 2328 Twelfth Avenue at 133rd Street, (212)
> 234–3883, Monday through Sunday from 8:00 A.M. to
> 11:00 P.M.
> **OVERALL:** Excellent

A mecca for all food lovers, Fairway is one store in NYC where gourmets can shop without breaking the bank. Downstairs at the flagship store on Broadway is practically a city block of every imaginable fresh fruit, vegetable, bread, cheese, and packaged good. (There's a reason people cross town or come in from the 'burbs to just to shop here.) But the second floor is a well-kept secret devoted natural goodness. An elevator leads to this haven of fresh organic produce and bulk grains and nuts, and there's even a health food bar that serves vegetarian/vegan favorites like wheat berry salad, vegan coleslaw, seaweed salad, and much, much more. There are aisles filled with veg specialties and alternative ingredients to meat, cheese, and sugar. Be sure to check out the vegan carob cupcakes.

Louie, Louie: The Non-Dairy King

ouie Lanza is late. And a few minutes after he strides into Josie's, the groundbreaking dairy-free restaurant he founded on the Upper West Side, his cell phone begins ringing. And ringing. The fast-talking, muscular Lanza, casual in a red T-shirt and jeans, is one busy guy.

Well, no wonder. As executive chef, he oversees a mini-empire of healthy restaurants, including the original Josie's (which opened in 1994), younger East Side Josie's, and its neighboring Better Burger. Plus Lanza has recently partnered with Equinox, the health club chain, to re-create Josie's at Equinox. And now he's developing his own energy bar and an organic crisp rice treat.

Lanza, just forty, did not set out to become the soy cheese king. "I learned traditional cooking—with butter and cream and cheese and all that kind of good stuff," he says. He and his partners originally operated a Cajun restaurant called Memphis. "The American Dairy Association would've given me a gold medal every year," he says with a laugh. But when a girlfriend with a thyroid problem inspired him to start cooking macrobiotic food, Lanza found he felt better without dairy.

"I started saying, wow, this is pretty wild—my whole life I thought it was good for you," he recalls. "But I realized that what we eat is not necessarily good for you just because the ADA or American cattle ranchers say it is." Though not veg, Lanza says he is now 85 percent organic and 85 to 90 percent dairy-free (save for the occasional pizza slice or scoop of ice cream).

Not coincidentally, Josie's, too, is 85 percent organic. Declaring yourself 100 percent organic is near impossible, Lanza explains. And while Josie's does serve animal products, Lanza considers it very veg-friendly. His staff is trained to be attentive to vegetarians' needs and requests. Unlike other restaurants, his don't use meat stocks in his vegetarian dishes. "I respect the vegetarian ways," he says. "That's the main thing."

Nearly a decade later, Josie's and its offshoots are at the center of a "clean food" scene—even the water used for cooking is purified. Still, Lanza insists on serving beer alongside the wheat grass. "Cooking is a gift," he says, "and I've been blessed with talents that apply to the masses." Ultimately, says the dairy-free king, "you cook for your customers."

—MELENA Z. RYZIK

8 The Health Nuts

2611 Broadway (at West 99th Street)

PHONE: (212) 678–0054
DAYS/HOURS: Monday through Friday from 9:00 A.M. to 9:00 P.M., Saturday and Sunday 11:00 A.M. to 7:00 P.M.
OTHER LOCATIONS: 835 Second Avenue (45th), (212) 490–2979, Monday through Friday from 8:00 A.M. to 8:00 P.M., Saturday 10:00 A.M. to 7:00 P.M., Sunday 11:00 A.M. to 7:00 P.M.; 2141 Broadway (75th), (212) 724–1972, Monday through Saturday from 9:00 A.M. to 9:00 P.M., Sunday 11:00 A.M. to 7:00 P.M.; 1208 Second Avenue (63rd), (212) 593-0116, Monday through Saturday from 9:00 A.M. to 9:00 P.M., Sunday 11:00 A.M. to 8:00 P.M.
OVERALL: Good

The Health Nuts can either be your everyday grocery store or your after-work pit stop. With four locations in Manhattan and one in Queens (718–593–0116), the stores range in size from a shoebox on Broadway and 75th to the superstore on Second Avenue and 63rd. Not all stores carry the same products, but all of them have towering aisles of dry foods, canned goods, snacks, drinks, health and beauty supplies, and vitamins. Some of the bigger stores have deli style counters in the back, where you can order a quarter pound of couscous, a shot of wheat grass juice, or a smoothie.

9 New Nutricerie

142 West 72nd Street (between Broadway and Columbus Avenue)

> **PHONE:** (212) 799–2454
> **DAYS/HOURS:** Monday through Saturday from 9:00 A.M. to 8:00 P.M., Sunday 11:00 A.M. to 7:00 P.M.
> **OVERALL:** Very good

Upon entering this 10-year-old Upper West Side institution, you'll instantly be intoxicated by the fresh and earthy aroma of vegetables and herbs. Unfortunately, the actual veggies are limited and not of the best quality, but at least they're all organic. The store utilizes a great economy of space—you'll easily be able to see most everything they offer at one glance. There is not much in the way of bulk (being in bins or large sizes), but it's great for the single person who is concerned about things spoiling before they can be finished.

The hot food that is served is very inexpensive and achieves a good balance of flavor—impressive considering that most dishes are made without salt, sugar, dairy, wheat, or oil. Fresh whole grains are used, rice dishes are kept warm in rice pots, and you can always count on your favorite sandwiches to be available, as they try to keep a consistent menu throughout the year. Although the salads and sandwiches are prewrapped, they are made fresh throughout the day, and you can ask to have one customized for you on the spot. There are a few seats available, which are used regularly by the neighborhood throng who visit for lunch on a daily basis.

10 Uptown Whole Foods

2421 Broadway (at 89th Street)

> **PHONE:** (212) 874–4000
> **DAYS/HOURS:** Monday through Saturday from 8:00 A.M. to 11:00 P.M.
> **OVERALL:** Excellent

This uptown establishment is a gem. Not only is it large and impeccably clean, with wide aisles and spotless displays, but the staff is remarkably helpful. This is the health superstore for all your needs: food, supplements, pet care, cleaning, and beauty. There are organic vegetables at startlingly low prices for a market of this caliber. What really catches one's eye, however, is the never-ending font of bulk items, from grains to dried fruit to carob rice cakes. There is also a terrific selection of local and prepackaged breads of all kinds (very fresh and delicious) and rennet-free cheeses, in addition to an enormous tea selection. A juice bar offers refreshing combinations, but the coup de grâce is the bounty of prepared kosher hot meals and salads that are mostly organic and delightfully flavorful.

Zabar's

2245 Broadway (at 80th Street)

> **PHONE:** (212) 787–2000
> **WEB ADDRESS:** www.zabars.com
> **DAYS/HOURS:** Monday through Friday from 8:00 A.M. to 7:30 P.M., Saturday 8:00 A.M. to 8:00 P.M., Sunday 9:00 A.M. to 6:00 P.M.
> **OVERALL:** Excellent

Be prepared to play bumper carts inside this market behemoth that began as a small counter in a local supermarket. Here you'll find Upper West Siders scouring the cluttered aisles for everything from Swiss quark to chipotle salsa to fresh challah bread—and all at competitive prices. Ready-made soups and salads are also on hand for a healthy but effortless meal. After admiring an eclectic produce section filled with delights like Israeli cucumbers and bright red and yellow Holland peppers, head upstairs to check out their extraordinary (and well-priced) selection of cookware or dart next door to Zabar's smoothie bar, where fruit concoctions like Apple Crisp and Orange Creamsicle await. This is a New York institution: One visit and you'll know why Brooklynites make pilgrammages to shop here.

Delivered to Your Doorstep

et's play the "if I won the lottery" game. You want a Jaguar and personal driver; Sam over there wants season tickets on the 50-yard line. But me, I can't imagine anything more luxurious than having amazing veg food specially prepared and delivered to my door. You don't have to win Powerball, though, for that to happen. Just set aside a mere $150 per week, pick up the phone, and wait for the miracle to arrive.

Busy professionals seeking healthy, flavorful vegetarian food at reasonable prices know where to turn in New York City. They call Lagusta's Luscious, an affordable alternative to eating out or hiring a private chef. Customers select from two different plans ($150 includes food and delivery in Manhattan; add another $25 for delivery to the outer boroughs). One plan offers three meals, each with one side dish, and the other provides two entrées, each with one side dish and either soup or dessert. Both provide enough food for three or four meals for two people or six or seven meals for a solo diner.

New clients fill out a food preference survey, and meals can be customized to accommodate individual tastes and dietary concerns. For those with more demanding restrictions, Lagusta is happy to work out alternative personalized plans.

Proprietress/chef Lagusta Yearwood, a graduate of the Natural Gourmet Cookery School, is a longtime vegan, and all her meals are vegan, organic, and seasonal (she does much of her shopping at Greenmarket). She eats the meals herself and calls them her "health insurance." Here's a sample to whet your appetite: coconut curried tempeh with sautéed market greens, wide rice noodles, Southern-style collard greens with sweet potatoes, biscuits, black-eyed peas, and a chocolate-coconut cake with chocolate fudge frosting (or maybe a rustic cranberry-apple galette). Lagusta also offers cooking classes and is willing to barter her services.

For more information, check out her Web site (but not on an empty stomach), www.lagustasluscious.com, or contact Lagusta at lagusta@lagustasluscious.com or (201) 530–0986.

—EMILY PARK

Places to Stay

12 Country Inn the City

270 West 77th Street (between West End and Amsterdam Avenues)

> **PHONE:** (212) 580–4183
> **PRICING:** Moderate

Landmark limestone townhouse with four individually decorated apartments. Luxury bed-and-breakfast accommodations at an affordable price and a great alternative to a hotel.

13 Lucerne Hotel

201 West 79th Street (at Amsterdam Avenue)

> **PHONE:** (212) 875–1000
> **PRICING:** Expensive

The 2003 *New York Times Travel Guide* named this luxury hotel No. 1 for service and value in its category. Need we say more? The Metropolitan Museum of Art and the Guggenheim are only a mile away.

14 Mayflower Hotel on the Park

15 Central Park West (between 61st and 62nd Streets)

> **PHONE:** (212) 265–0060
> **PRICING:** Expensive

First-class, traditional eighteen-story hotel with unparalleled views of Central Park—and they're pet-friendly, too! Two blocks from Lincoln Center.

Harlem

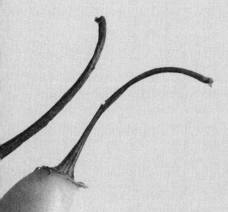

The epicenter of African-American culture is alive and well and thriving in Harlem. After decades in desolation and near poverty, the neighborhood is on its way back to its former glory. This district gained fame in the early part of the twentieth century as the birthplace of the Harlem Renaissance, the golden era when African-American artists, writers, and musicians earned world recognition for their talents. Gentrification has given a shot of vitality to this northernmost

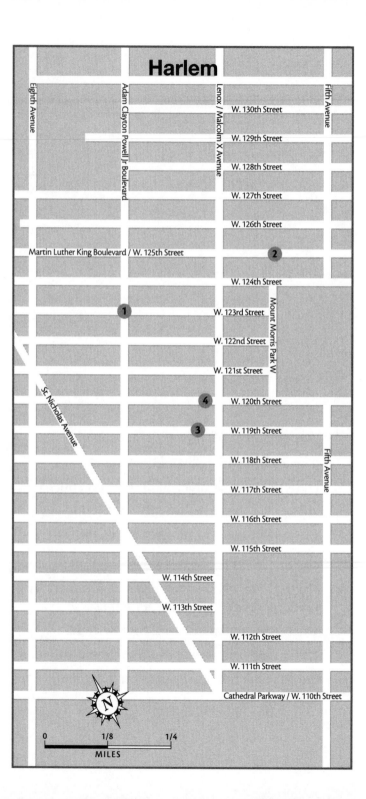

NYC neighborhood, with young families and mega chain stores making it safe to visit and explore.

The main drag here is 125th Street, home to the famed Apollo Theater, a rite of passage for emerging musicians and singers. Wednesday is Amateur Night, and you never know when you might catch the next Billie Holiday or Jackson Five (both got their starts here). Keep your eye out for Harlem Week/Harlem Jazz & Music Festival held every summer; the Malcolm Shabazz Harlem Market, an open-air market on 116th Street; and the Green Flea, a Saturday market on West 135th Street at Lenox Avenue. And if you're in the mood to sing your heart out, be sure to stop by the Abyssinian Baptist, Canaan Baptist, or Salem United Baptist churches for ear-bursting and soul-lifting gospel singing. Religion is also the force behind many of the burgeoning healthy restaurants in Harlem.

Places to Eat

① Strictly Roots

2058 Adam Clayton Powell Jr. Boulevard (at 123rd Street)

PHONE: (212) 864–8699

TYPE OF CUISINE: Organic global vegan

DAYS/HOURS: Monday through Saturday from 11:00 A.M. to 10:00 P.M., Sunday noon to 7:00 P.M.

VEGEBILITY: Excellent

RESERVATIONS: No

WHEELCHAIR ACCESS: Yes

KID-FRIENDLY: Yes

TYPE OF SERVICE: Cafeteria

PRICING: Inexpensive

PAYMENT ACCEPTED: Major credit cards

The motto at this homey uptown cafeteria is "We serve nothing that crawls, walks, swims, or flies." Their strict principle of veganism is pared down into the simplest of rules, bypassing all other agendas to pay homage to the lovable little creatures themselves. This matter-of-fact way of thinking is seen throughout Strictly Roots. The decor is similarly sparse and unassuming. In fact, the main "decoration" is a huge bulletin board reserved for community notices, humanitarian political agendas, and helpful vegetarian information, including a lengthy list of witty responses to a meat lover's barrage of excuses. A chessboard awaits a friendly game, and the sun-drenched storefront affords ample viewing of interesting passer-by activity. Don't arrive expecting a fancy meal in an elegant setting, but do come if you're in the mood for a no-frills café whose mission is serving reasonably priced vegetarian food that's fresh and delicious.

A quick glance at the all-organic menu reveals a broad range of global cuisine. From lightly seasoned to moderately spicy, there's something to appeal to all taste buds and diets. You can arrange your lunch or dinner as a smattering of tapas or select a few staples to create your own dinner plate. Particularly appealing are the baked veggie chicken, possessed of a marvelous firm texture and smoky flavor, and the tofu tempura, which was dipped into seasoned batter and fried to a crispy golden brown. Another specialty is the tart and tangy orange-ginger bread. There's also a good selection of dairy-free pastries and fresh juices.

The ample dining area is filled with neighborhood friends, weary businesspeople and others who value a healthy meal at the price of fast food. The employees are lifetime vegetarians who are both friendly and knowledgeable about different cultures and how alternative eating habits fit right into them. You'll feel right at home.

—BLAIR BARNETTE

2 Uptown Juice Bar
54 West 125th Street (between Fifth and Lenox Avenues)

PHONE: (212) 987–2660
TYPE OF CUISINE: Caribbean/American
DAYS/HOURS: Monday through Sunday from 7:00 A.M. to 10:00 P.M.
VEGEBILITY: Excellent
RESERVATIONS: No
WHEELCHAIR ACCESS: Yes
KID-FRIENDLY: Yes
TYPE OF SERVICE: Cafeteria
PRICING: Inexpensive
PAYMENT ACCEPTED: MC/V

Walking across 125th Street, one might expect to be bombarded by fast-food joints, fried chicken stands, and soul-food restaurants. So the nondescript healthy haven nestled in with all the bustle near Lenox Avenue comes as quite a pleasant surprise. Uptown Juice Bar's exterior may have all the charm of a Gray's Papaya, but the inside expands into a delicious little retreat that's far from ordinary.

The first thing you encounter is a juice bar in front of floor-to-ceiling columns of signs listing all the options. Scan the signs for whatever ails you and discover its juicy cure. I self-prescribed a carrot sea moss, which covered all sorts of malaise. It was frothy and light, with a hint of nutmeg adding a delightful zing. The ingredients are all hand-selected and when combined create marvelous refreshing drinks.

Off to the right is the food counter, where you can order your meal, prepared à la minute or from the numerous chafing dishes. Offerings include homemade organic vegan items like Cajun tofu, Italian stew, BBQ soy chunks, and curried "duck." If you come early, you can start your day with a tofu omelette, a favorite with the locals. Uptown Juice Bar uses not only seasonal organic produce but also fresh unbleached organic flour (delivered in small batches to ensure its freshness), organic soy, and unprocessed sea salt. At the counter you'll find a wide variety of nondairy pastries, the superstars being a pineapple slice tart and a dreamy tofu cheesecake.

After ordering then picking up your meal, head to the back, where the dining room opens up into a sunny little room. Changing exhibitions of work by neighborhood artists are displayed, and the proprietor is likely to be found ready to strike up a conversation about healthy living and soul-enriching music.

—BLAIR BARNETTE

Places to Stay

3 Crystal's Castle Bed & Breakfast

119 West 119th Street (between Adam Clayton Powell Jr. Boulevard and Lenox Avenue)

> **PHONE:** (212) 722–3637
> **WEB ADDRESS:** www.crystal-scastlebandb.com
> **PRICING:** Inexpensive

Owned and operated by a family of professional musicians. There are pets in residence, and in some cases guests may bring their own. Continental breakfast is served.

4 An Uptown Guest House

102 West 120th Street (between Adam Clayton Powell Jr. Boulevard and Lenox Avenue)

> **PHONE:** (212) 666–3650
> **PRICING:** Inexpensive

1890s town house with two one-bedroom apartments. Rooms include kitchens and sleep up to five guests.

Brooklyn

The 2.3 million souls crammed inside its borders make Brooklyn New York City's most populous borough. As with the rest of the city, it was the Dutch who originally settled the area in the 1600s (Brooklyn is Dutch for "broken land"). By 1860 Brooklyn was the third-largest city in the United States—until 1898 it was its own city, complete with its own city hall. The completion of the Brooklyn Bridge in 1883 helped to change Brooklyn's status from suburb to part of the city; until then ferries had shuttled people across the East River from home to work and back again. From the mid-1800s until the end of World War II, immigrants from the world over built their homes in different neighborhoods in Brooklyn and toiled in the manufacturing and shipping industries. After the war it became the trend for upwardly mobile folks to quit the cities for the 'burbs, and many neighborhoods in Brooklyn were left with people who couldn't afford to leave. In the late 1970s the affluent began to return to the cities, and with them came the gentrification of

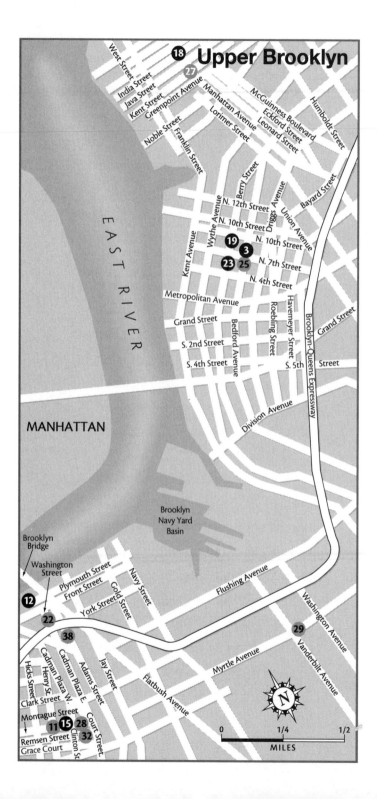

18 **Upper Brooklyn**

EAST RIVER

West Street
India Street
Java Street
Kent Street
Greenpoint Avenue
Noble Street
Franklin Street
Manhattan Avenue
Lorimer Street
McGuinness Boulevard
Eckford Street
Leonard Street
Humboldt Street
Bayard Street

Wythe Avenue
Berry Street
N. 12th Street
N. 10th Street
Driggs Avenue
Union Avenue
Kent Avenue

N. 10th Street
N. 7th Street
N. 4th Street

Metropolitan Avenue
Grand Street
S. 2nd Street
S. 4th Street
Bedford Avenue
Havemeyer Street
Roebling Street
S. 5th Street
Grand Street
Brooklyn-Queens Expressway

MANHATTAN

Division Avenue

Brooklyn Navy Yard Basin

Brooklyn Bridge

Washington Street

Plymouth Street
Front Street
Navy Street
Flushing Avenue
Washington Avenue
York Street
Gold Street

Vanderbilt Avenue

Myrtle Avenue

Jay Street
Flatbush Avenue

Cadman Plaza W.
Henry St.
Cadman Plaza E.
Adams Street
Court Street

Hicks Street
Clark Street
Montague Street
Remsen Street
Grace Court
Clinton St.

N

0   1/4   1/2
MILES

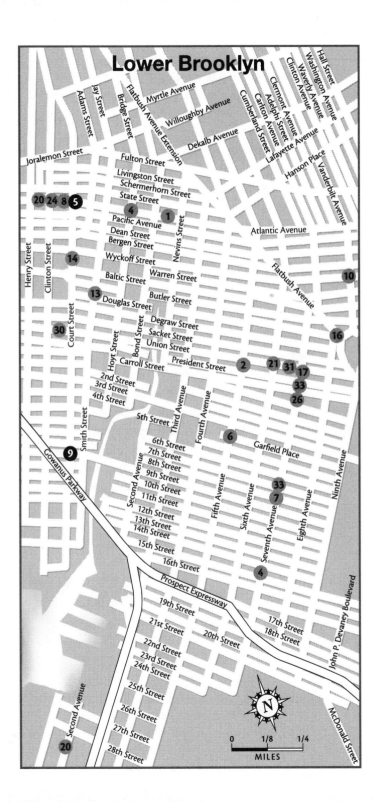

Lower Brooklyn

many ethnic neighborhoods. As real estate prices in Manhattan became more and more obscene, people bridged and tunneled their way to Brooklyn, where they found (in the early 1980s at least) more space for less money.

Boerum Hill, Brooklyn Heights, Carroll Gardens, Clinton Hill, Cobble Hill, DUMBO, Fort Greene, Greenpoint, Park Slope, Prospect Heights, and Williamsburg are some of the more upscale and trendy Brooklyn neighborhoods (most have been gentrified over the past twenty years). They are all fairly easy to access via public transportation and have lots of fun new restaurants popping up all the time. Montague Street in Brooklyn Heights, Smith Street in Carroll Gardens/Cobble Hill, and Fifth and Seventh Avenues in Park Slope are some restaurant-lined streets and are great hubs if you find yourself in the area with a rumbling stomach. Since the early 1980s the universe of well-known restaurants in Brooklyn has skyrocketed from a number you could count on both hands to well over a hundred.

Thanks to the ethnic influences of Jews, Poles, Italians, Middle Easterners, Africans, Russians, and people from all over Asia (and pretty much any other country you can think of), the food in Brooklyn is an impressive global smorgasbord. From smoky hummus in Boerum Hill to vegetarian kosher Chinese food in the Heights to po-mo diners in Williamsburg and Cobble Hill, Brooklyn's cuisine offers an enticing mix of tradition and innovation.

Places to Eat

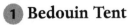 **Bedouin Tent**

405 Atlantic Avenue (between Bond and Nevins Streets, Brooklyn Heights/Cobble Hill border)

> **PHONE:** (718) 852–5555
> **TYPE OF CUISINE:** Middle Eastern
> **DAYS/HOURS:** Monday through Sunday from 11:00 A.M. to 11:00 P.M.
> **VEGEBILITY:** Very good
> **RESERVATIONS:** Not necessary
> **WHEELCHAIR ACCESS:** Yes (tight squeeze for a wheelchair, though)
> **KID-FRIENDLY:** Yes
> **TYPE OF SERVICE:** Table
> **PRICING:** Moderate
> **PAYMENT ACCEPTED:** Cash only

Located on a hodgepodge stretch of Atlantic Avenue that is teeming with antiques stores, trendy boutiques, and Middle Eastern merchants, Bedouin Tent (formerly Moustache) is a no-frills eatery specializing in pitza: individual-size pizzas made on freshly baked white flour pita bread.

When we say no-frills, we mean absolutely no frills—tables and chairs are plastic patio furniture, and beer and wine are BYOB—but Jordanian owner Walid Demis has livened up the decor by lining the ceiling of the dining area with colorful rugs, and festive Middle Eastern music on the sound system infuses the space with exotic flair. The back garden is a tranquil escape in the warmer months, but the best seats in the house are the three tables up front, where you can watch the freshly made pitas get rolled, topped, then magically transformed into light, crisp balloons by the 600-degree oven.

The majority of the menu selections are veg-friendly (vegans need only avoid the cheese-topped ones). Salads and dips, including the creamy hummus and smoky baba ghanoush, are wonderful to nosh on and easy to share. Don't miss the spinach and chickpea salad or the lentil and bulgur salad, both of which have a cooked-to-perfection al dente texture and lemony, sun-drenched tang. The pitzas themselves are pretty straightforward, but the Green Pitza (seasoned with fenugreek, the pungent ochre-colored spice used in curry powder) is a flavorful standout. And it's easy to add oomph to veggie pitzas by augmenting toppings with spinach, onion or garlic, and parsley.

To end, try a slice of baklava or basbousa, a honey-sweetened traditional cake with a crunchy texture, and a steaming mug of complimentary mint tea to put a sweet taste in your mouth before you slip away.

—MARY MARGARET CHAPPELL

2 Beso

210 Fifth Avenue (between Union and President Streets, Park Slope)

PHONE: (718) 783–4902

TYPE OF CUISINE: Nuevo Latino American

DAYS/HOURS: Monday through Friday from 10:00 a.m. to 3:00 P.M. and from 5:00 to 10:00 P.M., Saturday and Sunday 10:00 A.M. to 3:30 P.M.

VEGEBILITY: Good

RESERVATIONS: Recommended for dinner

WHEELCHAIR ACCESS: Yes

KID-FRIENDLY: Yes

TYPE OF SERVICE: Table

PRICING: Moderate

PAYMENT ACCEPTED: Major credit cards

Park Slope cognoscenti flock to this brightly colored, garage-size restaurant, which actually sports a garage door (opened in warm weather to give the illusion of outdoor seating). While Beso does have a few vegetarian options for dinner (and does serve beer and wine), weekend brunch is the real draw here. The chef's Nuevo Latino accents extend to even the most prosaic of breakfast foods, and the friendly (if overextended) staff and cheerful surroundings make for a great way to start a Saturday or Sunday.

It costs a little extra (only juice and regular coffee come with brunch), but splurge on a large café con leché, properly served in a bowl. Vegan options include the hot oatmeal served with quinoa and tropical fruit salad (request it with soy milk instead of condensed milk). Also available are the root vegetable fries, a crisp array of yucca, potato, and carrot fries spiced with cinnamon and chili pepper and served with homemade spicy ketchup. The fries come as a side with some of the entrées, but if they don't, be sure to order a plateful.

The unique made-to-order omelettes, coconut arroz con leche pancakes, pan dulce French toast, and cheese quesadillas with two kinds of queso are all evidence of the chef's Latin flair. Pay special attention to the empanadas: These flaky stuffed pastries are available with all sorts of veggie fillings. You have only to ask.

If you're not too stuffed from all that, end with a bowl of hot chocolate or some rich chocolate crema catalan, both of which are served with a sweet churro for dipping. Olé!

—MELENA Z. RYZIK

❸ Bliss

191 Bedford Avenue (between North 6th and North 7th Streets, Williamsburg)

> **PHONE:** (718) 599–2547
> **TYPE OF CUISINE:** Mostly organic vegan
> **DAYS/HOURS:** Monday through Friday from 9:00 A.M. to 11:00 P.M., Saturday and Sunday 10:00 A.M. to midnight
> **VEGEBILITY:** Excellent
> **RESERVATIONS:** Not necessary
> **WHEELCHAIR ACCESS:** No
> **KID-FRIENDLY:** Yes
> **TYPE OF SERVICE:** Table and take-out
> **PRICING:** Moderate
> **PAYMENT ACCEPTED:** Cash only

If the prospect of hydra-pressed juice, unprocessed foods, and desserts without refined sugar makes you salivate, get yourself to this cozy little Williamsburg café—pronto. At Bliss the kitchen uses almost exclusively organic ingredients, and the keyword is fresh; they even make their own vegan sour cream and seitan. In fact, nearly everything here is vegan, unless you want some real cheese (or eggs, available only during weekend brunch). The space is small but airy, with huge front windows and beautiful exposed brick walls, and the staff is friendly and helpful.

One caveat: Before you share this clean, simple food with people unaccustomed to such healthy eating, you may wish to salt liberally and go a little heavy on whatever sauce accompanies your dish (like the tasty miso-tahini or carrot-orange dressing). The signature Bliss Bowl, for example—a heaping helping of unseasoned steamed vegetables with beans on brown rice—may be just a tad too healthy-tasting for nonpurists. The thick and hearty three-bean chili is excellent with a few dashes of salt, and the truly amazing vegan sour cream (made from tofu) livens up the portobello burrito.

Don't forget about those hydra-pressed juices. Whether extra oxygen actually makes the juice better for you I cannot confirm, but it sure tastes good. Choose your own juice combination, or pick one of theirs. But if you like your beverages sweet, you'll want to add some honey. (If you like your beverages alcoholic, bring your own.)

Where the entrées and appetizers lack flavor, the desserts make up for it. Bliss serves some of the best vegan desserts around. Try the carrot cake and the apple crisp—unless you're a Twinkies junkie, you won't miss the refined sugar.

—JULIE HOLLAR

④ Brawta Cafe

347 Atlantic Avenue (at Hoyt Street, Boerum Hill)

PHONE: (718) 855-5515
OTHER LOCATIONS: 447 Seventh Avenue, (718) 788–4680
TYPE OF CUISINE: Jamaican
DAYS/HOURS: Atlantic Avenue: Monday through Thursday from noon to 11:00 P.M., Friday and Saturday noon to 11:30 P.M., Sunday noon to 10:30 P.M. Seventh Avenue: Monday through Sunday noon to 10:00 P.M.
VEGEBILITY: Fair
RESERVATIONS: Not necessary
WHEELCHAIR ACCESS: Yes
KID-FRIENDLY: Yes
TYPE OF SERVICE: Table, take-out, and bar
PRICING: Moderate
PAYMENT ACCEPTED: Major credit cards

This little Jamaican café is a tribute to spicy island home-cooking. Although it is not vegetarian, there are treats in store for all. The open kitchen exposes the authenticity of method and vibe, and a hip, youngish mix of Manhattan and Brooklyn diners make the scene a fun place to be. Vibrant Caribbean art and reggae music set the tone and pace for casual, unrushed dining.

Delicious juices are made from scratch, using fresh ginger, mint, sorrel, pineapple, lemon, and tamarind. Brawta's vegetarian ital stew is a mild, slow-cooked wonder with sweet potatoes, plantains, broad beans, carrots, and greens. It is delicious accompanied by the slightly sticky, spicy, and vinegary cabbage.

The vegetable roti—veggies like plantains, lima beans, celery, bok choy, and broccoli cooked in a base of coconut milk and wrapped in a whole-wheat flour pancake—make a rich and delectable lunch. For something sweet, try the traditional rum cake, a moist and dense infusion of island flavors. Equally luscious and delicious alternatives include sweet-potato pudding, carrot cake, and bread pudding.

If you happen to have grown up in the tropics, Brawta will taste like coming home. (Just remember to bring your own booze.)
—LARA OLCHANETZKY

5 Caravan

93 Atlantic Avenue (between Court and Clinton Streets, Brooklyn Heights)

PHONE: (718) 488–7111

TYPE OF CUISINE: North African/Middle Eastern

DAYS/HOURS: Monday through Thursday from 11:00 A.M. to 10:00 P.M., Friday 11:00 A.M. to 11:00 P.M., Saturday 11:30 A.M. to midnight, Sunday 11:30 A.M. to 10:30 P.M.

VEGEBILITY: Very good

RESERVATIONS: Not necessary, except Friday and Saturday nights

WHEELCHAIR ACCESS: Yes

KID-FRIENDLY: Yes

TYPE OF SERVICE: Table and take out

PRICING: Moderate

PAYMENT ACCEPTED: Major credit cards

Stop by Caravan sometime after 8:00 on a Saturday night and you'll find a crowd of convivial diners eating and enjoying the belly-dancing show. Any other time of the week, this French-Moroccan restaurant—outfitted with ornate mirrors on the walls and white cloths and napkins on the tables—feels positively demure on busy Atlantic Avenue. But don't let the crowd—or the quiet—keep you away.

Whatever else you order from the appetizer menu, be sure to try the mohamarah, a roasted red pepper and walnut dip sweetened with pomegranate juice that has a subtle, complex flavor that five-star chefs in the city would die to achieve. Hummus and baba ghanoush are tried-and-true dips that are smooth and citrusy with a nice garlic bite. Caravan's harira—a tomato-based vegetable soup made with lentils, celery, cilantro, chickpeas, and spices and traditionally served to break the daily fast during Ramadan—is a wonderful way to warm up when it's cold out yet filling enough for a light meal when it's warm.

For the ultimate in authentic North African flavor, try a vegetarian tagine—a seasoned, roasted vegetable dish with lemon and olives or onions, raisins, and prunes that is named for the cone-shaped clay dish it is cooked and served in. The vegetarian couscous are satisfying, but served Western-style on a plate with the couscous's on the side, the dish somehow lacks the spectacular quality of the rest of the food at Caravan.

—MARY MARGARET CHAPPELL

6 Cucina

256 Fifth Avenue (between Carroll Street and Garfield Place, Park Slope)

PHONE: (718) 230–0711

WEB ADDRESS: www.cucinarestaurant.com

TYPE OF CUISINE: Italian

DAYS/HOURS: Tuesday through Thursday from 5:30 to 10:00 P.M., Friday through Sunday 5:30 to 11:00 P.M.

VEGEBILITY: Good

RESERVATIONS: Recommended

WHEELCHAIR ACCESS: Yes

KID-FRIENDLY: Yes

TYPE OF SERVICE: Table and catering

PRICING: Moderate to expensive

PAYMENT ACCEPTED: Major credit cards

You might expect the interior of Cucina, a neighborhood favorite since the early 1990s, to feel homey and frozen in time, like a beloved Italian grandmother's kitchen. Instead, the ochre- and brick-colored walls, creamy leather banquettes, and Ikea-esque chairs give it a more contemporary feel, as if someone moved Grandma to a luxury high-rise apartment. Likewise, the food is a combination of classics (caprese salad, penne pomodoro) and more inventive fare that new chef Michael Fiore is still in the process of, well, inventing.

The best, and best value, starter is the Antipasti della Cucina, a generous combination plate of roasted vegetables, marsala mushrooms, mozzarella knots, and luscious fried ricotta balls. The veggies have a pleasant charcoal smokiness—as does another appetizer, the grilled portobello with goat cheese—but the standouts here are the cheeses. The thumb-size knots are chewy and mild, while the ricotta balls are the perfect combination of creamy cheese and crispy coating. (Like fried ice cream, it makes you wonder, How do they do it?)

If you haven't filled up on antipasti and Cucina's hearty bread—the onion focaccia with red pepper butter is particularly good—move on to the pasta section, which was still evolving at press time. While staples like pan-fried homemade gnocchi with peas and porcini mushrooms remain, Fiore plans to add new entrées, such as a delectable-sounding squash tortellini with sage butter. Vegans may need to make a meal out of sides or the Antipasti della Cucina (the penne pomodoro entree is also safe), but the kitchen is willing to work with you. One suggestion: Specify that dishes be cooked in olive oil instead of butter.

If, after all that, you still have room for dessert, try the torta ricotta, a real treat: mellow ricotta surrounded by walls of semi-sweet homemade dough and topped by a cluster of bright berries. If you're with a group, splurge on the chocolate truffle cake, a concoction so rich it takes at least four people to finish it off. Otherwise, prepare to bring some of this *cucina* back to yours.

—MELENA Z. RYZIK

Fava

336 Seventh Avenue (at 9th Street, Park Slope)

> **PHONE:** (718) 788–2756 or (718) 788–2758
> **TYPE OF CUISINE:** Mediterranean
> **DAYS/HOURS:** Monday through Sunday from 11:00 A.M. to 11:00 P.M.
> **VEGEBILITY:** Very good
> **RESERVATIONS:** Not necessary
> **WHEELCHAIR ACCESS:** One step at patio entrance; steps to rest room
> **KID-FRIENDLY:** Yes
> **TYPE OF SERVICE:** Counter, take-out, and delivery
> **PRICING:** Moderate
> **PAYMENT ACCEPTED:** Major credit cards

Fava is an indecisive diner's paradise. This eight-year-old neighborhood café offers everything from Indian and Mediterranean food to fresh-cooked pasta and vegan pizza. The peach-colored interior is dominated by a long mosaicked counter, where you choose your cuisine. At the far end is a brick oven churning out made-to-order pizzas.

After you order, grab one of the half-dozen tables inside or, in warmer months, head for the patio. Wherever you sit, don't skip the curried chickpeas, Fava's most popular dish, according to owner Ula Kesy. Pile them over bulgur, couscous, or a salty rice pilaf, or top them with bruschetta (a pico-de-gallo-like salad) or a creamy yogurt sauce. Also worth sampling are the falafels, which come in several flavors. The peanut falafel is pleasantly nutty, and the jalapeño version is surprisingly mild, with the flavor of the pepper coming through more than the heat.

The bulk of the menu is platters and sandwiches (there is meat served, but it's easily avoided). The curry platters, all of which can be made vegetarian or vegan, include rice, nan, and a small salad. Options include vindaloo (a spicy tomato sauce), makhani (a yogurt-based curry), and channa (a chickpea curry). In addition to the chickpeas, lentils and fava beans (of course), there are seven vegetable dishes for sandwiches and platters. Standouts include crisp broccoli, slightly spicy strips of cooked beets, and a vinegary three-bean salad. Sandwiches, served wrap-style in flat nan bread, are large and sloppily delightful. Choose from a simple and garlicky baba ghanoush, or go for the more elaborate eggplant combo,

which comes with spinach, rice, lettuce, bruschetta, and hot sauce. One unusual caveat for vegans: The spicy harissa sauce served on some sandwiches is dairy-based.

But if your heart's set on pizza, you'll find no less than twenty-eight varieties, all of which can be made with soy cheese upon request. (Watch for even more soy options in the future.) Beer and wine are available.

—MELENA Z. RYZIK

8 Fountain Café

183 Atlantic Avenue (between Court and Clinton Streets, Brooklyn Heights / Cobble Hill border)

PHONE: (718) 624–6764
TYPE OF CUISINE: Syrian
DAYS/HOURS: Monday through Sunday from 10:30 A.M. to 10:30 P.M.
VEGEBILITY: Very good
RESERVATIONS: Not necessary
WHEELCHAIR ACCESS: Yes
KID-FRIENDLY: Yes
TYPE OF SERVICE: Table and take-out
PRICING: Moderate
PAYMENT ACCEPTED: Cash only

Exotic smells and a warm welcome greet you the moment you walk through the doors of this simply decorated Syrian eatery. On a stretch of Atlantic Avenue that is peppered with Middle Eastern restaurants and specialty stores, Fountain Café is a friendly, flavorful standout featuring the best falafel on the block.

The Combination Veggie Platter is a fun, filling way to sample several of the vegetarian dishes on the menu, including creamy hummus, smoky baba ghanoush, tabouli, mint-laced stuffed grape leaves, and fried cauliflower. All platters are served with fresh white pitas (from the Damascus bakery down the street), which get crisped on the grill before being served. For a taste of the Middle East that you can savor as you stroll, try a vegetarian sandwich or wrap, served with french fries and salad.

If you're eating in, end your experience on a sweetly exotic note with baklava, knaffa (shredded wheat stuffed with Syrian cheese), a slice of semolina cake moistened with rosewater syrup, or the dairy-free apricot pudding, all of which are made in-house.

—MARY MARGARET CHAPPELL

❾ Goga

521 Court Street (between Huntington and West 9th Streets, Carroll Gardens

PHONE: (718) 260–8618

WEB ADDRESS: www.gogacafe.com

TYPE OF CUISINE: Mostly global vegan

DAYS/HOURS: Tuesday through Friday from 11:00 A.M. to 10:00 P.M., Saturday 11:00 A.M. to midnight, Sunday 11:00 A.M. to 9:00 P.M.

VEGEBILITY: Excellent

RESERVATIONS: Not necessary

WHEELCHAIR ACCESS: Yes

KID-FRIENDLY: Yes

TYPE OF SERVICE: Table, take-out, and delivery

PRICING: Moderate

PAYMENT ACCEPTED: Cash only

You take the F train to Smith and 9th Street in Brooklyn, but at Goga it feels more like Berkeley, California—in the '70s. This way cool Carroll Gardens café / lounge serves up live entertainment with its vegetarian cuisine and is a showcase for up-and-coming artists. The interior is a funky sanctuary of deep red walls, plush maroon couches with fluffy throw pillows, and colorful, changing wall art by emerging local artists.

The menu here is largely vegan, with a few dairy-based choices. The food is a hearty mix of tempeh and tofu plates, hummus, salads, veggie burgers, sandwiches, rice and beans, burritos, quesadillas, and soups. One of the most popular appetizers is the polenta, tasty wedges flavored with vegan pesto and sun-dried tomatoes that lend just the right kick. As an entrée, the barbequed tempeh is a winner, smothered in a homemade tomato-based sauce with a jolt of heat. This dish comes with mashed red potatoes and mixed greens. The taters are garlicky and chockful of chunks and skin. The greens are a hearty mix of organic spinach, kale, and broccoli and can easily feed two.

The best-selling dessert is the rice crispy dish, a sticky mix of crispies, berries, and carob that manages to satisfy the sweet tooth while still being healthy. There is also a variety of vegan cakes to choose from, in addition to beer and wine, juice blends, and an assortment of coffees and organic teas. Goga's goal is to not merely feed, but to also entertain. Every Saturday is live reggae night; Wednesdays feature DJ Durga, who spins world beats; the last Friday of the month is an event called Goga Soundsystem, featuring ritual grooves from a variety of DJs; and the last Wednesday of the month is reserved for Dawtaz, an all-female musical, poetry, and live performance review.

There is also a weekly Sunday brunch, complete with live jazz, blues, and Latin tunes—and a sizable menu. Go for the Goga Slam, a plate laden with three organic silver-dollar pancakes, scrambled tofu, home fries, and tempeh bacon. You can also have organic egg omelettes or fresh fruit salads that can be topped with either dairy or soy yogurt. Bagels get smeared with either dairy or tofu cream cheese.

So follow in the footsteps of the artsy clientele—and keep your third eye peeled for prominent members of the New York art world, who have been known to drop in.

—REBECCA KRASNEY STROPOLI

10 Green Paradise

609 Vanderbilt Avenue (between Bergen Street and St. Marks, Prospect Heights)

PHONE: (718) 230–5177

TYPE OF CUISINE: Raw vegan

DAYS/HOURS: Tuesday through Sunday from noon to 11:00 P.M.

VEGEBILITY: Excellent

RESERVATIONS: Not necessary

WHEELCHAIR ACCESS: No

KID-FRIENDLY: Yes

TYPE OF SERVICE: Counter seating and take-out

PRICING: Inexpensive

PAYMENT ACCEPTED: Cash only

There's a definite island theme at Green Paradise, a tiny but popular juice bar and vegan take-out joint. A counter and a few stools sit below a thatched roof, and lights carved out of coconuts and a steady reggae beat give the place its tropical feel. The only raw-foods restaurant in Brooklyn at press time, Green Paradise specializes in spicy West Indian cuisine, none of which is cooked above 108 degrees. Raw foodists like chef/owner Mawule Jobe-Simon, a veteran of Manhattan's Quintessence (see East Village), believe that not cooking food allows it to retain its natural enzymes. To the uninitiated, raw food can be intimidating, and if you're expecting the falafel and hummus to taste the same as they do at your corner stand, you may be disappointed. But Jobe-Simon's inventive pairings will also make you look at the produce stall in a whole new light.

Offering as many juices as entrées, Green Paradise has an abbreviated menu, but there are still several exemplary choices. The spinach pie is a dense rectangle of greens on a base of crunchy yams, topped by a spicy ginger sauce. Based on Jobe-Simon's grandmother's recipe, it's less spinach pie than spinach cake, but the "crust" and the sauce put it in a league of its own. Likewise, the wedge of curry tempeh has a grainy texture that's balanced by a flavorful tamarind sauce. The nappa sandwich—sliced tomatoes, cukes, and avocados with macadamia nut cheese served between two slices of crisp cabbage—will make you think cabbage should always be a sandwich option. It's messy, but it's more than worth it.

A lasagna special featured "noodles" composed of a creamy nut butter with layers of sun-dried tomatoes and zucchini; the sauce was fresh tomatoes and dates. It's nothing like regular lasagna, but it is oddly delicious. And there's a lot to be said for Green Paradise's desserts, like the rich mango coconut pie on a soft crust of nuts and dates. On a warm weekend day, pick up some mixed-berry "crepes" with coconut cream for brunch, and enjoy them in nearby Prospect Park.

—MELENA Z. RYZIK

⑪ The Green's

128 Montague Street (at Henry, Second Floor, Brooklyn Heights)

PHONE: (718) 246–0088, 246–1288; Fax: (718) 246–1500

TYPE OF CUISINE: Asian "mock meat" veg

DAYS/HOURS: Monday through Thursday from 11:00 A.M. to 10:30 P.M., Friday from 11:00 A.M. to 11:00 P.M., Saturday from noon to 11:00 P.M., Sunday from 1:00 P.M. to 10:30 P.M.

VEGEBILITY: Excellent

RESERVATIONS: Not necessary

WHEELCHAIR ACCESS: No (up full flight of stairs)

KID-FRIENDLY: Yes

TYPE OF SERVICE: Table, delivery, and take-out

PRICING: Moderate

PAYMENT ACCEPTED: Major credit cards

It's rare to find a vegan eatery whose approach to food is mainstream enough to succeed in a neighborhood where Chinese take-out joints are a dime a dozen—but that's part of the charm of the Green's. Its down-to-earth attitude about food, and downright cheap prices, have made it a favorite for vegetarians and health-minded diners.

Go for a table at one of the big bay windows so you can watch *le tout* Brooklyn Heights stroll along busy commercial Montague Street while you nosh on favorites like General Tso's Soy Gluten prepared by Taiwanese chef Long Huie Su. The soy gluten, protein and bean curd offerings are a faux-meat lover's dream. The Soy Protein Hunan-style is a particular standout, with its smoky sweetness of traditional ham.

Hidden in the extensive menu is an original gem that's well worth trying: Layer of Bean Crepe with Chinese Green Garden Vegetables with Bean Curd or just say Number 54. This mix of bean curd and leafy greens in a silky, soy-laced sauce is just the thing when you want something light or in place of a more traditional noodle soup.

When it comes to bargains, lunch specials at the Green's (served Monday through Friday from 11:00 A.M. to 3:00 P.M. and Saturday noon to 3:00 P.M.) can't be beat—your choice of soup, entrée and rice for just $5.50.

—MARY MARGARET CHAPPELL

"4-Course Vegan": Gourmet Home-Cooking

Inspired by a European practice that has flourished for years, a new trend is gaining momentum in New York City. As an alternative to dining out in restaurants, many foodies are enjoying meals cooked by top chefs in their own homes. One such feast is a vegan's delight in the heart of hipster Williamsburg. Chef Matteo Silverman offers an all-vegan meal cooked in his enormous loft. The feast is served downstairs in warehouselike surroundings that are kept separate from the living quarters. This weekly banquet, dubbed "4-Course Vegan," is held every Saturday and is usually limited to about twenty diners, though upwards of fifty have been accommodated

The menu changes every week, but it is consistently vegan-friendly. You might be served a first course of asparagus, five-spice tofu, nappa cabbage spring rolls with plum sauce, and pickled ginger. For a second course you may dig into a Chinese-style hot-and-sour soup with avocado and enoki mushrooms. The third course could be made up of Indonesian rice tamales with carrot-lemongrass sauce. And how about some cardamom-pistachio cookies and mango ice cream for dessert?

Chef Matteo also specializes in raw food and will sometimes prepare all-raw feasts. One such feast consisted of watermelon-radish ravioli with walnut rawcotta and summer pesto; green papaya creviche with three flavors and sunflower sprouts; young coconut pad thai with citrus-tamarind and almond-chile sauces; and cashew-mint ice cream with fruited-nut truffle disks.

Diners pay $25 a head, with an optional $10 for young coconut water service. Customers must reserve their space

by going to the Web site at www.4coursevegan.tripod.
com/menu or by calling (718) 599–5913. Portions of all
proceeds go to B.A.R.C., the Brooklyn Animal Rescue
Coalition.

—REBECCA KRASNEY STROPOLI

⑫ Grimaldi's Pizza

19 Old Fulton Street, (between Front and Water Streets, DUMBO)

PHONE: (718) 858–4300
WEB ADDRESS: www.grimaldis.com
TYPE OF CUISINE: Pizza
DAYS/HOURS: Sunday through Thursday from 11:30 A.M. to
10:45 P.M., Friday from 11:30 A.M. to 11:45 P.M., Saturday from
noon to 11:45 P.M.
VEGEBILITY: Very good
RESERVATIONS: No
WHEELCHAIR ACCESS: Yes
KID-FRIENDLY: Very
TYPE OF SERVICE: Table and take-out
PRICING: Inexpensive
PAYMENT ACCEPTED: Cash only

OK, so you're trying to cut back on carbs, especially white flour.
And no—you don't really need any more saturated fat. And yet
the pizza at Grimaldi's is so darn good, it's worth blowing your diet
for. If you think pizza is just pizza, you need to pay a visit to this classic little pizzeria tucked under the Brooklyn Bridge—arguably one
of the greatest culinary experiences you can have anywhere.

Consistently rated No. 1 in Zagat's NYC guide, Patsy Grimaldi's
pizza is outstanding. Crisp light crusts are topped with just four
things: freshly crushed tomatoes, basil leaves, a drizzle of olive oil,
and rounds of homemade mozzarella. More ambitious diners can
add such traditional toppings as mushrooms, peppers, black olives,
and onions. But the plain pie—the classic pizza Margherita, named
in 1889 for the queen of Italy and sporting the colors of the Italian
flag: red, white, and green—is a purist's delight. And there's good
news for vegans: Grimaldi's sauce and dough are both completely

dairy- and egg-free. Just request a cheeseless pie, top Patsy's legendary crust with sauce and veggies, and try to keep from drooling.

Dough is made fresh daily and can be seen rising in wooden boxes along the back wall, just beyond the red-checkered tablecloths and signed photos of Frank, Dino, Tony, and the gang. The real secret behind Grimaldi's perfect pies, however, is the coal-burning oven in which they're baked. Outlawed in Manhattan, coal-burning ovens produce extreme heat—more than 800 degrees—which allows the pizzas to be flash-cooked in three minutes. Heat that intense has an almost alchemical effect, transforming the dough, cheese and light coating of sauce into a heavenly taste combination. Pizza like this is so simple and so good—and so hard to find—that it will keep you coming back time and again.

If you fall into the usual trap of consuming a little too much of Patsy's pizza, take a stroll along the riverfront for one of the best views of Manhattan. If your appetite returns, pop into the Brooklyn Ice Cream Parlor, located in the old firehouse at the river's edge, or wander in the opposite direction to master pastry chef Jacques Torres's chocolate shop.

Words of warning: Bring cash; Grimaldi's doesn't accept any other form of payment. Don't bother trying to finagle a reservation; they're never accepted. And don't even *think* about ordering in; Grimaldi's doesn't deliver. They hold all the cards; you know it and they know it, but you don't care—you're hooked. You'll do anything they say, as long as they bring another steaming pizza to your table asap. (Also available: beer, soda, antipasto, calzone, spumoni, cannoli, espresso, and cappuccino.)

—SUSAN SHUMAKER

⑬ Halcyon Restaurant

227 Smith Street (between Butler and Douglass Streets, Cobble Hill)

PHONE: (718) 260-9299

TYPE OF CUISINE: Vegetarian snacks, café food

DAYS/HOURS: Monday through Saturday from noon to 2:00 A.M.

VEGEBILITY: Excellent

RESERVATIONS: No

WHEELCHAIR ACCESS: One small step

KID-FRIENDLY: Yes, but not at evening DJ events

TYPE OF SERVICE: Counter (lounge seating)

PRICING: Inexpensive

PAYMENT ACCEPTED: MC/V

This is an astonishing milieu that presents a number of interests to an inquisitive and conscious young crowd. It eludes definition, embracing a modern eclectic culture immersed in music, film, prose and art. Come here to browse through architecture and yoga magazines. Hear and buy vinyl and CDs. Halcyon is the real thing—a café opened by a tight group of (vegetarian) friends wanting to bring their passions together in a modest and creative business.

But come here to eat, too: There's a simple but tasty café menu. Sandwiches are made with good bread and (where cost permits) organic ingredients. Vegans should definitely try the sesame-tofu sandwich with a carrot-ginger dressing or the rosemary-portobello mushroom sandwich with a tasty paprika hummus. The fresh mozzarella sandwich is dressed with a tangy black olive tapenade, and the roasted vegetable comes with sun-dried tomatoes and pesto.

For breakfast, try the organic homemade granola with organic yogurt or soy milk or the zesty frittatas and quiches; and bagels are available all day long. For dessert, help yourself to an array of cookies ranging from the Health Freak (organic wheat and dairy-free, with rolled oats and organic fruit) to a sinfully chocolatey one smeared with Nutella. There are also teas, coffees, and wine and beer are available at reasonable prices.

Halcyon has you at heart. The DJs are famous, yet the entry is mostly free. You can lounge and listen, buy the hip retro paraphernalia and furniture, watch films, enjoy changing art exhibits and an outdoor courtyard in the summer, and mix with a hip, mixed, under-forty Brooklyn crowd. It is at once stimulating and relaxing, but be prepared for loud music (especially as it gets dark).

—LARA OLCHANETZKY

Smith Street

Back in the day when some of us pioneers first started moving out to Cobble Hill and Carroll Gardens, we were warned not to dally along Smith Street. Local thugs had been known to harass and even mug the unsuspecting. Basically we would dismount the F train, clutch our bags, and hightail it to Court Street and points west.

Today Smith Street is *the* destination on the F train. With dozens of fine dining, drinking, and shopping establishments—and more opening by the week, or so it seems—the 12-block strip from (roughly) Carroll Street to Atlantic Avenue has become the trendiest street in *le tout* Brooklyn, if not the entire city. In the early 1990s Patois, the first of the trailblazers, opened, with high-end French fare and Manhattan prices. Who'd have thunk: Something other than lasagna in the 'hood! Slowly but surely others followed suit, until practically all the bodegas, barbershops, and junk stores were gentrified into sleek eateries and snappy boutiques.

As with any hot trend, things change regularly; and as with any foodie hub, a lot of the offerings are not veg. But people of every dietary persuasion will find something to their liking—French, New American, Thai, Indian, Japanese, Pan-Asian, Italian, Middle Eastern, Caribbean—so it's worth a visit. In fact, spend an afternoon window-shopping and checking out menus. Here is a list, current at press time, of restaurants' addresses and phone numbers. We'll leave you to find your own hangouts and handbags.

—SUZANNE GERBER

Banania Café (New American), 241 Smith Street, (718) 237–9100

Bar Tabac (French bistro), 128 Smith Street, (718) 923–0918

Boerum Hill Food Company (American), 134 Smith Street, (718) 222–0140

Café Dore (Caribbean), 270 Smith Street, (718) 246–0505

Caserta Vecchia (Italian), 221 Smith Street, (718) 624–7549

Faan (Asian fusion), 209 Smith Street, (718) 694–2277

Fall Cafe (American), 307 Smith Street, (718) 403–0230

The Grocery (creative American), 288 Smith Street, (718) 596–3335

Halcyon Restaurant (vegetarian café; see review page 336), 227 Smith Street, (718) 260–9299

Paninoteca 275 (Italian), 275 Smith Street, (718) 237–2728

Patois (French), 255 Smith Street, (718) 855–1535

Raga (Indian), 142 Smith Street, (718) 522–3027

Rain Trees Cafe (juice), 130 Smith Street, (718) 858–4148

Robin de Bois (French), 195 Smith Street, (718) 596–1609

Saul Restaurant (New American), 140 Smith Street, (718) 935–9844

Savoia (Northern Italian), 277 Smith Street, (718) 797–2727

Sesame (Thai), 160 Smith Street, (718) 935–0101

Tuk Tuk (Thai), 204 Smith Street, (718) 222–5598

Wasabi (Japanese/sushi), 213 Smith Street, (718) 243–2028

Zaytoons (Middle Eastern), 283 Smith Street, (718) 875–1880

Joya

215 Court Street (at Warren Street, Cobble Hill)

PHONE: (718) 222–3484

TYPE OF CUISINE: Thai

DAYS/HOURS: Sunday through Thursday from 5:00 to 11:00 P.M., Friday and Saturday 5:00 P.M. to 12:30 A.M.

VEGEBILITY: Fair

RESERVATIONS: Suggested for parties of seven or more

WHEELCHAIR ACCESS: Yes

KID- FRIENDLY: Yes (families tend to come during the earlier hours, before it gets very crowded)

TYPE OF SERVICE: Table, take-out, and delivery (Sunday through Thursday) and bar

PRICING: Inexpensive

PAYMENT ACCEPTED: Cash only

Smack in the heart of lively Cobble Hill, Joya offers inexpensive Thai food in a hipster setting. Parting the thick blue curtains at the front door, you enter a world of modish brick walls adorned with splashy artwork and wooden tables complete with atmospheric candlelight. Very audible music, from alternative rock to mellow folk, plays at all times; weekends feature a DJ. Joya is open only for dinner, and the crowd tends toward the youngish, night-on-the-town variety, though families and older customers do populate the restaurant during the earliest dinner hours. When the weather is warm, the outdoor patio offers a quieter scene, ideal for intimate talks and romantic evenings. A fully stocked bar serves up cocktails aplenty, and during peak hours it's often packed with patrons waiting to be seated.

While Joya caters to carnivores as well, the vegetarian menu is ample and diverse. But beware—unless you ask for your dish to be prepared without fish sauce, all meals are cooked with it. No worries, though: All meals are cooked to order, and the kitchen is happy to honor veg requests. In fact, any meat-based dish can be prepared vegetarian. Try substituting tofu for chicken in the Gai Pad Khing, or dig into the Moo Kraprow sans pork.

For vegans, the vegetable curry—with its mix of eggplant, bamboo shoots, peppers, and carrots in a green or red coconut curry sauce—is a wise selection. The curry has a light and flavorful tang, and all of the veggies are cooked just enough to soak up the sauce without turning soggy and limp. Ovo-lactos will adore the spicy noodle dish with mixed veggies and egg in a chili-basil sauce. The noodles are thick and filling, and the sauce has just enough kick to satisfy but isn't so spicy that you'll need to down several Singhas to get through it. And how about that ginger tofu? The light, crispy fried tofu pieces absorb the flavorful sauce just enough to tickle the taste buds without overwhelming the senses.

For dessert, choose between the deep-fried banana with drizzled honey and whipped cream on the side and the vegan coconut sticky rice with fruit.

—REBECCA KRASNEY STROPOLI

⓯ Kapadokya

142 Montague Street, Second floor (between Clinton and Henry Streets, Brooklyn Heights)

> **PHONE:** (718) 875–2211
> **TYPE OF CUISINE:** Turkish
> **DAYS/HOURS:** Monday through Thursday from 11:30 A.M. to 11:30 P.M.; Friday through Saturday from 11:30 A.M. to midnight; Sunday 11:30 A.M. to 10:30 P.M.
> **VEGEBILITY:** Very good
> **RESERVATIONS:** Suggested
> **WHEELCHAIR ACCESS:** No
> **KID-FRIENDLY:** Yes
> **TYPE OF SERVICE:** Table
> **PRICING:** Moderate
> **PAYMENT ACCEPTED:** Major credit cards

From the owners of the Upper West Side gem Turkuaz comes a new Turkish restaurant and narghile (aka hookah) bar, Kapadokya. Located on the Brooklyn Heights commercial strip Montague Street, the restaurant features patio seating in the back, which is sure to add even more delight to the delectable food.

Kapadokya, which takes its name from an old civilization settlement in Middle Anatolia, has a heavy Turkish theme evident in the waitstaff's attire and the traditional copper and clay that are used in the decor. The extensive menu is filled with vegetarian choices: Twelve cold and three hot appetizers and four vegetarian entrées are featured. The mixed vegetarian plate is big enough to feed two grown-up appetites and includes baba ghanoush, hummus, ezme (spicy mashed vegetables), stuffed grape leaves, and spinach tarator (with haydari, a thick, creamy garlicky yogurt dip flavored with fresh mint and dill). For vegans, certain items on the platter can be substituted with nondairy ingredients.

One hot appetizer that stands out is the warm hummus with pine nuts, which is served straight from the oven with sizzling butter and crunchy nuts. It's melt-in-your-mouth delicious.

In addition to the traditional desserts—baklava, burnt custard, baked rice pudding—you also have the option of narghile for your after-dinner enjoyment. And if that's not fun enough, there's a belly dancer to entertain the guests on Friday and Saturday nights.

—SEZIN CAVUSOGLU

16 New Prospect Café

393 Flatbush Avenue (at Eighth Avenue, Park Slope)

PHONE: (718) 638–2148

TYPE OF CUISINE: New American

DAYS/HOURS: Monday through Friday from 11:00 A.M. to 10:00 P.M., Saturday and Sunday 11:00 A.M. to 11:00 P.M.

VEGEBILITY: Fair to good

RESERVATIONS: Not required

WHEELCHAIR ACCESS: No

KID-FRIENDLY: Yes

TYPE OF SERVICE: Table, take-out

PRICING: Moderate

PAYMENT ACCEPTED: Major credit cards

A Park Slope institution after eleven years on Flatbush Avenue, New Prospect is the kind of place locals treasure and nonlocals feel lucky to discover—a comfortable, quality, reasonably priced café to keep coming back to. Changing displays of local art adorn the walls, which are painted in mellow tones, and the giant bay window up front is a top spot for quality people-watching. New owner/manager Juan Salcedo, a former employee, has made improvements while keeping beloved old favorites on the menu, to the great relief of the regulars.

One must-have appetizer is the baked goat cheese in phyllo dough with pear and watercress salad. Three melt-in-your-mouth puffy triangles bursting with creamy goat cheese are beautifully presented on a verdant bed of watercress and pears. It could almost be a meal in itself, but then you'd miss out on too many exciting, always-changing entrées (like a homemade almond veggie burger or cheese and spinach ravioli with tomatoes, mushrooms, zucchini, and garlic). Even regular menu items, such as the cheese, scallion, and cilantro enchiladas with (veggie-safe) green mole, are far superior to what you will find at most restaurants, Mexican or otherwise.

Vegans had best like tempeh, because aside from an assortment of salads, there aren't a lot of options besides the grilled tempeh with a tamarind glaze, served on a bed of basmati rice with broccoli. (Not a bad dish, but uninspired compared with the yummy ovo-lacto entrées.) At the popular Sunday brunch, complete with $4.00 mimosas, you can feast on fresh fruit salad in yogurt and granola, poached eggs over English muffins with grilled zucchini and pesto hollandaise, Mexican omelettes with fresh salsa, and challah French toast with fresh fruit and real maple syrup. Also available: tempeh burgers, homemade veggie burgers, split pea soup, salads—and even muffins, coffee cake, and banana bread. (Beer and wine are available, too.)

—LISA POLIAK

17 Oshima Japanese Cuisine

71 Seventh Avenue (between Lincoln and Berkeley Streets, Park Slope)

PHONE: (718) 783–1888 or 783–4779

TYPE OF CUISINE: Japanese

DAYS/HOURS: Monday through Saturday from noon to 3:00 P.M., and from 4:30 to 11:30 P.M. Friday through Saturday, Sunday 2:00 to 10:30 P.M.

VEGEBILITY: Excellent

RESERVATIONS: Suggested for parties of six or more

WHEELCHAIR ACCESS: Yes

KID-FRIENDLY: Yes

TYPE OF SERVICE: Table, take-out

PRICING: Moderate

PAYMENT ACCEPTED: Major credit cards

Wedged between a Chinese and a Thai restaurant on a Pan-Asian block of Park Slope's bustling Seventh Avenue, Oshima offers a highly veg-friendly taste of Japanese flavors in an attractive, classic setting. The front room sports a sleek sushi bar and simple wood-and-bamboo furnishings; out back there's a romantic garden, illuminated by hanging red paper lanterns.

The seven entrées listed in the vegetarian section of the menu are actually all vegan, including Heavenly Chicken, soy chicken stir-fried with a variety of veggies and a tangy sauce. The Zen Duck (also soy) tastes so realistic, some veg customers have actually complained to owners John and Lydia Hwang. Other entrée options include Eggplant Lhasa, broiled Chinese eggplant with ginger black bean sauce, and Yaki Udon/Soba, vegetables stir-fried with udon or soba noodles. There is also a vegetable sushi menu with unusual rolls such as Ume Shisho Maki, a plum paste and shisho leaf roll; Kamyomaki, a pickled Japanese squash roll; and shiitake mushroom rolls, in addition to the more common avocado and cucumber rolls.

There are even more appetizer choices than entrées, the Harumaki (Japanese spring rolls) being a favorite. The wrapper is light and crisp and not at all greasy—unlike your typical spring roll. The Oshinko appetizer is an interesting variety of pickled Japanese vegetables, including Japanese carrot, radish, cucumber, and squash, and the Kaiso salad of assorted green seaweeds is a refreshing choice after the salty pickled veggies. Then there's the Broccoli Kuzhizashi, skewered broiled broccoli in a savory brown sauce, and Oshitashi, chilled spinach in tempura sauce topped with sesame seeds. (Vegans take note: The tempura batter is made with milk.) Choosing a salad may be difficult, as all the selections are terrific: two green salads; sesame noodles with mixed organic greens, seaweed salad, and organic tofu salad.

A haven for vegans and vegetarians, Oshima will win praise from diners for its top-quality fare and inviting setting. Lovers of mock meat will find true satisfaction in their soybean "meat" creations, and even those who never thought they liked faux meat will be very happily surprised if they try Oshima's take on it.

—LISA POLIAK

🔟 Ott

970 Manhattan Avenue (between Huron and India Streets, Greenpoint)

PHONE: (718) 609–2416; Fax: (718) 609–9495
TYPE OF CUISINE: Thai
DAYS/HOURS: Tuesday through Sunday from noon to 11:00 P.M.
VEGEBILITY: Excellent
RESERVATIONS: Suggested
WHEELCHAIR ACCESSIBLE: Yes
KID-FRIENDLY: Yes
TYPE OF SERVICE: Table
PRICING: Moderate
PAYMENT ACCEPTED: Cash only

Amid the Polish diners and kielbasa shops that line Manhattan Avenue, there's a new trend aimed at the neighborhood's burgeoning population of artists and hipsters escaping the soaring rents of Williamsburg: Thai restaurants. Ott, with its unassuming storefront, offers a pleasant surprise for vegetarians seeking unique fare. Named for the owner's son, the eatery is a mix of the traditional and the modern. Abstract paintings by a local artist hang next to Thai artifacts, and classic recipes vie for space on the menu with new inventions.

The spring rolls are served with an excellent sweet-and-sour sauce that's spiced with hot red pepper flakes. (Like most rolls, the wrap is made with an egg mixture.) The highlight of the salad menu is the reasonably priced ($3.50) papaya salad, light and fresh with a hint of heat. If you're a faux-meat fan, don't miss the Duck Panang. Doused in a thick currylike sauce, more artfully spicy than hot, the soy-based "duck" pieces are chewy and solid to the teeth. The vegetable pad thai, always a favorite, stacks up well, with a generous pile of crisp bean sprouts and shredded carrots, a perfect sprinkling of crushed peanuts, and a strong but not overpowering spiciness. The dish includes a heaping of egg but can be made without. The Tofu Basil offers large hunks of tofu, fried nearly crispy and coated with pungent basil.

Do try all three of the homemade table seasonings (they look spicy, but be brave). A great thing about Ott is that every selection and its level of spiciness is made-to-order. If the nine vegetarian entrées (plus appetizers, fried rice items, soups, and salads) don't suit you, you can order any of the meat entrées with tofu. In all, this is a worthy addition to Manhattan Avenue's growing Thai roster.

—PHIL ANDREWS

⑲ Oznot's Dish

79 Berry Street (at North 9th Street, Williamsburg)

PHONE: (718) 599–6596

TYPE OF CUISINE: New Mediterranean

DAYS/HOURS: Monday through Thursday from 11:00 A.M. to
11:00 P.M., Friday 11:00 A.M. to midnight, Saturday 10:00 A.M.
to midnight, Sunday 10:00 A.M. to 11:00 P.M.

VEGEBILITY: Very good

RESERVATIONS: No

WHEELCHAIR ACCESSIBLE: Yes

KID-FRIENDLY: Yes

TYPE OF SERVICE: Table, take-out, delivery, and bar

PRICING: Moderate

PAYMENT ACCEPTED: MC/V

Occupying a quiet street corner in the core of artsy Williamsburg, Oznot's Dish serves up New Mediterranean cuisine that
vegetarians have been embracing since the eatery opened in 1993.
Although carnivores also flock to Oznot's for its meatier fare, the
menu offers a slew of veg-friendly dishes that are steeped in flavor-
rich spices.

The first feast you'll enjoy when you walk through the door is
one for the eyes. The interior is a multihued mix of striking tile
design, elaborate murals, and space-enhancing mirrors; by night,
this milieu is complemented by soft candlelight. A narrow hallway is
lined with vintage seltzer bottles that add a quirky charm. In addition to a front room dominated by a well-stocked bar, Oznot's has a
winter garden and a small outside dining area that's always snatched
up first in summer.

The menu is heavily inspired by the cuisines of Spain, Italy,
Portugal, and North Africa. Flavorful appetizers include baby
spinach with goat cheese and blood orange (vegans can hold the
cheese); hummus and baba ghanoush served with olives, pita slices,
and savory nan bread; and the sumptuous baked Cypriot feta with
a roasted tomato dip, an outrageous concoction that blends fig
pesto with sizzling feta and is served with fleshy green amanida
olives and pita crisps.

You may want to dig into the roasted root vegetables in curry
sauce as a main dish. Served with basmati rice, cardamom, and
sautéed greens, it has a thick and creamy texture that belies its vegan

constitution. The porcini mushroom and pumpkin risotto is a sumptuous ovo-lacto plate flavored with roasted garlic and shaved Reggiano cheese.

The majority of food offered at Oznot's is made fresh on-site, including the bread and pasta. Complement your meal with a homemade chai or fresh-pressed apple cider. The wine list is extensive, and a variety of cocktails are made at the bar. The Saturday and Sunday brunches are a popular affair. Choose from a menu that includes cardamom French toast, Indian eggs with ginger and cilantro, and organic grits with butter and brown sugar or roasted peppers and jack cheese.

Oznot's prides itself on hiring "green" staffers; about half of the waitstaff is vegetarian or vegan, and an eco-friendly sentiment pervades.

—REBECCA KRASNEY STROPOLI

20 Pete's Waterfront Alehouse

155 Atlantic Avenue (between Clinton and Henry Streets, Brooklyn Heights-Cobble Hill)

PHONE: (718) 522-3794

OTHER LOCATION: 540 Second Avenue (at 30th Street, Red Hook), (718) 522–3794

TYPE OF CUISINE: Healthier-than-usual bar food

DAYS/HOURS: Monday through Sunday from 11:30 A.M. to 2:00 A.M. Kitchen closes Monday through Wednesday at 10:30 P.M., Thursday through Saturday at 11:30 p.m., and Sunday at 11:00 P.M.

VEGEBILITY: Fair

RESERVATIONS: No

WHEELCHAIR ACCESS: Yes

KID-FRIENDLY: Yes

TYPE OF SERVICE: Table and bar

PRICING: Moderate

PAYMENT ACCEPTED: AE/MC

The self-serve popcorn stand and the selection of draft microbrews and seasonal beers are big draws for neighborhood folk who know they can come to Pete's for bar-food favorites and fast service—and that suits sports fans and small fries alike (there's usually a family or two chowing down in one of the booths).

While the atmosphere is more end zone than Zen, the chefs strive to satisfy vegetarian palates with not one, but two types of meat-free burgers—a robust miso-flavored tempeh patty that's a flavor explosion all on its own and a smoky grilled portobello that you can kick up a notch with more than just ketchup (sauces include a spicy horseradish mustard and a real British HP curry). The most enlightened part of all: The veg burgers are cooked separately from the meat ones. (Frying is kept separate as well.) All burgers come with a side of fresh-cut fries, but consider splurging on the hand-cut sweet potato fries and creamy mustard slaw—which have a "cult following," according to assistant chef Larry Kohn.

If you have the guts to order "lite" fare at a bar, check the specials for vegetarian soups and sandwiches. The vegetable foccacia sandwich with fresh mozzarella and mushroom, eggplant, and goat cheese salad has a smoky Mediterranean flavor from the grill. You can also ask the kitchen to make its crispy, cheesy quesadillas without chicken or to whip up nachos without chili for Tex-Mex noshing. In fact, the chefs are happy to accommodate any appetite and will leave the cheese off veggie burgers and sandwiches for vegans.

—MARY MARGARET CHAPPELL

21 Rose Water

787 Union Street (between Fifth and Sixth Avenues, Park Slope)

PHONE: (718) 783–3800

TYPE OF CUISINE: New American

DAYS/HOURS: Monday and Tuesday from 5:30 to 10:00 P.M.,
Wednesday and Thursday 5:30 to 10:30 P.M., Friday 5:30 to
11:00 P.M., Saturday 11:00 A.M. to 3:00 P.M. and 5:30 to 11:00
P.M., Sunday 11:00 A.M. to 3:00 P.M. and 5:30 to 10:00 P.M.

VEGEBILITY: Good

RESERVATIONS: Suggested

WHEELCHAIR ACCESS: Yes

KID-FRIENDLY: Yes

TYPE OF SERVICE: Table

PRICING: Moderate

PAYMENT ACCEPTED: AE/MC/V

Rose Water is the kind of place that gives vegetarian food a good name, even among nonvegetarians. The cuisine is of the Alice Waters school—always seasonal and local and organic whenever possible. "I let the farmer tell *me* what I'm making," says chef/co-owner Neal O'Malley. The result is food that's fresh and inventive, served in a relaxed, welcoming setting.

The restaurant is such a local fixture that regulars pop in just to ask about the day's specials; the mercurial menu obviously satisfies a lot of repeat customers. One of the few constants is the small basket of warm bread, served with a high-quality olive oil instead of butter. The whole-wheat pita has a slightly sweet, nutty flavor that comes from ground black cherry pits called mahleb—a Middle Eastern flavoring for baked goods that O'Malley incorporates into his homemade bread.

With that kind of attention to detail, it's no wonder most dishes at Rose Water sparkle. Because the menu changes so frequently, it's hard to recommend a particular meal. There is always a vegetarian entrée available for dinner—in early spring, saffron noodles with mizuna, celery root, ramps, and a farm-fresh poached egg, for example—and though it's not on the menu, O'Malley is happy to whip up a vegetarian plate that combines the sides to his meat-based entrées. Twice-baked eggplant; green wheat kernels; roasted rhubarb, apple, and pear; sweet potato mash; and Jerusalem artichokes may all mingle happily on your plate.

Appetizers offer more veggie selections: A Portuguese "caldo verde" soup of kale and potato, served with yogurt and sesame pita chips, made a fan of a former kale hater, and the meaty porcini mushrooms in a salad served as a platform for the lighter flavors of watercress and thinly sliced pears. Rose Water is a restaurant with a philosophy: country-style cooking in the city. Nice to know it satisfies the palate as well as the principle.

—MELENA Z. RYZIK

22 Rice (see Soho/Tribeca)

81 Washington Street (between Front and York Streets)

PHONE: (718) 222–9880

23 Sea

114 North 6th Street (between Berry and Wythe Streets, Williamsburg)

PHONE: (718) 384–8850

TYPE OF CUISINE: Thai

DAYS/HOURS: Sunday through Thursday from 11:30 A.M. to 1:00 A.M., Friday and Saturday 11:30 A.M. to 2:00 A.M.

VEGEBILITY: Very good

RESERVATIONS: No

WHEELCHAIR ACCESS: Yes

KID-FRIENDLY: Yes

TYPE OF SERVICE: Table and bar

PRICING: Moderate

PAYMENT ACCEPTED: MC/V

SPECIAL NOTE: This Sea is affiliated with the Sea in the East Village as well as three other Thai restaurants in Manhattan all called Spice

Sea, a relatively new Thai restaurant in Williamsburg, is a noteworthy addition to the explosion of restaurants in this funky, not-so-cheap-anymore neighborhood. It is located in a former meatpacking factory—ironic because it is very veg-friendly—and its ski lodge/designer loft interior makes it a festive place to dine.

A surprising highlight of my meal was the Caesar salad. Thin strips of tender romaine lettuce drizzled with a vegan Caesar dressing (miso, vinegar, garlic, and ginger) was a tangy, refreshing alternative to the sesame-oil heaviness of the standard Thai carrot salad.

I can never resist a good peanut sauce dish, and Rama the King, an entrée of mixed veggies with a fish-free red curry peanut sauce, was substantial and satisfying. The smoky flavor of the lightly grilled tofu chunks and the basil undertone left a subtle and pleasant heat at the end of each bite. The house soup is plain in a simple way, which is good if you want a bowl full of fresh chunks of broccoli, tofu, carrots, and mung bean sprouts. This soup uses chicken stock, but the kitchen happily accommodates requests for a vegetarian stock.

The menu has many options for the pure vegetarian, and chef Tony Rarengjai (whose last name means "always happy heart") says the kitchen can make almost every dish vegan—and they don't even wince when asked. There are nightly specials, occasionally a vegetarian one. Interestingly, the curry pastes contain no fish sauce or other animal products, just pure, fresh ingredients.

Every night except Monday and Tuesday there's a DJ spinning, and diners wait, seated on the bubblelike stools that surround the elevated booth opposite the conical bamboo bar, for their chance to dine. Because Sea doesn't take reservations, order a drink and kick back. On weekends you might have a forty-five-minute wait.

—ANTRIM CASKEY

24 Tripoli

156 Atlantic Avenue (at Clinton Street, Brooklyn Heights/Cobble Hill)

PHONE: (718) 596–5800
TYPE OF CUISINE: Lebanese
DAYS/HOURS: Monday through Sunday from noon to 11:00 P.M.
VEGEBILITY: Very good
RESERVATIONS: Not necessary
WHEELCHAIR ACCESS: Yes
KID-FRIENDLY: Yes
TYPE OF SERVICE: Table
PRICING: Moderate
PAYMENT ACCEPTED: Cash only

The high ceilings, wall murals, and oak carved chairs (owner Mohammed Salem carved the restaurant's name into the backs himself) make Tripoli a more elegant destination than most of the Middle Eastern eateries that line the blocks of Atlantic Avenue between Court and Hicks Streets. Fortunately, the prices at this long-standing Lebanese restaurant, owned by the Salem family for thirty years, are comparable to the competition's, making it well worth taking the time to dine.

Start with an assortment of Middle Eastern standards, including a chunky and smoky baba ghanoush, a lemony foul (a salad of fava beans and parsley), and crispy falafel balls—and be sure to ask for extra olive oil. Tripoli imports its extra virgin oil from Lebanon, and its light, fruity flavor is perfect for dipping the white pita bread that's served with the meal.

In addition to appetizers, Tripoli offers an impressive selection of meatless main courses. Try the Kibee B'ziat (a vegetarian version of a Lebanese specialty), crispy fried ovals made with potatoes, cracked wheat, onions, nuts, and raisins. The stuffed grape leaves are prepared Lebanese-style: filled with rice, raisins, and pine nuts and cooked in a tomato broth. The Selek B'loubia, a veg favorite, is a surprisingly filling and flavorful sauté of celery and black-eyed peas seasoned with garlic and coriander.

Phyllo dough desserts (baklava, birds nests and ladyfingers) are all wonderful ways to finish your meal. For an even more authentic end, try a serving of the Pumpkin Delight kept on the bar. Just be forewarned: This thick, chewy, jamlike sweet is utterly addictive.

—MARY MARGARET CHAPPELL

25 Veracruz

195 Bedford Avenue (between North 7th and North 6th Streets, Williamsburg)

PHONE: (718) 599–7914

TYPE OF CUISINE: Tex-Mex

DAYS/HOURS: Monday through Thursday from 4:00 to 11:30 P.M., Friday and Saturday 4:00 P.M. to midnight, Sunday 3:00 to 11:30 P.M.

VEGEBILITY: Good

RESERVATIONS: Accepted weekdays only

WHEELCHAIR ACCESS: No

KID-FRIENDLY: Yes

TYPE OF SERVICE: Table, take-out, and bar

PRICING: Moderate

PAYMENT ACCEPTED: Major credit cards

Good Tex-Mex for vegetarians is excruciatingly hard to come by in New York City. Most of the options seem to be either Chinese-run fast-food affairs where "vegetarian taco" means "tortilla filled with snow peas and broccoli" or kitschy, overpriced joints where the food is so bland, you know the chef's never been south of New Jersey.

Enter Veracruz. This little Williamsburg hot spot offers better-than-average veg entrées, but what bumps it up into my short list of good Tex-Mex restaurants are the details: excellent chips and salsa, great margaritas, outdoor garden seating, and huge portions.

As something of a chips and salsa addict, I've scoured the city, and Veracruz delivers the best free chips and salsa I've found. The chips are warm, thin, and not too greasy; the salsa has just the right amount of onion, cilantro, and jalapeño; and both are made fresh daily. They're even complimentary at the bar, so in theory you could skip the entrées altogether and just nosh on chips while you suck down one of Veracruz's tasty margaritas, which don't suffer from the usual sugar overkill.

In the entrée realm, the enormous vegetarian burrito—filled with the vegetables of the day, beans, and guacamole—gets a tangy lift from the excellent green tomatillo salsa that covers it. The guac makes a great appetizer as well, served in a crispy tortilla bowl. The rice and black beans are veg-safe, but the refried beans, which only come as a separate side order, are made with lard.

Weekends can get crowded, but the outdoor seating at the back of the restaurant makes it worth the wait. The huge garden is open year-round, with a plastic tent and heaters to keep you warm in winter. But if you come in the middle of a New York summer, you can pretend you're actually sweltering in Mexico.

Veracruz's menu is very veg-friendly, with all the items color-coded: green for veggie, blue for seafood, red for meat. Most of the vegetarian items come with cheese or some other dairy product, but the staff will happily make just about anything vegan if you ask.

—JULIE HOLLAR

Organic Delivery Service

Sign up with Urban Organic and have fifteen to eighteen varieties of fresh, ripe organic fruits and vegetables delivered to your door fifty-two weeks a year.

The catch? They decide what you get based on what's in season, though you can, for example, elect never to have kale in your box. Here's how it works: If you can make it to their location or a street fair to sign up, there's no lifetime membership fee. If you join over the phone or Internet, you pay a onetime fee of $25.

Urban Organic's boxes of weekly produce are available in three sizes: A small one costs $21.49, a "value" box is $31.49, and the "extra value" costs $41.29. There's also a juice box for $31.49, and you can add on other grocery and bulk items like milk or bread or berries by phone or Internet.

Logistics: If you're not home at delivery time, you specify where to leave your box: on your stoop, with a neighbor, or even inside, if you provide a key. Also, you can suspend delivery when you're out of town. Your credit card is charged after your box is delivered (or you can prepay by check). The regularly scheduled delivery is free in Manhattan and Brooklyn; it costs $2.00 to $4.00 if you live in other boroughs, Long Island, New Jersey, or Connecticut.

Urban Organic
230A Seventh Avenue, Park Slope

PHONE: (718) 499–4321
WEB ADDRESS: www.urbanorganic.com

—MELENA Z. RYZIK

Places to Shop

26 Back to the Land
142 Seventh Avenue (between Carroll Street and Garfield Place, Park Slope)

> **PHONE:** (718) 768–5654
> **DAYS/HOURS:** Monday through Sunday from 9:00 A.M. to 9:00 P.M.
> **OVERALL:** Very good to excellent

This well-organized store has products clearly displayed on tall wooden shelves (a ladder is available to reach the high stuff), a good if basic produce selection and pre-bagged bulk grains, beans and spices. There's a wide range of supplements and pretty much everything you could ever want in a neighborhood natural foods store—except low prices. (Members of the nearby Park Slope Food Coop jokingly refer to it as "Back to the Bank." At least they deliver.)

27 The Garden
921 Manhattan Avenue (at Kent Street, Greenpoint)

> **PHONE:** (718) 389–6448
> **DAYS/HOURS:** Monday through Saturday from 8:00 A.M. to 8:00 P.M., Sunday 9:00 A.M. to 7:00 P.M.
> **OVERALL:** Excellent

You don't have to speak Polish to be understood at this surprisingly complete shop in the heart of Slavic Greenpoint. Upon entering you land in a wondrous organic produce section that's reasonably priced to boot. All kinds of fruits and vegetables can be had most of the year. Go deep and arrive at the prepared-food sections: not all veg but mostly so, and mostly all winners. Burritos, hummus, and potato pancakes coexist without squabbles over shared air space. Turn right and hit the coffee and bulk food zone and the always-deightful self-serve fresh peanut butter machine. (Do not grind it directly into your mouth, however tempting that may be.) Move on to pastas, a deli section (with an impressive collection of olives), teas, dairy, and then . . . the glorious bakery, which is hard evidence of the store's true Eastern European roots. Grab a loaf—or three—and you won't have to force a smile to all the pretty blond checkout women.

28 Garden of Eden (see Chelsea)

180 Montague Street (between Clinton and Court Streets, Brooklyn Heights)

> **PHONE:** (212) 222–1515

29 Karrot

431 Myrtle Avenue (at Clinton Street, Fort Greene)

> **PHONE:** (718) 522–9753
> **DAYS/HOURS:** Monday through Saturday from 8:30 A.M. to 8:00 P.M., Sunday 9:00 A.M. to 7:00 P.M.
> **OVERALL:** Good

Karrot celebrated its grand opening in November 2002, with support from the Myrtle Avenue Revitalization Project. This area of the Fort Greene/Clinton Hill neighborhood—overpopulated at the time by a glut of Chinese food joints, pizza parlors and fried chicken shacks, was sorely lacking in any kind of health food shop before Karrot came on the scene. This tiny store may not have a massive assortment of goods, but you will find a decent selection of soy-based "meat" products, whole-grain breads, veggie soups, natural cereals, fruit-juice-sweetened cookies and healthful beverages. There are a couple of shelves devoted to skin- and hair-care products as well. As is the case with most health food stores, some of the items are on the pricier side, but they are all within reason.

30 Park Natural

274 Union Street (between Court and Clinton Streets, Cobble Hill)

PHONE: (718) 802–1652

DAYS/HOURS: Monday through Saturday from 8:00 A.M. to 8:00 P.M., Sunday 8:00 A.M. to 7:00 P.M.

OVERALL: Very good and getting better

Regulars who've been shopping here since the midsize health shop opened in 2000 are in for a huge treat. In the winter of 2003–04, the store doubled in size. It now boasts an impressive organic produce section, bulk food, every kind of packaged good, and a truly stocked supplement section. (Bob, who manages the vitamins, is my go-to guy for everything from how much NAC I should be taking to which manufacturer makes a veggie DHEA.) If he doesn't have something you fancy, just ask and he'll order it for you. Cobble Hill is the hottest neighborhood in the area and it's nice to know its healthy offerings are finally as extensive as designer handbags.

31 Park Slope Food Coop

782 Union Street (between Sixth and Seventh Avenues, Park Slope)

PHONE: (718) 622–0560

WEB ADDRESS: www.foodcoop.com

DAYS/HOURS: Monday through Friday from 8:00 A.M. to 10:00 P.M.; Saturday and Sunday from 8:00 A.M. to 7:30 P.M.

OVERALL: Very good

The Holy Grail of health food markets, the Park Slope Food Coop is not just a store, it's a lifestyle. One of the oldest co-ops in the city, it prides itself on being entirely member-run. To keep prices low (20 percent above wholesale), the co-op is staffed by members who work about three hours, thirteen times a year. The produce selection is phenomenal: Everything from clementines to tomatillos to young Thai coconuts may be available seasonally. Produce prices are set weekly; most items are organic or minimally treated. Spices, grains, and beans are available in bulk, and there's a wide variety of local cheeses and breads. Because the co-op is so popular, members do complain about overcrowded aisles and long checkout lines, but for most, it's worth the wait.

32 Perelandra

175 Remsen Street (between Court and Clinton Streets, Brooklyn Heights)

PHONE: (718) 855–6068

DAYS/HOURS: Monday through Friday from 8:30 A.M. to 8:30 P.M., Saturday 9:30 A.M. to 8:30 P.M., Sunday 11:00 A.M. to 7:00 P.M.

OVERALL: Excellent

This clean, well-lit Brooklyn Heights store has everything you need under one large roof: an organic produce section that runs the entire length of the store; every fashion of pantry good, natural beauty product, and cleaning aid; a walk-in, climate-controlled bulk foods section; a supplement section that rivals produce on the other side of the store; and a mini-restaurant with a dozen daily specials (including wheat-free vegan desserts), juices, smoothies, and even fresh wheat grass juice. Staff, usually found stocking high shelves on the rolling ladders, happily come down from their perch to help you find that organic umeboshi paste or those black soybeans. Grab an alternative magazine from their huge selection on your way out as you start compiling next week's shopping list.

33 Uprising Bakery

328 Seventh Avenue (between 8th and 9th Streets, Park Slope)

PHONE: (718) 499–8665

OTHER LOCATION: 138 Seventh Avenue (between Carroll Street and Garfield Place, Park Slope), (718) 499–5242; 210 Court Street (at Warren Street), (718) 422–7676

DAYS/HOURS: Monday through Saturday from 7:30 A.M. to 9:00 P.M.; Sunday from 8:30 A.M. to 9:00 P.M.

OVERALL: excellent

"Prepare to meet your baker" was this shop's slogan when it first opened in 1998, and by all accounts, many Brooklyn residents have. The baked goods created by husband-and-wife team Nicole Lane and Joseph Rodriguez proved so popular that they opened a second Park Slope shop within a few years, and a third location opened on Court Street in Cobble Hill in 2003. Locals line up for breads like kalamata olive, country peasant, walnut-sage and herb focaccias. Not to be missed are goodies like cranberry-walnut scones, cupcakes, and daily bread specials (chocolate-cranberry on Tuesdays). Though the fare is no longer all organic, the service is friendly, the coffee is fresh, and the bread's as good as ever.

Places to Stay

Brooklyn Information and Culture (www.brooklynx.org), a site operated by a nonprofit group, has a decent selection of neighborhood bed-and-breakfasts.

34 Comfort Inn (not on map)
8315 Fourth Avenue (at 83rd Street, Bay Ridge)

> **PHONE:** (718) 238–3737
> **WEB ADDRESS:** www.comfortinn.com
> **PRICING:** Inexpensive

Erected in the 1920s as the Hotel Gregory, it has been beautifully renovated and is now part of the Comfort Inn chain. Luxurious guestrooms; refrigerator available in some rooms.

35 Marriott Brooklyn (not on map)
333 Adams Street (between Tillary and Fulton Streets, Brooklyn Heigts)

> **PHONE:** (718) 246–7000
> **WEB ADDRESS:** www.marriott.com/nycbk
> **PRICING:** Expensive

Literally on the access road to the Brooklyn Bridge, Brooklyn's largest hotel offers an Olympic-length lap pool and even a dedicated kosher kitchen. A five-minute walk to the bridge's pedestrian path and the charming neighborhood of Brooklyn Heights.

Queens

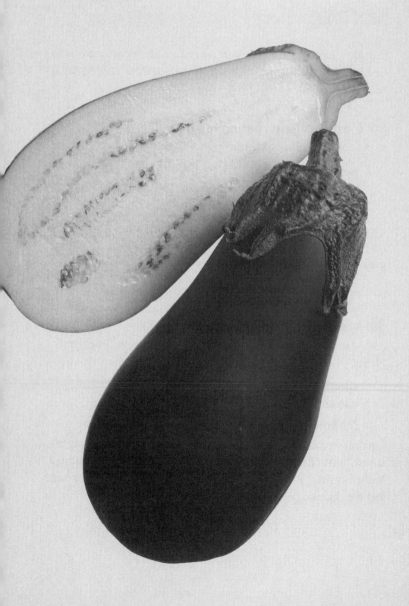

OK, so Queens lacks the hipness of Brooklyn and the excitement of Manhattan, but what it lacks in style, it makes up for with substance.

Just across the East River from Manhattan and north of Brooklyn, Queens is a residential borough, a collection of working- and middle-class neighborhoods with the most ethnically diverse population of any county in the country (and the dizzying array of cuisines to prove it). Queens was a Manhattan suburb before it was subsumed into New York City one-hundred-odd years ago, lending to the quieter, calmer atmosphere.

Quiet and calm doesn't mean boring, though: Queens has its share of attractions, from baseball to art to beaches. Long Island City (LIC), the first subway stop in the borough, is a recovering warehouse district that's gaining a reputation for its growing arts scene. P.S.1, housed in a converted public school building, is one of the coolest art museums in town, featuring experimental but accessible contemporary art in every nook and cranny from the

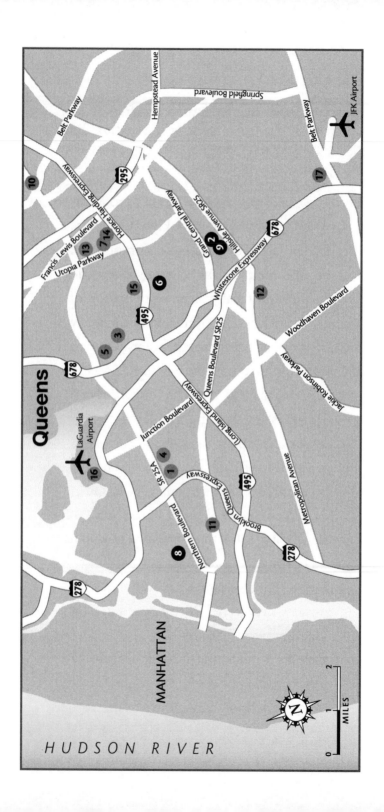

stairwells to the bathrooms. During the summer, hipsters flock to Queens for P.S.1's amazing (and cheap) outdoor parties with DJs, beer, and an art installation that always involves large quantities of cool water. Some little gems like the Isamu Noguchi Garden Museum and the American Museum of the Moving Image are not far away in Sunnyside and Astoria, respectively.

Astoria, just north of LIC, is home to a large Greek community and growing Latino and Arab populations. Here you'll find a plethora of Greek cafés jam-packed with people of all ages sipping tall glasses of coffee and munching on sweet pastries. Astoria also harbors the Bohemian, one of the last remaining beer gardens in the city, where the brew's cheap, the food's cheaper, and the outdoor garden is as big as a parking lot.

One of the best ways to explore Queens is to take the 7 train from Manhattan all the way to the end of the line, stopping along the way at random stations where interesting-looking people get off. The above-ground 7 cuts across so many different ethnic enclaves, it's known as the "International Express." Two great places to explore along the route are Jackson Heights and Flushing.

Get off at Roosevelt Avenue and you'll find yourself smack in the middle of Little India, replete with sari shops, gold jewelry, and restaurant after delicious restaurant. Go a few blocks in any direction, though, and you might stumble into a Peruvian, Colombian, or Chinese neighborhood.

I find Flushing to be one of the most interesting areas in Queens. It houses the largest Chinese population outside of Manhatten's Chinatown as well as large numbers of immigrants from Korea, India, Colombia, Afghanistan, Guyana, the Dominican Republic, Pakistan, the Philippines, and El Salvador. The streets are lively, and the only tourists you'll see will probably be visiting family members. If you think Manhattan is "real" New York, come visit Flushing to readjust your perspective (and get some seriously good and cheap food).

Even farther from Manhattan, near JFK airport, you'll find Jamaica. Home to a large Caribbean and African-American population, it should be high on the list of places to visit for aficionados of hip-hop and black culture. Charles Mingus, A Tribe Called Quest, LL Cool J, Run-DMC, and 50 Cent all hail from the streets of Jamaica and its environs, and they frequently reference their hometown in their music. In Jamaica you'll also find such lesser-known treasures as the Afrikan Poetry Theater, which holds regular workshops, performances, and lectures. Sadly, Jam Master Jay of Run-DMC was shot and killed in Jamaica in 2002—the area has something of a tough reputation—but most of the 'hood is relatively safe, especially during the day.

Fresh Meadows is an interesting little community just outside of Flushing: Built as a postwar planned community on a former country club golf course, this neighborhood has since expanded and evolved into a regular microsuburbia, complete with a Starbucks and Kmart.

There's much more in Queens—but we'll leave some of that exploring to you.

Places to Eat

 Anand Bhavan

35–66 73rd Street (between 35th and 37th Avenues, Jackson Heights)

PHONE: (718) 507–1600

TYPE OF CUISINE: South Indian vegetarian

DAYS/HOURS: Monday through Thursday from noon to 8:30 P.M., Friday through Sunday noon to 10:00 P.M.

VEGEBILITY: Excellent

RESERVATIONS: No

WHEELCHAIR ACCESS: No

KID-FRIENDLY: Yes

TYPE OF SERVICE: Table and take-out

PRICING: Inexpensive

PAYMENT ACCEPTED: Major credit cards

Indian-food lovers in the know satisfy their cravings in Jackson Heights (aka Little India), and the vegetarians among them head straight for Anand Bhavan. Afloat in a sea of Indian restaurants, this little café is the only strictly vegetarian local joint and one of the very few local South Indian places (most Indian restaurants serve primarily North Indian cuisine). The fare and decor are simple, but the low prices and the tasty dosas more than make up for that.

Anand Bhavan's dosas, thin pancakes rolled into gigantic tubes, are light, crispy, and never greasy. Made from rice and lentil flour, they come either plain or with a hefty dollop of filling and are accompanied by a tomato chutney and lentil soup. The potato masala is rather bland, so ask for extra coconut chutney, which is rich and spicy with a hint of ginger. If you crave more flavor, skip the appetizers and go straight for the rasam. This fiery broth soup is teeming with the pungent taste of tamarind and curry leaves, with a touch of coriander rounding out the flavor. Follow it all up with a cup of South Indian tea—this is what chai tasted like before it came in a carton.

The food is always a bargain, but lunch is a downright steal: A $7.00 dosa and appetizer will send you home stuffed. Anand Bhavan uses no eggs, but vegans need to avoid ghee (clarified butter). It is used in several dishes but not noted in the menu descriptions, so be sure to ask.

—JULIE HOLLAR

❷ Annam Brahma

84–43 164th Street (at 85th Avenue, Jamaica)

PHONE: (718) 523–2600

TYPE OF CUISINE: International vegetarian

DAYS/HOURS: Monday through Saturday from 11:00 A.M. to 10:00 P.M. (Wednesday to 4:00 P.M.), Sunday noon to 10:00 P.M.

VEGEBILITY: Excellent

RESERVATIONS: Not necessary

WHEELCHAIR ACCESS: Yes

KID-FRIENDLY: Yes

TYPE OF SERVICE: Table, take-out, and delivery (local, weekday lunch only)

PRICING: Moderate

PAYMENT ACCEPTED: Cash and personal checks (with photo ID)

Now in its fourth decade of operation, Annam Brahma (which means "food is god" in Sanskrit) is the oldest vegetarian restaurant in Queens. And given its exquisite food, friendly staff, and the oasis-like atmosphere that is the hallmark of all spiritual leader Sri Chinmoy's vegetarian restaurants, it's easy to see why.

Located on a leafy street just blocks from the Grand Central Parkway, Annam Brahma is a spiritual and gastronomic escape from the hustle and bustle of the outside world. Shephali, the restaurant's proprietor, points out that they do not serve "health food." Rather, he says, this is a vegetarian-style comfort zone, where the atmosphere is just as important as the quality of the food. As at other Sri Chinmoy establishments, the dining room is swathed in blue, the color of spirituality and consciousness. And, of course, the master's paintings and music fill the room, and his books of poetry are on display for purchase.

The regular menu is a mix of half American standards, half exotic Indian dishes. Tuesday is Chinese day; Thursdays are Italian. On Sundays, come for the international smorgasbord, an all-you-can-eat feast of dishes from around the globe. Annam Brahma is renowned for its imaginative salads: The tofu salad, for example, is vibrant mix of shredded beets and carrots, and ginger, garlic, tamari, and onion infuse it with a tasty kick.

The real specialty is the Indian delights, a treat for vegans (90 percent of the Indian dishes are egg- and dairy-free). You'll have a hard time choosing between the mustard and coriander samosa and the knish-like aloo chop, with a tomato-based chutney on the side. All the soups are vegan—even the "cream" ones are made with soy milk—and organic produce is used when available. Rounding out the meal are fresh juices, teas, and desserts.

—EILEEN REGAN

③ Buddha Bodhai
42–96 Main Street (between Blossom and Cherry Streets, Flushing)

PHONE: (718) 939–1188 or 2100

TYPE OF CUISINE: Chinese kosher vegetarian

DAYS/HOURS: Monday through Sunday from 11:00 A.M. to 11:00 P.M.

VEGEBILITY: Excellent

RESERVATIONS: Recommended on weekends

WHEELCHAIR ACCESS: Yes

KID-FRIENDLY: Yes

TYPE OF SERVICE: Table and take-out

PRICING: Moderate

PAYMENT ACCEPTED: MC/V

Buddha Bodhai is your run-of-the-mill Chinese restaurant in a strip mall section of Flushing. The only difference here is that the entire menu is not only strictly vegetarian, it is also strictly kosher. Be sure to mention to your server if you'd like your dish prepared vegan. Standard fare, standard service, standard decor; if you want your senses to be dazzled, look elsewhere.

—EILEEN REGAN

④ Dimple

35–68 73rd Street (between 35th and 37th Avenues, Jackson Heights)

PHONE: (718) 458-8144

TYPE OF CUISINE: Indian kosher vegetarian

DAYS/HOURS: Monday through Friday from 9:00 A.M. to 9:00 P.M., Saturday 10:00 A.M. to 9:00 P.M., Sunday 11:00 A.M. to 8:00 P.M.

VEGEBILITY: Excellent

RESERVATIONS: Not necessary

WHEELCHAIR ACCESS: No

KID-FRIENDLY: Yes

TYPE OF SERVICE: Take-out (some seats available)

PRICING: Moderate

PAYMENT ACCEPTED: Cash only

Dimple is nestled in the very Indian enclave of Jackson Heights. It's your typical greasy spoon (rough-and-ready seating, sparse decor), but with an Indian flavor. If you're a real aficionado of this type of cuisine, you'll find Dimple the real deal. But if you're looking to try something new or be enlightened, this is not the place to learn. Dimple is a prosperous business that's dependent on locals, so be sure to act like one when you're there.

—EILEEN REGAN

5 Happy Buddha

135–37 37th Avenue (between Main and Prince Streets, Flushing)

PHONE: (718) 358–0079
TYPE OF CUISINE: Chinese
DAYS/HOURS: Monday through Friday from noon to 10:00 P.M.,
Saturday and Sunday 11:00 A.M. to 10:00 P.M.
VEGEBILITY: Excellent
RESERVATIONS: Not necessary
WHEELCHAIR ACCESS: Yes
KID-FRIENDLY: Yes
TYPE OF SERVICE: Table
PRICING: Moderate
PAYMENT ACCEPTED: AE/MC/V

When it's vegetarian Chinese you're craving and don't want to travel for an hour into Manhattan, come here. You'll find all your old favorites, and they'll be served exactly how you like them. Szechuan mock chicken, a host of tofu dishes or Buddha's delight are done right—and cheaper than in the city. One extra-nice feature for this traffic-choked neighborhood: Happy Buddha has its own parking lot.

—EILEEN REGAN

❻ Oneness Fountain Heart

157–19 72nd Avenue (between Parsons and Aguilar Streets, Flushing)

PHONE: (718) 591–3663

TYPE OF CUISINE: Upscale vegetarian

DAYS/HOURS: Thursday through Tuesday from 11:30 A.M. to
9:00 P.M. Closed Wednesday.

VEGEBILITY: Excellent

RESERVATIONS: Suggested for Friday and Saturday nights

WHEELCHAIR ACCESS: Yes

KID-FRIENDLY: Yes

TYPE OF SERVICE: Table and take-out

PRICING: Moderate

PAYMENT ACCEPTED: Major credit cards

Oneness Fountain Heart is another offering from spiritual guru
Sri Chinmoy and his students. Situated on a tiny one-way street
in Flushing, this upscale vegetarian restaurant is a real find. A little
pricier and more elegant than the other Chinmoy establishments,
you might think of this as the family's sophisticated European cousin.

As at all Chinmoy restaurants, the presentation and quality of
the food—and the service—are impeccable. The decor is awash in a
quiet, contemplative pale blue, with two fountains smack in the
middle of the dining room. The atmosphere is conducive to quiet
reflection and keeps the focus where it counts: on the food.

We started with smoothies. They're delicious and thirst-
quenching, but you can skip the mango lassi—too much sour cream
to be refreshing. It's easy to see why the Grilled Vegetables alla
Mediterranea is the most popular appetizer. The eggplant, zucchini,
artichoke hearts, and red peppers are grilled to a perfect melt-in-your-
mouth texture, and the garlic makes your melting mouth water.

For entrées, we tried the Duck Surprise, Souvlaki Fountainopolis,
and Thai Heaven (popular with vegans, it comes with carrots, potatoes,
yams, and cashews in a mildly spicy coconut-cashew curry sauce). The
"duck" is sautéed in garlic and served with delightful butter-braised
broccoli, Royal rice, and a pineapple dipping sauce. The souvlaki would
do any Greek person proud. The "beef" is grilled and spiced with garlic, lemon juice, and oregano and served with cucumber-yogurt tsaziki,
brown rice pilaf, and a Greek salad garnish.

Oneness Fountain Heart is famous for two things, the first being
its version of the classic American meat loaf, Neat Loaf. It consists of

baked rice, grains, eggs, ricotta cheese, and tofu and is topped with a zesty secret sauce and served with a mom-size helping of mashed potatoes and hearty mushroom gravy. The second claim to fame is the tiramisu. As the menu puts it, "We make it . . . and it's to die for."

There are also numerous veggie burgers, sandwiches, and salads, ranging from your standard Greek to the eclectic Infinite Bleu. If you're in a sandwich mood, you can try the Neatwich, their version of a meat loaf sandwich, or the classic BLT done vegetarian-style. If none of that works as is, just ask for what you want. The always-accommodating staff will do its best to make your taste buds happy.

—EILEEN REGAN

7 Quantum Leap

65–60 Fresh Meadows Lane (between 65th and 67th Avenues, Fresh Meadows)

PHONE: (718) 461–1307
TYPE OF CUISINE: International macrobiotic vegetarian
DAYS/HOURS: Monday through Thursday from 11:30 A.M. to 10:00 P.M., Friday and Saturday 11:30 A.M. to 11:00 P.M., Sunday 10:00 A.M. to 10:00 P.M.
VEGEBILITY: Excellent
RESERVATIONS: Recommended for parties of six or more
WHEELCHAIR ACCESS: Yes
KID-FRIENDLY: Yes
TYPE OF SERVICE: Table and take-out
PRICING: Moderate
PAYMENT ACCEPTED: AE/MC/V
SPECIAL NOTE: Not affilliated with the Quantum Leap in Greenwich Village

Quantum Leap may be the best-looking vegetarian restaurant in Queens. The dining room is open, airy, and light. Tables and booths are of a blond wood that gives the place a casual and warm ambiance. But the menu—a smattering of Thai, Mexican, Chinese, and Japanese—is even more appealing. For the less adventurous, there are the requisite burgers, spaghetti and potato skins. About 80 percent of the menu is vegan, and the staff happily accommodates any vegan requests. (Two best-sellers are the BBQ tempeh and the

veggie thai curry.) Many people who eat macrobiotic come here; a favorite among them is the Japanese soba noodles.

In addition to menu staples, there are daily specials, consisting of two soups, one casserole, one quiche, five entrées, and five desserts. The dessert menu offers fruit pies, tofu pies, and dairy treats, none of which is made with sugar—just honey, maple syrup, and natural fruit juices. In the summer you can have a nondairy shake. Organic coffee and a wide variety of teas are available year-round.

But the most impressive feature may be the brunch menu—as extensive as some restaurants' regular menus. There are fifteen brunch specials and as many first courses and platters. Choose from a wide range of pancakes, waffles, omelettes, scrambled tofu, soy sausages...the list is almost endless.

Quantum Leap is a family-owned restaurant that takes its customer's satisfaction seriously. The chef periodically comes up with new dishes and tests them out on the locals via the daily specials. If something is a hit, it becomes a menu fixture. Adjoining the restaurant is Quantum Leap Natural Market, so you can do your shopping and have a delicious meal under the same roof.

—EILEEN REGAN

8 S'Agapo Taverna
34–21 34th Avenue (at 35th Street, Astoria)

PHONE: (718) 626–0303
TYPE OF CUISINE: Traditional Greek
DAYS/HOURS: Monday through Sunday from noon to midnight
VEGEBILITY: Good
RESERVATIONS: Recommended for parties of six or more
WHEELCHAIR ACCESS: Yes
KID-FRIENDLY: Yes
TYPE OF SERVICE: Table and take-out
PRICING: Moderate
PAYMENT ACCEPTED: All credit cards

If the idea of Greek food conjures up images of spinning skewers of gristly meat, it's time for a visit to S'Agapo. Owners Barbara and Kostas Lambrakis opened their family-run restaurant in Astoria in 1995 to bring a taste of real Greek home-cooking back to the neighborhood, an enclave of Greek immigrants for more than a century.

And real Greek home-cooking includes a surprising amount of meatless food.

The meze, or appetizers, are the veggie stars at S'Agapo, and vegetarians will probably want to build their meal out of them. The variety plate (pikilia orektikon) is Barbara's personal work of art, with six different spreads sectioned off by slices of fresh cucumber and apple, making a colorful wheel that looks as good as it tastes. The warm triangles of pita are perfect scoops for spreads made of chickpeas, eggplant, beets, parsley, or red pepper; ovo-lacto vegetarians can also try the rich yogurt-based tzatziki. The grape leaf dip, a concoction of finely processed grape leaves and spices, stands out for its aromatic, slightly sweet simplicity. There are also seven kinds of bean or green salads (all of which can be made vegan), grilled veggies, cheese dumplings, and the soup of the day—always vegetarian and sometimes vegan. Don't miss the sautéed spinach: Fennel and top-shelf olive oil make this a seriously mouth-watering treat.

S'Agapo buys all of its produce locally at the Greek markets that litter Astoria and uses almost no butter in its recipes, relying on high-quality olive oil instead. The place isn't particularly cozy or romantic, but it does have a homey feel to it; all the recipes are family recipes, and you'll spot family photos on the walls. The prices are moderate, and the owners don't cut corners on quality. Barbara makes her own phyllo dough from scratch, and Kostas makes some of the only Cretan Raki—an ouzo-like liqueur—you'll find in New York. The wine selection includes more than twenty Greek reds and whites.

Weekends are busy, but weeknights tend to be quiet. If you come in the summer, try to get an outdoor table and enjoy the weather and the relative quiet of Queens. And a special little hint for vegans: During the last week of Greek Lent (usually in April), almost all the veggie items are made vegan to observe the Greek Orthodox tradition.

—JULIE HOLLAR

⑨ The Smile of the Beyond

86–14 Parsons Boulevard (between 86th and 87th Avenues, Jamaica)

PHONE: (718) 739–7453

DAYS/HOURS: Monday through Friday from 7:00 A.M. to 4:00 P.M., Saturday 7:00 A.M. to 3:00 P.M.

TYPE OF CUISINE: Global vegetarian

VEGEBILITY: Excellent

RESERVATIONS: Not necessary

WHEELCHAIR ACCESS: Yes

KID-FRIENDLY: Yes

TYPE OF SERVICE: Table, counter, and take-out

PRICING: Moderate

PAYMENT ACCEPTED: Cash only

This quiet little place in an even quieter section of Jamaica could well be the best-kept culinary secret in Queens. The coffee-shop-style vegetarian café is a delightful gem in an otherwise nondescript neighborhood.

The Smile of the Beyond is owned and operated by the followers of Sri Chinmoy, a spiritual leader and teacher who emigrated from India forty years ago. His influence is unmistakable, from his artwork adorning the walls to his music playing softly in the background. But not to worry: The only thing you'll have to swallow is the scrumptious food.

A favorite with the locals, the luncheonette has a real community feel. Parents drift in with their children, and neighbors chat as they tuck into their meals at the counter. The food is always fresh, and nothing is premade, not even the salads. The manager, who's been there for nearly twenty years, buys organic produce as often as he can, depending on season and price. About one-quarter of the all-veg menu is vegan, and the staff is happy to accommodate any vegan requests.

One of the most popular vegan dishes is the rice and (spicy, chunky, taste-bud-kicking) chili, and the "steak burger" (a soy fry patty) is a hit with ovo-lactos. But the real star is the hummus. Served over lettuce with tomatoes, cucumbers, green peppers, onions, and mushrooms, this warm-weather delight is pure ecstasy sans dressing, but you would be remiss not to try the white sauce (a blend of egg-based mayonnaise, filtered water, and aged soy sauce) or the herbal dressing (corn oil, red wine vinegar, soy sauce, rosemary, basil, oregano, and chopped parsley).

Complete your meal with a dessert from the irresistible selection of cakes and pies, several of them vegan. The rum pound cake is crumbly, moist, and packed with a wallop of real rum and is served with a scoop of whipped cream. You almost feel guilty indulging in such earthly pleasures in such an otherworldly atmosphere, but you get over it with first bite.

There is one small shortcoming, however. The restaurant was established before the mandated restroom law was passed, so there is no lavatory. But customers are welcome at the health food store just a few doors down. It, like most of the other businesses on the block, is owned and operated by Sri Chinmoy's students.

The Smile of the Beyond is diamond in the rough, off the beaten path indeed. But like most rare treats, it's worth the extra effort.

—EILEEN REGAN

⑩ Zen Pavilion

251–15 Northern Boulevard (between Cornell and Browvale Streets, Little Neck)

PHONE: (718) 281–1500; Fax: (718) 281–9695
TYPE OF CUISINE: Asian kosher vegetarian
DAYS/HOURS: Sunday through Thursday from 11:30 A.M. to 10:00 P.M., Friday and Saturday 11:30 A.M. to 11:00 P.M.
VEGEBILITY: Excellent
RESERVATIONS: Not necessary
WHEELCHAIR ACCESS: Yes
KID-FRIENDLY: Yes
TYPE OF SERVICE: Table, take-out, and delivery
PRICING: Moderate
PAYMENT ACCEPTED: Major credit cards

Located very close to the Long Island border, Zen Pavilion is about as far as you can get from Manhattan while still being within the city limits. That said, this kosher-certified establishment is definitely worth the trip. Here you'll find Asian vegetarian cuisine at its best. There is even a message on the front of the menu about simplicity, happiness, and good homemade meals.

The menu offers a terrific selection of soups, appetizers, and salads as well as sushi, all-organic dishes, and five house specialties. These "Zen recommendations" include the General Medallions, perfectly crisped soy nuggets with crunchy peppers in a spicy sauce; the Sizzling Sensation, crispy wheat gluten and cauliflower in the house brown-orange sauce; and the Taro Bowl a-la-King, veggie seafood and chicken, soy protein, black mushrooms, nuts, and diced mixed vegetables sautéed in an edible taro bowl.

Zen Pavilion is only three years old, but it has already established a following from Manhattan and Long Island. The decor is sparkly and clean; the service is attentive and friendly, without being pushy; and best of all, the menu is 90 percent vegan—and all requests are happily accommodated.

—EILEEN REGAN

Places to Shop

11 Go Natural

45–03 Queens Boulevard (between 45th and 46th Streets, Sunnyside)

PHONE: (718) 482–0008

DAYS/HOURS: Monday through Friday from 10:00 A.M. to 8:30
P.M., Saturday 10:00 A.M. to 8:00 P.M., Sunday 11:00 A.M. to
6:00 P.M.

OVERALL: Good

Go Natural is a great find on the bustling but rather generic
thoroughfare of Queens Boulevard. It's your typical natural
food store with the requisite shelves of vitamins, natural remedies,
and supplements. What's unique is their fresh sandwiches and wraps
in the refrigerator section. Egg rolls, tofu "chicken" salad sandwiches—all your deli favorites are here. Made daily, there is an extensive selection for the vegetarian and vegan palate. The produce
selection is rather small, but it is all organic, very clean, and very
fresh. There is a wide variety of prepackaged foods, from frozen dinners to yummy vegetable chips. The store itself is quite clean, and
the staff is pleasant and helpful.

12 Linda's Natural Kitchen & Market

81–22 Lefferts Boulevard (between 83rd Avenue and Austin, Kew
Gardens)

PHONE: (718) 847–2233

DAYS/HOURS: Monday through Friday from 10:00 A.M. to 7:00
P.M. (Wednesday to 8:00 P.M.), Saturday 10:00 A.M. to 6:00 P.M.,
Sunday 11:00 A.M. to 5:30 P.M.

OVERALL: Excellent

Linda's is exactly what you would expect to find on a quiet little
gentrified street with a café and an indie movie house. This
health food market is a bustling center for the local community.
From hummus to fresh-baked carob cookies to fresh-squeezed
juices, the food—not to mention the service and the vibe—are top-
notch. The store caters to all your supplement, vitamin, dietary, and
beauty needs. The produce is all organic and luscious-looking, but

the real attraction is the deli counter. Neighbors come here to catch up and chat, with each other and the owners—the food is an added bonus! Be sure to save room for the homemade desserts.

13 Neil's Natural Market

4610 Hollis Court Boulevard (between Utopia Parkway and 46th Avenue, Flushing)

> **PHONE:** (718) 321–2088
> **DAYS/HOURS:** Monday through Saturday from 9:00 A.M. to 9:00 P.M., Sunday 9:00 A.M. to 7:00 P.M.
> **OVERALL:** Excellent (except for produce)

What Neil's lacks in fresh produce (look elsewhere for your fruits and veggies), it more than makes up for in frozen and prepackaged foods. It's just like your typical deli, quick snacks and premade meals, but for those of us who care about our furry friends and our green earth. The produce section is just a wire shelf in one corner with a few yams, onions, avocados, and bananas thrown in loosely and no signs with prices. There is no to-go service here either, but there's a huge freezer section with shelves upon shelves to tempt you (like organic chocolate cookie dough). The prepackaged items are just as extensive, from cookies to chips to sweets. Just like most health food businesses, Neil's is chock-full of vitamins and natural supplements. The health and beauty section is quite extensive, too, right down to the cruelty-free eye drops.

14 Quantum Leap Natural Market

65–60 Fresh Meadows Lane (between 175th Street and 67th Avenue, Fresh Meadows)

> **PHONE:** (718) 762–3572
> **DAYS/HOURS:** Sunday through Thursday from 10:00 A.M. to 10:00 P.M., Friday and Saturday 10:00 A.M. to 11:00 P.M.
> **OVERALL:** Excellent

Connected to Quantum Leap restaurant by a doorway, this natural market is the place for your one-stop shopping. The produce section is quite extensive, and the fruits and vegetables are fresh, inviting, and certified organic. They have a decent-size freezer section and a wide variety of premade wraps and sandwiches. From an impressive bulk food selection to organic pet food, this market has it all. The aisles are wide, the store is clean, and the staff is friendly and helpful. Be sure to check out the market after a delicious meal next door.

⓯ Queens Health Emporium

159–01 Horace Harding Expressway (between Parsons Boulevard and 160th Street, Fresh Meadows)

> **PHONE:** (718) 358–6500
> **DAYS/HOURS:** Monday through Saturday from 9:30 A.M. to 8:00 P.M., Sunday 10:00 A.M. to 6:00 P.M.
> **OVERALL:** Very good

Located on the north-side service road of the Long Island Expressway, this is a natural foods mammoth. The Emporium has everything your local Stop & Shop has—only everything here is organic, kind to the earth, and cruelty-free. Two entire aisles are devoted to cereal and soy milk, the freezer section runs the width of the store, and the produce section is enormous and exquisite. The deli counter serves hot and cold vegetarian foods and sweets and boasts an organic juice and salad bar. Food can be eaten in or taken out. The book section is located upstairs near the seats, which is convenient if you have nothing to read while you eat. There is also an extensive health and beauty section, from natural hair coloring to a complete line of cosmetics, and the herbs and vitamins shelves literally reach the ceiling.

Places to Stay

Although Queens is one of the most vibrant and culturally rich communities in the world, the accommodations are sadly lacking. With a plethora of taxis to whisk you away from the Big Apple to either LaGuardia or JFK in minutes, there's really no need for you to stay in Queens. Take our word for it. But if you must...

16 Courtyard LaGuardia Airport Hotel
On Grand Central Parkway across from LaGuardia Airport

PRICING: Expensive
Designed by business travelers; pets welcome.

17 Hampton Inn JFK Airport
144–10 135th Avenue (between 143rd and 145th Streets, Jamaica)

PRICING: Moderate
Close to JFK Airport. Indoor heated swimming pool.

Contributors

Alia Akkam's passion for food was ignited as a child, when she would spend hours in the kitchen with her father, a Syrian native, as he prepared exotic Middle Eastern specialties while she looked on in fascination. She also remembers thumbing through the family's well-worn copy of *The Art of Syrian Cookery* and being mesmerized by pictures of women making pita bread in brick ovens. Having grown up spoiled by home-cooked meals, she couldn't handle college dorm food and so, though broke, became obsessed with restaurants. She interned at the Food Network and at a scary New York City theme restaurant, where she got her first glimpse into restaurant culture. Today she lives in Brooklyn and writes about food and restaurants for FoodTV.com, *Time Out New York*, Forbes.com, and other publications.

A lifelong foodie, **Phil Andrews** went veg in 1998 and has never looked back. He loves to cook and has a strange habit of organizing veggie potlucks everywhere he goes. His tastes include, but are not limited to, Mexican, Indian, Thai, Japanese, Italian, and Southwestern. He spent five years in Baltimore living in a Food Not Bombs house, which hosted weekly vegan recovered-food meals for the hungry. As a labor organizer, photographer, freelance writer, activist, and musician, he still finds time to chew his food properly.

Blair Barnette was raised in south Georgia, where a vegetarian meal consisted of collard greens stewed with ham hocks, whipped potatoes with bacon and beef gravy, and cracklin' corn bread made with roast pan drippings. At fifteen she single-handedly initiated the installment of a salad bar in her high school lunchroom by handcuffing herself to the school mascot and threatening to force-feed it gazpacho. In college she gave up the fight, claiming that she would sooner live on veggie burger slices in a can than stomach another bowl of iceberg lettuce. Today, thrilled with the more universal acceptance of meatless fare and the wide world of delectable options, she has settled into the life of a jazz singer in New York, coining the phrase "Monk, not meat!"

It's no wonder **Diana Bocco** has a fascination with food. Growing up with two European grandmothers meant a lot of hours spent in the kitchen. Grandma Elise made a luscious ricotta cheese strudel, and Grandma Mercedes loved to cook so much, she prepared extra food and fed the neighbors. When Diana turned vegetarian at sixteen, she realized she'd better learn how to cook for herself. Since then, she's taken classes at the Natural Gourmet Cookery School, the NY Open Center, and the New School and has even learned how to make vegan strudel. She is currently at work on her own vegan cookbook.

As a child, **Antrim Caskey** would only eat hamburgers. In college she adapted to the Colorado customs of granola life and started eating tofu and brown rice on a regular basis. From there, her vegetarianism took its own unique forms in China and India and, since 1999, New York City. Wherever she is, she enjoys the search and rewards of a well-cooked vegetarian meal, and those close to her know of her sturdy appetite.

Growing up in Istanbul, where food is only mentioned about sixteen times a day and weekly feasts are part of the family tradition, **Sezin Cavusoglu** was practically raised in her grandmothers' kitchens, baking delicacies by the age of five. Her transition into vegetarianism wasn't a smooth one, as meat is the focal part of a Turkish dinner table. She persevered, however, and by age eighteen was completely meat-free and by twenty-two a vegan. She likes to experiment with green vegetables and grains in her cooking and believes if a dish can't be done with some form of soy, it can't be done at all.

Brian Cazeneuve became a vegetarian twenty-two years ago, at age fifteen. As a staff writer for *Sports Illustrated,* he has traversed thirty countries, locating meatless fare from the American South to South America to Liverpool (which sounds simply hostile to vegetarians). A waiter in Moscow once told him that his restaurant had no plain omelettes or cheese omelettes but could fire up a ham omelette in no time. A French bistro owner once threatened to pelt him with a crepe (rhymes with "step") if he dared rhyme it with "shape" again. His favorite foods are chocolate, cheesecake, and anything with pesto, though his attempts to create a palatable pesto-infused chocolate cheesecake have failed miserably. He lives in New York with his tofu.

Mary Margaret Chappell spends her weekdays trying to sneak vegetarian recipes into the food pages of *First for Women* magazine (where she is a senior editor), her weekends doing cooking demonstrations at New York City's Greenmarkets, and every other free moment reading, writing, and talking about food. A trained pastry chef, she spent seven years in Brittany, France, where she learned to cherish fruits and vegetables by shopping in the open-air markets. Today she will order any menu item that contains leeks (unless it also has beets) and has been known to consume pounds of fresh cherries in a single sitting.

Eureka Freeman has been a dilettante vegetarian (with special credit for Asian cuisine) and a New Yorker for thirty-three years. She writes restaurant reviews for the *Walt Disney World Information Guide* under the nom de plume Czarina. She is also a playwright, director, and puppeteer. Her interest in offbeat food began at an early age. Her British mother's idea of American cuisine was to boil ears of corn for five hours, until the cobs were tender. Fortunately, Eureka married the Okra King, who will eat anything as long as it's Asian, searingly hot, or slimy.

Suzanne Gerber embarked on a vegetarian lifestyle at age four, when she discovered the relationship between lamb chops and baby lambs. During the '70s in upstate New York, she was considered something of a freak for her unwillingness to not pull pepperonis off pizzas and just "eat around the meat." Over the past thirty years she has managed to find delicious—OK, edible—vegetarian food everywhere from Northern Ireland to Eastern Europe to Central America to southern Germany to Kentucky. The freelance writer/editor, professional astrologer, and former editor in chief of *Vegetarian Times* claims she has yet to meet a vegetable she couldn't learn to love.

Vegetarian since age twelve, **Rebecca Gould** wants the world to know there's a lot more to Russian cuisine than blinis and borscht. She holds the distinction of being the first vegetarian her host family in St. Petersburg had ever met. After finally succeeding in translating "vegetarian" to her hosts, she spent the next three months eating crème brûlée, ice cream, and soup and adding her favorite cheese in the world (tvorog) to every main course. She hopes to buy a dacha in Russia someday with no electricity but with mushrooms, blueberries, and birch trees.

Astoria resident **Julie Hollar** has been hunting down good vegetarian restaurants in New York City since her arrival on the scene in 2001. Meat-free since the age of twenty and occasionally vegan here and there, her current obsession is finding the best bibimbap (in a hot stone pot, of course) in the city. Julie learned her culinary ropes at a vegetarian housing co-op in Austin, Texas, where she cooked devastatingly delicious meals for thirty people every week out of pots larger than her current bedroom. Her writing can also be found in such publications as *The Texas Observer* and *SparkNotes*.

Esther James divides her time between her home base of Washington, D.C., and various urban and rural adventures, including working with New York City's Greenmarket and on organic vegetable farms in Maryland and Virginia. A sometime writing tutor and book reviewer, she is passionate about vegetarian cuisine and getting locally grown food into kitchens, restaurants and school cafeterias. A childhood spent slurping dandelion soup and other suburban backyard delicacies has prepared her well as she forages for Manhattan's best vegetarian joints.

Carlos Lopez, an amateur cook and a vegetarian since 1991, enjoys exploring nonmeat offerings from different cultures and breaking free from the "pasta and salad" mentality that many folks seem to have. Carlos recently studied under chef Hans Welker in his Artisinal Breadmaking seminar at the French Culinary Institute in New York City and plans to continue his studies as soon as he recovers from buying a home. He also hopes to open a small vegetarian café. He and his wife, Kathleen, reside in southern New Jersey with their son, Alejandro (and more on the way).

Kathleen Lopez is a massage therapist and aspiring nutritionist whose professional focus is working with pregnant women and infants. The same woman who once ate an entire ham in one sitting during her pregnancy is now raising a vegetarian son and participating in outreach programs promoting meat-free lifestyles. She is married to Carlos Lopez and is becoming a self-proclaimed expert on organic gardening in small spaces.

Christina Massey grew up in northern California and has been a vegetarian by choice her entire life. The only vegetarian in her family, she promotes healthy eating and healthy lifestyles. She has cooked and served vegetarian meals in restaurants, over campfires, and in Dutch ovens. Christina received a B.F.A. in painting and critiqued gallery exhibits, theater productions, and outdoor adventures before moving to New York City.

Lara Olchanetzky grew up in a family of foodies. Her parents owned a small Relais and Chateaux hotel and restaurant in Cape Town, South Africa, and she worked in a little vegetarian restaurant in Morgantown, West Virginia, cooking and baking organic and vegan yummies. Since moving to Brooklyn four years ago, she has been relishing all that NYC has to offer. But that didn't stop her from moving to Paris in 2003, with her husband and child. Thankfully, she finished all her reviews before crossing the pond.

Emily Park grew up the daughter of a Korean immigrant father and a Tennesseean mother, so food was bound to be a source of both pleasure and some contention. A vegetarian since the age of fourteen (though now a pescatarian), Emily is currently an assistant editor at NYU Press, with culinary and writerly aspirations.

Jewel Elizabeth Partridge can hold forth for hours about the benefits of soy products and whole grains. A professional dancer and fitness instructor based in Chelsea, she has written for *Dance Spirit, Pointe,* and *Dance Teacher* magazines. She strives to find balance in this crazy city while teaching others about keeping a healthy spirit and body, full of isoflavones and endorphins.

Brooklynite **Lisa Poliak** is a freelance writer and editor and devotee of fine food. She has a longtime interest in healthy, organic, and ethnic cuisine and organic gardening. Tasting local dishes has been a highlight of her travels to countries including Costa Rica, Cote d'Ivoire, Italy, Morocco, Portugal, Spain, and St. Maartin. Her writing has been featured in several national magazines as well as *The Princeton Review.* She received an M.F.A. in creative writing from

Brooklyn College, writes short stories, and has edited everything from *Scholastic* classroom magazines to consumer Web articles to poetry collections.

Eileen Regan has been an almost-vegetarian for more than a decade. She has lived her entire life in New York, minus a few months testing the waters in Cork, Ireland, where she learned the art and technique of cooking from her aunt and uncle, Mary and Chris, two internationally known chefs. From ratatouille to crème brûlée, she mastered and fell in love with all things culinary. Her heroes are Jamie Oliver and Nigella Lawson, and her favorite place in the world is Tea & Sympathy in Manhattan. This Anglophile is an editor for Hatherleigh Press and currently lives in Brooklyn.

Emily Rubin, a business writer but not a strict vegetarian, would describe herself as extremely veg-friendly. She has to be, as she frequently travels to exotic locales with the author of this book, and over the years has learned how to say "no meat, no fish, no chicken" in Turkish, Arabic, and Portuguese, among other languages. On a dare in southern Mexico several years ago, the native New Yorker ate a fried grasshopper—a local delicacy—which she found truly disgusting in both taste and texture, as well as a compelling argument for eating veg while traveling.

Melena Z. Ryzik loves to cook but rarely does, since a new restaurant opens in New York roughly every three minutes. She never says no to dessert and once ate ice cream every day for an entire summer. A writer, reporter, and epicure, she has written for the *New York Times* and a host of print and on-line magazines. She often interviews celebrities but rarely sees them eat, leading her to believe she will never be celebrated for her sophisticated palate. Melena lives in Brooklyn with her ice-cream maker.

A college professor once told **Marianne Semchuk** that she was born to be a critic. (Unfortunately, it was her singing teacher.) Most noted for her theater reviews, she also submits tongue-in-cheek commentaries on business, wellness, and dating to local publications. Marianne's large Jewish family has provided her with a lifetime of overeating experience. Her mother was even named an honorary Italian for her mastery of that cuisine. In her eight years living in

NYC, Marianne has eaten at all the finest establishments, from four-star restaurants to roadside vendors.

Founders and series editors of Vegetarian World Guides, **Susan Shumaker** and **Than Saffel** are a waiter's worst nightmare. Their styles as food writers, restaurant reviewers, and tireless researchers complement each other as they sniff out every last ingredient and any possible substitution a vegetarian or vegan could want. They ask the tough questions, playing good cop/bad cop with servers, chefs, and managers so readers won't have to. Authors of *Vegetarian Walt Disney World and Greater Orlando* (The Globe Pequot Press, second edition, 2003), they currently live on a farm in West Virginia with their daughter, Rhowyn, and two very friendly border collies.

Rebecca Krasney Stropoli is a Brooklyn-based writer/editor who has been an ovo-lacto vegetarian since the age of seventeen. While she appreciates fine cuisine, her childhood reverence for Tater Tots and Kraft Macaroni and Cheese remains intact. Her food passions also include Ben & Jerry's (any flavor), feta cheese, and falafel. As a teenager she moved from Boston to Florida, where she discovered the considerable value of the early-bird dinner. She graduated from UF Gainesville with a B.A. in English. Her pop cultural reviews have appeared in the independent Fort Lauderdale–based *Discourse* magazine, and she is a contract writer for AOL/Digital City as well as an editor at the Manhattan-based *Business Wire*. She currently makes her home in the Brooklyn neighborhood of Fort Greene.

Thanks to *Charlotte's Web,* **Jessica Wurwarg** has been a vegetarian since she was eight years old. The Long Island native is interested in all aspects of food, from growing it to harvesting it to cooking it to eating it. She worked on organic farms in Denmark, France, Italy, Switzerland, and Oregon, planting, feeding sheep, and making cheese. She has also worked as a chef in a London restaurant, interned at Zagat's, and wrote restaurant reviews for *Around and About Providence,* a guidebook to that Rhode Island city. In 2003 Jessica left her job at Greenmarket to pursue a master's degree in city design and social science in London.

Index

MARKETS

LODGING

OTHER ESTABLISHMENTS

BY CUISINE

AMERICAN

ASIAN

BY VEGEBILITY

EXCELLENT

VERY GOOD

BY PRICE

About the Author

Suzanne Gerber is the former editor in chief of *Vegetarian Times* and a staff editor at *InStyle, Redbook,* and *New York Woman* magazines. Currently a freelance writer and editor living in Brooklyn, New York, she writes magazine articles about food, natural health, relationships, and lifestyle issues. This book is the marriage of two of her greatest passions: vegetarianism (since 1973) and dining out in NYC (since 1982).